THE PROJECT MANAGEMENT INSTITUTE

PROJECT MANAGEMENT HANDBOOK

THE PROJECT MANAGEMENT INSTITUTE

PROJECT MANAGEMENT HANDBOOK

Jeffrey K. Pinto, *Editor*

Foreword by Lewis R. Ireland

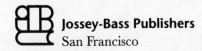

Jossey-Bass Publishers
San Francisco

Jossey-Bass books and products are available through most bookstores. To contact Jossey-Bass directly, call (888) 378-2537, fax to (800) 605-2665, or visit our website at www.josseybass.com.

Substantial discounts on bulk quantities of Jossey-Bass books are available to corporations, professional associations, and other organizations. For details and discount information, contact the special sales department at Jossey-Bass.

 Manufactured in the United States of America on Lyons Falls Turin Book. This paper is acid-free and 100 percent totally chlorine-free.

Library of Congress Cataloging-in-Publication Data

The Project Management Institute : project management handbook /
  Jeffrey K. Pinto, editor ; foreword by Lewis R. Ireland. — 1st ed.
      p.   cm. — (The Jossey-Bass business & management series)
    Includes bibliographical references and index.
    ISBN 0-7879-4013-5
    1. Industrial project management.   2. Project Management
Institute.   I. Pinto, Jeffrey K.   II. Series.
    HD69.P75P735   1998
    658.4'04—dc21   98-12381

FIRST EDITION
HB Printing 10 9 8 7 6 5 4 3

A JOINT PUBLICATION OF

THE JOSSEY-BASS BUSINESS & MANAGEMENT SERIES

AND

THE PROJECT MANAGEMENT INSTITUTE

CONTENTS

PART FOUR: INTEGRATIVE ISSUES IN PROJECT MANAGEMENT

To Joseph Barber Pinto,
our wonderful surprise and red-haired delight

FOREWORD

More and more, organizations around the world are turning to project management as a solution to their business challenges. The powerful nature of project management has been recognized, and it is increasing in use in all fields of endeavor. Global markets and competition dictate that only the most effective measures be employed to bring goods and services to consumers in a timely, cost-effective manner. Both developed and emerging nations are embracing project management as the system of choice to deliver the benefits of domestic and international commence.

The Project Management Institute, a global professional association, encourages the advancement of the art and science of project management. As the largest professional project management organization in the world, its programs and activities are designed to deliver the benefits of project management knowledge to its members and to support their career advancements. Formal education, certification, accreditation, and standards programs are only some of the benefits provided to members. Important components include 120 chapters located on six continents and 14 specific interest groups promoting industry interests within project management.

This book, *The Project Management Institute Project Management Handbook,* is an important contribution to project management literature. Readers will find valuable and useful information in every chapter. This book offers comprehensive and insightful advice for both seasoned project management professionals and new project managers just starting their careers in this rapidly expanding profession. Chapter authors are recognized international authorities in our field, and I hope you will agree that their experience and advice are indispensable for all persons involved in the complex but rewarding field of project management.

Denver, Colorado   Lewis R. Ireland
September 1998   President
                                                            Project Management Institute

PREFACE

The field of project management as a professional discipline has truly come into its own. Indeed, a recent *Fortune* magazine article rated project management as the number one career choice for the next decade. Project management is by no means a new field, but there are a number of reasons for the recent upsurge in its popularity. The increasing complexity of products, the demand for integrated organizational teamwork, the dramatically shortened time-to-market windows, and the need for ever higher levels of organizational efficiency all combine to present corporations with both challenges and opportunities. The challenges are obvious; the opportunities stem from the ability of some organizations to exploit this new business environment through operating both efficiently and effectively. I am convinced that the successful organizations of the future will remain so based on their willingness to adopt project management principles.

This book is the result of a long-term effort to bring together some of the foremost scholars and writers in the project management field and ask them to take a critical look at some of the most important aspects of project management and lend their expertise to finding ways to do it better. Project management is a complex process that requires managers to be both technically and managerially adept. The technocrat who understands the technical side of project management is no more likely to negotiate the myriad minefields than a good "people" manager who has no understanding of how to run a project. These important skills, technical and people, are two sides of the same coin.

The organization of this book reflects a desire to approach project management as comprehensively as possible. It addresses the main topics in the project management field:

1. The project context, consisting of six chapters that explore the unique aspects of projects and the role they play in organizational success
2. Scope management and project planning, consisting of eight chapters that explore several of the key aspects of the project planning role
3. Human resource management, consisting of eight chapters that address some of the distinctive "people" challenges that managing projects presents
4. Integrative issues, consisting of three chapters that look at the project management processes from a general viewpoint to understand its unique characteristics

The goal of this book is to present a comprehensive guide that addresses the key features in the field of project management and provides up-to-date and (perhaps more important) practical information on every page.

This work bears the unmistakable stamp of the Project Management Institute (PMI), the leading professional project management organization in the world today. Indeed, the structure of the book is similar to the main points outlined in PMI's Body of Knowledge document: its systematic organization of the material necessary to become fully conversant with the practice of project management. As a result, this book contains chapters that span the broad avenues of project management, exploring the technical, organizational, administrative, and behavioral dimensions of the discipline.

The writing style is purposely varied. When I asked the various authors to contribute to this book, I made it clear that I wanted them to write in the manner they were most comfortable with—one that was not too academic but was up to date on current project management theory. They took me at my word and did a wonderful job of writing in a way that not only is accessible to novice project management readers but also contains new insights for seasoned professionals. The blend of authors from academia, consulting, and private industry gives this book a unique style and usability that should appeal to all levels of readers.

Acknowledgments

That this book was first conceived and finally completed is due in no small part to the efforts of a number of individuals who truly went above and beyond the call of duty in order to bring this work to fruition. Cedric Crocker, of Jossey-Bass, was the catalyst behind the idea and served at various points as the sole anchor of sanity in a sea of competing demands and seemingly insoluble difficulties. Thank you, Cedric. Byron Schneider has worked tirelessly to move this project through to fruition. Jim Pennypacker, of the PMI, remains a good friend and was a terrific person to bounce ideas off. When bottlenecks threatened to slow our progress to a crawl, Jim was usually the person to get us back on track. For that I thank him sincerely. The editorial staff at Jossey-Bass faced a huge challenge in working on this book, and they came through admirably. I thank them for their dedication and professionalism. In particular, Sheryl Fullerton did a wonderful job copyediting the chapters. The work has benefited greatly from her suggestions.

I would be remiss in not thanking the chapter authors; each added a tremendous amount of value to the project. I was both gratified and humbled by their willingness to get involved and the quality of the work that each contributed. Indeed, much of my excitement over this book results from reading the marvelous chapters prepared by these dedicated individuals, whose sole motivation was to do their part to strengthen our understanding of project management. I offer each of them my heartfelt thanks.

Finally, as ever, I reserve my biggest thanks for my family, who have given me the greatest blessing any individual could ask for: a happy home life and the encouragement to do my best in the challenges I accept. Emily, AJ, and Joey bring new delight to each day of my life and demonstrate that children are truly God's gift to us. For my wife, Mary Beth, I reserve the biggest thanks, something that words alone cannot adequately express.

Erie, Pennsylvania   Jeffrey K. Pinto
September 1998

THE AUTHORS

Jeffrey K. Pinto is the Samuel A. and Elizabeth B. Breene Fellow in Management and associate professor of management in the School of Business at Penn State Erie, the Behrend College. He has consulted widely with a number of organizations, both domestically and internationally, and has authored or coauthored seven books and numerous articles on a variety of topics, including project management, information systems implementation, innovation and change, leadership, and learning theory.

David F. Caldwell is a professor of organization analysis and management at the Leavey School of Business and Administration, Santa Clara University. His current research interests include the effects of structural and individual variables on the performance of groups. He has published widely in his field.

David I. Cleland is the Ernest E. Roth Professor and professor of engineering management at the University of Pittsburgh. He is the author or editor of twenty-eight books in the fields of project management, engineering management, and manufacturing management. He has served as a consultant for both national and foreign companies and is recognized as one of the best-known members of Project Management Institute. He has been described as the Father of Project Management. He has both a national and international reputation in his field, and has been honored for his original and continuing contributions to his disciplines. In

1997 he was honored with the establishment of the David I. Cleland Excellence in Project Management Literature Award sponsored by the Project Management Institute.

James P. Clements is the chairperson of the Department of Computer and Information Sciences at Towson University and serves as an adjunct professor of information systems and technology for the Whiting School of Engineering at the Johns Hopkins University. His research and consulting interests have led to associations with a variety of organizations, including the Applied Physics Lab at the Johns Hopkins University and Bell Atlantic Corp.

Kenneth G. Cooper is president of Pugh-Roberts Associates, a division of PA Consulting Group, Inc. His management consulting career spans over twenty years, specializing in the development and application of computer simulation models to a variety of strategic business issues. He has directed over one hundred consulting engagements, among them analyses of major commercial and defense development projects.

Dorla A. Evans is professor of finance at the University of Alabama in Huntsville. She has several years of industrial experience in financial analysis and has published extensively in various journals.

Robert C. Ford is the associate dean for graduate and external programs at the University of Central Florida. He has authored or coauthored nearly one hundred articles, presentations, and books on a variety of topics, including management by objectives, organizational design project organization, and human resource management topics. His current work is in guest service management, and he is now completing a text on that topic.

J. Davidson Frame is academic dean and professor at the newly established University of Management and Technology (UMT). Prior to joining UMT, he served as professor of management science at George Washington University for nineteen years. He has also served as director of certification and director of education service at the Project Management Institute. Frame has authored six books and more than forty scholarly publications.

Jack Gido is director of the Pennsylvania Technical Assistance Program at Penn State University. His twenty years of industrial management experience includes the management of productivity improvement and manufacturing technology programs. He has authored three books on project management and has taught workshops on project management.

Joan Knutson is president and founder of Project Mentors, a San Francisco–based training and consulting firm that specializes in helping its clients to implement project management practices through consulting, training, and software products. She has over twenty-five years of project management and consulting experience in both the public and private sectors. She has developed courses addressing topics ranging from fundamental tools and techniques to risk, estimating, and multiple project management.

James M. Kouzes is chairman of Tom Peters Group/Learning Systems, which makes leadership work through practical, performance-oriented learning programs. He is coauthor with Barry Posner of the award-winning and best-selling book, *The Leadership Challenge: How to Keep Getting Extraordinary Things Done in Organizations.* Prior to joining the Tom Peters Group, he was the director of the Executive Development Center in the Leavey School of Business and Administration at Santa Clara University.

Christopher M. Lucarelli is a doctoral student in the Lally School of Management and Technology.

Rolf A. Lundin is professor of business administration in the School of Business and Economics at the University of Umea, Sweden. A prolific author in the field of project management, his current research interests include the study of organization theory, particularly temporary organizations. He is also interested in the use of corporate audits as a model effort to renew companies.

John M. Magenau is an associate professor and director of the School of Business at Penn State Erie, the Behrend College. He has published several research articles and book chapters on negotiation and dispute resolution, workers' patterns of commitment to employer and union, and decision making processes in police departments.

Peter W. G. Morris is an executive director of INDECO Ltd. and professor of project management at the University of Manchester Institute of Science and Technology. He is also deputy chairman of the International Project Management Association and vice president of the UK's Association for Project Management.

Barry Z. Posner is dean of the Leavey School of Business and Administration, Santa Clara University, and professor of organizational behavior. He is the coauthor of several award-winning leadership books, including *The Leadership Challenge: How to Keep Getting Extraordinary Things Done in Organizations* and *Credibility: How Leaders Gain and Lose It, Why People Demand It,* along with two noted and informative books on project management: *Getting the Job Done: Managing Successfully Teams and Task Forces* and *Project Planning and Management.*

W. Alan Randolph is a professor of management in the Robert G. Merrick School of Business, University of Baltimore. He is also a senior associate with Blanchard Training and Development of San Diego, California. He has served as a consultant with a wide variety of companies, in both the United States and internationally.

Marie Scotto is president of the Scotto Group, a consortium of management consultants and business trainers. She has been a management consultant and trainer for more than twenty years. In addition to training, the Scotto Group conducts capability assessments, consults on specific projects, designs project organization implementations, and works with clients throughout the implementation of organization and methodology adjustments.

Gene R. Simons has been associated with Rensselaer Polytechnic Institute for thirty-two years, where he has chaired the Industrial and Management Engineering Program, developed the graduate programs in manufacturing systems engineering, and founded the Northeast Manufacturing Technology Center. He is currently associate dean for special graduate programs in the Lally School of Management and Technology and director of Manufacturing Outreach for the NYS Center for Advanced Technology in Automation, Robotics, and Manufacturing.

Dennis P. Slevin is professor of business administration at the Katz Graduate School of Business, University of Pittsburgh. His research interests focus on entrepreneurship in both large and small strategic business units, strategy, structure, and their impact on organizational effectiveness. He has also done work in the area of project management and the keys to successful project implementation.

Anders Soderholm is an associate professor of business administration in the School of Business and Economics at the University of Umea, Sweden. He is the author of numerous papers and conference presentations on issues including research into project organizations, temporary organizations, project management, new organizational forms, and issues in organizational renewal.

William E. Souder is the Alabama Eminent Scholar Endowed Professor in Management of Technology and director of the Center for the Management of Science and Technology at the University of Alabama in Huntsville (UAH). He also holds appointments as professor of management and professor of engineering at UAH. He has many years of varied industrial experience, is the author of over two hundred research papers and six books, founded three start-up firms, and has received numerous awards, including one from the White House for his research accomplishments.

Hans J. Thamhain is professor of management at Bentley College in Waltham, Massachusetts, and is well known for his research and writings in project management. He has held engineering and project management positions with GTE, General Electric, Westinghouse, and ITT and has written over seventy research papers and five professional reference books in project and engineering management.

Peg Thoms is an assistant professor of management in the School of Business, Penn State Erie, the Behrend College. She has sixteen years of management experience in the private sector and has managed numerous special projects. Her research interests are leadership and leadership development, self-managed work teams, and human resources selection.

Vijay K. Verma is a group leader at a Canadian national laboratory where he provides project management services for projects varying in size, complexity, and diversity. He is a well-known speaker, trainer, consultant, and author and has written a three-volume series on the human aspects of project management.

R. Max Wideman is a practicing consultant with over forty years of project management experience. During his career, he has served in the capacity of executive, project director, and project manager to a range of clients in public, private, and nonprofit enterprises. His projects have ranged from heavy civil engineering, through buildings to administrative, software, and intellectual projects.

David Wilemon is professor of marketing and innovation management in the School of Management at Syracuse University. He also serves as director of the Snyder Innovation Management Center. He has conducted extensive research on new product development, high-performing teamwork, management, and innovation management.

THE PROJECT MANAGEMENT INSTITUTE

PROJECT MANAGEMENT HANDBOOK

PART ONE

THE PROJECT CONTEXT

CHAPTER ONE

KEY ISSUES IN PROJECT MANAGEMENT

Peter W. G. Morris

Project management has traditionally been thought of as the process of accomplishing a task on time, in budget, and to technical specification. This view reflects project management's origins in contract administration and task management. Today that view is changing to something much more ambitious, exciting, and challenging.

A New View of the Discipline of Managing Projects

Project management evolved in the 1950s, 1960s, and 1970s essentially as a discipline for managing, to time, budget, and specification, quite complex engineering projects.[1] The project management task was essentially taken as a given: the project manager's job was to do it. For many, project management is still primarily a set of tools, techniques, and activities that are applied almost regardless of where in the project life cycle one is.

You plan, using the work breakdown structure (WBS) and various scheduling and budgeting techniques; you organize, allocating WBS tasks to organizational units by using an organization breakdown structure (and task responsibility matrix) and structuring units with project or matrix organizations; you form teams, exercise leadership, and deal with conflict; and you monitor progress using various measurement and reporting techniques.

Much of standard project management training is focused at this level. The trouble is that managing projects is much more complicated than this. And by no means do all project managers feel the need for all these techniques. Too frequently project management is described with too little attention paid to real practice. In the real world, project staff have to be much more sophisticated in using project management.

In particular, too many people see project management as basically downstream implementation. Too few recognize the important contributions that project management professionals can make in the key early definition stages of the project life cycle. This chapter explores some of these challenges, showing the vital role that project management has to play from the very earliest moments of project inception, through the time that contracts are let and traditional implementation begins, to commissioning, testing, and handover, and into operation.

But it does more than that, for the traditional view of project management is no longer good enough. Today's world of project management is much more demanding than the old "on time, in budget, to spec" one. It is about managing projects as entities. Its focus is the project. It is about accomplishing projects successfully. It is about managing change and transition. And today, as never before, it is value driven. It is about meeting and exceeding customer expectations; about getting the best bang for the buck, creating value, and shortening implementation schedules (time to market).

The skills demanded of today's top project managers are now often much more demanding than have traditionally been required. They are, typically, those of ensuring the following:

- A project *definition*, which is strategically thought out and makes business sense
- A *design* that is optimally matched to customer needs, with production input fully integrated to ensure the most efficient development and delivery times
- *Technology* that is properly chosen and proved
- A design process that evolves smoothly, with firm configuration management and iron *change control*
- Effective *risk management*
- Value-enhancing *procurement*
- Superefficient *implementation*

These are the themes we shall be exploring. Let us follow the project life cycle (see Figure 1.1) and examine some of the issues and lessons from the contemporary management of projects (see Figures 1.2 and 1.3).

Too many people see project management as beginning when the project is set up. Yet all the lessons of modern management—and indeed all the lessons of project management history—show that time spent up front in defining needs, exploring

FIGURE 1.1. PROJECT LIFE CYCLE.

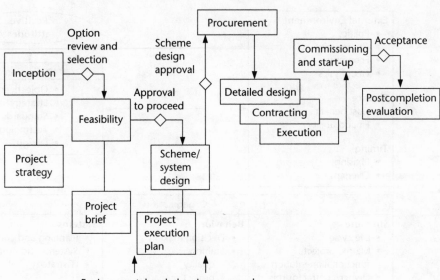

Environmental and planning approvals

options, modeling, testing, and looking at different business benefits is central to producing a successful project. The decisions made at the early definition stages set the strategic framework within which the project will subsequently develop.[2] Get it wrong here, and the project will be wrong for a long time—perhaps forever. Get it right, and you are halfway there. (Defining the problem is half the solution; 90 percent of the outcome is defined in the first 10 percent of the project.) This is potentially one of the most crucial areas of project management professional input.

Project management professionals are the experts in the management of projects. Harnessing their professional expertise from the very beginning of the project is only logical, yet it is a new idea to many people. Indeed, one of the most important issues in the management of projects today is that of deciding what the role of project management is in managing the front-end stages of projects.

Role of Project Management in Project Definition

Integration is one of the most basic functions of project management. It brings together the skills that are necessary to achieve project success and ensure that the activities that need doing are accomplished properly. Integrating marketing, design, production, and other functions in project definition cannot logically be queried.

FIGURE 1.2. MAJOR ISSUES IN PROJECT MANAGEMENT.

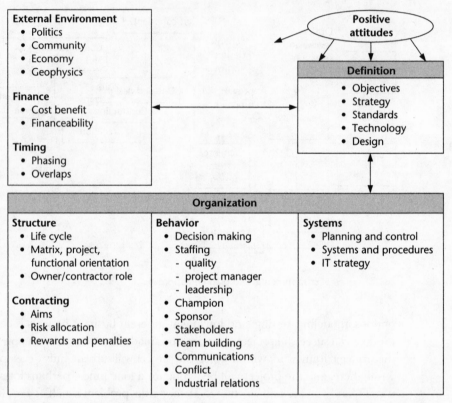

Source: Morris, P. W. G., & Hough, G. H. (1987). *The anatomy of major projects.* New York: Wiley.

Does this not mean that project managers should be involved from the very earliest stages of a project? Not everyone has been so convinced.

Such has been the traditional view and practice of project management (basically as contract implementation) that many people see a potential conflict of interest in having the same project manager involved in the presanction stage of a project as in the later implementation stages.[3] There is a danger, some believe, that the project manager may be biased toward going ahead where a less interested party might recommend that the project not proceed.[4] But the error arises by conflating contract or implementation project management with the generic discipline of project management.

Project management is not simply implementation management. It is the discipline of defining and delivering successful projects. Perhaps it would be better if the discipline was called "the management of projects," for then it would be clear

FIGURE 1.3. CURRENT ISSUES IN PROJECT MANAGEMENT.

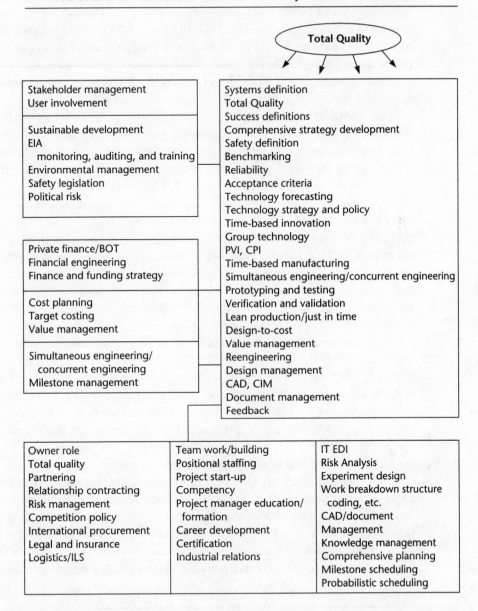

that the object was the project and how to manage it successfully—more an outside-looking-in, holistic discipline than an internal, process-driven activity.

Project management as a generic discipline applies at all stages of the project life cycle, and it can be practiced at all levels of management. The three most important uses of project management, however, are in project definition and development; project implementation and execution; and commissioning, testing, and start-up. These three overlap. They all focus on the project, and they all use project management. But they have slightly different, though enormously valid, perspectives. Though different, however, the generic skills are the same.

Project management is practiced by many groups: owners, consultants, suppliers, and others. Project management in the first and last of the three stages is essentially applied from an owner's perspective, although it neither should be nor is confined to just owners. Owners' project management may be a little different from suppliers', but it is still the same generic discipline, just as the marketing or finance disciplines vary depending on the type of organization performing them.

(In fact, the trend today is increasingly for owners to hone their form of project management by employing quite sophisticated though small project teams, primarily in the role of definition and development managers, with suppliers providing the more skill- and technology-specific implementation project management. BAA, a major worldwide airport owner and operator company, employs a project management strategy very much in this mold. This brings two dangers, however. One, which is a very old one in project management, is of getting effective project definition. The other is of maintaining a level of overview and involvement that is positive and value creating.)

Project management, as the discipline of managing projects optimally, has an important role in the front-end definition of projects. Project management professionals should be the people who understand the project process and best practice; who can form and shape project strategy; who can judge how best to procure resources, arrange work flows, optimize cash flows and financial returns; and who can motivate teams, monitor, and replan. All of these actions, performed from the earliest stages of project concept definition and options investigation, should benefit hugely if conducted by someone who understands projects.

In bringing their expertise to bear in managing the front end, project managers must use their professional skills to create the conditions for realizing a successful project and advising the client (internal or external) on the potential risks and difficulties, as well as the options and possibilities. Ford, for example, used an overt project management structure from the very earliest stages of new car project definition to integrate its traditional functional organization chimneys.

The Project Sponsor and Project Management

Roles at the front end also raise another important issue in project management: the difference between a project manager and a project sponsor. Understanding this difference, and the role of the project sponsor, helps one tackle an old question of project management—the proper relation between project management and operations.

Projects need owners. Owners, in fact, typically have two kinds of project roles: someone responsible for the business case for investing in and creating the project, increasingly known as the project sponsor, and a project manager for delivering the best project within those business case parameters. For example, an automobile company decides it wants to build a new factory somewhere in Europe to produce X thousand trucks a year in four years. The vice president for Europe is given responsibility for the capital investment project. This is just one of his management responsibilities, however. He clearly has no time himself to do all the work of managing, specifying, contracting, reviewing, and so on, so he appoints a project manager from within the company to do this. This project manager is appointed from the very outset; probably it is not even clear yet which country the plant is to be in. (Indeed, based on information that may be subsequently generated, it could be that the company decides not to go ahead with the project.) It is the project manager's job to do everything necessary on behalf of his boss, the vice president for Europe, to fulfill the board's decision— specifically, to provide the definition of a plant that will produce X thousand trucks a year for $600 million in four years' time. (In practice, the specifications will soon be a lot more detailed than that, of course.) Should the project manager find that the business case has to change, he must inform his boss, the sponsor—the holder of the business case. (U.K. government departments have, under Treasury guidance, recently put considerable emphasis on the role of the sponsor.)

The sponsor is particularly responsible for ensuring that the brief (or project instruction document) accurately reflects his needs. The sponsor must approve the brief as it evolves as the project definition and design develop. (There will often be three or four formal brief approval points.) And it is he who must decide (in consultation with the board) if the brief should change as the project unfolds— for example, whether extra capacity needs to be added, the schedule needs to be accelerated, additional cost should be incurred, and so forth. The sponsor will also need to be kept informed of and may require approval for changes in the way the project is to be implemented, particularly if these will affect the owner's business or corporate responsibilities. (Better brief management is one of the areas now receiving increased attention in the U.K. construction industry.)

One of the sponsor's major responsibilities is integrating the needs and wishes of operations and users into the project management process. This is a crucial area. Time and again in the history of project management, problems have developed because operations have requested changes late in the project life cycle; as a result, projects have been gold-plated (over-engineered) or delays have been incurred. (This has been one of the biggest problems in delivering defense projects. The military officers have often insisted on technically demanding operational requirements, generally overruling the procurement project manager, and often ordering changes during design.)

If integrating operations' needs into an effective project definition is difficult, integrating those of users is generally even more challenging. Users' needs are represented, or managed, in different ways in different project industries. In many situations, users' needs are best reflected by the marketing function. Often, though, it does not work this way. In commercial building and civil engineering, for example, the user link may be quite weak. In either case, integrating the needs of operations and users into the project is one of the most important duties of the project sponsor—and one of the least well done.

The project manager (and the sponsor) must explore many different options at the definition stage: of configuration, specification, schedule, procurement, funding, and so forth. The aim is to find the best scheme and to identify the weak spots in potential options. Proposals should be rigorously tested and new ideas explored. Many options should in fact be investigated at the early prefeasibility and inception stage, with the number reducing substantially as the project moves to the feasibility stage. The process is highly creative, involving a mix of synthesis (new design) and analysis (as options are dissected and evaluated). The range of issues covered, and probably the kind of people and styles one will be working with, are substantially different from the later implementation stages of the project. And although the skills are still very similar—integration, process, and people management—the project manager must still be involved sufficiently in the detail to be sure no mistakes are being made or options overlooked and that the recommendation will stand detailed scrutiny.

Testing and evaluation of the options at this time will focus particularly on technical performance, environmental issues, finance and economics, commercial risks, and likelihood of business success (using that term in its widest sense: meeting functionality, competitiveness, investment return, and cost-benefit criteria).

Risk management should be a major preoccupation at this stage. If you look at the owner's record of actual project outturn results compared with the case put at the time of capital investment approval, the result is very often worse than had been forecast, in many cases substantially so. This has to suggest that most owner companies do not perform risk analysis effectively.

All major risks should be identified and assessed as early as possible. Where not acceptable, risks should be laid off to third parties (but be realistic on how much they are really being laid off), insured against, designed out, or otherwise eliminated. Inevitably there will be residual risk. The project manager should ensure that the sponsor is happy to bear this. This risk process should continue throughout the project life cycle.

Modeling

Business, technical, financial, environmental, and other dimensions of the proposed project should be modeled as far as possible, and as cost-effectively as possible, before committing either significant resources to the project or indeed to irrevocable go-ahead. Developments in computer-assisted design, in so-called 5D (three-dimensional plus cost and time), and virtual reality are significantly enhancing our ability to "prebuild" the project before committing to final go-ahead. Rolls Royce, for example, has quoted its ability to prebuild a new engine electronically as probably the single biggest breakthrough in its project management in the past decade.

Although I say to model as fully as possible before committing significant resources, be under no mistake that the project definition stage ought to be well funded. This probably means more fully funded than most organizations normally realize. Three to 6 percent of the final capital cost of the project could be spent in prefeasibility, feasibility, and preliminary design proofs. (The amount spent on subsequent design prior to full commitment varies. For example, on software projects it will be much higher—on the order of 20 percent or even more—than on capital construction projects where the high cost of plant and equipment pushes it down to 10 percent or so.) The problem in practice, however, is that while this holds in theory, in reality the development team is often not at all sure what the final capital cost of the project will be, and is, in any case, hoping that it will be rather less than the amounts being suggested. There is hence a natural inclination to spend less than what ultimately proves to be the 3 to 5 (or less) percent. Guard against this. Remember that money spent early in the project can be a fortune saved later. Unfortunately, the less experienced the owner is, the less willing he or she generally is to accept this.

Project Strategy

The project manager at this early stage of project definition must ensure that project planning is as comprehensive as possible. A project strategy document should be prepared very early in the life cycle, with an outline strategy sketched for each project option. Certainly by the time the single proposed option is chosen, it should have a comprehensive preliminary strategy. The strategy should cover at least the following elements:

- Clear identification of sponsor and project objectives
- Statements on how these are to be achieved
- Environmental issues and strategy for addressing these

- Quality policy and strategy for implementation
- Safety policy
- Owner's role and the role of third parties, such as consultants and contractors
- Financial and economic objectives, financial strategy, funding strategy, and cost targets
- Legal and insurance issues and strategy
- Technical strategy, technical policy, and design philosophy
- Project and work breakdown structure
- Milestone and summary-level schedule
- Risk management strategy
- Contracting and procurement strategy
- Logistics policy
- Employment and industrial relations strategy
- Communications policy, particularly regarding external policy
- Information technology policy

As the project develops, the strategy should be progressively updated. By the time of moving into procurement, the strategy will have evolved into a formal project execution plan (PEP), which, among other things, will give a detailed method statement of how the project is to be executed. Any deviations from the strategy should be noted and approved by the project manager (and his or her management, as appropriate—for example, the project board if there is one, and in certain instances the project sponsor).

Environmental and Other Approvals

On many projects, and by no means just construction ones, considerable work is legally necessary at the definition stage on analyzing, presenting, and obtaining the approval for the environmental impact of the project. (In the context of this chapter, this term includes the health, safety, planning, easements, and other legal approvals required of the project before it may proceed.) Often these requirements may have a considerable impact on the project budget, and to an extent that can be quite difficult to assess accurately. The final effects of decisions on the cost of compulsory purchases or redesign to meet planning approvals can be significant.

Over the past decade or two, these requirements have increased in most countries and states by several orders of magnitude. Actually, in project terms, this is not a bad thing, for it forces the project team to spend time at the front end doing detailed planning and then to put its project proposals out to scrutiny. In the past, too many projects have gone forward with far too little front-end planning. Peer review gives the project the opportunity to test its plans quite rigorously. Again, time spent at the front end pays off.

Finance

No discussion of contemporary project management could avoid reference to the very strong trends toward private sector finance in almost all sectors and in most countries. In some sectors, of course—pharmaceuticals for example—finance has always come from the private sector.[5] But in many, and particularly in infrastructure—such as power, water, roads, telecommunications, and rail—there has been an enormous swing across a whole swath of government sectors toward the use of private sector financing in place of the traditional public sector sources.[6]

BOT/BOOT (Build Own [Operate] Transfer) is the term probably most frequently employed in this regard. It refers to the practice of offering project opportunities that were traditionally in the public sector domain to private companies or groups on the basis that they raise the funds, build the project, and then operate the facilities for a period that is sufficiently long to recoup the funds and make a profit. Attractive though this idea is to many governments, it is a lot easier to say than to do. The devil is in the detail, particularly the legal and contractual detail of the arrangements among the governmental entities, the contracting group, and those funding the undertaking. Getting the detail right, and acceptable to the parties, can be enormously expensive.

This said, there is little doubt that the move toward private sector disciplines and project finance—that is, finance guaranteed primarily by the ability of the project alone to meet its repayment commitments—is good for project management. Accountability is clearer. The focus is on outturn costs. Risk analysis becomes central. (The three different risks of concessionaire, developer, and builder or supplier should be clearly and separately appraised.) Managing the project as an integrated whole comes into play from the outset. There is a stronger focus on commercial success, with the owner group typically concentrating on the business case, giving maximum attention to setting up the project optimally and devolving implementation responsibility more—though by no means completely—onto the suppliers. The suppliers, in turn, probably operating in a Total Quality framework, work closely with the owner and are rewarded or penalized according to their performance.

Design

Designing what is to be built, or done, is clearly one of the most critical parts of the project. It is also one of the parts that most commonly goes wrong, or at least one where it is often felt it could have gone a lot better. It is certainly one that is least well understood. Yet it is hardly ever treated in the project management literature, or even in project management training or education courses.

Design covers several stages of the overall project life cycle. Early design work involves defining the customer requirements and investigating these within the context of the overall project strategy. This definition goes variously under the names of *briefing, project identification, system engineering,* and the like. The important points to recognize are these:

- Design begins at the very earliest of stages in the life cycle. Even at the prefeasibility stage, different configurations will be being developed and explored.
- It is holistic.
- It is intimately interwoven with establishing the user needs and assuring the viability of the project business case.
- It involves not just shape (and configuration) or aesthetics but also fitness for purpose and choice and management of technology, including technical risk management, selection of materials, systems, electronics, and so forth.
- The process is iterative and interactive.
- But clear milestone review points can, and must, be established.

Today, design is generally a team-based activity. And designers have to design very consciously to cost and to schedule. Indeed, it is more than just designing to cost; design is about improving value. Hence value engineering (or value management)—the discipline of maximizing value or, slightly differently, the functionality-to-cost ratio—is becoming increasingly recognized as a central input in the design process.[7] So too is production management, particularly in managing the design process more effectively and in integrating downstream manufacturing and production know-how. Hence there is growing recognition of design for manufacturability and buildability. *Concurrent engineering* is widely, if sometimes confusingly, used as a term to capture these ideas.[8]

Concomitant with value is reliability. Huge effort is put into ensuring reliability. How often is it that a car or a television set, let alone a pharmaceutical product or an aircraft, is unreliable compared with ten or fifteen years ago? These products are much more reliable now. Designers must be clear on the reliability standards they are being expected to meet. Equally, project management should define at an early stage of the design process what the acceptance criteria will be for handover of the project to operations.

Technology

One of the greatest sources of problems in projects has historically been using inappropriate or unproven technology.[9] All project managers should recognize that using unproved technology in their projects will increase the likelihood of problems, delays, or overruns dramatically. (Hence private sector financiers are extremely cautious about funding projects that have unproved technology in them.) The rule must be to develop new technology "off-line," on R&D or prototype projects, for example, and to avoid at all costs incorporating unproved technology into production projects. Pretesting through prototyping and modeling has become much more common project practice. Prototyping is being used routinely now in information systems projects, for example, as well as in manufacturing in general and new product development in particular.

Proper verification and validation—sometimes, as in software, done independently by a third party, hence referred to as independent verification and validation (IV&V)—should be planned from the outset. Although most commonly applied during implementation, such independent reviews should happen throughout the project. Independent design reviews, for example, are an extremely valuable means of improving the design at minimal cost. Effective design review meetings are at the absolute heart of a properly conceived and soundly managed project. These are the gates—the milestone review points—that the project must go through to check that the design is within budget and giving optimal value, and that the overall schedule has been compressed to a commercially realistic point and tied to relevant target dates. At the conclusion of each review, the design should be frozen; change to the design should be allowed under only the very strictest of circumstances, with full appreciation of the proposed change's impacts, and presumably only for very good reason.

Recognition of upcoming innovations and the effect these will have on the project is another critical aspect of effective design management; doing this formally is sometimes referred to as preplanned product improvement (P^3I). Management may identify, for example, that a new version of a component in the product design will be available in several months' time. Deciding how and when to incorporate that technology needs careful handling, not just technically but in terms of marketing, pricing, supply chain management, and a host of other dimensions. Dealing with this problem over a portfolio of upcoming products is an important issue in contemporary manufacturing management, an area that has recently received much attention in product development research.[10]

Configuration Management

That poor control of changes is another major source of project difficulty is now widely recognized. Change control is thus now commonly seen as a core project management practice. Changes often arise from design, and it is extremely important that designers and design managers recognize the damage that poor change control can cause to a project. Configuration management—the term used in aerospace and electronics and other high-tech industries for the management of project documentation, change control, interface management, configuration status, accounting, and auditing—further strengthens project management's ability to control the identification and status of every element in the project, including, obviously, all changes.

Document management is an integral part of configuration management. There are dramatic improvements occurring in the way we can prepare, store, coordinate, and transmit documents and other information electronically. We are now genuinely capable of moving into the era of the paperless project, as the Boeing 777 was said to be, though total paperlessness may not in fact necessarily be very desirable. Tying the overall project documentation and the design documentation together electronically has major benefits for design management. Configuration management is consequently now being extended to become configuration of the total project documentation, including the information technology infrastructure and procedures that are to be used. Hence, with information being held increasingly in predominantly electronic form, modern configuration management is becoming more infocentric than documentcentric.

Software project development in some ways has been leading the field in integrating project management with product design. Certain CASE[11] management tools incorporate best project management practice integrally with systems engineering. I believe, however, that we shall shortly be seeing the development of similar tools in other project-based industries using sophisticated knowledge-based project management information systems to tie in rules, procedures, and help lines to project design, procurement, budgeting, and other project management activities and routines.

Overlapping Design and Production

Concurrency was the old term used to describe beginning implementation before the technology was proved and the design stable. It almost always led to major cost overruns. (Modern "concurrent engineering" stems from this, but is much more. It connotes team working of production, design, marketing, and other facets without starting production implementation before the design is stable.) The danger represented by concurrency does not have to mean that implementation need never start before all design is ready, however. "Fast track" is an example of how production and design can safely be overlapped.[12]

The essence of fast track/fast build is that the overall, or scheme/system, design is firmed up before moving to detailed design and production, but the detailed design and production of individual packages then proceeds on a phased basis. Implementation on early packages may even be complete before detailed design on later packages has been started. In this way, considerable schedule benefit can be obtained without incurring the risks of later design changes.

Integrated Logistics Support and Operations Input

Integrated logistics support (ILS) is another dimension of overall product or program planning that is familiar in some project industries, though not in all. Its central ideas are self-evidently sensible and deserve to be applied generically. Like most other project management practices, it needs to be initiated in the project definition stage but emerges forcibly only in design. The practice, from the defense and manufacturing industries, refers to the need when specifying equipment and other product components to consider how the long-term supply handling and maintenance during operations should be optimized. The emphasis on operational costs and management is sound and at last beginning to become fairly widely accepted as good project management practice. Value management and value engineering, for example, now routinely look at operational costs.[13]

After the design is established, most projects need to import external resources, to supply needed equipment and materials, specialist skills, or additional labor. These must be procured either from within the organization or from outside.[14]

Procurement

Like so much else in the management of projects, procurement practices have been undergoing profound changes recently. Until the mid–1980s, most project industries had their own ways of procurement and contracting. The defense industries worked largely on a cost-reimbursable basis. The oil and gas industries largely procured on the basis of cheapest bidder, as did the building and civil engineering industries. The fact that a bid might clearly be too low was the bidder's problem. The North Sea procurement practices of the late 1980s even encouraged concurrency by asking the bidder to bid on incomplete design information and to take price and completion risk. But then things changed—radically, and for the better.

Total Quality Management (TQM) began to affect project-based industries from the mid-1980s. TQM involves a whole raft of value-creating management practices: focusing on customers, management by fact, measuring along the whole production process (the total life cycle), teamwork, and continuous improvement. Continuous improvement means what it says: continuously improving—not just meeting one-time targets but relentless year-on-year improvement. If you are looking for long-term continuous improvement, then choosing a supplier on the basis of the cheapest bid alone simply cannot make sense. Instead, you would do better to select on the basis of long-term ability to perform and improve, organizational compatibility, quality, and a price that is competitive today but can be even more so tomorrow.

Total Quality and Continuous Improvement—lean management—was pioneered by the Japanese, largely in the automobile industry. The focus was on capturing value and retaining margin by improving the way a company worked with its suppliers. This works more self-evidently in manufacturing, where products are developed for sale in an open, competitive market. It is harder in the capital development industries, such as construction, where the link among quality, value, selling price, and margin may be harder to see. Nevertheless, at the very least, practices such as two-stage tendering became more common: select first on the basis of technical ability and then on price. But newer ideas, such as partnering, alliancing, and framework contracts, also began to become more in vogue.[15]

Partnering is still a poorly understood practice, although the principle is simple enough: performance will be improved by buyers' and suppliers' working together closely on a long-term Total Quality basis. If aims are matched, resources pooled, teamwork promoted, and planning integrated, then surely the end result will be better than simply taking the cheapest bidder. But what has not received so consistent attention in many industries is the nature of the incentives, and demands, that ought to be put on the parties.

There are many who see partnering as some kind of warm and comfortable relationship between purchaser and supplier where everything will be better. This vagueness hides potential opportunity for improving performance. The trick is to identify what performance targets are being sought and what programs of action will be initiated to realize these improvements. The owner (buyer) and supplier(s) both work closely together, jointly and openly, to try to reach these targets. The owner benefits because his real long-term business needs are being addressed, and he is harnessing the in-depth know-how of his supplier base. But there ought to be some incentive to reach those improvement targets: both a reward for achieving them and a penalty for not doing so. Partnering agreements in the auto industry, for example, have had very steep performance improvement targets; failure to meet these incurs serious financial penalty.

The recent trend for organizations to "reengineer"—which, in effect, means to reduce costs—has caused, and is causing, substantial procurement challenges. In today's environment of pressure on costs, one of the first areas to receive attention is overhead. The result is a marked trend toward outsourcing, an overt objective being to gain cost reduction from suppliers. And this leads directly to one of today's management tension areas. Reengineering and outsourcing lead readily to cost minimization and organizational uncertainty; TQM, on the other hand, aims to create teamwork, long-term relationships, and an overriding concern with quality. The two are not, in fact, incompatible, but they can easily slip into opposition. Efficiency gains and costs reduction need setting in a TQM environment. While customer needs dominate, competition is promoted, along with incentives and penalties; there is heavy concentration on early and intense planning and performance measurement; and teamwork is central, even in difficult, competitively demanding circumstances. The aim is to release supplier value—for the supplier's benefit but also for the buyer's.

Like almost everything else in project management, the trend in procurement has been to shift to the left—to begin the procurement process earlier and take advantage of earlier preplanning. Procurement is the stage where major commitments are made. Get it wrong in design, and you have an suboptimal product. Get it wrong in procurement, and you can have a commercial and financial mess. Because the risks of getting it wrong are so significant, it is prudent to rely as far as possible on proved and tested terms and conditions. (But do not stick with known contract forms if, even though known, they do not follow best project management practice.) And do perform careful risk analysis of the proposed procurement package.

Risk Management

The identification, assessment, allocation, and management of risk is central to effective procurement management. This said, it is important to recognize from the outset that risk management is a generic management tool that can be applied at any stage and to any set of project management problems. I mentioned it briefly in relation to the need to develop and maintain a comprehensive project strategy. It can also be applied to design, safety, finance, and many other parts of the process. Each one of these risk dimensions can pose substantial risk; failure of design, safety, or finance can have disastrous consequences. It is particularly important at the procurement stage, because it is here that major decisions are taken on the commercial and organizational allocation of risks and responsibilities. These decisions will have a major impact on the conduct of the project—on organizational structures, freedom to manage, attitudes, and responsibilities—and not least on final cost liability and its impact on commercial and financial performance. (The allocation between supplier and buyer may not be as final and secure as hoped; claims are generally possible, and in some situations likely.)

Historically, normal practice has been to put delivery risk as far as possible onto suppliers. Often this has resulted in major problems that then arise as suppliers found that they had misjudged circumstances or been forced to take risk on matters that they were not capable of handling, either managerially or financially. This was deemed "fair enough" by purchasers, generally because there was—and indeed still often is—a sufficiently large pool of other suppliers to top up those in trouble. In short, a crude buyers' market attitude prevailed. Inevitably things went wrong more frequently in such an environment: claims arose, and teamwork and project performance suffered. The only real exception to this fixed-price risk transfer philosophy of procurement was the defense sector, where the high technical risk caused by the developmental nature of so many defense contracts and the limited number of capable suppliers drove the industry for a long time to a cost-reimbursable mode. (In the United States, an attempt was made in the late 1960s and early 1970s to change this but with near-disastrous consequences; U.S. procurement now tends to follow a reimbursable mode up to agreed scope definition and then switches to firm price. In the United Kingdom, cost-reimbursable forms held until the mid–1980s but then switched to firm price, coupled with strong risk analysis.) The late 1980s and 1990s have seen a subtler approach to risk allocation in procurement.

Basic tenets of good risk management in today's procurement are that all parties should be clear on the long-term aims of the purchaser. The risks posed by the project should be appraised fully and allocated openly to the parties best able to bear them. Risk should not unreasonably be put on parties that cannot properly bear that risk. It is wrong and ill advised, for example, to put delivery risk on a supplier if that supplier is not capable (commercially, managerially, technically, and so on) of bearing it; if neither the suppliers nor the owner has the capability of bearing the risk, it is probably better not to proceed. Many project managers require suppliers formally to undertake risk analysis and report on the risks they see in the project. (Of course, project managers should be doing the same for their management.) Additional risk should cost more; the supplier ought to be covering the cost of the additional risk in his price, and it is right for the purchaser to pay for this. Once the risks are allocated, let the parties have the freedom to manage them. Except as specified in the contract, firm price contracting would normally limit the buyer's right to direct the supplier on how to perform the work or what information he should supply; it should be more expensive to request changes to fixed-price contracts. Incentives and penalties are to be encouraged. These may usefully be related to operating costs and revenues, but not unreasonably so; for example, it is ludicrous to try to tie large consequential damages to a weakly capitalized supplier.

Supplier Selection and Project Start-Up

A great deal of the project's implementation success depends on the selection and induction of its contractors, consultants, and suppliers. The key to much of this is careful warming of the market to the project and good supplier preselection. By warming, I mean advising potential suppliers and contractors of the upcoming project, describing its particular needs and features, and exciting those whom you want to bid to do so with a good offer. Preselection involves ensuring that only those bid who have the requisite abilities and upcoming capacity, and not wasting time with suppliers who do not.

Bid terms should be clear and consistent, as should the evaluation criteria. If possible, avoid negotiation of bids. Seek clarification rather than negotiation. Sometimes, however, negotiation is impossible to avoid, particularly on complex or imprecisely defined bids. If negotiation is required, be professional about it. Know your objectives, and have a negotiating strategy formulated.

Once selected, third parties and other new entrants to the project must be oriented, fired up, and mobilized. The generic term *project start-up* is increasingly being used to describe this activity. It ranges variously from "tool box" meetings to more sophisticated workshops combining team building and project planning. The aim is partly to provide an opportunity to plan the strategy and tactics of how implementation will now proceed and partly to deal with instruction on housekeeping issues, including project procedures; most specifically, it seeks to fire up the new team and inject a "kick" into the project.

Implementation and Handover

Once the project is in "go" mode, the goal is to give it the kick: to get it going flat out. With the design stable and the contracts let, the whole tenor of the project changes—or at least it should change. There is a fundamental and pronounced transition: from conception to execution, from synthesis to action, from exploring options to implementing solutions.

In a way, of course, there will already have been considerable implementation from the very earliest stages of the project. Undertaking feasibility studies, developing designs, modeling, and letting contracts, for example, all require active implementation management. This is part of the point I was making at the outset about project management's role beginning at the front end of the project. But this said, there is undoubtedly a qualitative change as the project cusps and begins its race toward completion.

And race it must be, for the goal now is to finish as quickly as economically possible. (Obviously at some point, the increased cost of speeding up the project will outweigh the economic benefits of quicker completion, but as a rule, the cash flow and competitive positioning advantages of early completion are extremely strong.) The operational philosophy of the project from now on should be as follows:

- No design changes unless they are absolutely necessary
- Teamworking to find the quickest implementation schedules
- Deployment of an analytic, practical problem-solving approach to resolving difficulties before they compromise schedules or budgets
- Every attempt made to keep costs down within the terms of the specifications and to increase delivery value

Today's huge focus on productivity has led to considerable improvements in production management. Robotics, increased standardization, new work group patterns and relationships, and process reengineering are now common areas of attention and innovation. And this applies throughout the project life cycle, of course, with implementation applying as much to design, bidding and procurement, and handover, testing, and commissioning as to manufacturing, construction, coding, and other areas.

Managers are particularly keen now on seeking out and comparing best practices from other industries. Benchmarking is increasingly common, with the real benefits arising when benchmarking between industries. There is considerable latent potential here with project management, since one of the great strengths of project management is the lessons it throws up from the interindustry nature of the discipline.[16] One of the major areas of project management development over the next few years, I believe, will be in establishing and refining interindustry metrics for quantifying performance improvements. Much of this work will be IT related.

High performance requires high competency. There is a strong interest now in improving competencies, both organizationally and individually. Competency comprises knowledge, skill, personal attitudes, and experience. Project-based organizations increasingly are putting more effort into ensuring that their employees gain appropriate experience as their careers develop.

Knowledge management too is becoming much more sophisticated. While skills' and needs' assessment practices have developed strongly in recent years, a major area of development opportunity is in IT's ability to provide relevant information much more efficiently. Multimedia, Internet technology, and computer-supported work sharing techniques are beginning to revolutionize knowledge distribution and learning. Combine this with distance learning, and the improvements we can make in taking training and education to the work site, in manageable and powerfully easy-to-digest forms, are dramatic. This is changing radically not just the learning organization but the practices of universities and colleges, and the way they interact with industry. This trend is reinforced by moves in society toward continuous education, with individuals' recognizing the need to learn continuously during their careers. Training increasingly is not something just done periodically, off-site. It is becoming integrated into project operations.

Leadership and teamwork at all levels are the essence of effective implementation. A large number of people will now be working on the project, under considerable pressure, to accomplish difficult tasks as efficiently and productively as possible. Whether or not modern management jargon is used to explain why, the reality is that the more clearly everyone can understand the overall project objective and their part in accomplishing it, the better it will be. Leadership at all levels in the project plays a crucial role in defining and communicating objectives and in motivating people to put in extra effort. And by working together synergistically, teams will achieve much more than working in compartmentalized groups. Worse, of course, is where contractual disputes or other factors cause people actively not to work together effectively. Modern contract forms should explicitly encourage teamwork. The best ones do.

The emphasis now as the project races through production is on tight progress monitoring and short-term planning. The project management team will be looking at actual or potential matters that might prejudice the project's completion on time, in budget, and to spec. Project management must have the flexibility to change direction or speed up or slow down as circumstances require. Contract forms should allow this to happen on equitable terms. Similarly, arrangements for handling contractual disputes should be such as to keep parties working together effectively and the project moving forward. Recent trends toward alternative dispute resolution procedures are a welcome example of this.

It is essential that management knows what progress is actually being made and what the trends are with respect to meeting budget and schedule. Cost and schedule performance measurement must be linked; C-Spec (performance-management-based) earned value analysis is one of the more common project management techniques for achieving this, but others exist (and are often more appropriate).[17] The control emphasis must be rigorously on estimated completion cost to date and the trend(s) toward meeting these. Controlling variations and changes, allocating different resources, use of contingencies: all are important management actions at this time. Cash is particularly important. The time value of money is so great that early completion is financially enormously worth struggling for; late completion can wreck the project's financial viability. (The English Channel tunnel is a clear example.)

The considerable expenditure of resources at this stage of the project brings its own challenges. Cash management is one; logistics and materials handling are also frequently important topics; but I am thinking more of the various matters associated with employing large numbers of people—that is, labor law and health and safety.

The project documentation may well be totally IT based. Certainly effective document management is central to the effective management of the project at this stage. Project documentation can be integrated with facilities and operations documentation by means of the ILS systems or plant "as-builts."

As we have seen, project documentation is increasingly totally IT based. The configuration management task is now not so much issuing current versions of drawings and other documents as maintaining the current operating versions of the project technical information and ensuring project participants can effectively browse and comment on this version as appropriate.

Integration with operations is generally an important issue. Sometimes there is a direct impact, as in rail, airports, and many manufacturing situations, so ensuring there is minimal or no interruption of operations is essential. Management will be giving particular attention to efficient project completion: handover, commissioning, and so forth. As the project moves toward handover, project management at one level will be focusing harder and harder on product completion; at a higher sponsor level, it will be ensuring that training, staffing, operating materials and equipment, moving plans, and everything else is in place, and on time; and that the business and revenue-generating activities are effectively initiated.

When the project is at last completed, the project management task is still not quite yet done. Lessons should be learned. One has, after all, just spent a huge effort in undertaking something of great importance. It would be foolish not to review what happened and to try to learn from the experience. Yet until recently that is what normally did happen. Postcompletion evaluations were very rare; to find an organization taking the lessons seriously, evaluating them, and where necessary changing practice was even rarer. Fortunately this too seems to be changing. Postcompletion reviews, often quite systematic and sophisticated, involving teams and with lessons learned being carefully documented and fed into an organizational knowledge base, are now much more common. The results themselves may well be benchmarked.

The welcome rise in the practice of formal postproject evaluations is partly a consequence of management's generally increased attention to performance, by suppliers and owners alike, and partly due to the new practices of TQM and partnering. Partly it is helped by the new ideas of knowledge management and organizational learning, and in part it is the direct result of the increased professionalism of project management.

Improving Project Performance and Competency

Much that I have just reviewed is relatively new to management and to project management. The discipline of managing projects is clearly alive and well. Initially developed for accomplishing a given undertaking in budget, on time, and to specifications, it is now more holistic and more value driven. Drawing on best practices from many industries, it is a discipline that now transcends its earlier, more mechanistic focus. It is now about defining and delivering successful projects to clients—projects that give optimal value. Developing fast, evolving in a TQM, process improvement environment toward new levels of performance, it demands new work styles and attitudes.

The following will be key issues as project management heads into the twenty-first century:

- *Project definition:* Managing the development of options, identifying and managing risk, and integrating comprehensively the interplay of multiple issues (including engineering and design, finance and commercial, health, safety and environmental, schedule and phasing, and organizational matters)

- *Procurement:* Developing and implementing an effective procurement and contracting strategy in a post-TQM environment where value enhancement and cost reduction are essential
- *Implementation and competency improvement:* Designing and creating an effective project organization; delivering effective projects; creating the conditions for competency improvement through better positioning of staff and improving skills, knowledge, and experience; providing the information needed for empowering people and the systems required to manage projects effectively; and better systems for evaluating, reviewing, and benchmarking

CHAPTER TWO

STRATEGIC PROJECT MANAGEMENT

David I. Cleland

Because organizations achieve their goals through the projects that they produce, project management must be an integral part of strategic management. It might seem that project and strategic management are separate, that they occur on different levels within the organization, and that project management is concrete while strategic management is conceptual, but that is not the case. At least it should not be the case for organizations facing the kind of intense global competition and relentless change that are features of the business environment. In this chapter, we review some basic concepts within strategic management and project management to see where the two intersect. From that understanding, project managers can expand their own thinking about their role and the importance of their work in the strategic management of their organization.

Strategic Management

Selecting and establishing the future direction of the enterprise through the development of future products, services, and supporting organizational processes is a key challenge facing managers today. Strategic management has three basic components: (1) it is directly related to the overall purposes of the enterprise; (2) it is future oriented, dealing with decisions whose impact will be felt in the future, usually a year or more out; and (3) it involves assessment of the possibilities and probabilities of environmental and competitive factors. The design and development of strategic management involves the explicit consideration of new or modified organizational mission, objectives, goals, and strategies. Strategic management decisions will ultimately affect the entire enterprise and its subdivisions and components. As well it facilitates other changes—for example:

- Development of improved or new products, services, or organizational processes
- Acquisition and disposition of facilities and equipment
- Identification and pursuit of new markets
- Development of new distribution channels
- Reengineering initiatives
- Organizational restructuring, downsizing, and realignments
- Mergers, acquisitions, and strategic partnerships
- Recapitalization
- Total Quality Management (TQM) programs
- Use of alternative teams
- Upgrading of personnel knowledge, skills, and attitudes
- Divestment of existing products or services
- Long-term alliances with customers and suppliers

Project Management

Because of the potential for projects to change the purpose and future direction of the enterprise, project management plays a key role in strategic management. By pulling together organizational resources to create something that did not exist before, they provide, through completed projects, a new performance capability for the enterprise. Project management oversees the use of resources from a project's conceptual beginnings through a distinct life cycle, culminating in the delivery of the results that support and sharpen the organization's strategic direction. Four key considerations are always involved in a project:

1. What will the project cost?
2. What time is required to complete the project?
3. What technical performance capability will the results of the project provide?
4. How will the results of the project fit into the design and execution of the enterprise's strategies?

Project management makes it possible for the enterprise to design, develop, and execute improved strategies for future products, services, and organizational processes. Strategic management and project management are thus intertwined in the organizational process of dealing with the inevitable strategic and operational changes, clearly the toughest job that any manager encounters in contemporary organizations. Even when they recognize those changes, managers have to develop strategies to modify the use of resources so that the organization can respond successfully, whether through mergers, acquisitions, downsizing, reengineering, concurrent engineering, benchmarking, self-directed manufacturing initiatives, strategic alliances, or the greatest of all changes—globalization.

Strategic management and project management, interdependently linked, provide the framework for preparing the enterprise to deal with its future, and develop and execute survival and growth initiatives in the marketplace.

Beating Obsolescence and Managing Change

The record is clear that all too many once-agile, competitive enterprises developed flaws in their performance and their ability to survive in an increasingly competitive marketplace, as these examples from industrial history show:

- General Motors's complacency and bloat augmented by the internal needs of its intricate bureaucracy caused progress in new strategies to take an eternity because of a hopelessly entangled complex corporate structure that resisted change.
- Digital Equipment found itself mired in obsolete products and services that were once remarkable, aggravated by a ponderous bureaucratic muck. The founder, Kenneth Olson, who built the company, never did adjust to change in the marketplace, and he was finally ousted from his leadership of the once innovative company.
- IBM lost touch with its most important customers. It was still pushing giant mainframes when the computer world was cutting costs with desktops.
- Sears tried modest discounts associated with business-as-usual strategies to capture middle-class shoppers who sought savings in purchasing at more innovative stores like Wal-Mart.

Many other examples could be given of enterprises that failed to anticipate the changes in their marketplaces. Failing to keep touch with their customers, reinforced by failure to have a vision and a strategy for how to anticipate and deal with change, accelerated their decline.

Having a vision for dealing with change—and a management philosophy and a management system to focus the use of resources to accomplish that vision—is critical. In this respect projects play an important part.

The Strategic Role of Projects

Project teams manage many operational and strategic initiatives in the enterprise, including, for example:

- Construction and enhancement or modernization of facilities such as a new manufacturing plant, warehouse, or computer or telecommunication support
- Reengineering initiatives to bring about a fundamental rethinking and radical redesign of business processes to achieve extraordinary improvements in cost, quality, service, speed, and other performance measures
- Concurrent engineering of the simultaneous design and development of organizational products and services and processes
- Self-directed production activities to improve quality and productivity in manufacturing and production operations through the use of self-directed teams
- Ongoing benchmarking processes that measure organizational products and services and processes against the most notable competitors and industry leaders
- TQM using cross-functional organizational designs to integrate quality improvement efforts
- New business development ventures for the enterprise
- Strategic planning assessments (for example, determining the expected pathway of future technological changes in the marketplace) and use of project teams to design and carry out strategic planning processes
- Negotiation and finalization of strategic alliances with other enterprises, suppliers, and major customers
- Reverse engineering evaluations of competitors' products and services
- Other enterprise initiatives, such as reorganization efforts, liquidation strategies, initiation of new training programs, and downsizing actions

A Strategic Management Road Map

Project teams play a vital role in preparing and facilitating the future of the enterprise. Many of the opportunities for teams arise from the design and execution of strategic initiatives for the enterprise through the use of strategic management road maps to prepare the enterprise for its future.[1] Such a road map outlines a general route for the future of the enterprise and contains several strategies and checkpoints on the road to changes in the enterprise's purposes:

- *Foresight.* The orderly development and anticipation of the possible and probable changes in the markets in which the organization would like to provide products and services. Performance in the desired markets will be affected by changes in the political, social, economic, legal, and technological forces in such markets. Foresight includes consideration of both existing markets and those markets likely to develop. The purpose of foresight, as the act of looking forward with concern or prudence, is to predict events and forces likely to affect the enterprise's business. Nothing else is more important to the organization than its future—assuming, of course, that it has demonstrated operational competence in providing current quality products or services to its customers. Effective foresight can give the enterprise an opportunity to get its products or services to the future first and stake out a leadership position. Foresight is based on deep insights into those forces and events that have a good chance of changing competitive practices.

- *Competitive assessment.* A rigorous examination and evaluation of the strengths, weaknesses, and probable strategies of competitors in their products or services, organizational processes, and market performance.
- *Organizational strengths and weaknesses.* Assessment of the strengths and weaknesses of the enterprise, particularly regarding the ability to deliver competitive products or services through the use of effective organizational processes.
- *Benchmarking.* Review of the performance of competitors and other organizations that are considered the best in the industry, to determine what operational and strategic abilities enable them to perform so well.
- *Strategic performance standards.* Identification, development, and dissemination of the elements required to establish strategic performance standards and guide the use of resources in the enterprise. These standards include the organizational mission, objectives, goals, strategies, and design; individual and collective roles; leader and follower style; supporting systems; and the quality and quantity of organizational resources.
- *Functional expertise.* The ability to develop and maintain centers of excellence in the disciplines needed to support operational and strategic initiatives.
- *Vision quest.* The ability to envision what the future should be for the enterprise—that is, the general direction the enterprise should follow to become what organizational leaders want it to be.
- *Stakeholder interfaces.* Discovery, development, and maintenance of common boundaries with the people and organizations that have a vested interest in the products or services and processes provided by the enterprise. Customers and suppliers are the principal stakeholders with whom close working relationships need to be maintained.
- *Market needs.* Assessment of the probabilities and possibilities of the marketplace, including the potential for products and services for markets that do not currently exist.
- *Product and service and process development.* The use of project teams to focus cross-functional and cross-organizational resources to conceptualize, design, develop,

and initiate continuous improvements in existing products and services and organizational processes, as well as the development of new initiatives in such products and services and processes.

- *Feedback.* Ongoing insight into how well the strategic road map elements are being developed and implemented in positioning the organization for its future purposes.

Figure 2.1 shows a model of this strategic road map. The effective use of this model requires alternative types of teams to focus resources for operational and strategic purposes.

FIGURE 2.1. ROAD MAP FOR STRATEGIC MANAGEMENT.

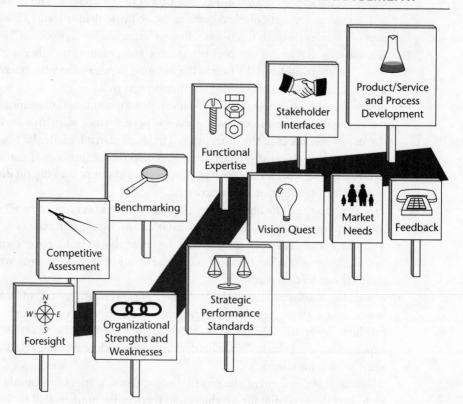

Source: D. I. Cleland, *The strategic management of teams,* p. 9. Copyright © 1996 John Wiley & Sons, Inc. Reprinted by permission of John Wiley & Sons, Inc.

Components of Strategic Management

Strategic management is concerned with designating the fundamental, essential components of strategy formulation and implementation. Strategy formulation encompasses these components:[2]

- Vision
- Mission
- Objectives
- Goals
- Strategies

And strategy implementation encompasses these components:

- Organizational design
- Individual and collective roles
- Management style
- Supporting systems
- Organizational resources

Vision

The vision is a mental image produced by the imagination. A vision is a dream of what might be for a person or an organization. A metals processing company describes its vision as doing what it needs to do to make the company a world-class competitor—and to keep it that way. Another company described its vision for the quality of its products, services, and processes as making it possible to have exceptional quality that seeks to exceed customer expectations.

A lack of vision for the enterprise is sometimes given as one of the reasons that companies fail.[3] But even a well-founded vision must be supported by strategies on how that vision can be realized.

The decline of Apple Computer is sad testimony that product innovation and bold vision are sometimes not enough for long-term survival. The lessons of Apple's decline are extremely important: its core renegade culture planted the seeds of its decline. The expert creators of technology held experienced managers and marketers in disdain. The result? An inward-looking, closed culture that kept Apple from expanding into the larger marketplace. The company remained aloof from the marketplace and let its core technology stagnate. Innovation and vision could not make up for hubris, weak management, and the inadequacies of senior managers who let once-precious assets rot on the vine.[4]

Mission

An organizational mission is a statement of the business that the enterprise pursues. One company described its mission thus: "We are in the business of designing, developing, and installing energy management systems and services for the Power Generation industry." The Boeing Company, which uses project management widely, describes the mission of the company as "to be the number one aerospace company in the world, and among the premier industrial firms, as measured by quality, profitability, and growth."

Objectives

The organizational mission is supported by objectives. Organizational objectives are the target and critical results that must be achieved in the long term in an enterprise to enable accomplishing the mission. Objectives can be stated in quantitative or qualitative terms. A computer company defines one of its objectives as leading the state of the art in personal computers. Wal-Mart describes one of its objectives as "providing customers with quality goods, and make the goods available when and where customers want them."

Goals

Organizational objectives are supported by goals. The goal of an organization is a time-sensitive milestone, such as a financial performance goal of 15 percent return on investment by a specific date. One company described one of its goals as "designing, engineering, constructing and putting into operation a 'greenfield' manufacturing plant by the end of 1995." When an organizational goal has been attained, measurable progress has been made toward the satisfaction of the organizational objectives. In the design and construction of the greenfield plant, a project team was used as a focal point to bring together the human and nonhuman resources to make the plant an operating entity. If an organizational goal involves the use of resources to create something for the enterprise that does not currently exist, then the use of project management to bring a focus to the use of those resources is a valuable strategy.

Strategy

Strategies are the design of the means to attain organizational purposes. An organizational strategy is the design of the means through the allocation of resources to accomplish the goals, objectives, and mission of the enterprise. Strategies include operational (short-term) plans, programs, policies, procedures, and projects, which are basic building blocks in the design and execution of organizational strategies. Projects that have cost, schedule, and technical performance objectives are the direct means for designing and implementing strategies. Changes in the enterprise's products and services and its organizational processes are brought about through the use of project teams that bring together resources from within the organization and from outside sources to create new or improved products and services and processes. Thus, projects are a direct line for the accomplishment of organizational goals and objectives. For example, at the Swiss Corporation for Microelectronics and Watchmaking, project teams have made extraordinary contributions to one of the most spectacular industrial comebacks in the world: the revitalization of the Swiss watch industry. The chief executive officer, Nicolas G. Hayek, states, "We are big believers in project teams." He believes that the whole process of using projects works only if the entire management team focuses on developing products and improving operations, not fighting with each other.[5]

Jasinowski and Hamrin describe what they call the "Ten Paths to Success" of the fifty companies that they examined that had participated in American industry's comeback. Two of these paths were the ability to "empower employees" and "envision new products and markets," both directly related to the use of project teams to bring about change in the enterprise.[6]

At the 3M Corporation three project management approaches are used to develop new products: (1) "skunk works" projects, spearheaded by employee project teams; (2) traditional development in which business unit managers and researchers work together as a team to create new products sand improve existing ones; and (3) pacing programs, which consist of a small number of products and technologies that promise to produce substantial profits fast—usually in two years or less.[7]

Organizational Design

This refers to the alignment of people, specialized activities, and resources of the enterprise through a process of decentralization of authority, responsibility, and accountability. The organizational chart, which portrays the alignment of resources within the enterprise, is the most visible evidence of the organizational structure. Organizational designs use various schemes of departmentalization to gather together resources to accomplish organizational purposes—for example:

- *Functional.* Organizational units are based on common specialties such as finance, engineering, and manufacturing.
- *Product.* Units are responsible for major products or product lines.

- *Customer.* Resources are centered around customer groups, such as the Department of Defense.
- *Territorial.* The organizational units are based on geographical lines, such as the Western U.S. Marketing Zone.
- *Process.* The resources are organized on the flow of work, such as in a manufacturing plant or an oil refinery.
- *Matrix.* This is a blend of the functional and other departmentalizations and a designated focal point for managing the various project activities within an enterprise.

Roles

Within any organizational design, the performance of individual and collective roles brings life to the enterprise. Organizational roles are the individual and collective parts played by the members of the organization. These roles take on special significance when teams are used as elements of enterprise strategy. The performance of organizational roles brings life to the organizational design of the enterprise as people play their respective parts in working with people in the enterprise and with outside stakeholders.

Style

Each person occupying an organizational role has an individual and unique style. The manager and follower style is the manner in which knowledge, skills, and attitudes are expressed by the people who play roles in the enterprise. The styles followed by leaders and followers in the enterprise can range from bureaucratic to highly participative. With the growing use of project teams in contemporary organizations, managerial and supervisor styles are changing from being in charge of people to being coaches, teachers, mentors, and facilitators who provide the environment and resources for the team members who are doing the work of the enterprise. For example, at General Electric's huge Louisville, Kentucky, manufacturing site, the reorganization from assembly lines into self-directed project teams has produced stellar results. In GE's new Maxus line of washers, 40 percent fewer parts are used, resulting in simpler assembly and less manufacturing inventory. Other team-based improvements have been designed and implemented at GE. The Louisville facility, which lost $40 million in 1992, is now making over $50 million.[8]

Supporting Systems

An important part of any enterprise is its supporting systems: those associated with the organizational processes, such as manufacturing, finance, marketing, and research and development. Information systems, production planning and control systems, and accounting systems, among others, facilitate and assist in the design and execution of the many organizational systems that support the performance standards of the enterprise. Computers have greatly changed the operation of these systems, with likely future changes to be as impressive as those that currently exist.

Resources

The bottom line of organizational performance is the resources. The quality and quantity of human and nonhuman resources is the basis of the ability of the enterprise to be successful. The efficient and effective use of these resources is critical, as is the development of strategies to improve the contribution of the resources, such as training for updating the knowledge, skills, and attitudes of all the people working in the enterprise.

The components of strategic management just outlined provide the foundation for the enterprise to use in determining if it is reaching its purposes through the ability to deliver competitive products and services and supporting organizational processes. Whether the organizational entity will attain these components is dependent on many forces and factors in coping with the inevitable change facing the enterprise. The use of project teams can assist in dealing with this change.

Team Results

The results likely to be produced by project teams have both operational and strategic importance. At the Lord Corporation's Dayton plant, chosen as one of *Industry Week*'s ten best plants in 1991, the use of an empowered team workplace made dramatic performance improvement between 1986 and 1990: (1) productivity was up 30 percent; (2) absenteeism was down 70 percent; (3) setup time was reduced more than 75 percent; (4) no-lost-time accidents occurred in the four years; (5) there was an 85 percent reduction in scrap; (6) the manufacturing cycle time was reduced from seventy-five days to seven days; and (7) work in process was reduced by 75 percent.[9]

At the Johnson & Johnson Company, decentralization is practiced with a vengeance: 166 decentralized units act independently, scrambling relentlessly for new products and new markets through an empowerment process that uses project teams as the basic organizational design.

Rubbermaid Corporation's business teams are the basic business units and the drivers of innovation. Each product line has a business team that is managed by a core of four representatives: one each from marketing, R&D, manufacturing, and finance. The team makes the decision as to what product areas they want to go into; wholly new business makes it to the corporate level for the final decision.[10]

At the 3M Corporation, innovative ideas are evaluated for commercial potential by people with hierarchical responsibility for them and by a technical audit team of scientists, manufacturing folk, and marketers. The audit has a dual purpose: to second-guess the hierarchy and to expose the idea to other businesses in a company that might want it.[11]

At Yokogawa Electric, the CEO has successfully pushed teams of workers to meet seemingly impossible cost-cutting goals through reengineering and the redesign of products.[12]

Strategic decision-making teams have become a familiar feature on the corporate landscape.[13] Teams produce results and in the process create trigger effects.

Trigger Effect

One of the effects of the use of project teams in the design and execution of strategies has been the development of the matrix form of organizational design. The pace of change in contemporary business organizations has made traditional, formal organizational structures anachronisms. Such traditional structures tend to be slow, inflexible, and bureaucratic—hardly an organizational design to facilitate dealing with the changes facing business organizations in today's global marketplace.

These traditional organizational designs also create barriers between the companies and the many stakeholders with which they must deal in managing change in the enterprise. For example, at Asea Brown Boveri (ABB), a global matrix has been created that encompasses thirteen hundred separate operating companies. Each front-line operating company manager has a dual reporting relationship: to a regional manager and to a worldwide business head. This reporting relationship helps ABB to be both global and local. In such relationships, the individual front-line units are able to create a culture in which entrepreneurship can flourish, and these operating units can be linked across organizational boundaries in creating and providing customers with innovative products, as well as organizational processes to develop and deliver products and services to users on a timely basis with competitive costs.[14]

As contemporary businesses introduce and accelerate the use of project teams as elements of organizational strategy, other effects are set in motion that change the manner in which the management system operates and the organizational structure of the enterprise. Indeed the very culture of the enterprise changes in direct and subtle ways. Some of the more important of these changes include these:

- There is more entrepreneurship at front-line operating units.
- The organizational competence and competitive strengths in the operating units are better linked across organizational boundaries, extending outward to customers, suppliers, and other key stakeholders.
- The development and propagation of horizontal communication channels and processes are strengthened, resulting in a greater sharing of resources, problems, opportunities, authority, responsibility, and rewards of successful competition.
- There is less predisposition to continue to do things as they have always been done. Rather, there is a greater tendency to discard old ideas and assumptions as they become obsolete, to be replaced by new ideas, strategies, assumptions, and products and organizational processes.
- There is less resistance to change, and the use of project teams as organizational units to facilitate change has become a way of life in many enterprises.
- The formalization of informal horizontal processes that cut across organizational boundaries changes the way things are done. Under traditional management philosophies and organizational designs, such horizontal processes received limited, and in some cases scant, managerial attention.
- People in the organization tend to look at their companies and see less structure and more processes.
- Professional competence is built around technical areas of expertise as well as being integrated across organizational boundaries.
- Creativity, innovation, and a flourishing entrepreneurial culture are found throughout the organization, often existing deep in the organization as the company has grown into a large entity.
- Organizational leaders recognize that their organization's survival and growth depend much less on top-down direction and delegation and more on the development and propagation of an organizational culture that encourages and facilitates bottom-up ideas and innovative initiatives.
- The organization is viewed as growing up from the bottom, where project teams that are successful help the company to change. Ideas managed by project teams during their life cycle grow and contribute to new or improved organizational products and processes, ultimately growing into new departments, new businesses, and new divisions.

- Since much of the organizational work has been assigned to alternative project teams working in the context of new products and processes, fewer senior managerial levels are needed, and the operating units take on added budget responsibility for research and development and financial autonomy.
- Managers learn to develop a tolerance for reducing reliance on formal control systems and foster self-discipline at the operating unit levels.
- Project teams become the instruments by which senior managers challenge the status quo and facilitate a renewal process for the organization reflected in new and improved products and services and supporting organizational processes.
- There is a dedication to make existing products and services and processes obsolete before the competition does.
- Downsizing and restructuring allow subordinate units to operate almost as independent companies, with senior managers playing principal roles of facilitators, resource providers, and strategic management of the enterprise.
- Organizational charts show project teams as well as the more traditional functional or disciplinary groups.
- Project management has become a distinctive career path for those people aspiring to dwell in the land of CEOs, presidents, executive vice presidents, and general managers.

Summary

In this chapter the concepts of strategic management and project management have been described and linked to show how project teams support the strategic management of the enterprise. Strategic management is the management of the enterprise as if its future mattered through the design, development, and execution of explicit strategies to assess future environments and prepare strategies to position the enterprise to take advantage of future opportunities.

Project management is a concept and process for pulling together diverse activities across functional and organizational structures to create something for the enterprise that did not previously exist. Projects are defined as building blocks in the design and execution of organizational strategies. Examples were given of the context in which projects are used to develop and execute new initiatives for the enterprise.

This chapter closed with a description of some of the trigger effects of using project teams in the management of the enterprise.

CHAPTER THREE

MANAGING THE BLACK BOXES OF THE PROJECT ENVIRONMENT

Rolf A. Lundin, Anders Söderholm

Scholars or practitioners dealing with organizational matters are sometimes accused of viewing organizations as black boxes. They seem to focus only on input to and output from these organizational black boxes, and ignore what goes on inside them. Project management techniques, in contrast, seem to work the other way around. They are constructed to emphasize primarily internal aspects of projects, and to stress efficiency as the main requirement for handling those internal aspects (see, for example, the Project Management Institute's *Project Management Body of Knowledge*).[1]

This preoccupation with efficiency means that the much broader context of projects tends to be disregarded. Prescriptive project management theories and techniques tend to concentrate on unfolding the mysteries of a project and aim to make its workings transparent. In so doing, they may view the project environment as an inverted black box—a "black environment" that more or less can be disregarded. This means, for example, that questions about how the task was decided on, what other project ideas were considered, what parallel activities are carried out, relations to host organizations, activities to be carried out after project termination, and so forth are not considered despite the fact that they might have an impact on the project. As a consequence, the understanding of projects is limited to internal project mechanisms during implementation and essentially ignores phases before and after implementation (see Figure 3.1.).

FIGURE 3.1. THE INVERTED BLACK BOX OF PROJECT MANAGEMENT AND THE PROJECT MANAGEMENT ENVIRONMENT.

The black environment of projects	The illuminated inside of projects	The black environment of projects

The stress on techniques we know, such as critical path method and earned value, further emphasizes efficiency concerns in project management. The view of a project as something that has to be isolated from its environment and limited in terms of time and resources also stresses techniques aimed at improving efficiency. And so does the use of a master plan and schedules. But producing relevant specifications for a project, delimiting a project in time and in space, and allocating resources (such as a special team) to it are all very difficult assignments that can have important consequences for how the project can be handled and evaluated in its wider context. Moreover, use of experiences from previous project efforts might be of primary importance for the success of the project. Ignoring postproject activities might be a mistake in the long run.

We believe that concerns about effectiveness (that is, the success of a project in its context) should be a prominent aspect of the project manager's work. Activities before and after the project that have been less well defined should be regarded as fundamental for project work and should be an integral part of the project manager's responsibilities. This extended view of project management coincides with what project management professionals actually believe they should do. In other words, investigating the project environment and pre- and postproject activities might also be a way out of the powerlessness that project managers seem to suffer from in general.[2] This broader view is shown in Figure 3.2.

In this chapter we use experiences from various projects that we have come in contact with to conceptualize some of the pitfalls of being too concerned with efficiency instead of paying enough attention to phases that occur before and after projects. In particular, we concentrate on relationships between projects and their environments in time and space when it comes to matters like conceptualization, decoupling, learning, and recoupling.

FIGURE 3.2. A BROADER VIEW OF PROJECT MANAGEMENT.

Preproject activities— effectiveness consideration	Project management activities— efficiency considerations	Postproject activities— effectiveness consideration

The Heart of Project Management

Conventional wisdom in project management suggests that the notion of action in a project is central. In fact, the very popularity of projects as an organizing principle appears related to the stress on action. Action, as opposed to decisions or discussions, is the prime requirement in project management. Accomplishments are almost always measured in terms of action, not talking, and then mostly in terms of very concrete results. Projects are often defined as a specified area of action that is demarcated from other areas of action (such as other projects or activities in an organization). This demarcation is needed to secure a project's survival and completion and takes four different forms: task definition, time limits, team, and transition: the four T's of project management and project work.[3]

These four T's are not action in themselves but definitions of arenas for action. According to popular belief, project managers must have a good grasp of those four T's in order to push the project to completion and keep control of it. Most of the time, others define these four T's for a particular project, but if someone has failed to define them, properly trained project managers should ask for clarification from their superiors. We suggest that project managers not only should ask for and expect clarification, but should also question the 4T premises of the project and use these demarcations to support the desires that project managers have for appropriate action. For example, definitions on task given to a project manager might be decided on as a result of negotiations among different parties and thus are not necessarily task definitions that promote action. Team members might have been selected on different criteria from those that a project manager might use. Time limits could be inappropriate according to task definitions or resources provided. Since given definitions are not always helpful for promoting action and success, project managers should carefully investigate the four T's and be aware of how they were reached and what consequences they have.

Task

As the raison d'être for the project, the task is without doubt the most fundamental aspect. Certainly task is the project equivalent of an organization's goal structure, but the task is possibly even more important. It defines in an explicit way what should be accomplished. Without a task, there cannot be a proper project, nor will the project retain its identity. The task not only defines action, implicitly or explicitly, but it also forms a basis for the evaluation of the project, the project manager, and the accomplishments of the project team. In other words, it defines on a very basic level what are acceptable results and what are not. Task definitions are also used to allocate all the necessary human, technical, and economic resources to the project.

The task gives the project a distinguishable identity for both project team members and those who work with them outside the project, for example, by being recognized as those "developing the new car" or "building the new apartment complex." Task and action are obviously closely linked, since task gives the basic reason for action and also gives hints on how to organize action. If task is defined in a traditional manner ("building another house"), it also implies what methods to use to achieve the goal. If, on the other hand, the task is defined differently ("building a house that provides new relations between companies, environment, and people"), that might be used to find and employ new methods as well.

Time

The task must be defined in such a way that it can be attained in a limited and predetermined time period. Projects should never be allowed to continue forever since they then no longer will be projects and, consequently, they will lose their focus on action. By definition, they must have a definite termination point when their mission is to have been accomplished. The pressure to keep time schedules is partly also a way to control and limit costs. Time then carries a very clear significance for action and gives project members and management an opportunity to evaluate progress and results.

Team

Any project of importance is typically a venture that involves multimember teams and demands a considerable amount of coordination among them. Most typically, team members are experts who represent different and complementary competencies. In fact, role behaviors are prescribed, at least in projects that are well known to participants, like construction projects, where teams are formed in such a way that all the phases of the work can be taken care of. At the same time, the team is fluid and changes over time with the status of the project. To many in the organization, the team personifies the project, and the selection of a team indicates the real start of a project, even though the entire team seldom stays close to the project for its entire lifetime.

This fluidity within the team has implications for the members' motivation, and it might be a threat to feelings of responsibility and individual involvement. Team issues also highlight the question of action. Members are assigned to the project because they are supposed to act in accordance with task and transition definitions. And implicitly or explicitly, team members pressure each other to deliver what is due. Teams are normally configured with respect to the task, but the team also affects the meaning of the task because members will use their specific competencies to deal with problems that occur.

Transition

Inevitably action involved in projects will lead to some type of transition of the real world, at least if the project has not stalled completely. Transition in this sense means that some changes are made or some achievements are accomplished that make a difference to the world outside the project. The project manager needs a good grasp of the transition to be accomplished. Transition is related to the task but differs in that it also concerns the progression toward task completion. Thus, the transition might be regarded not only as the main result of the project work but, more important, as the path leading to the fulfillment of the task. In the latter meaning, transition stands for a cognitive view of cause-and-effect relationships that are important for the fulfillment of the project task.

The project manager has to grasp both the path and the result in order to function well. Even if only technical matters appear to be at stake, symbolic matters are important as well. If "before" the project is compared with "after," one would expect there to be a leap (a bridge has been built, or a new accounting system has been developed) as a result. Something will be expected to have changed as a consequence of the project.

Implications of the 4T Framework for Conception and Termination

Besides their importance in demarcating action, the four T's of project management also have implications for implementation of project plans, for example, as prescribed by available guidelines for project management. When task, time, team, and transition have been given a content, something is also said about implementation. The selection of team includes selection of certain skills that give priority to some implementation strategies at the expense of others. In the same way, task, time, and transition have implications for implementation. Moreover, the four T's boost the general efficiency concerns in the project by stressing internal aspects and neglecting those that occurred before, parallel to, and after the project. In this chapter, we are primarily interested in how the 4T framework can be harnessed to improve activities before and after a project, that is, the borderlines between projects and their environments in terms of parent organizations and past, parallel, and future projects.

The professional project manager usually gains his or her reputation being skilled to manage the project after it has been initiated (and implicitly or explicitly defined), control it through implementation, and eventually ensure its completion. We believe that there is more to it than that. The professionalism should also come from being able to sort out all important experiences of project work and systematically apply those experiences on any new project. For example, insight about the malfunctioning of certain building materials should ideally be transferred to decisions about material so that future projects can be designed differently. Such an approach should also foster a critical attitude to taking project specifications as given in project work. Since many project owners, especially outside project-oriented companies, are quite inexperienced when it comes to controlling and managing project work, they should not be expected to have a full grasp of the fundamental details of project specification.

Basically the project manager's role can be described under four general headlines concerning pre- or postproject matters. Preproject activities focus on the actual creation of a project and the allocation of resources to it. The core of this is *conceptualization* of the project. Much of the momentum for the project is in fact created very early in the process, and the project manager should play a conspicuous role at that stage. The project also needs to be *decoupled* from its environment in the parent organization. Conceptualization and decoupling are certainly related to each other, but they should be attended to separately, since conceptualization mainly involves rhetorical and cognitive aspects of projects, while decoupling involves power to set the project in motion by allocating resources and by "setting up walls" around it. Those "walls" are needed in order to secure the project's isolation from the kind of disturbances that projects in general are bombarded with.

Postproject activities, in contrast, focus on terminating a project and linking experiences, resources, or results to other contexts. One definite challenge is to make sure that *learning* from project work facilitates future endeavors and satisfies customers. Such learning pertains to both the project work as such and the area of the project task, such as learning about procedures and about how to define tasks. There are solid indications that when projects are seen as well known beforehand, no learning occurs, at least not in such a way that it can be retrieved for future use. (This is the so-called learning paradox, according to which opportunities for experimentation never seem to be used in projects that are well known to those involved.)[4] This holds true for both kinds of learning. The handling of learning and storing of knowledge for future use are formidable challenges for project managers.

Another prominent challenge in the postproject phase concerns *recoupling* of resources, mainly personnel but also material resources. One aspect of recoupling is delivery of project results; other aspects are connected, for example, to the team (returning to assignments in other parts of the organization or transferring to other projects). If recoupling is not taken care of appropriately, project participants might mentally leave it prematurely, thereby destroying the sense of "being in this together if they are left to worry about what will happen when project life is over. Moreover, the responsibility of using personnel in a way that conforms with their own interests is related to a range of ethical questions that should be a major concern for professional project managers. The task of recoupling also has a learning twist, which means that learning and recoupling are related to each other much as conceptualization and decoupling are. Recoupling is a way to see to it that members of the project group learn from it and use that learning in future projects or in the parent organization. Moreover, the knowledge that is embedded in the tools and in other material resources used in a project might in fact be transferred between consecutive projects in this way.

Preproject Considerations

Conceptualizing

The conception phase is not very well understood or well handled in most projects. For one thing, project managers seem to have some difficulties in using and integrating the rhetorical aspects of projects with the need for practical action. Of course, the stress on action is a hallmark, but conceptualization is more about rhetoric (that is, gaining support for the project and mobilizing and motivating potential team members).

During conceptualization, single project ideas compete with each other, as well as with other ongoing projects or activities that are related to any of the four T's. Tasks might be compared, transition goals and difficulties can be looked at together with tasks in order to find the least costly alternative, competition might arise for team members, time limits can be argued in favor of specific projects, and so on.

Competition occurs not just between projects of exactly the same kind, but also because at any given point in time, there is simply not space enough for an unlimited number of projects, whether in product development, corporate renewal, or construction. There are limitations in resources in terms of personnel, machinery, and mental and cognitive capacities. Too many projects might make the process of rational choice among them break down.

Choices among projects to work with have to be made in advance, which is why rhetorical conceptualization is an important preproject activity. By stressing conceptualization, we also introduce the notion of management by projects. Management by projects means that a manager involved in several projects will be concerned about how to handle interdependencies among them. Regardless of whether the project manager is responsible for one or more projects, conceptualization is important for several reasons:

- During conceptualization, expectations about project outcome are formed and defined. Superiors to project managers form their evaluation criteria based on issues brought up during conceptualization.
- The outcome of conceptualization might not always mirror a practical way to carry out the project once it comes to implementation. Conceptualization provides the project manager with an arena for action, but this is not necessarily the same as a model for action. By being part of preproject activities, project managers might be able to judge which parts of a project conceptualization are essential for carrying it out and which parts will basically be used for evaluation or maybe not used at all.
- During conceptualization, projects are the most receptive in terms of how to demarcate the arena for action. Project managers might find it easier to affect these issues during conceptualization than during implementation, when many issues are no longer on the agenda.
- Motivation and commitment from both team members and the parent organization can be promoted by successful conceptualization and discouraged by poor conceptualization. Project managers can play an important role in building and transmitting commitment if they are involved in conceptualization, especially if they can also involve others, such as potential team members.

Decoupling

Whereas conceptualization mostly involves rhetorical and cognitive matters on how projects get born, decoupling involves making decisions on what is to be regarded as part of the project and what is not. Decoupling is thus prerequisite for action and the basis for dividing resources into two categories: project and not project.

Depending on decoupling, a project may get the best resources that are available or only the resources that can be spared in the context of other ongoing projects.

From the viewpoint of the potential project manager, getting the best available resources is clearly preferable. To this person it is a matter of streamlining the project from the very beginning rather than having to adapt to whatever has been made available because the project has somehow been downgraded in importance and in relation to his or her own expectations. A project manager can upgrade the importance of a project by playing an active part in conceptualization. Thus, good initial support of a project plays a necessary but not sufficient role in securing useful resources for the project work.

Conceptualization and decoupling are mutually dependent on each other. A project that is well argued might be regarded as so essential to the fate of the parent organization that it is never contested. Similarly, a project that has already been allocated resources is easily regarded as a given and not in need of support. In the latter case, without discussion of the project before decoupling, it is more vulnerable later on. The argument that "I knew nothing about this" is a powerful battering ram that potential competing managers use against the walls around a project.

Decoupling is important for four additional reasons:

1. It is a moment of truth since it is when the project becomes real for the rest of the organization and receives its identity. That moment of truth occurs when the task of the project gets an official status in the parent organization and the fight about scarce resources with competing projects or regular activities of the parent organization becomes a reality that has to be resolved and given room for real action on the project.
2. It is a situation when the prospective project manager must have a good grasp of time and transition in relation to the task, since they have to be balanced with the relevant resources. He or she must be able to answer questions about plans for the realization of this project. In that sense, decoupling is a kind of negotiation.
3. Decoupling activities demand participation (or at least consent) by top management. The project manager must insist that decoupling does not lead to vague premises for the project. Allocated resources cannot be announced as tentative because that will weaken the walls around the project that shelter it from attacks from those who promote other activities. The project manager must demand certainty for his or her future work and insist that decoupling be irrevocable.
4. It might be wise for the project manager to regard at least some of the decoupling, like allocating of resources, as tentative for the part of the project.

The problem with the preproject phase is that much of what is going to happen during the course of the project is uncertain (which means that there is an asymmetry between preproject and postproject phases). This uncertainty puts restraints on the project manager, but he or she can also use them to provide for leeway and provide space for future tactics.

Postproject Considerations

Learning from Projects

Efficiency concerns are important. Once we know what should be done, everyone appreciates efficiency in doing just that. But when most projects reach termination, only individuals seem to learn. Projects end, and most parent organizations lack adequate mechanisms for taking care of how to transform project experiences into organizational learning for use in future project work. Projects are allowed to die without leaving any serious traces.

This seems to hold true even for organizations that deal with projects that can be characterized as repetitive, such as in the construction industry, where there is a close resemblance among consecutive projects and where the usefulness of learning appears obvious. This "renewal paradox" applies in spite of apparently excellent opportunities to renew project procedures as well as construction techniques.[5]

The need for learning is obvious, and in many cases learning does occur. The point is that traditional project management approaches do not focus on learning from projects or storing knowledge generated. Generally learning is a question of how to create a bridge from finished projects and postproject evaluations to the future. To project managers, the postproject activity of learning should be of crucial importance.

Evaluation of projects depends heavily on the outcome in terms of learning. Although the result might be remarkable in terms of technical or administrative elegance, postproject performance is normally part of the evaluation and thus part of the project's results. Depending on the character of the project outcome, project managers should get themselves involved in bridging project results to and from end users even though the project might be delayed or even if project costs increase as a result.

Project managers might also want to consider returning to reevaluate their project's results some time after project completion. They might gain valuable insights into how to organize projects as well as into how to conceptualize them, especially in cooperation with customers. Returning to old projects from a distance is useful; once the nitty-gritty of the detailed project work has been forgotten, the essentials tend to stand out.

Another type of learning not very often considered in the traditional project management literature is the concurrent evaluation of projects throughout their life cycles. Such learning is normally considered a part of applying tacit knowledge, but it should be more explicitly and deliberately possible by making these kinds of activities part of the project manager's work. Among other aspects, this includes deliberate changes of the arena of action during the project life cycle and corresponding changes in the four T's. Another aspect is that it might help in setting the agenda for the final evaluation due to changes over time.

Maybe the most important implication of the learning is the possibility of improving future project work. By being part of a project after formal termination, many insights might be gathered that are useful for the future. Project managers should in fact demand evaluations of the projects to be done in order to facilitate such learning.

Recoupling

Recoupling of personnel as well as of material resources used in a project is very much a problem of ensuring that resources on a companywide level are used effectively. Project managers should be more than facilitators; they should also be instrumental in seeing that resources are properly transferred back to other productive uses.

Recoupling and decoupling are in a sense reciprocal. Decoupling has to do with the beginning of the project and recoupling with the end. Moreover, both phases occur sequentially. Decoupling is likely to be decided in its entirety as part of a deal when the project is initiated (even though resources are to be made available later). It is taken to be a clear commitment on the part of the top management, whereas recoupling is a commitment on the part of the project manager.

Learning and recoupling are, of course, related to each other in various ways. The resources returned to the host organization for new assignments are by no means the same ones that were originally decoupled for the particular project that the project manager has been responsible for. Personal learning has occurred. The apprentice is no longer a newcomer, and the most valuable project participants have probably gained in usefulness as a result of this particular project experience. The project manager should see that the advances made by the individuals are regarded as assets for the company as a whole. But the project manager also has to be alert to the deterioration that might occur. Deterioration might be most easily observed when it comes to machinery or equipment, but it also happens with human resources, especially if the project has faced serious crises.

Recoupling is a second moment of truth for a project, at least when most of it is done and the project approaches its conclusion. At that time the project's stated purpose or task and outcome are compared and evaluated. During recoupling, the project manager's reputation for being professional becomes known. This manager can publicize his or her accomplishments with regard to the project and skill as a manager to the project environment.

Personnel leaving the project should get recognition for their contributions to solving problems in the project and pushing it forward to completion. Project managers should assist their staff members in managing their reputation for future assignments. In particular, those who assumed responsibilities beyond what was expected on the project should be recognized officially for their contributions. This recognition should be a regular part of the human resource planning of the project-oriented company.

When the recoupling occurs, the project manager in a sense loses control of the project because the resources for carrying it to completion are dissolved. In order not to jeopardize the completion of the project, the project manager has to see that recoupling is not done prematurely. Fulfilling the task is still the most important task, and it gives the manager an advantage when it comes to orchestrating the recoupling.

Top management in the parent organization would never allow the project manager to control resources too long. As part of the decoupling procedure, plans are usually set up for when various resources can be made available to other parties again, and the project manager is committed to those plans. During the course of a project, the project manager should develop a sense of responsibility for the rest of the organization by informing top management if and how decoupling has to be rescheduled as a result of the actual development of the project.

Extending Project Manager Responsibilities into the Black Environment

We claimed at the start of the chapter that project management's concern with internal efficiency tends to overlook the importance of the project environment, with negative impact on effectiveness. The framework presented here in no way fully describes the environment, but it does propose a few directions for deliberately extending project management into relevant parts of the environment. Figure 3.3 presents an elaborated version of Figure 3.2, where these concerns have been combined with the four T's. The general picture of project management thus consists of three major parts: preproject (where conceptualization and decoupling pertain), project, and postproject (where learning and recoupling pertain).

The four T's provide a guideline for extending project managers' work to include environmental skills. This extension might be a more fruitful direction for

FIGURE 3.3. PROJECT ACTIVITIES EXTENDED WITH THE FOUR T'S.

competence development and for parent company effectiveness than further development of implementation procedures and planning tools.

Challenges in Extending Responsibilities

There are at least three important challenges in extending project manager responsibilities into the preproject and the postproject phases along the lines indicated in this chapter:

1. The project manager has to come to some form of agreement with his or her superiors about how to extend the responsibilities. They, as well as the project manager, may play new roles.
2. The work that the project manager has to perform becomes much more difficult and demanding. All the new factors that the manager has to relate to make the job more complex. And it might well be that the manager best suited for extending project management may not be the one who is good at getting things done.
3. All of these complex matters leave the project manager with less time and effort to spend on what he or she traditionally is very good at doing: getting things done and taking action. This new role will be more demanding for the project manager than for the parent organization because it opens up new forms of evaluation. It will never do for a project manager of this new species to say, "I followed all the procedures and the rules according to the book." Rather, the project manager has to argue that he or she did the right things considering what was best for the company and its employees.

Just how much of the black box of the environment should be regarded as the project manager's responsibilities is an open question. We believe that the preproject and postproject aspects should be included. Nevertheless, this also means that the notion of project success and project failure will be changed. The new breed of project manager is in need of a broader perspective than the previous, overly efficiency oriented project manager. It might even be that the project management world should be looking for another type of manager in the future.

CHAPTER FOUR

STAKEHOLDER MANAGEMENT

David I. Cleland

When the Enron Corporation launched an initiative to build, own, and operate a megapower unit in India, it discovered, to its dismay, that it had not given adequate consideration or planning to a number of political factors. A rising backlash against foreign investments by an opposition coalition led by the Bharatiya Janata party resulted in a delay of the project. The company had not teamed up with a local partner, nor had it been entirely above board in the way it awarded contracts, without competitive bidding. When a successful lawsuit by a Bombay consumer group forced disclosure, Enron offered to renegotiate to make the power cheaper.[1]

Enron's failure to account for political factors and players, as well as the fact that it had not lined up a local partner or conducted contract bidding in an open manner, are prime examples of how organizations ignore the importance of stakeholders in project management. Stakeholders are people or groups that have, or believe they have, legitimate claims against the substantive aspects of a project. A stake is an interest or share or claim in a project; it can range from

Note: Portions of this chapter are paraphrased from David I. Cleland, "Project Stakeholder Management." *Project Management Journal,* Sept. 1986, pp. 36–43, with permission of the Project Management Institute, Four Campus Boulevard, Newton Square, Pennsylvania 19073-3299, a worldwide organization advancing the state-of-the-art in project management. Phone: (610) 356-4600, Fax: (610) 356-4647.

informal interest in the undertaking, at one extreme, to a legal claim of owner-ship at the other extreme. In Enron's case, stakeholders included (but were not limited to) local and national politicians, other local companies, and contrac-tors that would be eligible to work on different aspects of the megapower unit. Other stakeholders might include environmentalists, stockholders, creditors, in-vestors and bankers, employees, future customers, suppliers and vendors, com-petitors, and local communities.

Project stakeholders are identified by their interests in the project resources and how those resources are likely to affect their well-being. Stakeholder man-agement is a crucial part of successful project management from inception through completion and beyond. In this chapter, we look at how stakeholders are identi-fied, what hierarchies exist among groups of stakeholders, and keys to planning and carrying out successful project stakeholder management.

Origins of the Stakeholder Concept

The concept of stakeholders has grown out of the context of business organiza-tions. Table 4.1 shows a model of generic organizational claimants (stakeholders) and their claims (stake) in a typical business organization. Successful stakeholder management in organizations requires that the following initiatives be carried out by the key managers:

- Identify appropriate stakeholders that have, or believe that they have, a vested interest in those things of value that are provided by the enterprise.
- Specify the nature of the stakeholders' claim (for example, in the case of em-ployees, fair wages and appropriate fringe benefits). A creditor would expect to receive interest and principal payments when due.
- Measure and assess the stakeholders' interest, such as the degree of customer satisfaction, delivery terms, price, and payment policies for vendors.
- Manage the stakeholders through the development of a strategy that identifies and manages stakeholders so that they are supportive of the goals and objec-tives of the enterprise.

Project Stakeholders and Their Management

Project stakeholders, like organizational stakeholders, believe they have a legiti-mate claim and are identified by their interests in the project resources and how those resources are likely to affect them and their well-being. Stakeholder

TABLE 4.1. ORGANIZATIONAL CLAIMANTS AND THEIR CLAIMS.

Claimants	*Claims*
Stakeholders	Participation in distribution of profits, additional stock offerings, assets on liquidation, vote of stock, inspection of company books, transfer of stock, election of board of directors, and such additional rights as established in the contract with the corporation.
Creditors	Participation in legal proportion of interest payments due and return of principal from the investment. Security of pledged assets; relative priority in event of liquidation. Participation in certain management and owner prerogatives if certain conditions exist within the company (such as default of interest payments).
Employees	Economic, social, and psychological satisfaction in the place of employment. Freedom from arbitrary and capricious behavior on the part of company officials. Share of fringe benefits, freedom to join union and participate in collective bargaining, individual freedom in offering services through an employment contract. Adequate working conditions.
Customers	Service or product provided; technical data to use the product; suitable warranties; spare parts to support the product during customer use; R&D leading to product improvement; facilitation of consumer credit.
Supplier	Continuing source of business; timely consummation of trade credit obligations; professional relationship in contracting for, purchasing, and receiving goods and services.
Governments	Taxes (income, property, and so on). Fair competition and adherence to the letter and intent of public policy dealing with the requirements of "fair and free" competition. Legal obligation for businesspeople (and business organizations) to obey antitrust laws.
Union	Recognition as the negotiating agent for the employees. Opportunity to perpetuate the union as a participant in the business organization.
Competitors	Norms established by society and the industry for competitive conduct. Business statesmanship on the part of contemporaries.
Local communities	Productive and healthful employment in the local community. Participation of company officials in community affairs, regular employment, fair play, local purchase of reasonable portion of the products of the local community, interest in and support of local government, support of local government, support of cultural and charity projects.
General public	Participation in and contribution to the government process of society as a whole. Creative communications between government and business units designed for reciprocal understanding. Bearing fair proportion of the burden of government and society. Fair price for products and advancement of the art in the technology that the product line offers.

Source: Cleland, D. I. (1986, September). Project stakeholder management. *Project Management Journal*, pp. 36–43.

management requires attention to their legitimate and perceived interests during the time the project is conceived, through planning, organizing, and fulfilling its goals, as well as in providing value to its owner and other entities that share in its results. A successful project requires that diverse stakeholders work together to accomplish multiple and not always entirely congruent purposes, for without their support, the project will not achieve its goals.

The Hidrovia Project in Brazil is a proposal to reengineer the natural infrastructure of a continent. The project is planned to run the entire length of the Paraguay-Parana River system, some thirty-four hundred kilometers of it, as a superefficient shipping lane. As would be expected, conservationists in South America and throughout the rest of the world are alarmed about the potential social and environmental impacts of this project, which will open up the heart of South America to private investment and raise interest in the continent's natural resources. Major issues concerning investment, social, and economic considerations are being evaluated to determine the long-term implications of the changes this project will cause. Unfortunately, detailed information needed to assess these changes has become notoriously difficult to obtain. Nevertheless, construction will likely start sometime before the end of 1997.[2]

Project stakeholder management develops and implements strategies to influence stakeholder activities that could favorably or adversely affect the projects and executes the strategies that enable the organization to take advantage of stakeholder issues and opportunities. Managing a project's stakeholders means describing it in terms of the individuals and institutions that share a stake or an interest in it. Project team members, subcontractors, suppliers, and customers are all stakeholders who will be affected by decisions and thus must be considered. But management must also consider other stakeholders who have an interest in the project and are often outside the formal authority of the project manager. They can present serious management problems and challenges.

It is vital that the project team have a specific delineation of the various strategies that a particular stakeholder, such as an environmental group, intends to employ in satisfying its goals and objectives, along with a prediction of the future impact of its actions on the project's outcome. For example, a project manager who must make a recommendation concerning the design of a new plant must be aware of state and local land use, plant design, tax laws, and the area's likely pattern of growth. The project manager must also be aware of the local political climate, availability of a skilled labor force, and public attitudes toward the location of the plant in the community. To put all these aspects together requires an understanding of how to apply the management process in dealing with project stakeholders.

Defining the Stake and Levels of Stakeholding

A stake is an interest or a share or a claim—the right to something of value of the project—and in the project and its results. It can range from an informal interest in the undertaking, at one extreme, to a legal claim of ownership at the other extreme. The claim may be legal or moral, or based on the impact that a person or group says the project will have on them.

Not all stakes or stakeholders are equal in their claims of ownership, rights, or interests in a project and its activities. *Primary stakeholders* have a legal contractual relationship to the project and include the project owner, suppliers, functional groups, investors, and those from the public domain (such as communities and institutions) that provide infrastructures and markets, whose laws and regulations must be obeyed, and to whom taxes and other obligations are owed. *Secondary stakeholders* are those who influence, or who are influenced or affected by, the project but are not regularly engaged in transactions with it and may not be essential for its survival. The media and special interest groups are secondary stakeholders who can mobilize public opinion in favor of or in opposition to the project's purposes and performance.

Identifying the Stakeholders

The management of a project inevitably entails bringing into the picture those persons and groups that have both contractual interests and vested interests in the management of the project as well as its outcome. These persons and groups come from a wide variety of organizational settings and include the following:

- Senior organizational managers, including corporate directors
- General managers
- Functional managers
- Project managers
- Work package managers
- Project team members
- Customers (users)
- Suppliers, contractors, and subcontractors
- Local, state, and federal agencies; commissions; and judicial, legislative, and executive organizations
- Employees
- Creditors

- Shareholders
- Unions
- Social organizations
- Political organizations
- Environmentalists
- Competitors
- Local communities
- The general public
- Consumer groups
- "Intervenor" groups, such as the Sierra Club
- Private citizens
- Tourists
- Professional organizations, such as the Project Management Institute
- Schools, universities, hospitals, churches, the chamber of commerce, civic groups, minority groups, activists, the American Civil Liberties Union, and other institutions
- Media
- Families
- Anyone else who believes that they have a stake in the project.

A model of the project stakeholders is shown in Figure 4.1. In a sense, the secondary stakeholders comprise a "virtual organization"—one that exists in essence or effect though not in actual fact, form, or name. The secondary stakeholder virtual organization lurks under the surface—a sort of potential organization that exists between the lines and structure of the formal organization. Despite their virtual status, the secondary stakeholders can exert a powerful influence over the project's planning and outcome.

Responsibilities of Primary Stakeholders

Primary stakeholders have more than a contractual or legal obligation to the project team; they also have the responsibility and authority to manage and commit resources according to schedule, cost, and technical performance objectives. Such stakeholders have direct strategic and operational roles through participating in the design, engineering, development, construction (production), and after-sales logistic support of the project outcomes. Primary stakeholders belong to the project team and its supporting organizational infrastructure. They serve as functional managers, general managers, senior managers, customer and supplier officials, and so forth. These stakeholders' responsibilities and authority follow:

FIGURE 4.1. PROJECT STAKEHOLDERS.

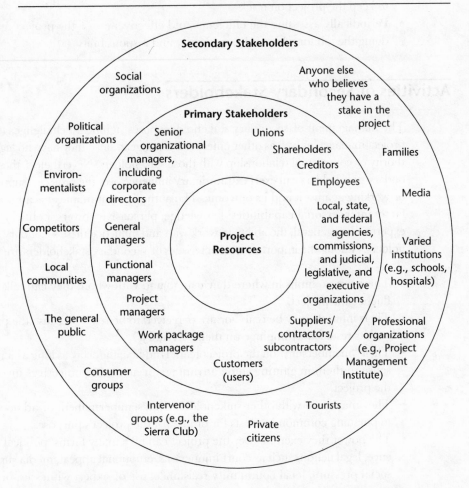

- Leading the project team members
- Allocating resources to be used in the design, development, and construction (production) of the project results
- Building and maintaining relationships with all stakeholders
- Managing the decision context in the design and execution of strategies to commit project resources
- Leading by example to set the cultural ambiance of the project in order to bring out the best in people and provide high-quality professional resources
- Maintaining ongoing and effective oversight of the project's progress in meeting its schedule, cost, and technical performance objectives, and, where

necessary, instituting reprogramming and reallocation of resources as required to keep the project on track
- Periodically assessing the efficiency and effectiveness of the project team in doing the job for which it has authority and responsibility

Activities of Secondary Stakeholders

The management of secondary stakeholders poses significant challenges for the project manager, as well as other enterprise managers, since they have no legal authority or contractual relationship with those stakeholders. Nevertheless, these secondary stakeholders can exert extraordinary influence over the project—supporting or working against it and its outcome. The authority that managers can use is de facto: interpersonal capabilities, knowledge, persuasive powers, political savvy, expertise—in general, the ability to work with and influence these secondary stakeholders. Among the important characteristics of secondary stakeholders are these:

- There are no limits in where they can go and with whom they can talk to influence the project.
- Their interests may be real—or are perceived to be real—because the project and its results may impinge on their "territory."
- Their "membership" on the project team is ad hoc; they stay as long as it makes sense to them in gaining some advantage or achieving objectives involving the project.
- They may team with other stakeholders on a semipermanent or ad hoc basis in pursuing common interests for or against the project's purposes.
- The power they exercise over the project can take many forms: political influence, legal actions such as court injunctions, emotional appeal, media support, social pressure, local community resistance, use of expert witnesses, or even scare tactics.
- It is up to them whether they will accept responsibility for their strategies and actions.

Examples of Successful Stakeholder Management

The Milwaukee Water Pollution Abatement Program (MWPAP), a $2.2 billion project to renovate and upgrade the sewage system of Milwaukee and its suburbs, all without disrupting service, is a classic case of successful stakeholder management. In this project, the Environmental Protection Agency (EPA) recognized the need for the citizenry to be involved in the planning of major public works projects and required their involvement in this grant-supported project. In doing so, they had a firm groundwork for stakeholder involvement.

Despite the enormity of the project and a tight timetable, stakeholder involvement in the MWPAP was achieved in several key ways:

- The highly experienced CH2M Hill, an international firm of engineers, planners, economists, and scientists and its consortium of principal associate-consultants, was selected to manage the project.
- All twenty-seven separate municipalities that were affected were involved from the project's inception.
- Care was taken to listen carefully to all stakeholder concerns and to address those concerns in the planning and execution of the MWPAP.
- The program management team placed speakers on key local community platforms, gained editorial support from local media, and worked carefully to gain the endorsement of key stakeholders in the top political, business, and public interest organizations. The public was kept informed of every step.
- Project management focused on balancing the interests of all the stakeholders with those of the program manager. The fact that stakeholders' interests were recognized and dealt with by the project team was considered one of the key factors in its success.[3]

The 12.5–mile $490 million highway project through Glenwood Canyon in Colorado is one of the most expensive nonurban sections of the interstate system. This project has no operations component. As such, there is no added level of liability or risk to markets or investors on its completion. It required more than a decade of planning and twelve years to construct. The project involved an unprecedented degree of cooperation among the project team, environmentalists, and tourists to create a major highway that preserved and even enhanced one of the nation's premier natural settings. The construction of the highway through a scenic gorge overcame fierce initial opposition, a wide variety of design changes and physical constraints, plus remarkable cooperation in creating a four-lane highway that even the environmentalists love.[4]

Bechtel planned, designed, engineered, and managed the procurement, right-of-way acquisition, and construction of a second gas pipeline extending 875 miles from Canada into central California. This included the construction of a new compressor station and the retrofit of seventeen compressor stations and three major meter stations, at a cost of approximately $1.6 billion. This new pipeline parallels the first completed in the early 1960s. Throughout the pipeline expansion, concern about the wide range of environmental factors was paramount.

Careful planning by Bechtel resulted in the development of extensive safeguarding of environmental factors on the pipeline. Certain measures dealt with the control of erosion, noxious weeds, hazardous material and construction noise, as well as extensive training for all personnel on environmental awareness of work practices.[5]

Strategies for Successful Stakeholder Management

Developing a strategy to manage stakeholders starts with putting forth a few key questions designed to guide the thinking and actions of the project team. When these questions have been appropriately answered, real progress has been made in managing the stakeholders:

- Who are the project stakeholders, both primary and secondary?
- What stake, right, or claim do they have in the project?
- What opportunities and challenges do the stakeholders provide to the project team?
- What obligations or responsibilities does the project team have toward its stakeholders?
- What are the strengths, weaknesses, and probable strategies that the stakeholders might employ to realize their objectives?
- What resources are at the stakeholders' disposal to implement their strategies?
- Do any of these factors give the stakeholders a distinctly favorable position in influencing the project outcome?
- What strategies should the project team develop and implement to deal with the opportunities and challenges presented by the stakeholders?
- Will the project team know if it is successfully managing the project stakeholders?

Developing the Stakeholder Management Plan

A formal stakeholder plan is essential. Multiyear projects are subject to so much change that informal means are inadequate. Reliance on informal or hit-or-miss methods for obtaining information will not lead to effective management of issues that can arise. Similarly, the plan should be complete. It should provide the project team with adequate intelligence to help them select realistic options. Information on project stakeholders can be gained from a variety of sources, some of which might superficially seem to be unprofitable.

Several questions can be asked to ensure that decisions on a project consider stakeholder interests:

- Will the decision lead to action that is justifiable with regard to the benefits of the project stakeholders?
- Are any of the real or perceived rights of project stakeholders likely to be harmed?
- Does the project decision jeopardize the fair treatment of any of the project stakeholders?
- What might happen if a key stakeholder takes exception to a decision being made?

Identifying Specific Project Stakeholders

Some stakeholders are obvious in a project, but others have to be sought out and identified. Environmental interest groups, neighborhood and historic associations, and business organizations are mindful that nearly any project will affect stakeholder groups that are unknown at the beginning of the project. For example, on one highway improvement project, data were gathered concerning known and potential stakeholders through the following means:

- Visits to businesses
- Inspection drives through the area
- Consultations with local social groups, governmental officials, and educational, ecclesiastical, and association groups
- Meetings with local contractors, banks, and suppliers and vendors
- Visits to institutions and residences

Besides identifying as many stakeholders as possible, the project team put extra effort into publicity efforts and the formation of a technical group to act as a focus to ensure representation of geographic and special interests. The project team found that remaining flexible regarding the study of stakeholder issues was advisable. By regularly briefing officials of stakeholder groups and citizenry, new stakeholders began to surface. A technical group, acting on behalf of the project team, carried out the following meetings to spread the word on the project and to identify stakeholders and their concerns:

- Executive briefings for senior government officials
- Briefings and working sessions for department of transportation officials
- Meetings with local governments, institutions, industries, and other agencies
- Presentations to city councils and planning agencies

- Meetings with local hospitals, chambers of commerce, the Salvation Army, and the area's largest employers
- Formal public information and local public hearings

The technical group was supported by a mailing list of stakeholders who received regular newsletters. They also:

- Established local drop-in centers to provide basic project information
- Took great care in defining the scope of the project for stakeholders
- Generated "contentious issues" to be considered during the work with the stakeholders on an ongoing basis
- Created ongoing profiles of a willingness and commitment to meet and work with concerned stakeholder groups.

The work with the stakeholders on this project resulted in almost complete acceptance by agencies and the general public.[6]

Gathering Information

Part of identifying project stakeholders is getting information about them, a process that is similar to collecting information on competitors.[7] A systematic approach will include answering the following questions:

- What needs to be known about the stakeholder?
- Where and how can the information be obtained?
- Who will have responsibility for the gathering, analysis, and interpretation of the information?
- How and to whom will the information be distributed?
- Who will use the information to make decisions?
- How can the information be protected from leaking or misuse?

In obtaining such information, the highest standards of ethical conduct should be followed. The potential sources of stakeholder information and the uses to which such information can be put are so numerous that it would not be practical to list all sources and uses here, but the following sources are representative and can be augmented according to a particular project's needs:

- Project team members
- Key managers
- Business periodicals such as the *Wall Street Journal, Fortune, Business Week,* and *Forbes*

- Business reference services, including *Moody's Industrial Manual* and *Value Line Investment Security*
- Internet
- Professional associations
- Customers and other users
- Suppliers
- Trade associations
- Local press
- Trade press
- Annual corporate reports
- Articles and papers presented at professional meetings
- Public meetings
- Government sources[8]

Once the information has been collected, it must be analyzed and interpreted by the appropriate experts. The project manager should draw on the company's professional personnel for help in doing this analysis. Once the analysis has been completed, the specific target of the stakeholder's mission can be determined.

Some of the information collected on the project's external stakeholders may include sensitive material. One cannot conclude that all such stakeholders will operate in an ethical fashion. Consequently, all information collected should be assumed to be sensitive until proved otherwise and protected accordingly. This suggests the need for a security system patterned after a company's intelligence system. Some information should be available only on a need-to-know basis, and some should be available to all interested parties. The following precautions should be considered:

- One individual is responsible for security.
- Internal checks and balances are in place.
- Documents are classified and controlled through periodic inventory, constant records of their whereabouts, and prompt return.
- Files and desks are locked.
- Shredding or burning of outdated or outmoded documents is supervised.
- Confidential envelopes are used for internal transmission of confidential documents.
- Strict security is maintained for offices containing sensitive information.

In gathering information about stakeholders, it is essential to know how it will be used. Project management must ensure the availability of timely, credible, and comprehensive information about the capabilities and the options open to each stakeholder and continue to identify their probable strategies and how those strategies might affect current project interests. Project management must also monitor and provide comprehensive information about probable actions in the project-stakeholder environment that might affect it.

Evaluating Stakeholders and Their Strategies

Once the stakeholders' purpose is understood, their strengths and weaknesses should be evaluated in order to understand their strategies and their potential for success. This analysis is a summary of the most important strengths on which the stakeholders base their strategy and the most significant weaknesses they will try to avoid in pursuing their interests. Identifying five or six strengths and weaknesses of a stakeholder should be enough to make a judgment about their strategy.

An adversary stakeholder's strength may be based on such factors as these:

- The availability and effective use of resources
- Political alliances
- Public support
- Quality of strategies
- Dedication of members

Accordingly, an adversary stakeholder's weaknesses may emanate from:

- Lack of political support
- Disorganization
- Lack of coherent strategy
- Uncommitted, scattered membership
- Unproductive use of resources

Once these factors have been analyzed, each strategy for coping with the stakeholders can be tested by asking the following questions:

- Does this strategy adequately cope with a strength of the stakeholder?
- Does this strategy take advantage of an adversary stakeholder's weakness?
- What is the relative contribution of a particular stakeholder's strength in countering the project strategy?
- Does the adversary stakeholder's weakness detract from the successful implementation of his or her strategy? If so, can the project manager develop a counterstrategy that will benefit the project?

Devising Strategies for Dealing with Stakeholders

The strength-weakness analysis is important to developing project strategy but it must also extend to a full understanding of all stakeholder strategies.

A stakeholder's strategy is a series of prescriptions that provide the means and set the general direction for accomplishing stakeholder goals, objectives, and mission. These prescriptions stipulate what resource allocations are required; why, when, and where they will be required; and how they will be used. These resource allocations include plans for using resources, policies and procedures to be employed, and tactics used to accomplish the stakeholder's purposes.

Based on an understanding of external stakeholder strategy, the project team can proceed to predict stakeholder behavior in implementing its strategy. How will the stakeholder use resources to affect the project? Will an intervenor stakeholder picket the construction site or attempt to use the courts to delay or shut down the project? Will a petition be circulated to stop further construction? Will an attempt be made to influence future legislation? These are the kinds of questions that, when properly asked and answered, provide a basis for the project team to develop specific countervailing strategies to deal with adversary stakeholder influence.

Implementing Stakeholder Management Strategy

The final step in managing the project stakeholders is developing implementation strategies that will do the following:

- Ensure that the key managers and professionals fully appreciate the potential impact that both supportive and adverse stakeholders can have on the project outcome.
- Manage the project review meetings so that stakeholder status is an integral part of determining the project status.
- Maintain contact with key external stakeholders to improve the chances of managing their perception of the project and analyzing their probable strategies.
- Ensure an explicit evaluation of probable stakeholder response to major project decisions.
- Provide an ongoing and up-to-date status report on stakeholder status to key managers and professionals for use in developing and implementing project strategy.
- Provide a suitable security system to protect sensitive project information that might be used by adverse stakeholders to the detriment of the project.

Henry F. Padgham, former president and chairman of the Project Management Institute, who has managed many successful large projects, believes that "project management today demands that we pay attention to all who have a stake in our projects."[9]

The Commitment Factor

The successful management of the project stakeholders requires an extraordinary sense of commitment, conviction, loyalty, and trust. The project manager has to be a champion in creating the conditions that bring stakeholders to support the project and keep everything together and moving in the right direction. The project manager and team need to:

- Play an active role in developing strategies for dealing with stakeholders and regularly review the efficacy of such strategies during the life cycle of the project.
- Accept and become advocates of the concept and process of the stakeholder "virtual" organization.
- Keep information flowing throughout the project team and senior management concerning what is going on relative to the stakeholders' strategies and interests.
- Sustain quality virtual relationships with the stakeholder groups, recognizing their key roles in aiding or negating the strategies being developed and implemented by the project team.

The measurement of project performance has traditionally been limited to the satisfaction of the project owner with the project results. No longer can the project's results and performance be done at the expense of stakeholder organizations. This means that the project manager and the team must take the opportunity to resolve inevitable conflicts between the project and the stakeholder interests. Fairness and balance are key criteria for the project team to use in resolving the conflict with stakeholders, with the desirable outcome of preserving the integrity of the project to serve the maximum of total stakeholders.

Future Opportunities

The ongoing acceptance of project management as a key enterprise strategy means that stakeholders will continue to grow in importance. In the management of megaprojects, this is becoming abundantly clear. Not only is there a phenomenal growth in the application of project management principles within organizations, but there are also major opportunities for the use of project management in building competitive infrastructures in world markets. For example, the International Finance Corporation (an affiliate of World Bank) projected in its 1992 Annual Report that $200 billion per year in infrastructure investment would occur in the 1990s, half of which would be for electricity. The Asian Development Bank calls for $1 trillion infrastructure development for the region by the end of this century. About two-thirds of the world's growth will come from emerging nations. This is a trend that is unlikely to be reversed since it is based on market demand to satisfy the needs of many people and organizations.[10]

In the United States most cities face a gap between infrastructure funding and needs, with the major needs being seen in New York, Boston, Philadelphia, and other northeastern cities, where age, winter weather, and road salt have taken a toll on the infrastructure. The Infrastructure Institute of Cooper Union estimates that there is a need for $6 billion to $7 billion annually over the next thirty years to meet infrastructure needs of the northeastern cities, where less than $5 billion is spent currently.[11]

The demand for the improvement of infrastructure around the world will continue to accelerate. This demand is particularly strong in the emerging nations for establishing infrastructure to support economic growth. Much of this demand will center around major power, water, and transportation initiatives. For the United States and the European community, social infrastructure programs such as health care must also be tackled.

Since 1950, the expectations of developing countries and the opportunities for market development have coincided with the increasing numbers of Third World youth participating in and completing Western educations. Through their leadership, greater use of technology and more training to advance production, creating skilled opportunities and financial partnering, requires a greater dependence on transportation, communications, and power infrastructure. Yet governments' experience in launching, financing, and designing specific infrastructure or operations management capabilities was low or uneven. The result was a hierarchy of economic dependence among the multilateral banking institutions, regional development agencies, and the private sector.

The financing of megaprojects will continue to become more critical as public funds increasingly are used to develop economic and social infrastructure to help meet the growing needs of population increases, resource shortages, resource exploration and use, and increases in global standards of living.

Summary

A stakeholder is an individual or group with one or more stakes in a project. Stakeholders may be affected by the actions, decisions, policies, or practices of the project. These stakeholders also may affect the project's actions, decisions, policies, or practices. With the project stakeholders, there is a potential two-way interaction or exchange of influence. A stakeholder may be thought of as any individual or group who can affect or is affected by the actions, decisions, policies, practices, or goals of the project.

Stakeholders can be classified as primary, with a formal, official, or contractual relationship with the project; and secondary, with an interest, although an informal one, in the project. Both primary and secondary stakeholders can have an impact on the project. It is the latter kind of stakeholder that the project manager so often underestimates.

Stakeholders can be in favor of the strategies coming forth from the project, or they can be against the project and perceive that their interests can best be served if the project does not achieve its goals. Stakeholders act in a manner that they believe will further their interests in their endeavors. Stakeholders can be active in that they attempt to develop strategies to maximize benefits to themselves. They may simply be aware of what is going on regarding the project and, in general, recognize the advantages or disadvantages associated with the project. Finally, they may be ambivalent in their attitude toward the project; they find nothing particularly good or irksome about the project. Usually active stakeholders will act when they believe that they have the power to bring about desired changes.

The management of the project stakeholder community has become important as many vested interest groups have discovered that their interests have to be relatively satisfied for the project to meet its objectives. The challenge for project managers is to see to it that the primary project stakeholders achieve their objectives, while other stakeholders are also satisfied or their potentially negative impact is minimized.

CHAPTER FIVE

DEVELOPING WINNING PROPOSALS

Joan Knutson

In a dramatically changing business environment, certain markets disappear for some companies and new business opportunities appear for others. Both of these situations suggest that organizations issuing requests for proposal (RFPs) and requests for quotation (RFQs) can expect highly competitive responses. Regardless of how strong you think your company or division is in the marketplace, misjudging business opportunities or submitting less than a quality proposal can lose business that is critical to success.

What may separate the winner from the loser in this bidding process is the bidder's degree of foresight into changing industry trends and the impact and quality of the submitted proposal. Therefore, program managers involved in the bidding and proposal preparation processes must become sharper in analyzing business opportunities and more professional in how they generate the proposal.

Although the terminology of proposal generation is most often equated with external supplier or consulting firms, the concepts are germane to everyone in program management who must sell their projects to management, an internal client group, or their boss. Internally, the information systems division must issue proposals to obtain funding for projects to support their user groups. And the marketing organization is taking the pulse of its customers and making proposals for new or better products, while the engineering department may bid a job so that the divisions do not go to an external contractor to acquire engineering expertise. As resources become scarcer, project managers must develop the skills and abilities to look for business opportunities, either internally or externally, and then be able to write the proposal, cost-benefit analysis, or business case necessary to justify that project.

This chapter presents a generic model that is as suitable for use internally as it is for use by consulting firms, research and development firms, or construction contractors. The process requires a time commitment for up-front planning and analysis before writing the actual proposal. To guide the up-front analysis of business opportunities, this chapter suggests questions to consider in developing a winning proposal. Each reader will interpret these questions differently depending on his or her industry, competitive position within the marketplace and the prevailing economic trends affecting that industry. The second half of the chapter covers proposal infrastructure and protocols. These are guidelines only; if a client specifies the format for the proposal, it must be followed to the letter.

Analyzing Business Opportunities

There are two key components of this process: (1) being chosen by the client as a bidder and (2) choosing what is or is not appropriate to bid on.

Am I on the Radar Screen?

Requests for services do not automatically show up in your mailbox; you must be positioned to be considered in the bidding process. Cultivate prospects by engaging everyone in your organization in marketing the organization's talents. A tool that may help your organization prospect for leads or referrals is a one-page synopsis with bullet points listing the characteristics of your ideal client. This information is helpful especially when talking with informal sources of information (friends, other clients, vendors). Newspaper articles or even minutes from a steering committee meeting can provide information or ideas on places to develop new business.

Make a customer contact plan, and then take the steps necessary to create visibility in your potential marketplace. Once you establish your contacts, make sure you maintain that network. Keep regular contact through advertising, newsletters, periodic mailings, telephone calls, or by stopping in for a brief visit. Awareness is paramount, so that when new business opportunities arise, the potential customer thinks of you as the viable candidate.

Cultivate a network of people who recommend you and your talents. Be gracious with tangible and intangible recognition for their help. Maintain cordial relations even with your competition. They may want to team with you at some point, or perhaps they may not be able to handle a job and recommend you as a show of good faith to the client. Building positive word of mouth about your firm's abilities is one of the most important steps you can take to get more RFPs coming through your door.

Is This a Viable Project?

In the most simplistic terms, determining whether the prospective customer meets the following BANC criteria will help you assess the viability of the project both now and in the future:

- *Budget.* Does the customer have the money to pay for the job? If not, when will the funding be available? If the near-term position is unfavorable, think seriously before you put a lot of time and effort into writing a lengthy proposal. Still, this might be a good future business opportunity, so do not lose touch with the prospect.
- *Authority to commit resources.* Does your prospect have the authority to approve the project? If not, how far up the line does your prospect need to go to obtain approval? If your contact is not the decision maker, does not have formal or informal power to fund the project, or does not have direct access to the decision maker, then this business opportunity may not be worth a lot of effort now— maybe later, but not now.
- *Need that matches your skill set.* Is there an identified need on which everyone is in agreement? If not, can you help define the need? And will you and your prospect be able to sell the need once it is substantiated? The next step is to determine whether your organization can satisfy the need with its current expertise and products. If not, how much risk is involved in acquiring the skills and products to fulfill the contract without exceeding the time and dollar requirement? If the evaluation indicates an unfavorable risk-to-reward on this venture, it is preferable to pass up this situation.
- *Cycle.* When will the customer act? Where is the customer in the decision process? Is this type of project a priority? Is the money currently allocated for your type of project, or will it be next quarter or next year before the money is made available? The closer the customer is to the end of the procurement cycle, the more you want to offer. The further away the cycle, the less time you want to spend now; however, when the cycle is imminent, be positioned to respond with a full proposal.

Here is a hypothetical scenario: A prospective customer has approached you with a business opportunity. He is extremely enthusiastic. He assures you that you and your group are absolutely the right people to do this work, and he needs a proposal by Friday at 5 o'clock. So before the prospective customer's hype overwhelms you, you start asking some questions. First you ask, "Is there money to pay for a job of this magnitude?" (Budget) Your prospect responds that he hasn't gotten that far yet, but he is sure that there should be some money available to accommodate this endeavor. Your next question is very direct: "Are you the person who will make the decision? If not, have you been delegated the authority to make this deal?" (Authority) Your prospect is starting to calm down a little and confesses that he is not the decision maker. In fact, he believes that four different departments will have to agree before any decision will be made. Next, you inquire if these four departments agree on the statement of work (Need), at which time your potential customer admits that he is really doing more of a fact-finding mission than actually responding to a defined need within the organization. Last, you ask when they will act (Cycle), and you find out that the budgets for the next fiscal year were submitted last week without this as a budgeted project.

Can you see that if you had allowed the enthusiasm of your customer contact to sweep you away without asking the BANC question set, you would have put time and effort into writing a proposal with minimal chance of it culminating in a real assignment?

Do I Really Want This Business?

Not every opportunity may be worth doing. Think very carefully and do some extra analysis before venturing beyond the parameters of your mission statement and core competencies. Some years ago, a successful data processing consulting and training firm took an opportunity to start a data entry business. It turned out to be a bad decision. The data entry business was not consistent with the company's mission, the company did not have the expertise, and the venture diluted its energy and financial resources, which adversely affected their growth. With more insightful analysis, the firm could have determined that although data entry is tangentially related to data processing, it was not its primary business function.

Do not be a gambler unless you have the resources to absorb a loss. If the business opportunity still seems enticing after evaluating the above questions, consider once more the risk and what the chances are of being awarded the contract. Producing a winning proposal takes time and energy. It is not worth undertaking unless you are convinced you have a good chance and want to get involved in that business opportunity.

Also, do not let your desire to win cloud your good sense. Do not pursue a business opportunity that you will not be able to respond to or complete competently. Not only is it embarrassing to the client, but word gets around the industry.

Finally, if profit is not guaranteed or there is not a compelling intangible reason, then pass the opportunity by.

Can I Put Pen to Paper Yet?

Do not put pen to paper unless you have done the research necessary to understand your customer. In today's market, the criteria applied to the selection of a firm or internal resource are both technical expertise and knowledge of the client's company, business, and market. Executives who may be evaluating your proposal are most concerned with their own company's profitability and competitiveness. Obtain as much documentation as you can about the customer: its industry, the market, its style of management, and its key concerns.

Do not ever deceive yourself that you are smarter than your customer. The customer's executives have a vision of their needs, and their perception is their reality. You can either bid the job they are asking for or bid the job you think they need. If you choose the latter, be prepared to lose. If you cannot ethically bid the job they are asking, then do not bid at all.

Proposal Infrastructure and Protocols

Let us say that you know the business opportunity fits your area of expertise, you have qualified the prospect, and you know your client's needs. Now take the time to plan the proposal preparation. Following five steps will help to ensure the success of your proposal process: (1) staff the proposal team; (2) critique and learn from past experiences; (3) establish administrative discipline; (4) establish protocols; and (5) set up an advisory and review team.

Staff the Proposal Team

Writing a winning proposal is a project. Assign a proposal leader, assemble a balanced team of business and technical professionals, and put together a project plan. The team members can be chosen for any of the following reasons: they are intimately familiar with that part of the business, they know the customer, they have submitted successful proposals, or they are skilled resource estimators.

Critique and Learn from Past Experiences

Pull together every piece of documented history that you can. Critique any similar proposal, whether or not it was successful. In addition, collect any history on previous projects that can provide schedule and cost information. The team should also debrief any past experiences your firm has had with the client.

Before the team moves forward, consider what may have changed. Time has elapsed since this business opportunity was evaluated and the decision made to bid on the job. If there are new players, policies, predicaments, or predilections, there may be a new situation. Take any new policies, organizational changes, or changes in the business environment, either yours or the customer's, into consideration.

Establish Administrative Discipline

The time to establish the systems that everyone will use while putting the proposal together is before starting, not while developing the proposal. In addition to making sure that all the appropriate information is collected, determine the format and font for all materials. At a minimum, have your boilerplate sections—company qualifications, résumés of key consultants, and so forth—ready and formatted for inclusion in the proposal. Develop pricing templates or guidelines (such as, all dollars will be figured on a ten-year payback, or volume pricing can discount by only a certain percentage). Once you establish the guidelines, make sure you conform to them; otherwise consciously change them.

Establish Protocols

Protocols are the disciplines that must be followed during the proposal process—for example, discuss no dollars with anyone outside the team; meetings will be held on Tuesdays at 1:00 P.M. and all members must be present; or only the proposal leader talks to the client. The protocols should cover both the proposal preparation process and the period after the proposal is submitted. For example, once the proposal is submitted, the responsibility to communicate with the client may stay with the proposal leader or switch to the person with the authority to sign the proposal.

Set Up an Advisory and Review Team

Everyone who needs to contribute to the proposal may not be available or appropriate for the team. Designate certain contributors as advisers, who, when their skills are required, can help prepare specific sections. Another option is to form advisers into a "red pencil team" to edit and suggest improvements to the document. It is better for this team rather than the client to tear up your draft proposal.

A thorough process involves review and approval at various stages while the proposal is being prepared. In the initial stages, review for accuracy, readability, and consistency with the evaluation criteria set forth in the RFP. Once the proposal is near completion, have an adviser review the financial data and a lawyer review for legal issues. Finally, have the highest levels of management examine the proposal from a strictly business perspective. Top management needs to determine whether the organization is willing to commit to these promises and whether it has used every technique it has to win the bid.

Since a proposal is an official offer of services or product, define who has the authority to approve the dollars and conditions within the proposal. Then make sure that the approver is available to review and approve the proposal in its final stages. Who has the authority to sign the proposal representing the company? If this offer is not well conceived because of faulty assumptions or commitments, there can be embarrassing as well as legal consequences.

Writing the Proposal

A proposal should include four sections (see Exhibit 5.1), with the emphasis and order dependent on the decision criteria or format specifications set forth by the client:

- Section 1, the response requirements, answers the question, "How well does the bidder understand my business situation and the project?" It should include a response, point by point, to the evaluation criteria.
- Section 2, the technical section, is a specific response to the product or service requested. It explains how you intend to solve the problem or complete the project. This section contains the statement of work, tasks, definition of who is responsible, and the time line and sequence of activities.
- Section 3, the management section, includes your firm's capabilities as they relate to the project. It also provides a description of the company, the credentials of the team assigned to the project, and the justification for awarding the contract.
- Section 4, often the first section read, lays out the cost or price and the terms of payment.

The objective of your proposal is to differentiate yourself from the competition. Make sure your proposal stands out and is memorable in a positive way. One way is through the use of graphics, pie charts, project plans, and models, or you may find proposal preparation software that can help with the organization and visual presentation of your proposal, and with price estimating and reporting. If you are generating proposals for large projects or making proposals to government

EXHIBIT 5.1. PROPOSAL TEMPLATE.

Client: Client contact:
Source: Client decision maker:
Proposal leader:
Proposal team:
Phone: Fax: E-mail:

Client's Business Needs:

Evaluation Criteria (by weight)	**Company response and unique capabilities to meet this need**
1st	1st
2nd	2nd
3rd	3rd

Statement of Work:

Deliverables (quantitative, if possible):

Exclusions, if any:

Special requests and requirements (for example, proof of insurance):

Other unique qualifications of company and people assigned to the project:

Price Estimating Template

Task Description	Consultant Name Est Days $/Day	Support Staff Est Days $/Day	Other Costs (billable nonlabor costs) Unit $
Contingencies			

Compliance Matrix

Deliverables Our Company Produces	Work Provided or Produced by Client

Progress Payments

Milestone Date	Deliverable	Invoice Amount

Special Arrangements

Any agreed-on discounts or special arrangements:

Who owns what:

References:
Name   Phone Number   Name of Project Referenced

agencies, you may consider investing in software that systematizes price estimating and cost report generation.

Do not confine yourself to an exclusively paper-based product. Depending on your type of work or the client, consider a video or computer presentation that visually displays your work. For an executive who is on the road a lot, you may even consider creating a cassette with an audio proposal. However, do not let creativity compromise the clarity or the professional appearance.

Let's review each of the sections in more detail.

Response Requirements

Evaluation criteria are the points on which the prospective client will ultimately judge the proposal. In some RFPs, these criteria are clearly stated; in others, one has to ferret out those variables that are most important in the choice of a supplier. A prospective client's most important evaluation criterion might be the ability to meet the schedule, or adhere to budget constraints, or produce the highest-quality product or service possible. Their evaluation criteria might focus on the number of years of experience or the degrees your project manager or team members bring to the project. Another focus might be having project management processes in place that will assure professional management of the assignment.

If you did the early phases of the proposal preparation process well, the team has dissected the RFP's evaluation criteria, asked clarifying questions of the prospective client, and now thoroughly understands the client's decision criteria. If there was no RFP, then there needs to be a series of long, probing conversations with the client to be sure the business need and criteria on which the bid is to be evaluated are completely understood.

Once you isolate the evaluation criteria, find out which criteria will be given heavier weighting. Sometimes pricing is weighted higher than adherence to requirements. Although obtaining the weighting of criteria may be difficult, attempt to get the client to share this information because the weighting of criteria may become a tiebreaker. Balance your response to the weighted criteria. For example, if the customer indicates that the most important criterion is cost, then do not weight your response toward a description of the impressive qualifications of every consultant and technician on your staff.

Technical Requirements

Have your review team double-check that your statement of work is totally responsive to the RFP. Go back to the RFP one more time and make sure that it addresses the requests and requirements. For example, is there a need for proof of insurance or minority contractors? Do not expect all requirements to be clearly identified; there may be an important issue that the customer wants addressed that is buried in the RFP.

Your technical expertise or response to the requirements of the product or service requested by the client must be clearly laid out. Often, in addition to this section, your technical response may be summarized in the point-by-point response requirements.

Do not forget to include a project plan. What are the tasks? Who is responsible? What is the amount of effort required and the time line? In the past, the adage was to provide enough information to show that you understand the project and have good ideas, but without detailing the solution. In this post-downsizing era, it is likely that the client's in-house team is so small that the members not only cannot take your ideas and implement them, they are, in fact, looking to you for ideas, development, and implementation services. Use your good judgment in spelling out your solution, especially the details that differentiate you from the competition.

Management

Describe what is unique about your company or services that justifies being awarded the contract. Company history focused on past performance with this client or similar clients is especially important. Also, describe who will manage the project, and provide information on the experience of the project team, including subcontractors.

If you do not have all the talent to cover all facets of the assignment, do not try to fake it. Find, within your network, other people or firms that can team with you on this contract or to whom you would be willing to subcontract. Be careful in choosing subcontractors, because once you subcontract, you are not totally in control. Also, be sure that you leave enough time in the proposal preparation process for your subcontractor to contribute to the proposal. As our world increases in complexity, more and more people are considering teaming with others to respond to opportunities. The upside is that the other firm brings expertise that may help you get the contract and break into a new area of business. The downside is that if it does not work, breaking up is hard to do.

Another area to address in the management section is the compliance matrix, which graphically shows what the customer will be responsible for and what your organization will be responsible for. Indicate what tests or products will ensure compliance, how they will be measured, who will measure them, and who will sign off.

Give references of clients and other people who are going to say only wonderful things about you. Remember to tell your references to expect a telephone call from your prospective client, and preferably, brief your references about the business opportunity. If at all possible, provide samples or examples of similar work you have done. Remember that the customer is trying to find some tangible reason that he or she should pick you above all the others.

Price and Financials

In developing your pricing section, take advantage of all the history that is available relative to pricing the job. Use past job logs, personnel and payroll reports, and change control logs. Conduct a risk assessment, and define contingencies. Think of everything that caused extra expenditures of dollars and hours, and take those into account when estimating the job. Also, look at those unknowns where innovation, technology, or just good luck is involved. Be sure to factor everything into the equation.

Position the financial part of the proposal to be realistic yet persuasive. It might include a risk-reward analysis, a cost-benefit evaluation, or a cost comparison of different approaches. Remember that the word *realistic*. No bid is worth winning if you lose money in the end or do not professionally meet your commitments to your customer. Always bid the job high enough that if you do get it, there are sufficient funds for the expertise, technology, and time to do the job right.

Verifying and Certifying the Proposal

Pick a proposal theme—for example: "We are the best in the business and will supply you with the strongest talent available," or "We give you the most for your money," or "We have the technical expertise and the ability to provide you with a variety of options." Whatever your theme is, keep coming back to it throughout all the sections of the proposal. Trying to juggle multiple themes at the same time will probably confuse the customer. Take a calculated risk, and choose a theme that is both tied to the evaluation criteria and will sell.

Double-check your calculations. One mathematical error can undermine the best proposal. Have several people check the data: someone old, someone new, someone borrowed, and someone blue—in other words, someone who has worked on the team, someone who knows nothing about the proposal, someone from finance or the estimating group, and your resident cynic, that nitpicker who will find the slightest error.

Now that you, your team, and your advisers have reviewed the document thoroughly, bring in some other people (often called a "red team"), who have not been involved until now. In addition to checking the numbers, have them go through the proposal looking for statements that are illogical, unsubstantiated, or do not jive with other statements. Bring in people with good critical thinking skills to perform this check. And leave your ego at home. The document will probably be substantially changed by the time the final review is done, but it will be a better proposal.

Submitting the Proposal and Follow-Up

If it is a written proposal, print it, make sure the pages are in the right order, bind it, give whatever ritualistic blessing you use, and deliver it, preferably in person. Proposals are part of the sales process, and every proposal should have the benefit of a verbal explanation. When making your verbal presentation or submitting an oral proposal, show up on time, and be prepared with a professional standalone presentation and a handout. Also, do not do all the talking; ask open-ended questions and listen.

Always call a few days after submitting a proposal. The telephone call serves two purposes: to ensure that the proposal has not been lost and gets into the customer's hands before the deadline internally or externally, and to reemphasize your interest in getting the contract.

Another value-added service that you could provide your client is a proposal evaluation checklist. A sample is provided in Exhibit 5.2. Think in terms of what the client can use to justify its selection decision to potential detractors. Keep the checklist criteria balanced (it should not just be a listing of your company's attributes) and make sure it addresses the criteria listed in the RFP.

Contract Award

All that hard work paid off, and your organization has been awarded the contract! Take some time to celebrate, and then do two things before racing headlong into the assignment.

Before you put the structure and plans in place to move into the program management of the actual job, debrief the proposal process. What did we do right? What will we do better next time? Create an archive of parts of the proposal that can be excerpted for future opportunities.

Take the time to work this continuous improvement process through. This process will be invaluable for the next proposal that needs to be developed and in how you relate to your new current client.

EXHIBIT 5.2. PROPOSAL EVALUATION CHECKLIST.

Key
Vendor 1: Your Company Name
Vendor 2: _____
Vendor 3: _____

Selection Criteria	Response	Weighted Evaluation Criteria	Vendor 1	Vendor 2	Vendor 3
Is vendor stable? Number of years in business					
Do they offer a full range of services?					
Are they geographically available? Do they have representation beyond this area? Nationwide? International?					
Is there breadth and depth in their client list? Have they had long-term relationships with their clients?					
Are any of their clients in an industry similar to ours?					
Does the vendor understand our business and the competitive challenges we face?					
Client References • Did the job meet requirements? • Did the job stay within budget? Within schedule? • Was the project team professional in the relationship?					
Is vendor a minority- or women-owned business?					
Are they willing to conduct interviews to become familiar with our culture?					

Selection Criteria	Response	Weighted Evaluation Criteria	Vendor 1	Vendor 2	Vendor 3
Did the vendor provide a project plan for the job?					
Have they dedicated the appropriate amount of time and staff talent to the job?					
Are they willing to invest time to support us in detailing the scope of the project?					
Does the vendor have one focal point of contact for the job? At the appropriate level?					
Is our contact "listening" to us?					
Has vendor prepared thoughtfully before meeting with us?					
Did vendor prepare a professional proposal?					
Do they believe in their product and talk about it intelligently?					
Does vendor show concern for our needs and success? Do they quickly grasp important concepts and requirements?					
Are they willing to follow our lead? Not a hard sell?					
Are we comfortable in presenting this vendor to management?					
Is their philosophy or concept consistent with or is it able to be tailored to be consistent with corporate policies and procedures?					
Are pricing options available?					
Is vendor willing to negotiate? Are quantity discounts available?					

CHAPTER SIX

ORGANIZATIONAL STRUCTURE AND PROJECT MANAGEMENT

Robert C. Ford, W. Alan Randolph

The major organizational challenge of the next century is to manage increasingly limited resources in a highly aggressive and rapidly changing environment. As competitors become more willing and able to give the customers what they want, when they want it, and at the price they want to pay, organizations will need to find a way to respond quickly or be driven out of business. That is especially true when it comes to managing projects—on time, on budget, and according to the customer's specifications.

The key to meeting these challenges is increasingly flexible organization forms. One of the most responsive organizational structural forms available today is the cross-functional organization, which allows companies simultaneously to gain the advantages of the traditional functionally focused organization while retaining the flexibility of the project and matrix structures. The cross-functional forms of organization, matrix, and project structures make it possible to reassign human and financial resources quickly to meet the ever-changing dynamics of market competition, technological advances, governmental rules and regulations, and customer expectations.

This chapter describes the forces that have led to the increased interest in cross-functional organizational forms, the characteristics of these new organizational forms, their advantages and disadvantages, the circumstances that make these structures the best solution for meeting modern organizational challenges, and their particular value in project management. The hope is that organizations can find guidance in the lessons of those who have used cross-functional forms of organization.

Forces in the Current Business Environment

To those who are hoping that their traditional hierarchical functionally organized structures will successfully survive into the next century, there is reason to be concerned. The reality is that these traditional bureaucratic structures will be increasingly unable to cope with the trends first categorized by Hammer and Champy in their best-selling book, *Reengineering the Corporation.*[1] They identify three major forces that have created the modern complex and dynamic business environment: customers, competition, and change.

The first force, *customers*, refers to the emergence of the power of customers to tell suppliers what they want, what they will pay for it, when they want it, and in what form they want it. And because customers have so many choices available to them from so many different sources, organizations need to respond quickly to their needs and expectations. Furthermore, the availability of sophisticated information systems means that it is possible to identify increasingly small niches in the marketplace and market a uniquely tailored product or service directly to that group of customers. Only flexible organization structures can satisfy the customer demand for individualized products and services with precision. As Hammer and Champy point out, international competitors introduced this variety, and now American consumers expect it.

The second force refers to *competition*. With the increasing sophistication of customers have come increasing opportunities for competitors to focus their entire energy on marketing a product or service to a specific niche in the market. These new, smaller, and nimble competitors are able to dissect markets for any product or service into smaller and smaller segments, making it increasingly difficult for the large, traditional organization to compete. The globalization of trade means that the number of potential competitors will continue to increase at a geometric rate. A company may enjoy a profitable market share today, but competitors invent ideas that lower cost, increase quality, and expand service at such a pace that a company's market share is not secure for very long. Indeed, start-up companies rewrite the rules of competition, raising the expectations of customers at each step along the way. What was excellent service, high quality, and a good price yesterday may not even be close to meeting today's customers' expectations.

The third force is the recognition that *change* has become constant. Companies are continuously seeking and finding changes in the technology used to produce their products, the technological characteristics of the product itself, and even the way the product is distributed and marketed to the final customer. These changes lead to changes in customer expectations as to what the product ought to be, how the product is produced, and how much it should cost. Technological change even influences how the organization is structured. A company that is using just-in-time manufacturing processes to reduce its costs and improve quality will need to be organized differently and far more responsively than a manufacturing organization using more traditional methods. Similarly, changes in market expectations have necessitated the reduction in product life cycles from years to months, forcing the adoption of new organizational forms and technology to compress product development time frames substantially.

Companies that cannot move fast and flexibly will probably not be moving at all within a short period of time. And to make matters even more challenging for the traditional organizational structures, changes come from a number of different directions—not only are competitors and technological innovations but customers' expectations. Customers may like the product the company makes, but become unhappy with the service associated with the product or the way the product is distributed in the marketplace. Saturn provides a telling illustration of a company that both created a better product and found a better way to sell it. It forced the major automobile companies to rethink their marketing strategies, products, and organizations. Finally, the environment also continues to change. Not only are state and federal laws and regulations in a state of continuous change, but companies must now learn how to respond to various special interest groups as well.

As Hammer and Champy conclude, these three C's have created a world of business that is completely new and different. The solution, they suggest, is to find a new way to structure the organization. The necessary innovation, speed, low cost, high quality, and customer responsiveness cannot be achieved by hierarchical organizations. Companies of the future will need cross-functional forms of organization that make use of sophisticated technologies, while also drawing on the full capabilities of people's expertise and skills to compete.

Cross-Functional Organizational Forms

A large literature discusses and describes the cross-functional forms of organization under various terms. In this literature, the terms *matrix management, project management, matrix organization,* and *project organization* are frequently interchanged. All of these terms refer to some type of cross-functional organization because they invariably involve bringing people together from two or more normally separated organizational functional areas to undertake tasks on either a temporary basis (as in a project team) or a relatively permanent basis (as in a matrix organization). A thorough review of this literature reveals certain characteristics that generally apply to these forms of organization. Let us review these characteristics and then return to a working definition to tie together the discussion of the advantages, disadvantages, and circumstances under which these forms of organization can be best used.

Characteristics of Cross-Functional Forms

One of the most common characteristics of cross-functional forms of organization is the mixed or overlay, in which a traditional, vertical hierarchy is "overlaid by some form of lateral authority, influence, or communication."[2] As depicted in Figure 6.1, the vertical hierarchy is traditionally functional, and the horizontal overlay typically consists of projects, products, or a defined business or customer focus. Along these two dimensions, the matrix form of the cross-functional structure typically has a second common characteristic: dual lines of authority, responsibility, and accountability that violate the traditional principle of management of only one boss per employee.[3] Indeed, this is the key characteristic of matrix management. The matrix structure, then, "constructively blends the program orientation of project staffs with the specialty orientation of functional personnel in a new and synergistic relationship."[4]

Most writers place matrix organizations at the center of a continuum, as seen in Figure 6.2, between purely functional type organizations and purely product type organizations.[5] On the functional end of this continuum is the traditional hierarchical structure divided along functional lines, such as marketing, production, and accounting. On the other end of the continuum is the pure product organization. Here, a separate team is formed, duplicating the functional structure but organized under a product manager.[6] Matrix organizations are somewhere in between these end points. They are temporary in nature and focused on a specific project, which is scheduled to be completed within some defined time, cost, and performance standards.

The structures represented by each end of this continuum have their benefits and costs. A functional structure, for example, enables individuals to remain aware of new technical developments in their respective areas of expertise and allows them to concentrate their efforts and interactions in their areas of interest. A cost of functional structure, however, is the difficulty created in coordinating across these distinct functional disciplines, task orientations, and organizational loyalties. The product structure eliminates or reduces the coordination difficulties by concentrating all team members' attention on the requirements of the product. At the same time, such concentration on the product makes

FIGURE 6.1. MATRIX ORGANIZATIONAL STRUCTURE.

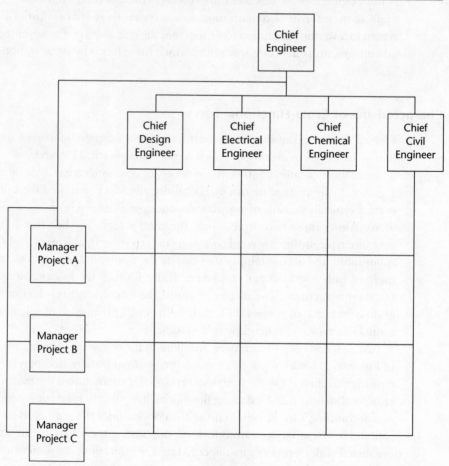

it more difficult for the individual members to stay current with their own particular functional expertise and may result in their technological obsolescence. The dilemma is that when one structure is chosen, the benefits of the other structure are lost. Organization writers view the cross-functional form of matrix as a solution to this dilemma. A matrix combines the benefits of both structures by providing proper project coordination while maintaining a continuing linkage with a functional expertise.[7]

Gobeli and Larson refined this functional-product continuum by developing three subclasses of matrix—functional, balanced, and project—that identify the

FIGURE 6.2. FUNCTION, MATRIX, AND PRODUCT:
A CONTINUUM OF ALTERNATIVES.

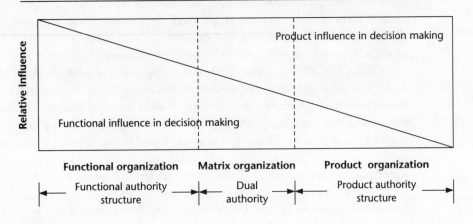

primary source of decision authority.[8] In the functional matrix, the matrix manager relies on personal influence and communication skills to coordinate the different functional areas of the project in the absence of real organizational power. The functional manager retains ultimate decision-making authority over what the matrix unit does, its personnel, and other aspects of the project. Under project matrix (or what is commonly termed project management), the project manager has primary control over the project's resources and direction. The functional groups' managers serve largely in a supporting or advisory role. The balanced matrix splits authority midway between the two. The project manager directs and sets control for the project with some shared authority over the functional personnel. Functional management retains control over much of the team and is responsible for carrying out the plans and controls established by the project manager.[9]

Some researchers have observed that matrix systems evolve over time.[10] These writers argue that this evolutionary process typically covers five stages. In the first stage, the organization begins as a traditional or a functional type of hierarchy. As that structure becomes inadequate to deal with the complex, dynamic conditions it faces, the organization moves into the next phase, *project organization* or *temporary overlay,* in which the traditional functional hierarchy remains the cornerstone of the organization and project management is added as a secondary, temporary overlay to deal with the new complexities faced by the organization. As the level of environmental complexity and turbulence increases, some organizations move to the next stage, where they make this overlay permanent. This third phase, labeled *matrix organization* or *permanent overlay*, makes project management the permanent form of the organization, although the functional hierarchy is still considered primary. The next phase of evolution is labeled the *mature matrix*. In this phase, a balance of authority exists between the functional hierarchy and the project organization. The last phase, termed *beyond the matrix*, may entail organizational forms that are unique to the particular organizations that are facing unique challenges from their customers, competitors, or other forces of change.[11] An organization may stop evolving at any point in this process if the driving forces noted earlier are not present. These structures are found in organizations that produce more than one product or service or that must modify their product or service frequently in response to changing environmental, technological, or other conditions.

Building on this discussion, it is possible to develop a definition of cross-functional structures that incorporates the key characteristics of these types of structures: cross-functional organizations are functional overlays with multiple lines of authority that place people in teams to work on projects for finite periods of time. This broad definition includes the many varieties of cross-functional organization forms. One key to understanding the distinctions among the variety of cross-functional forms is the time element. Project management forms typically have the most finite time frame. A project has a deadline, definable costs, and completion standards within that time frame. Project organizations are an extension of project management, and they come into play as an organization finds itself regularly managing multiple projects. Similarly, matrix management is a more temporary application than matrix organization.

The distinction between matrix and project is that project structures form around specific finite tasks, such as a cross-functional project, whereas matrix structures tend to form around repeating tasks that use similar but not identical resources, such as managing an engineering consulting firm or manufacturing a complex product (as aerospace companies do). Overall, then, these cross-functional organization forms have a great deal in common: an overlay on the traditional hierarchy, multiple lines of authority, and teams working on tasks for finite time periods. With this definition, let us proceed to review what the literature has suggested regarding advantages and disadvantages of cross-functional structures.

Advantages and Disadvantages of Cross-Functional Structures

The literature abounds with lists, tables, and anecdotal stories of advantages and disadvantages of cross-functional structures.[12] Although only a few of these lists are empirically based, over time the lists of both advantages and disadvantages have become commonly accepted as definitive.[13] What little empirical evidence exists is sparse and limited in scope. Most of the advantages are derived from the creation of horizontal communication linkages, whereas most of the disadvantages spring from the creation of dual or multiple authority and influence.

A primary advantage of the cross-functional form of organization is that it expands the organization's ability to process information laterally.[14] At the same time, the cross-functional structure reduces the need for vertical communication by creating self-contained task teams focused on a specific, finite project. It improves communication among departments and projects by forcing managers to maintain close contact with all organizational groups on whose support they must rely for project success. A related communication benefit of matrix is that the increased contact among departments allows information to permeate the organization, improving decision making and response time, which translates into an organization that can quickly and flexibly adapt to a dynamic situation.[15]

Improved information flow and flexibility of responses by team members in a matrix can allow resources to be disengaged quickly and easily from unproductive uses and applied to new opportunities as they are discovered.[16] Expensive specialists and equipment can be assigned in a flexible manner over a changing array of project teams.[17] Functional expertise is not lost because these specialists typically retain their associations with their functional areas while they are assigned to various projects.[18]

Related to these communication and information flow advantages are its advantages for individuals. In particular, several writers argue that a matrix should positively influence motivation, job satisfaction, commitment, and personal development because individuals have the opportunity to work on a variety of projects with a variety of individuals from across the organization.[19] In sharing ideas, knowledge, and perspectives, the group relationships enlarge an individual's experience and outlook, increase responsibility and involvement in decision making, and offer a greater opportunity to display capabilities and skills.[20] Other individual benefits include the development of interpersonal and group skills, problem-solving abilities, planning, and improved career paths.[21]

The final advantage claimed for the matrix is technical excellence.[22] Improved information processing facilitates the sharing of technical information by those who need it and assists in the communication and consideration of critical, technical information for a project. Greater flexibility allows an organization to make appropriate technical decisions quickly, adapt to changing technical conditions, and use resources efficiently across projects.[23] The multidisciplinary approach allows functional expertise to be maintained in ways not possible in other organizational forms. In other words, projects benefit from the use of functional economies of scale while remaining small and task oriented enough to stay technically innovative.[24] Finally, a matrix assists in the development of knowl-edgeable, technically competent individuals who eventually become matrix com-petent and comfortable. In combination, these advantages facilitate technical excellence.[25]

The disadvantages of cross-functional structures are as varied and as anec-dotal as the advantages, but on closer inspection many of them are a product of the same dual or multiple overlay of authority and influence characteristic that yields the advantages. In traditional structures, two classical principles of orga-nization clearly stand out: (1) "Authority should equal responsibility" and (2) "Every subordinate should be assigned to a single boss." Cross-functional forms of or-ganization tend to violate both of these deeply ingrained principles, creating prob-lems for both the organization and its individual members.[26] In the matrix form specifically, the boundaries of authority and responsibility are split or shared be-tween functional and project managers, creating ambiguity, conflict, and power struggles over areas such as resources, technical issues, salaries and promotions, and personnel assignments.[27]

Several studies have sought to identify the sources of organizational conflict created by a matrix.[28] The most common authority conflicts are those between functional and project managers over project priorities, administrative procedures, technical perfection versus performance trade-offs, personnel resources, cost esti-mates, scheduling, and personalities. The Barker and Associates study focused on the intensity of these conflicts over the project life cycle.[29] They found that the three most intense areas of conflict (schedules, priorities, and personnel resources) result from the split-authority problem between project managers and functional departments. Thus, the way to minimize conflict is to clarify authority and re-sponsibility for the project.

Conflict can also exist at the individual level. The interaction of people with different work orientations (such as project or task versus functional or profes-sional), different professional affiliations, different time horizons (such as long term versus short term), and different values are all potential causes of conflict.[30] In a matrix, individuals find themselves working across various projects under differ-ent managers. This situation creates multiple reporting relationships (role conflict), conflicting and confusing expectations (role ambiguity), and excessive demands (role overload).

A final issue in individual conflict can arise when functional managers experi-ence insecurity and an erosion of autonomy. According to Davis and Lawrence, when functional managers view a matrix organization as a loss of status, authority, and control over their traditional domain, they react with resistance and hostility.[31]

Another major disadvantage is cost. Matrix management can be costly for both organizations and the individuals. Dual authority creates additional management overhead and additional staff, mainly administrative.[32] Matrix also leads to costs associated with organizational "heaviness," including excessive meetings or "groupitis," which can lead to delayed decision making and increased information processing costs.[33] The costs of unused or underused resources, both physical and human, are also likely to increase, as well as the costs for extra training of project and matrix managers and the costs associated with monitoring, controlling, and coordinating the people and project within the matrix.[34] Although solid empirical data are rare, a matrix does appear to have more organizational costs than traditional structures.

Matrix structures also create costs for individuals. Although these costs are difficult to quantify and their effects on the organization are even more difficult to measure, writers generally believe that individuals pay a price for working in a matrix. Specifically, the dynamic, ambiguous nature of authority in a matrix leads to individual role ambiguity, conflict, and stress for functional and project managers, as well as their subordinates.[35] Individuals are expected to take more personal initiative in defining roles, negotiating conflicts, taking responsibilities, and making personal decisions, but the downside of such freedom is stress. If the matrix is not properly managed, problems with motivation and satisfaction can surface, negatively affecting the quality of working life and resulting in lost productivity.[36] Table 6.1 summarizes the advantages and disadvantages for cross functional organizations.

In reviewing the advantages and disadvantages, it is apparent that they share some similarities. For example, the benefit of increased information processing capacity of cross-functional organizations creates an additional cost. The lesson is that cross-functional structures should be used with caution. It is useful, however, to review the environmental, organizational, task or project, and task or project team characteristics that the many writers on this topic have concluded are better suited for the use of cross-functional structures. If such structures are more appropriately used or seem to be more successful in particular circumstances, then the organization may find that its circumstances mean that the advantages outweigh the disadvantages.

Factors That Facilitate Using Cross-Functional Structures in Projects

Implementing a matrix is a complex process and involves more than just changing the organizational structure, systems, culture, and behaviors over time. According to Davis and Lawrence, choosing a matrix is a serious, top-level decision requiring commitment to a thorough implementation. They state, "Matrix is an

TABLE 6.1. ADVANTAGES AND DISADVANTAGES OF CROSS-FUNCTIONAL STRUCTURES.

Advantages	Disadvantages
Create lateral communication channels that increase frequency of communication across functional areas	Violate principles of traditional single line of authority and authority equal to responsibility
Increase quality and quantity of information up and down the vertical hierarchy	Lead to ambiguity over control of resources, responsibility for technical issues, and human resource management issues
Increase flexibility in utilization of human expertise and capital resources	Create organizational conflict between function and project managers
Increase individual motivation, job satisfaction, commitment, and personal development	Create interpersonal conflict among individuals who must work together but have very different backgrounds, perspectives on work, time horizons, and goals
Achieve technical excellence more easily	Create loss of status, insecurity for functional managers, and feelings of erosion of authority
	More costly for the organization in increased overhead and staff, more meetings, delayed decisions, more information processing
	More costly for individuals in terms of role ambiguity, conflict, and stress

exceedingly complex form that is not for everybody. To put it bluntly, if you do not really need it, leave it alone."[37] The advantages and disadvantages must be weighed and the process managed if the cross-functional form is to work. Therefore, it is imperative for organizations to understand what factors facilitate or influence the adoption of a matrix before they choose it.

The argument over which factors influence structural choice is by no means a new or a simple one. The task is particularly difficult with cross-functional forms because several interrelated factors may be involved. In its simplest sense, the optimal organizational form is that which best suits the organizational environment, the organizational characteristics, the task to be accomplished, and the skills of the team leader and members. The question we wish to address, then, is what the environmental, organizational, project and task characteristics, and project and task team characteristics are that contribute to the successful use of cross-functional organizations.

Environmental Influences

The environments that organizations face can be categorized into sociocultural, economic, physical, and technological. These elements combine to define an environment that has four basic properties: complexity (number of elements), diversity (variety of elements), rate of change (stable or dynamic), and uncertainty (predictability of changes).

Simple environments are characterized by a small number of similar, unchanging elements that are relatively predictable. Complex environments are characterized by a large number of diverse, rapidly changing elements that are relatively unpredictable.[38] When an organization's environment is relatively simple, a traditional hierarchical form works well. As its environment grows more complex, the traditional and less flexible structure may become overloaded by having to process the quantity of information necessary to adjust to the changing environment.[39] In the more complex environment, the organization should adopt a more organic organizational form, such as the matrix.

Another important environmental factor is the influence of a dominant stakeholder. The history of project management indicates that much of the initial impetus for its use was a function of the stipulation of the U.S. Defense Department's and the National Aeronautics and Space Administration that project management be used as a requirement of the contract acquisition process.[40] It was believed that this organizational arrangement would best allow the organizations bidding on large, unique, complex, government projects to complete them within the expected time and budget constraints. Because so many of these projects were pushing back the frontiers of knowledge into areas where it was difficult, if not impossible, to know with certainty the costs, technology, time to complete, and resources required (on a major project like a space shuttle or moon landing), this approach made considerable sense as a coordinating mechanism and a control measure.

The internal environmental factors, such as technology, can also influence the decision to adopt a matrix. Technology can be viewed in many ways. To some it may be physical (machinery, tools), whereas to others it may be knowledge (information and know-how). Technology also exists at various levels: individual, departmental, organizational, and industrial. An organization's technology is its set of techniques (both material and mental) used to transform the system's inputs into its outputs.[41] Traditionally, researchers have viewed the functional form as most effective when technical expertise is critical to organizational success.[42] Simple technology is characterized by a slow rate of change, little interdependence of disciplines, and technical expertise in efficiency. Complex technology is characterized by a rapid rate of change, high interdependence of disciplines, and technical expertise in innovation. Traditional functional structures are most efficient when technology is relatively simple. However, as technology becomes more complex, the functional structure may be unable to provide the degree of flexibility and innovation across disciplines that matrix can provide.[43]

Organizational Characteristics

Another factor that influences the applicability of cross-functional structure is the nature of the organization, in particular its culture. According to Cleland, an organizational culture "is the environment of beliefs, customs, knowledge, practices, and the conventional behavior of a particular social group. Every organization, every corporation has its distinct character."[44] Organizational culture is important because it unites individuals with a purpose under a "set of principles and standards to live and work by." It exists at all levels of the organization and is shaped by its various subcultures, as well as by the society in which it exists.[45] Certain organizational cultures are more receptive to cross-functional structures than others. Organizational cultures characterized by a rigid bureaucracy, minimal interdepartmental interaction, strong vertical reporting lines, and little tradition of change are not very receptive to cross-functional structures.[46] In fact, unless the culture can be changed, the matrix may face resistance or open hostility. Organizations with a tradition of openness and change are more compatible with the requirements of matrix structures. The move to a matrix is often easier for these organizations.[47] Burns and Wholey point out a related issue to culture that identifies the influence of organizational peers on a particular organization's decision to adopt or not adopt a cross-functional matrix organization.[48]

Also associated with cross-functional success is the way in which ambiguity in authority and responsibility has been clarified by the organization. Most researchers argue that ambiguity in a matrix is harmful and should be controlled by a clear definition of organizational roles.[49] Otherwise, the organization invites unnecessary and unproductive conflict due to the resulting ambiguity.

A related organizational issue is the division of authority between project and functional managers.[50] A study by Larson and Gobeli measured the relative effectiveness of different project structures (such as project matrix, balanced matrix, and functional matrix). Project matrix was rated the most effective, although the other two matrix forms were used almost as frequently. These researchers attribute the apparent contradiction to the existence of the evolutionary development of the matrix forms, beginning with functional and ending up at project. A related explanation is that since project matrix, though most effective, is not politically feasible for many organizations because of the authority and organizational realignments required, functional or balanced matrix may be more widely used.[51]

The research evidence seems to indicate that the balanced structure is least effective and the project matrix is the most effective. It does confirm the traditional organizational thinking that someone has to be in charge of the project to ensure accountability and responsibility. Indeed, the work on sources of project conflict seems to indicate that the greatest conflict occurs when there is uncertainty over who is in charge or when one manager is held responsible for a situation but the other manager has the authority to make the decisions.[52]

The authority issue is only one organizational characteristic, and many other areas of investigation await inquiry. The elements of culture deserve a great deal of research attention. In addition, such issues as size of organization, size of project, private versus public, and the multidimensional relationships among these issues represent a few of the largely unexplored and untouched subjects of future research.

Characteristics of the Project

A third element issue in the use of cross-functional structures (Figure 6.3)[53] is the project's characteristics. Organizations are no longer providing a single product or a single service to a single customer or area. Markets have diversified and customer demands have become more stringent. As a result, organizational tasks have become more complex.[54] Determination of the nature of an organization's tasks rests on the combination of four properties: task complexity (number of tasks), task diversity (variety of tasks), rate of task change (slow or rapid), and task size (defined by cost or time needed to complete the task).[55] Simple tasks are small in number, limited in diversity, relatively unchanging, and relatively small in cost or time. Complex tasks are large in number, highly diverse, rapidly changing, and large in cost or time.[56] Functional structures, although well suited for simple tasks, experience difficulty integrating multiple, complex tasks. Matrix structures provide an alternative for handling the coordination of complex and diverse tasks.[57] Clearly, the research on project characteristics needs to be more extensive.

The essential factors in successful cross-functional organizations are summarized in Table 6.2.

Project Team Characteristics

Of the many possible variables that could be considered under this heading, one of the few empirical works focuses on communications.[58] This study of professionals in a research and development facility was designed to investigate the relationship of communication, especially communication within the project, to project success. The study found that although there was no significant differ-

FIGURE 6.3. A MODEL OF CROSS-FUNCTIONAL STRUCTURES.

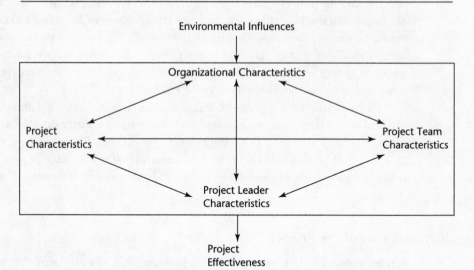

ence in the relationship of project performance and the amount of communication within the project, it made a great deal of difference in the way that information and decision-making involvement was distributed. More equal team member participation was related to greater project success. Thus, one characteristic of successful cross-functional teams would appear to be that they are participative in nature and allow their members free and equal access to communications.

A later interpretation of the data by Katz suggests that there is a difference between research and development teams in how they organize themselves to communicate with others outside the project team.[59] Development projects are defined and operationalized in terms of the particular strengths, interests, and experiences of the organization's subculture. As a result, the need to communicate externally is relatively less than it would be for a research group that relies on access to the scientific community at large. In terms of the project team characteristics, therefore, it would seem reasonable to conclude, as Katz does, that the longer groups are together, the more they tend to rely on each other and the less they seek to communicate outside the group. They become, as Katz terms it, "increasingly isolated from outside sources of information and influence."[60] On the basis of these data, Katz concludes that group longevity is related to project team performance in that

TABLE 6.2. FACTORS ASSOCIATED WITH THE SUCCESSFUL USE OF CROSS-FUNCTIONAL ORGANIZATION.

Category	Facilitating Factors
External Environmental Complex, diverse, rapidly changing, unpredictable	Competitors and customers Stakeholder requirements Peer organization pressure
Technological Environment Complex technology (sophisticated and rapidly changing)	Highly interdependent technology High-level technical expertise required High information processing needs to coordinate
Organizational Culture Tradition of openness and change	Clearly defined organizational roles and goals Clearly defined assignment of authority and responsibility Top management commitment to make cross-functional structure work
Task/Project Complex with multiple parts requiring high level of skill or professional expertise from different functional parts of organization	Finite with defined beginning and end Rapidly changing and nonroutine
Project/Task Team High levels of team member participation	Free and equal access to information for team Members located in physical proximity Longer in duration Have necessary expertise included

for all types of research and development groups in the study, performance of the long-tenured project groups was significantly lower.

In a 1986 study of thirty-two R&D project groups, Keller found that group cohesiveness, innovative orientation, and job satisfaction have a positive relationship to project group performance. He concludes that managers of research and development project teams should encourage group cohesiveness through minimizing physical distances between group members, using a participative leadership style, and maintaining stable group membership.[61]

Beside these few studies focusing entirely on research and development project teams, there is surprisingly little in the literature to help practicing managers design effective cross-functional teams. White suggests that project team members should represent all types of cognitive styles if they expect to be effective.[62] The work of Pinto and Slevin identifies competence of team members as one factor for project success.[63]

The area of project team characteristics offers an important and largely undeveloped area for future research. Although there is a large literature on the structuring and development of effective groups, this literature has not found its way into research focused on cross-functional teams.[64] Clearly, the structure, composition, size, attitudes, training, and length of association are issues that could be fruitfully pursued. Even such elementary and easily measured factors as age, sex, and similar demographic characteristics remain important areas for investigation.

Project Effectiveness

The reason to use cross-functional structures is to achieve project effectiveness. The literature provides a variety of discussions about factors that lead to project success.[65] Perhaps the most extensive is represented by the work of Slevin and Pinto.[66] These writers have sought to identify, measure, and investigate factors that are critical to project management success. The ten factors they empirically identified include several noted in the four areas reviewed above. From their studies, they developed a Project Implementation Profile and used it to investigate the relative importance of these factors across the project life cycle. They found that project mission clarification factor and the factors representing communicating with clients showed up as significant in a regression analysis using project performance as the dependent variable across all stages of the project life cycle. The only other factors to enter into the regression equation were top management support (in the planning stage), technical expertise (in the execution and termination stage), and troubleshooting and planning (in the execution stage). Although the concept of identifying the critical tasks in implementing successful project management is an important one, there is need for more research

Pinto and Slevin reviewed five other conceptual approaches to identifying factors that are critical to the success of project implementation.[67] Although there is some obvious overlap in these lists, some differences show up too. Overall, the critical factors can be categorized into two general areas. The first factor is the clear definition of the project's mission. Because all else really flows from this in terms of justification for resource acquisition, rationale for time schedules, and criteria for evaluation of project success, this factor becomes paramount in project management.[68]

The second critical factor in project management success is top management support for the project and its willingness to show that support by committing resources to the project. This factor would include the general managerial and organizational culture that supports the projects. Although Pinto and Slevin identify some of these critical factors, which refer back to those noted in Table 6.2, the empirical results are still too limited to make strong claims about which factors are definitely related to project success

Another body of research looking into the characteristics of effective project organization is that of Larson and Gobeli.[69] They have investigated the relative effectiveness of project matrix, functional matrix, and balanced matrix forms across industry, size, and other demographic and contextual factors. In terms of effectiveness, these two writers report that the project matrix is the most effective, although they note that all three forms are used extensively. Of the contextual factors studied, only clearly defined objectives was significantly related to success.[70]

Summary and Conclusions

From this review of the substantial body of literature, one major conclusion seems clear: there is much to learn about the circumstances and practices that relate to the successful use of cross-functional organizations. Still, it is safe to say that these writings do provide some guidance to practicing managers. Pinto and Slevin, for example, have created a generic, empirical framework of success factors. Their Project Implementation Profile (PIP) and subsequent studies indicate that their identified factors do have a relationship to project effectiveness and that the relative impact of several of the factors appears to vary across the phases of the project life cycle.[71]

Davis and Lawrence warn that "a successful matrix must be grown instead of installed."[72] An organization simply cannot plug a matrix into its existing structure and expect success. Matrix structures should be uniquely developed for a particular application in a particular organization, and this development will likely follow the evolutionary path described earlier. There is also evidence to suggest that contingencies based on the structural, systems, behavioral, and cultural contexts of the organization in general and the matrix structures in particular have positive and negative influences on the effectiveness of the cross-functional structure.[73] Managers would do well to consider the contingencies summarized in Table 6.2.

Thus, in conclusion, the literature does provide some guidance for practicing project leaders. Although far too little of this material is empirically derived, there are a large number of anecdotal accounts and single firm experiences that lend some credence to the factors noted in this chapter. Clearly cross-functional organizations work better than functional forms or even product forms in certain circumstances. These circumstances seem to reflect the same characteristics that are associated with organizations faced with rapidly changing customers, competition, and other types of change.

Cross-functional organizations are not an insignificant or isolated phenomenon. They are intensively and extensively used today by organizations looking for help in adapting to the challenges of a highly competitive and rapidly changing environment. Those organizations facing the environmental conditions noted above and that have the organizational, tasks or projects, and project team characteristics associated with successful use of cross-functional structures may find that these forms of organization can make the difference for them in meeting the challenges they will face.

PART TWO

SCOPE MANAGEMENT AND PLANNING

CHAPTER SEVEN

PROJECT SCOPE MANAGEMENT

Jeffrey K. Pinto

Emmitt Smith, the All-Pro running back for the Dallas Cowboys, has always attributed his remarkable success to his commitment to developing and working toward a series of personal goals. He likes to tell the story of his high school days and the impact they had on his future success. When Smith was a student at Escambia High in Pensacola, Florida, his football coach used to say, "It's a dream until you write it down. Then it's a goal."

For successful projects, scope management functions in a similar manner. Until a detailed set of specifications is enumerated, recorded, and controlled for, a project is just an expensive dream. It is only when systematic planning occurs that projects evolve to an operational level where they can begin to be developed. Scope management represents the foundation on which all project work is based. It is therefore the culmination of predevelopment planning. "The scope of a project can be either the work content or component of a project. It can be fully described by naming all activities performed, the end products which result and the resources 'consumed.'"[1]

This chapter details the key components of project scope management, which, when properly done, seeks to leave as little as possible to chance, through eliminating project errors resulting from ambiguous goals, unclear reporting structures, and poor communication, while efficiently developing the necessary action steps for project development.

Scope management consists of several distinct activities, all based on creating a systematic set of plans for the upcoming project. Among the activities associated with scope management are conceptual development, the scope statement, work authorization, scope reporting, control systems, and project closeout (see Exhibit 7.1).[2] These activities are key to comprehensive planning and project development.

Conceptual Development

The Project Management Institute's Body of Knowledge defines conceptual development as the "process of choosing/documenting the best approach to achieving the project objectives."[3] In order to create an accurate model of conceptual development for the project, several pieces of information must be collected by the project manager and the team:

- *Problem or need statement.* A project's scope management begins with a goal statement: what the project intends to do, why there is a need in search of a solution, and what the underlying problem consists of.
- *Information gathering.* This step consists of engaging in an information search to gather all relevant data or information on the circumstances and the targets set for the project. It is clearly pointless to expect a project to be effectively initi-

EXHIBIT 7.1. ELEMENTS IN PROJECT SCOPE MANAGEMENT.

1. **Conceptual development**
   - Problem statement
   - Information gathering
   - Constraints
   - Alternative analysis
   - Project objectives

2. **Scope statement**
   - Goal criteria
   - Management plan
   - Work breakdown structure
   - Scope baseline

3. **Work authorization**
   - Contractual requirements
   - Valid consideration
   - Contracted terms

4. **Scope reporting**
   - Cost, schedule, technical performance status
   - S curves
   - Earned value
   - Variance or exception reports

5. **Control systems**
   - Configuration control
   - Design control
   - Trend monitoring
   - Document control
   - Acquisition control
   - Specification control

6. **Project closeout**
   - Historical records
   - Postproject analysis
   - Financial closeout

ated if the project manager does not have a clear understanding of the current state of affairs.

- *Constraints.* Coupled with the goal statement, project managers should work diligently to understand the restrictions that will affect their ability to create their projects. Time constraints, budget shrinkages, and client demands can serve as serious constraints on project development.

- *Alternative analysis.* Problems usually offer alternative methods for their solution. In project management, alternative analysis consists of first clearly understanding the nature of the problem statement and then working to generate alternative solutions. These solutions, in addition to giving all involved a clearer understanding of the project's characteristics, also offer a choice of approaches for addressing how the project should be undertaken.

- *Project objectives.* Conceptual development should conclude with a clear statement of the final objectives for the project in terms of outputs, required resources, and timing. If the previous steps have been well done, the objectives will logically follow from the analysis. Novice project managers should take care that they have not limited their alternative analysis information search. If the information search has been done well, the final objectives for the project should be clear.

Do's and Don'ts of Conceptual Development

It is vital that project managers set the stage for their projects as completely as possible. Clearly establishing the conceptual development for a project is often based on being able to reduce the complexity of the overall project to a more basic level, in which problem statements and goals and objects are clearly stated and easily understood by all team members. Unfortunately, many projects are initiated with less than a clear understanding of the problem the project seeks to address. I am familiar with a number of projects that have far exceeded their initial budgets and schedules due to a vague understanding among team members as to exactly what the project was attempting to accomplish. Creating a reasonable and complete problem statement is important for establishing the nature of the project, its purpose, and set of concrete goals.

Part of the problem statement consists of the ability to analyze multiple alternatives. It is dangerous and often wrong to lock in to "one best" approach for solving a problem through a project. In fact, until a fuller understanding of the problem is generated, there is a very real likelihood that the projects being developed will not, in fact, serve the purpose for which they were created.

To be effective, problem statements should be kept simple and based on clearly understood needs in search of solutions. A project goal that is vague or excessively optimistic does not satisfy the criterion of simplicity. For example, a goal that suggests the project is intended to "improve corporate profitability while maintaining quality and efficiency of resources" does not have the virtue of simplicity. It does not give the project team a reference point when problems occur over the course of project development.

Scope Statement

The scope statement, the heart of scope management, consists of the best attempts at creating the documentation and approval of all important project parameters prior to proceeding to the development phase. There are a number of key steps attached to the scope statement process, including the following:

1. *Establishing the project goal criteria,* including cost, schedule, performance and deliverables, and key interfaces with important project stakeholders (particularly the clients). The goal criteria represent the significant constraints of the project around which the project team and organization must labor.

2. *Developing the management plan.* This plan consists of the organizational structure for the project team, the policies and procedures under which team members will be expected to operate, their job descriptions, and a well-understood reporting structure for each member of the team. The management plan is essentially the bureaucratic step in the project of creating control systems to ensure that all team members know their roles, their responsibilities, and professional relationships.

3. *Establishing a work breakdown structure.* The work breakdown structure (WBS) is one of the most vital planning mechanisms. It breaks the project down into its component substeps in order to begin establishing critical interrelationships among activities. Put more simply, until a project has gone through WBS, it is impossible to determine the relationships among the various activities (which steps must precede others, which steps are independent of previous tasks, and so forth). Accurate scheduling can begin only with accurate and meaningful WBS.

4. *Creating a scope baseline.* The scope baseline contains a summary description of each component of the project's goal, including basic budget and schedule information for each activity. This is the final step of systematically laying out all prework information, in which each subroutine of the project has been identified and given its control parameters of cost and schedule.

Do's and Don'ts of the Scope Statement

The main point for project managers to keep in mind about the scope statement is the need to spend adequate up-front time preparing their schedules and budgets based on accurate and reasonable estimation. This estimation can be adequately performed only if project managers have worked through the WBS and project goals statements thoroughly. There are fewer sure-fire ways to create the atmosphere for a project destined to fail than to do a cursory and incomplete WBS. When steps are left out, ignored, or underestimated during the WBS phase, they are underbudgeted or underestimated in scheduling. The resulting project will almost certainly have a sliding schedule, rapidly inflating budget, and confusion during the development phase. Much of this chaos can be avoided if the project manager has spent enough time with the scope statement to ensure that there are no missing elements.

A second point to bear in mind concerns the development of the project's management plan. Be sure to consider all relevant information in developing the reporting structure—not just the relationships *within* the project team but *between* the project team and the rest of the organization. I have witnessed countless examples of frustrated project managers who thought they had a sound reporting structure, only to discover that they had not taken into consideration the impact of external functional managers and department heads on members of their project team. We need to understand that in many organizations, it is necessary to allow for the intrusive effects of these functional bosses on team members' time and ability to commit to our projects for extended periods of time.

Work Authorization

Work authorization consists of the formal go-ahead given to the project once the scope definition, planning documents, management plans, and other contract documents have been prepared and approved. Work authorization typically includes some contractual obligations in the case of projects developed for external clients or the establishment of an audit trail for internal clients. It is beyond the scope of this chapter to examine all components of contractual obligations between the project organization and clients but among the key points are legal features such as the following:[4]

- *Contractual requirements.* What is the accepted definition by both parties of "specific performance"? In other words, do all concerned parties understand the expected level or degree of project performance as specified by contract? Are the terms of performance clearly understood and identified by both parties? The more ambiguous the definition of project performance is, the greater the likelihood is of downstream conflict and even potential legal action if the two parties have developed dramatically different views of how the project should perform.

- *Valid consideration.* This refers to something voluntarily promised in exchange for a reciprocal commitment by another party. Does the work authorization contract make clear the commitments agreed to by both parties?
- *Contracted terms.* This includes excusable delays, allowable costs, statements of liquidated damages in the case of nonperformance, inspection and responsibility for correction of defects, steps necessary to resolve disputes, and so forth. The contracted terms often have clear legal meanings that encourage both parties to communicate efficiently.

Do's and Don'ts of Work Authorization

The key point to bear in mind about work authorization has to do with the nature of stated terms for project development. Especially when dealing with external clients, it is both prudent and reasonable to draw up contracts that clearly stipulate the work agreed to, the nature of the project development process, steps to resolve any disputes that may arise, and clearly identified criteria for successfully completing the project. To the degree that work authorization is clearly stated, this step can be an important help for project development downstream. On the other hand, the more ambiguous are the terms employed or milestones to be met, the greater the likelihood is that work authorization will bring with it a string of arguments, negotiations, and potentially legal action, all guaranteed to slow project development to a crawl or add tremendous costs to the back end of completed projects.

Scope Reporting

Scope reporting consists of determining at the project's kickoff, the types of information that will be regularly reported, who will receive copies of this information, and how this information will be acquired and disseminated. Scope reporting prepares the project team and key clients for the amount and regularity of project updates they will have access to.

A wide variety of different forms of project reports can be tracked and itemized. Among the more common types of project parameter information that may be included in these reports are the following:[5]

- *Cost status.* Updates on budget performance. On a timely basis, project cost figures must be updated. Typically, auditors work with projects either after the fact or on an ad hoc basis. Regular approaches to adjusting and reporting budget status (weekly, monthly, or some other time frame) are much more useful and can pinpoint potential problem areas while there is still time to correct them, rather than waiting until there are no avenues left for project correction.

- *Schedule status.* Updates on schedule adherence. Similar to maintaining timely reporting of cost, schedule status requires project managers or administrators to stay on top of the schedule. A clearly specified program for schedule evaluation and reporting ensures that all stakeholders in the project are receiving the same timely updates on project schedule.
- *Technical performance status.* Updates on technical challenges and solutions. Another important report concerns determining how and to what level of sophistication technical performance will be reported. Some of the important issues to be settled include whether technical updates are just for engineering staff or whether they will be prepared in such a way that they are understandable by all parties involved in the project's development. Another is which technical aspects are deemed worthy of reporting.
- *S curves.* Graphical displays of costs (including labor hours and other costs) against project schedule. S curves offer a good visual representation of project status based on plotting costs against development time.
- *Earned value.* Reporting project status in terms of both cost and time. Earned value is the budgeted value of work performed regardless of actual costs incurred.
- *Variance or exception reports.* Documenting any slippages in time, performance, or cost against planned measures. Some of the important questions to be settled behind variance reports include who will receive them, what items will be included in them, what measures will be widely employed for the reports, and what specific mechanisms the project team will use to report variances (for example, meetings, memos, or informal communications). Because variance reports give the project team early warning signs of potential problems, it is vital that not just the reports but avenues for communicating this information be clearly specified.

Do's and Don'ts of Scope Reporting

One of the most important points to remember about effective scope reporting is to avoid the temptation to operate in a communications vacuum, in which project status information is carefully limited to a handful of individuals. This process is similar to a management practice referred to as "mushroom management," in which the supervisor treats subordinates the same way that mushrooms are grown: by keeping them in the dark and feeding them a steady diet of manure. Just as mushroom management is ineffective for creating a motivated subordinate, so too does limiting project reporting guarantee a disconnected and ultimately indifferent project team. Project managers should judiciously consider who will benefit from receiving regular project updates and plan their reporting structure appropriately. For example, some stakeholders I encourage project leaders to include in their regular reporting are members of the project team, project clients, upper management, other groups within the organization affected by the project, and any external stakeholders who have an interest in project development. All of these groups have a stake in the development of the project or will be affected by the implementation process. It is a mistake to limit information that can only fuel misunderstandings, rumors, or organizational resistance to the project.

Control Systems

Another important element in effective scope management is to identify the types of project control systems that will operate for its development. Control systems are vital to ensure that any changes to the project baseline are conducted in a systematic and thorough manner, rather than as a series of disjointed reactions. There are a number of types of project control that project managers may choose to employ in tracking the status of their projects, including the following:[6]

- *Configuration control.* Procedures that monitor emerging project scope against the original baseline scope. Is the project following its initial goals, or are they being allowed to drift as status changes alter the original project intent?
- *Design control.* Systems for monitoring the project's scope, schedule, and costs during the design stage.
- *Trend monitoring.* A system for tracking the estimated costs, schedule, and resources needed against those planned. Trend monitoring reveals significant deviations from norms for any of these important project metrics.
- *Document control.* Systems for ensuring that important documentation is compiled and executed in an orderly and timely fashion. Document control verifies the existence of and adherence to important contractual or other documents that guide scope development.
- *Acquisition control.* Any system used to acquire necessary project equipment, materials, or services needed for project development and implementation.
- *Specification control.* Systems for ensuring that project specifications are prepared clearly, communicated to all concerned parties, and changed only with proper authorization.

Do's and Don'ts of Control Systems

One of the most important pieces of advice for novice project managers regarding control systems is to establish a reasonable level of control, including reporting structures, at the beginning of the project and maintain them. "Reasonable" means avoiding the urge to overdevelop these systems and seek to control everything.

Excessive control system reports can inhibit project managers' ability to mange the day-to-day activities of the project by forcing them to spend undue amounts of time filling out reports. On the other hand, it is equally important to avoid the mistake of ignoring control systems as taking up too much time. Judicious use of project control systems (knowing the right ones to use and how often to employ them) can eliminate much of the guesswork when dealing with project delays or cost over-runs. Poor project managers are often those who have ignored these control systems until it is too late, when their projects have fallen behind and they are unsure as to the causes or steps to take in bringing them back on line.

Project Closeout

Perhaps ironically, effective scope management, which occurs at the beginning of the project, also includes an acknowledgment of the importance of a project's termination. Project closeout considerations require project managers to consider the types of records and reports that they will require at the completion of the project. The earlier in the project scope development that these decisions are made, the more useful information can be collected over the project's development. Such information can be important for a number of reasons. In the case of contractual disputes after the project has been completed, the more thorough the project records are, the less likely it is that the organization will be held liable for alleged violations. These records can then serve as a useful training tool for post-project analysis of either successes or failures, and they make project auditing tasks easier by showing the flow of expenses in and out of various project accounts.

Among the important types of documentation a project leader may decide to track as part of project closeout are these:

- *Historical records.* Project documentation that can be used to predict trends, an-alyze feasibility, and highlight problem areas for similar future projects.
- *Postproject analysis.* A formal reporting structure, including analysis and docu-mentation of the project's performance in terms of cost, schedule adherence, and technical specification performance.
- *Financial closeout.* The accounting analysis of how funds were dispersed on the project.

Do's and Don'ts of Project Closeout

One of the most important lessons for successful project managers is to start with the end in mind. In other words, effective project development begins with a clear understanding of the goals of the project; hence, the importance of scope management. Although the purpose of this chapter has been to suggest the importance of devoting sufficient time at the beginning of the project to make these goals clear, one important aspect of clear goals is to make equally clear what the project's completion will require. The purpose of project closeout is to prepare the ground for a project's successful termination. I have mentioned a number of reasons that it is important to consider project closeout at the beginning (for example, it requires a consideration a priori of the types and amounts of information that will be regularly collected during project development). The wise project manager will develop a sound project tracking and filing system to ensure that when the project is in its closeout, time is not wasted scrambling for old project records and other information that is needed but missing.

Conclusions

A project is just a dream until it is written down. Until the project's plans are laid out, its purposes specified, its constraints considered, and its impacts anticipated, a project is nothing more than the fanciful expression of an organization's hope for commercial success. Project scope management is the systematic process of turning these dreams into a workable reality by formally developing the goals toward which the project manager and team will labor. Successful project management requires that adequate time be spent up front in creating a thorough and workable project scope document that can be used as a lighthouse, illuminating the safety of eventual project completion even while that team is being tossed on the waves of numerous crises and concerns. As long as that lighthouse continues to shine, as long as the project manager works to develop and maintain the various elements of project scope, the likelihood of passage to successful project completion is strong.

CHAPTER EIGHT

METHODS OF SELECTING AND EVALUATING PROJECTS

Dorla A. Evans, William E. Souder

Research, development, and engineering (RD&E) projects may vary widely in their nature, ranging from small laboratory-scale research and design efforts to multinational engineering construction projects. One of the major responsibilities of project managers is to make decisions on which RD&E projects the firm will undertake. In today's globally competitive world, even small-scale RD&E projects can entail large organizational commitments and carry substantial risks of failure. A wrong choice of RD&E projects can jeopardize the future of the entire organization. However, undertaking the right RD&E projects and avoiding the wrong ones is fraught with many uncertainties, often compounded by the need to consider many different aspects in balancing conflicting organizational objectives.

This chapter reviews the state of the art in project selection and evaluation methods. Proven techniques are presented for assisting project managers in distinguishing superior from inferior projects and selecting the best project opportunities.

Project Selection: The Problem and Its Issues

Project selection can have many connotations and meanings. In the context used here, the term refers to the process of choosing the best RD&E projects from the available candidates for funding. For most organizations, more alternative candidate projects exist than can be funded at any one time. Moreover, additional candidates are usually regularly suggested by the RD&E personnel, the company's own sales force, customers, competitors, and consultants. Thus, the selection decision is typically compounded by the presence of an array of choices, each varying in the degree of detail and familiarity to the organization. Project selection is often viewed as a problem of "too many alternatives with incompletely defined potentials chasing too little money."[1]

In such situations, an appropriate decision paradigm is to follow a hierarchy of project selection decision aids that economizes on the time and expense of analysis by stepping all the candidates through a series of sequentially more challenging hurdles. Candidates that survive earlier screens successively encounter more rigorous screens that sequentially weed out the weaker candidates. Weaker candidates are thus discarded at each screen, automatically focusing decision attention and resources on the surviving candidate projects.[2]

The Project Selection Screening Hierarchy

The project selection screening hierarchy runs from simple to increasingly complex models. Candidate projects are passed through the system, with some projects surviving each model to go on to the next, while other projects are screened out and placed in a holding pen. The holding pen allows screened-out projects to be resurrected and returned to the evaluation system at some later time. Resurrections from the holding pen may occur for many reasons. For example, economic conditions may change, casting a different light on those previously screened-out projects. This notion of a hierarchy with a holding pen allows flexibility in the project selection system, accommodating varying real-world conditions that may emerge.[3]

Checklists

A checklist is the least rigorous project selection decision aid, and therefore it is a good starting point for the project selection screening hierarchy. A checklist consists of a set of criteria for making preliminary judgments about candidate projects, along with a qualitative scale for rating candidates. Checklists are simple devices for documenting opinions and catalyzing productive discussion. Thus, they are best used in a consensus group setting, where each manager shares individual ratings, exchanges opinions and information, and works toward a consensus.

Table 8.1 presents an example of a checklist for three hypothetical candidates: projects X_1, X_2, and X_3. The criteria are reliability, safety, and durability. The table documents the conclusion that project X_3 is a holding pen candidate.

Although checklists are effective within their designed purposes, they cannot resolve trade-off issues. For example, the checklist results in Figure 8.1 do not clarify whether project X_1 or X_2 is the superior choice. This is the purpose of a scoring model.

Scoring Models

It is a short step to go from a checklist to a scoring model (see Table 8.2). All that is needed are suitable numerical scale equivalences of the high, medium, and low positions used in the checklist (see Table 8.1), along with importance weights for the criteria. Multiplying the importance weight by the respective score on each criterion gives a weighted score for each criterion, which can then be summed to a total score for each project.

A comparison of Tables 8.1 and 8.2 demonstrates how the scoring model allows finite distinctions to be made between the total scores for projects X_1 and X_2, as well as the components of these scores. The impacts of project X_2's lower reliability are numerically apparent from Table 8.2.

We caution project managers in interpreting scoring models. Unless the scales and importance weights are carefully anchored and justified, only ordinal levels of measurement are achieved. It can only be said that larger numbers are just that: larger. For example, if reliability is not three times as important as durability in Table 8.2, then the total score of 16 for project X_1 may only be said to be larger

TABLE 8.1. A CHECKLIST.

Project	Criteria	Performance on Criteria		
		High	Medium	Low
X_1	Reliability	✔		
	Safety	✔		
	Durability			✔
X_2	Reliability		✔	
	Safety	✔		
	Durability			✔
X_3	Reliability			✔
	Safety			✔
	Durability			✔

TABLE 8.2. A SCORING MODEL.

Project	Criteria	Importance Weight	Score	Weighted Score
X_1	Reliability	3	3	9
	Safety	2	3	6
	Durability	1	1	1
			Total Score	16
X_2	Reliability	3	2	6
	Safety	2	3	6
	Durability	1	1	1
			Total Score	13

than the total score of 13 for project X_2. When the numbers are only orders of magnitude (ordinal), it cannot justifiably be said that project X_1 is $3/13 = 23$ percent better than project X_2. Rules for designing scoring models are detailed elsewhere.[4]

Profile Models

Figure 8.1 illustrates the use of a profile model in plotting the risk-return profiles of six hypothetical candidate projects. Risk may be expressed in various ways. Typically, it is expressed as the likelihood that the project will fail. Return may also be expressed in a number of alternative ways, such as the profits expected if the project succeeds. The choices of risk and return definitions are organizational matters, depending on the dimensions that are most meaningful within the particular organization or for the set of projects under consideration.

Like checklists and scoring models, profile models are aids to judgment rather than answer machines. Figure 8.1 makes it apparent that projects X_1 and X_6 should go into the holding pen since they are outside the desired return and risk boundaries, respectively. Projects X_2 and X_4 should also go to the holding pen because they are inferior to respective alternative projects X_3 and X_5. Project X_3 yields the same return as project X_2, but with lower risk. Project X_5 yields a higher return than project X_4, but with the same risk.

Although pictures like Figure 8.1 are clearly revealing, it is the give-and-take discussion of such pictures among the involved parties that puts real value into the analyses. The result is often a reconsideration of the desired risk-return trade-offs. For example, Figure 8.1 makes it apparent that a slight lowering of the desired return would allow the low-risk project, X_1, to become an acceptable candidate.

FIGURE 8.1. A PROFILE MODEL.

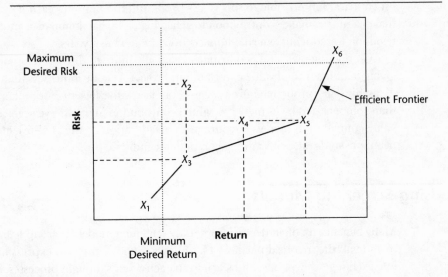

TABLE 8.3. VALUE CONTRIBUTION MODEL.

	Value	Project X_1	Project X_2
This year's goals	**60**		
Maximize profit	35	35	30
Maintain cash flow	25	25	25
Five-year goals	**40**		
Achieve technical dominance	25	10	25
Reduce external impacts	15	0	5
Total value contribution	100	70	85

Value Contribution Models

Value contribution models are a way of estimating and examining the relative contributions that projects make to achieving various organizational goals. To develop a value contribution model, first list the hierarchy of organizational goals. Table 8.3 shows a hierarchy of short-term and long-term goals, ranging from maximizing this year's profit to achieving longer-term technical dominance.

The second step in developing a value contribution model is value weighting the goals. This is done by allocating a hypothetical 100 points across the short-term and long-term goals, and then allocating their sums across the subsidiary goals. Projects are then valued according to their degree of contribution to the various goals. For example, in Table 8.3, project X_1 is judged to make the highest contribution possible to this year's profit and maintaining cash flows. But it makes a much smaller contribution to achieving technical dominance and no contribution to reducing external impacts over the next five years.

Competing project X_2 contributes relatively more to the five-year goals, thus giving it a higher total value contribution. Project X_2 contributes less than project X_1 to this year's profit maximization goal, but its relative lower contribution is more than compensated by its higher weighted contribution to the five-year goals. Thus, value contribution models encourage a consideration of the goal-oriented contributions and trade-offs among competing candidate projects.

Using Screening Models

Many benefits are often derived from using screening models in group settings that include all the involved parties.[5] This allows each manager to express an opinion, exchange viewpoints, and learn from each other's thought processes. Screening models are most appropriately used when the candidate project has not been fully detailed and only preliminary information is available about its costs and benefits. Thus, screening models can play a vital role in structuring constructive discussions and exchanges during these formative periods.

Group settings are excellent situations for designing and developing screening models that are the most appropriate for the organization and for gaining commitment to the future use of models that the users themselves have designed. As an artifact of this design process, participants have the opportunity to gain insights into organizational goals and objectives, discover relationships between projects and goals, and gain greater understandings of each other's roles and positions.

Project managers using project selection screening models should bear in mind that pure forms of checklists, scoring models, and other types of models may not exist in practice, nor are pure forms necessarily desirable. For example, value contribution models have elements of scoring models and checklists. All of the models have some related features, and users are free to mix various features as needed in designing models that best suit their particular organizational or decision-making needs. The objective is to develop and make good use of a decision aid that rapidly and inexpensively distinguishes acceptable from unacceptable candidates.

Discounted Cash Flow Models and Associated Analyses

Once a project has successfully passed all the models in the project screening system, it is ready for the much more stringent test of discounted cash flow models. Project managers (and their analysts who prepare much of the analysis) require much more information to apply these models than to apply screening models. Specifically, detailed data are needed on all relevant cash flows, their timing, and their riskiness. Relevant cash flows include only those caused by the addition of the project, such as increased labor costs. Costs incurred prior to the analysis, such as expenditures for an architectural design, are considered irrelevant sunk costs. Also irrelevant are costs the firm has already incurred but wishes to allocate over all projects, such as overhead costs consisting of executive pay and staff salaries.

Analysts require detailed estimates of one-time and annual cash flows and the appropriate discount rate. One-time cash flows may include environmental studies prior to building on a site, construction costs, purchase of equipment, R&D costs, costs to reclaim land, and revenue from salvaging equipment. Annual cash flows include the unit price of the product, number of units sold, labor costs, raw materials and component costs, utilities, and taxes. Depreciation is not a cash flow, but it is included in the analysis to derive the tax savings earned from deducting depreciation from taxable income. Interest expense and dividends paid are cash flows but are not included because they are already incorporated in the discount rate.

The relevant discount rate is typically based on the firm's cost of capital, which is the weighted average cost of all sources of capital. The costs of each source of capital are weighted by the percentage of market value the source contributes to total capital. The weighted average cost of capital, k_a, is calculated as follows:

$$k_a = (w_d)(k_d)(1 - t) + (w_e)(k_e), \tag{8.1}$$

where W_d and W_e are the percentage of capital derived from debt and equity sources, respectively; k_d and k_e are the percentage costs of debt and equity; and t is the firm's marginal tax rate. The cost of debt is computed after taxes because interest payments are tax deductible.

The cost of capital is the rate of return the firm should earn on a project with risk equal to the average risk of all of its projects. If the risk of the project under consideration is higher or lower than this average, analysts should adjust the cost of capital to a higher or lower discount rate, called a risk-adjusted discount rate (RADR).

Cash Flow Decision Models

The following models will be described: payback and discounted payback period, accounting rate of return, net present value, internal rate of return, modified internal rate of return, and option models. Then we will offer some analytical techniques in applying the models.

Payback and Discounted Payback Period. In its most basic form, the payback period is defined as the number of years required to recoup the original investment and net working capital when the discount rate is zero. Criticisms that the payback period ignores the time value of money resulted in the development of the discounted payback period, defined as the number of years required to recoup the original investment and net working capital when the discount rate is either the cost of capital or RADR.

Independent projects with payback periods less than the internally established maximum standard are accepted. When the projects are mutually exclusive (both projects cannot be accepted), decision makers should accept the project with the shorter payback period that also meets the standard.

Organizations frequently use the payback period in conjunction with one or more other cash flow techniques. It is used because it captures liquidity, an aspect of risk.[6]

Accounting Rate of Return. Unlike the other project decision methods described here, the accounting rate of return (ARR) is based on net income rather than cash flows. Because net income varies over time, ARR requires analysts to calculate an average income:

$$ARR = \frac{Average\ income}{Average\ investment}. \tag{8.2}$$

Decision makers compare the ARR against an internally established minimum ARR. Independent projects that meet or exceed the minimum ARR are accepted. In a mutually exclusive pair of projects, the project with the higher ARR that meets the minimum is accepted. Because net income is not an acceptable substitute for cash flow, the ARR is not considered an appropriate decision method, although it is frequently used.

Net Present Value. The net present value (NPV) is the preferred project decision method of finance professionals. The future cash flows and the depreciation tax benefits are discounted at the cost of capital or at the RADR and then netted against the initial cost. The NPV provides the dollar change expected in the firm's stock value if the project is undertaken. Therefore, a positive NPV means that the value of the firm will rise by the NPV. Independent projects with positive NPVs are accepted. From a mutually exclusive pair of projects, the one with the higher positive NPV is accepted:

$$NPV = \sum_{t=1}^{n} \frac{Cash\ flow_t}{(1+k)^t} + \sum_{t=1}^{n} \frac{Depr_t \times Tax_t}{(1+k)^t} - I_0. \tag{8.3}$$

Internal Rate of Return. The internal rate of return (IRR) is the discount rate that makes the NPV equal to zero. If the IRR is greater than the hurdle rate, either the cost of capital or the RADR, then decision makers should accept the project. When a pair of projects is mutually exclusive, decision makers should accept the project with the higher IRR if it is greater than the hurdle rate:

$$NPV = 0 = \sum_{t=1}^{n} \frac{Cash\,flow_t}{(1 + IRR)^t} + \sum_{t=1}^{n} \frac{Depr_t \times Tax_t}{(1 + IRR)^t} - I_0 \tag{8.4}$$

Many decision makers incorrectly interpret the IRR as the rate of return on the project. The IRR equals the project's rate of return only when the firm can reinvest the cash inflows from the project into new projects at the IRR. If the firm can reinvest only at a rate lower then the IRR, the real return on the project is lower than the IRR.

Decision makers using the IRR and NPV will make the same investment recommendations if the projects under consideration are independent. If they are mutually exclusive, then it is possible for the IRR and the NPV to rank projects differently. Finance academicians argue that the NPV is the appropriate technique because it is not subject to the problems inherent in the IRR.

The IRR may have multiple solutions if the cash flows are not normal, that is, if net cash outflows follow a period of net cash inflows during the life of the project. An example of nonnormal cash flows occurs when a firm must pay large costs to reclaim strip-mining land to its original condition during the last few years of the project. The cause of the multiple solutions is found in equation 8.4 for the IRR. The equation is a polynomial with degree n. Therefore, there are n solutions to the equation, only one of which is real when the cash flows are normal. When the cash flows are not normal, the number of real solutions is equal to the number of times the signs of the cash flows change. The NPV, on the other hand, has one solution for any given discount rate.

Another reason the NPV is preferred over the IRR is based on their respective reinvestment rate assumptions. In the IRR, cash inflows are assumed reinvested at the IRR; with the NPV, cash flows are reinvested at the cost of capital or the RADR. The NPV assumption is more feasible on a consistent basis.

Nevertheless, practitioners prefer using the IRR, presumably because a rate of return is easier to use and understand than the NPV.[7] Hence, a modified IRR (MIRR) has been developed to eliminate the problem of multiple IRRs. The MIRR requires analysts to find the terminal value of the project. That is, they must compute the future value of all the annual cash inflows and outflows as of the ending period of the project. The MIRR is the discount rate that makes the terminal value equal to the initial cost. Decision makers should recommend an independent project if the MIRR is higher than the hurdle rate. To be selected, a mutually exclusive project must have the higher IRR and an IRR above the hurdle rate.

Option Models. Investment decisions based on the NPV or IRR neglect a key aspect of projects: they may be irreversible. That is, it may be impossible to recoup the investment if the project is not as productive as planned. For example, if a firm builds a very specialized plant in a highly competitive industry and then finds it cannot earn an economic profit, it will be difficult to find a buyer that can do so. Therefore, decision makers who are considering irreversible projects should determine whether (1) the firm has the flexibility to postpone implementing the project and (2) information will become available later that will clarify whether the project is worthwhile.[8]

Suppose a computer chip firm is evaluating whether to buy a license to market a technology exclusively that could substantially improve the computational capacity of a chip. The cost of the license is $5 million, which will generate estimated net cash flows of $800,000 per year indefinitely. The firm requires a 10 percent return on its investment. Assume the license is purchased and implemented instantaneously, and the firm sells its first improved chip next year. Currently the firm forecasts it may earn $800,000 annually from the chips, but next year it might get new information. It might earn $1.2 million with probability of 50 percent, or only $400,000.

Analysts can calculate the expected NPV of the licensing project. The expected cash flow each year, $800,000, and the NPV are calculated below. Because the $800,000 is a perpetuity that begins in Year 1, analysts divide it by the discount rate of 10 percent to determine the value of the perpetuity:

$$E(\text{Cash flows}) = .5(\$1{,}200\text{K}) + .5(\$400\text{K}) = \$800\text{K}. \qquad (8.5)$$

$$NPV = -\$5{,}000\text{K} + \sum_{t=1}^{\infty} \frac{\$800\text{K}}{(1.1)^t}.$$

$$= -\$5{,}000 + (\$800\text{K}/.1) \qquad (8.6)$$

$$= -\$5{,}000\text{K} + \$8{,}000\text{K}$$

$$= \$3{,}000\text{K}.$$

According to the NPV, the firm should accept the project. But by neglecting the possibility of postponing the purchase of the chip license so the firm may determine the future market for such a product, decision makers neglect important information available in the future. By waiting a year, they will know whether the earnings will rise (50 percent chance) or drop, in which case the firm will not invest in the license. If the earnings from the license rise, the NPV of the project is:

$$NPV = .5 \times \left[\frac{-\$5,000K}{1.1} + \sum_{t=2}^{\infty} \frac{\$1,200}{(1.1)^t} \right]$$

$$= .5 \times \left[\frac{-\$5,000K}{1.1} + \frac{(\$1,200K/.1)}{(1.1)} \right] \qquad (8.7)$$

$$= .5 \times (-\$4,545K + \$10,909K)$$

$$= \$3,182K$$

If the firm must invest today or not invest, it should prefer a project with an expected NPV of $3,000,000 to no project. But if it has the choice of delaying one year, it should do so because its NPV rises to $3,182,000.

How much is this flexibility worth? That is, what is the value of the option to purchase the license? It is the difference between $3,182,000 and $3,000,000, or $182,000. The firm should be willing to pay $182,000 more for the licensing opportunity if it is flexible than if it is not.

Model Implementation Issues

There are three common implementation issues decision makers frequently confront. First, many projects to be analyzed are for equipment to replace currently existing equipment. Second, projects may have optimal economic lives different from their physical lives. It may be in the firm's best interest to accept a project and then abandon it prior to the end of its physical life. Third, many project selection decisions are made within the context of resource constraints. All of these situations require different approaches from other situations.

Replacement Decisions. Often decision makers are faced with the issue of replacing existing equipment that is not fully depreciated yet with new equipment that has operating cost advantages. In this case, the analyst computes an NPV for the difference in cash flows between the new equipment and the old equipment.

Assume that new technology allows a firm to automate a large portion of its pipeline business. It currently uses people to open valves to release product from and introduce product into the tanks. It will cost $60,000 in equipment to automate the tank farm. The equipment has a five-year life but will be sold after Year 4 with salvage value of $14,000. The tax rate is 34 percent, and the cost of capital is

20 percent. Operating costs under the current and automated systems are listed in Table 8.4. The question for decision makers to answer is whether the large decrease in operating costs with the automated system is worth the initial cost of $60,000. Analysts calculate the incremental costs and savings from automating versus the current system and then calculate an NPV on the increment. Assume the firm uses straight line depreciation so that annual depreciation is $12,000.

Analysts set up a table showing cash flows gained through the introduction of automation and cash flows lost from eliminating the current system. Table 8.5 shows these cash flows and the NPV of the automated system over the current system. The positive NPV, $840,000, indicates the firm is better off with the automated system.

TABLE 8.4. COST DATA FOR EXAMPLE REPLACEMENT DECISION (IN THOUSANDS).

Year	Automated	Current
1	$10	$40
2	$12	$42
3	$14	$44
4	$16	$46

TABLE 8.5. REPLACEMENT DECISIONS ANALYSIS (IN THOUSANDS).

Year	0	1	2	3	4
Salvage new					$14
Operating costs new		$(10)	$(12)	$(14)	(16)
Saved operating costs old		40	42	44	46
Write off remaining depreciation on new					(12)
Depreciation new		(12)	(12)	(12)	(12)
Saved depreciation old		0	0	0	0
Earnings before interest and taxes		18	18	18	20
Taxes at 34 percent		(6)	(6)	(6)	(7)
Net income		12	12	12	13
Add back depreciation		12	12	12	12
Add back write-off					12
Operating cash flow		24	24	24	37
Cost of automation	$(60)				
Lost salvage on old	0				
Net cash flow	$(60)	$ 24	$ 24	$ 24	$37

Net present value at 20 percent is $8.4

Abandonment Decisions. Frequently neglected in investment decision analyses is the determination of the optimum abandonment period. The firm should abandon a project whenever its current salvage, or abandonment value, is greater than the present value of the future cash flows discounted to the abandonment decision period.

Suppose analysts collected the project data shown in Table 8.6. The NPV of the project over its entire four-year physical life with a discount rate of 20 percent is −$2,000. Therefore, the decision maker would find the project unacceptable.

Before reaching that conclusion, however, the decision maker should check the NPV of the project assuming it is abandoned after each year. The NPV after holding the project one year is computed with the initial outflow of $50,000 and the inflow of $25,000 in the first year, plus the value of the abandoned project at the end of that year, $40,000. The NPV is a positive $4,000. The NPVs with abandonment at Years 2 and 3 are both $2,000. Therefore, the decision maker should accept the project, hold it for one year, and then abandon it. The project's economic life is one year.

Decisions with Resource Constraints. Theoretically, a firm should be able to raise any amount of capital needed to invest in projects with positive NPVs. In an informationally efficient market, investors will invest in firms that have positive NPV projects because the projects will increase stock values. But practically, firms often limit resources. Reasons may include restricting the growth rate of the firm so it can be managed properly, minimizing the cost of capital by restricting capital sources to internally retained earnings,[9] and markets' not being completely informationally efficient.

Hence, the firm may be capital rationed. That is, it does not have all the money it needs to undertake every project with a positive NPV. Conceptually it is easy to deal with the problem. The firm should undertake the combination of projects that gives the highest NPV that can be purchased with the funds available.

TABLE 8.6. CASH FLOW DATA FOR THE ABANDONMENT DECISION (IN THOUSANDS).

Year	Cash Flows	Net Abandonment Value at End of Year t
0	$(50)	$50
1	25	40
2	20	25
3	15	15
4	10	0

Suppose a firm's capital budget is $2 million, and it has the projects shown in Table 8.7. The firm should accept projects B and D, which give the highest total NPV possible: $2.2 million, with a budget of $1.5 million.

Incorporating Risk

Risk arises because decision makers cannot know the size or timing of the cash flows. Risk is most often defined as experiencing an outcome different from what was forecast. Therefore, the standard deviation often is used to operationalize risk. In practice, most decision makers would agree that risk is experiencing an outcome *lower* than expected, or the semivariance. Because the standard deviation is more widely understood, most risk models are based on it as the definition of risk.

Most well-developed risk models address the risk of the individual project (stand-alone risk), disregarding the project's being only one asset in the firm's portfolio of assets, which, in turn, are only a small component of an investor's diversified portfolio of stocks (market risk).[10] The type of risk addressed will be identified with the models described below.

TABLE 8.7. CAPITAL RATIONING EXAMPLE (IN MILLIONS).

Project	Initial Cost	NPV
A	$1.2	$ .9
B	.5	1.0
C	.8	.6
D	1.0	1.2

Combination	Total Cost	Total NPV
A	$1.2	$ .9
B	.5	1.0
C	.8	.6
D	1.0	1.2
AB	1.7	1.9
AC	2.0	1.5
AD	2.2[a]	—
BC	1.3	1.6
BD	1.5	2.2 Best
CD	1.8	1.8
ABC	2.5[a]	—
BCD	2.3[a]	—
ACD	3.0[a]	—
ABD	2.7[a]	—
ABCD	3.5[a]	—

[a] Not feasible within resource constraints.

Scenario Analysis. Scenario analysis is a stand-alone risk model. Analysts develop three scenarios: best, worst, and most likely. In the best case, the values of every variable included in the analysis are the best possible: low costs with high revenues. An NPV is calculated for each scenario.

Scenario analysis provides decision makers with the most likely NPV bounded within the range of the most extreme outcomes. Often probabilities totaling 100 percent are assigned to the scenarios, allowing analysts to compute the expected NPV and its standard deviation. However, decision makers should be aware that the probability of these particular outcomes is very low. The outcome is much more likely to have variables at a mixture of levels: best, worst, and most likely. Moreover, scenario analysis does not provide an objective decision rule. Decision makers will decide subjectively whether the expected and best-case NPVs are sufficiently high to offset the worst-case NPV.

Sensitivity Analysis. To conduct a sensitivity analysis (stand-alone risk), analysts begin with the most likely case scenario, with all its built-in assumptions. Next, they explore how sensitive the most likely NPV is to the assumptions behind the variables by changing one assumption at a time. For example, analysts will increase sales by 5 percent and by 10 percent. Then they will decrease sales by 5 percent and 10 percent. Each time sales is changed, the NPV is recalculated. Then sales are set back to their most likely value, and the process is repeated with labor costs, and so on until all the variables have been adjusted.

Sensitivity analysis identifies which assumptions will have the largest impact on NPV. Variables with small impacts may be ignored. The assumption bases behind variables with large impacts should be carefully reexamined. However, just because a variable could have a large impact on NPV does not mean it will. For example, the firm may have contracts that essentially eliminate any variation in some of the assumptions. Note also that sensitivity analysis does not provide an objective decision rule.

Risk-Adjusted Discount Rates. RADR, a stand-alone risk assessment method, is fairly simple. Analysts use the cost of capital as the discount rate when projects under consideration have risks equivalent to the average risk of projects within the firm. The cost of capital will reflect the required rates of return demanded by the firm's stockholders and bondholders based on the level of risk they perceive the firm to have. If from now on the firm accepts only projects with risks higher or lower than its average, investors will perceive its risk as higher or lower and raise or lower their return demands. The firm's cost of capital will rise or fall.

The RADR uses this principle. If a particular project has a higher or lower risk than average, analysts will adjust the discount rate upward or downward. A higher-risk project will have to perform better with a higher discount rate in order to achieve a positive NPV. The firm establishes different categories of projects based on risk level. Analysts determine the category within which a project falls in order to identify the RADR. Analysts use the RADR as either the discount rate in NPV analyses or the hurdle rate in IRR analyses. The established NPV and IRR decision rules then apply.

Simulation. Simulation is the most complex of the stand-alone risk methods. Analysts estimate a probability distribution for each variable in the cash flow forecast. From the distributions, the simulation program randomly selects values (one from each distribution) and then computes the NPV. The process will be repeated five hundred or more times. Values for each variable will be chosen randomly, so each value should show up in NPV calculations in the approximate proportion as set in the probabilities. All combinations will not be tried.

The simulation software then reports information about the probability distribution of NPVs, including the mean, standard deviation, skewness, kurtosis, and NPV at given cumulative probability levels. The output provides information on whether the project has met the firm's established targets, by which the decision is made. For example, the target may be a probability of 15 percent or less of a negative NPV.

Simulation provides the greatest amount of detail for evaluating projects, but it also has the heaviest data input requirement. If variable distributions have no basis, then the NPV results of the simulation are suspect.

Market Risk. Total (stand-alone) risk of a project is composed of market and unsystematic risk. Unsystematic risk derives from factors specific to the project (such as demand for the product or risk of injury to the consumer) and can be eliminated by diversification. Market risk derives from factors that affect all securities in the market, caused by events such as unexpected inflation and interest rate changes. It cannot be eliminated through diversification.

To understand the relationship between returns from projects and the market's return, one must understand how portfolios reduce unsystematic risk. Consider the two projects shown in Figure 8.2. Each project has variation in its return caused by the unknown future economic condition, but when combined into a portfolio, they have no variation, or risk. When project cash flows are less than perfectly positively correlated, their combined risk is less than the average of their stand-alone risk. Shown in the figure are projects with returns that are perfectly negatively correlated, a very unlikely event, but illustrative of the salient effects of diversification.

FIGURE 8.2. ILLUSTRATION OF PORTFOLIO EFFECTS.

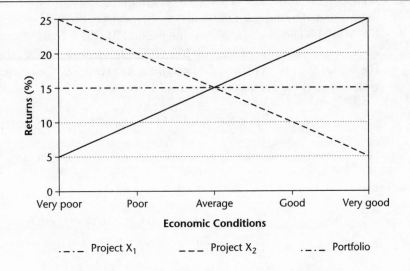

The market risk of a project is the variation of the project's returns relative to the variation of the market's returns: β_P, project's beta. β_P may be calculated as follows:

$$\beta_P = \frac{\sigma_P}{\sigma_M} \rho_{P,M} \tag{8.8}$$

where σ_P and σ_M are the standard deviations of the project and market returns, respectively, and $\rho_{P,M}$ is the correlation between the project and market returns. β_P also may be estimated using the regression option in a spreadsheet package. Define the independent variable as the market's return, define the dependent variable as the project's return, and specify the Y intercept to be calculated. The value of the X coefficient is beta.

The beta is then used in the capital asset pricing model (CAPM) to compute the cost of equity within the weighted average cost of capital equation (8.1). The resulting cost of capital is used either as an RADR for the NPV or as the hurdle rate for the IRR. The CAPM, shown below, holds that the expected return on a project, $E(R_P)$, is proportional to its market risk:

$$E(R_P) = \text{RF} + \beta_P (R_M - \text{RF}). \tag{8.9}$$

RF is the risk-free rate of return, often approximated by the rate on U.S. Treasury bonds, and R_M is the expected return on a portfolio made of all assets with value, approximated by a market index like the Standard & Poor's 500.

With this information, analysts use the CAPM to determine the project's cost of equity. For example, if the risk-free rate of return is 5 percent, the return on the market is 14 percent, and the beta of the project is 1.6, then the expected return on equity capital for the project is 19.4 percent:

$$k_e = E(R_P) = .05 + (.14 - .05) \times 1.6 = .194. \qquad (8.10)$$

With the cost of equity, analysts can compute the project's cost of capital:

$$\begin{aligned} k_a &= (w_d)(k_d)(1 - t) + (w_e)(k_e) \\ &= (.4)(.1)(1 - .34) + (.6)(.194) \qquad (8.11) \\ &= .1428 \end{aligned}$$

Analysts will then use 14.28 percent as the RADR in NPV or as the hurdle rate for the IRR.

Although relying on the CAPM is theoretically superior to stand-alone risk models, it is extremely difficult to implement. Future project returns, market returns, and their correlation are difficult to estimate.

International Issues

International projects add complexities to project analysis. Although cash flows may be generated in a different country from the parent company, investors in the parent company provide funding for the project. Therefore, cash flows should be analyzed from the parent company's perspective.

Unlike simple domestic investment decisions, parent company cash flows must explicitly incorporate financing in the foreign country. For example, Brazil may offer loans at below-market rates as an incentive to invest. The analysis should include this advantage.

Differential rates of inflation in the countries involved in the project must be considered over time, as must changes in exchange rates. The movement of funds from the project to the parent company needs to consider differential tax rates, political and legal impediments to transferring money, and so forth.

The parent company should invest only if it can earn a risk-adjusted rate of return greater than that earned by its competitors in the foreign country that is investing in a project with similar risks. If the parent company cannot earn a rate greater than its competitors, investors would be better off individually buying stock in the competitors.

There are several types of risk that are unique to international transactions: exchange rate risk, convertibility of funds, and political risk. Decision makers need to study these risks and learn methods used to handle them.[11]

Conclusions

This chapter has demonstrated a variety of analytical tools to aid project selection decision making. The tools range from simple screening devices, which are most useful during the early stages of project analysis, to more complex discounted cash flow and risk assessment models, which are appropriate for projects that have survived earlier screens. Users of all these tools must be sure that the models reflect the factors that are important to the firm and the culture of the organization. Users of discounted cash flow and risk analysis techniques must be especially diligent in making detailed estimates of cash flows, probabilities, and cost of capital. Unlike screening models, where precision of information is less critical, reliable information is essential for accurate discounted cash flow analyses.

CHAPTER NINE

PROJECT RISK MANAGEMENT

R. Max Wideman

Risk by definition is only an estimate of the probability of loss from a large population of unwanted circumstances. It predicts neither what will happen nor when. Project risk management is about being ready for the unwanted event, especially when the most obvious happens. Project risk management, or the avoidance or mitigation of risk, requires communication, understanding, and teamwork.

Projects are surrounded by uncertainty. Can a project be completed on time, within budget? Will some event occur that will derail its progress? Will the product of the project perform as expected? Indeed, is the product appropriate to the circumstances? Will the project be perceived as successful after it is finished? That depends on how the observer defines success.

Consequently, managing risk in project work is as much an art as it is a science. It involves identifying, analyzing, and being ready to respond to risk events. As far as possible, the goal of project risk management is to forecast the various sources of risk to the project, especially those with the most serious adverse impacts, and seek to reduce their consequences.

In the rush to get a project established, risks tend to be underestimated or overlooked. Therefore, good practice requires that a deliberate sequence of identification followed by planned mitigation is adopted, especially during project formulation. Depending on the size and nature of the project, effective risk management may require quite detailed quantitative assessments of the impacts of various uncertainties. Such practice will not only improve the chances of project success, but will also help in getting the project launched in the first place.

This chapter examines the major issues in managing project risks: opportunity and risk identification, quantification, response development, and control.

Uncertainty, Opportunity, and Risk

Do not overlook the possibility that uncertainty also leads to opportunity. Uncertainty is simply the sum of unknowns about the future, that is, lack of knowledge of future events, and these events may be either favorable or unfavorable. Those outcomes that are favorable result from opportunity; outcomes that are unfavorable result from risk.[1]

An opportunity, the reason for most projects in the first place, always carries associated risks, and generally the greater the opportunity is, the greater the risk is. Indeed, one may be seen as the corollary of the other. Visualize the relationship between uncertainty, opportunity, and risk as shown in Figure 9.1. In this context, project risk may be defined as the cumulative effect of the chances of uncertain occurrences' adversely affecting project objectives. It is the exposure to negative events and their probable consequences. Three risk factors characterize project risks: the risk event, its probability, and the amount at stake. These elements will be discussed later in this chapter.

Both risk and opportunity are highest at the start of a project, while the amount at stake is lowest. As the project progresses and uncertainties are translated into certainties, opportunity and risk fall. Simultaneously, the amount at stake

FIGURE 9.1. UNCERTAINTY, OPPORTUNITY, AND RISK.

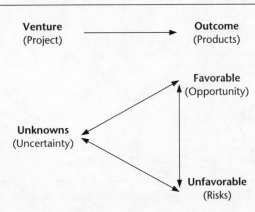

steadily rises as resources are consumed and the value of the investment increases. These trends are shown in Figure 9.2.

Many project risks that become unexpected events could have been turned into opportunities with a little foresight and ingenuity. When project risks are ignored and left to be handled reactively, the possibility of an opportunity gets overlooked. The justification for project risk management is to be proactive in mitigating the adverse effects of risk events and moving them toward opportunity.

The Nature of Risk Management

A risk should be taken only when the potential benefit and chances of winning exceed the remedial cost of an unsuccessful decision, or the chances of losing, by a satisfactory margin. Ask these questions:[2]

FIGURE 9.2. RISK VERSUS AMOUNT AT STAKE: TYPICAL LIFE CYCLE PROFILES.

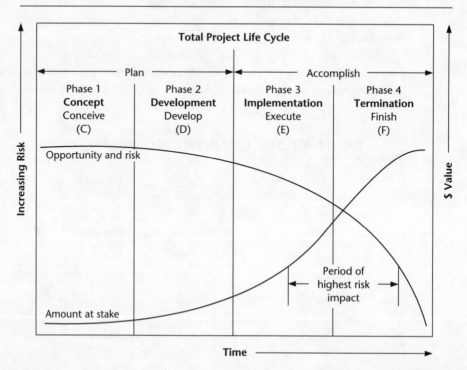

- Why take the risk?
- What will be gained?
- What could be lost?
- What is the chance of success (or failure)?
- What can be done if the desired result is not achieved?
- Is the potential reward worth the risk?

Project managers vary in their attitudes to risk. Some are risk averse, and others are risk inclined. Attitudes to risk are affected by these factors:[3]

- Potential frequency of loss
- Amount and reliability of information available
- Potential severity of loss
- Manageability of the risk
- Vividness of the consequences
- Potential for (adverse) publicity
- Ability to measure the consequences
- Whose money it is

However, there should be a careful avoidance of an attitude of unwarranted optimism, prejudice, ignorance, or self-interest. These are the questions to answer:[4]

- Has it been done before?
- How close is the analogy?
- Do we have corroborative evidence?
- Have we held personal interviews with those with experience?
- Have we obtained alternative opinions?
- Are these assessments quantitative and written?

Helpful rules of thumb for when not to take the risk follow:[5]

- The organization cannot afford to lose.
- The exposure to the outcome is too great.
- The situation or the project is just not worth it.
- The odds are not in the project's favor.
- Being successful is no more than a fair bet.
- The benefits are not identified.
- There appear to be many acceptable alternatives. (The greater the number, the more the uncertainty.)
- The risk does not achieve a project objective.
- The expected value from the baseline assumptions is negative or becomes negative with small changes in assumptions.
- The data are unorganized, without structure or pattern.

- There are not enough data to compute the results. (In this case, get more data or do research.)
- A contingency plan for recovery is not in place should the results prove to be less than satisfactory.

The best protection is to identify the project success criteria by which the project will be ultimately judged. As part of the project's front-end planning, make sure that these criteria are the important ones to the project's principal stakeholders. These success criteria then provide project management with the proper basis for decision making.

Four-Stage Approach

Project risk management consists essentially of four stages: risk identification, assessment and quantification, response development, and documentation and control.

Stage 1: Risk Identification

First identify all the possible risks that could significantly affect the success of the project. Conceptually, these may range from high impact and high probability through low impact and low probability. Give most attention to high and medium risks, including accumulations under any one item. However, do not overlook combinations of lower risk that together pose a greater threat than each individually. Also, beware of fatal flaws: risks that seem to be remote but could bring the project to a standstill. In current jargon, these are sometimes called showstoppers. Potential intervenors in environmental hearings who have other vested interests in obstructing the project are a case in point.

A good practice is to hold a brainstorming workshop early in the project with the members of the project team and others with knowledge and experience. Have them develop a list of project risks and their collective and intuitive opinion of relative importance on a scale of one to ten. Then ask for their assessment of priorities. This workshop will provide both a team-building opportunity and a good reference for risk assessment.

Stage 2: Assessment and Quantification

Assess and quantify the identified risks, and categorize them in terms of type, impact, and probability. This may range from a simple attempt at subjective evaluation on a smaller project, to a more serious attempt at measurement on a larger one. Some significant risks may defy direct measurement, and a more in-depth impact analysis may be necessary.

Stage 3: Response Development

Establish a strategy for dealing with the various categories of risk identified. Then deal with each appropriately by avoidance workarounds (that is, by finding alternative solutions to each potential problem), such as taking out insurance, transferring risks that are transferable through contract arrangements, or by contingent planning. Deal with each in order of priority until an acceptable level of comfort is obtained. The sponsoring organization should assume responsibility for high-impact but very low-probability risks such as government intervention or labor, material, or cash flow shortfalls.

Stage 4: Documentation and Control

Carefully document the data collected and mitigation strategies recommended. The objective is to build a reference source for the continuing evaluation of risk on the project and for use should any of the risks materialize. It is an interesting reflection that the more a risk is carefully planned for, the less likely it is to happen. Teams on subsequent similar projects will also find these data invaluable.

Risk Factors in Project Management

All project risks are characterized by three risk factors:[6]

1. *Risk event*: Precisely what might happen to the detriment of the project
2. *Risk probability*: How likely the event is to occur
3. *Amount at stake*: The severity of the consequences

With these data, the risk event status (criterion value or ranking) of a given risk event can be determined by the following relationship: (*Risk event status*) = (*Risk probability*) (*Amount at stake*). Some risk events are characterized by low probability and high severity, and others are the reverse. Clearly the most serious are those involving both high probability and high severity. These risks may require more careful examination and special analytical techniques.

Risk interaction can increase the amount at stake well beyond the sum of the individual risk events. These events may also cross traditional functional responsibility boundaries so that total project risk is not given sufficient attention. This becomes especially evident when viewed from the individual perspectives of scope, quality, time, and cost. The project manager, and ultimately the project sponsor, are responsible for ensuring that this does not happen.

A typical case might be an action to keep the project on schedule (or within budget) when the consequences of the action are not well understood. Perhaps the requisite information is too costly, too time-consuming, or simply too slow in arriving. Such actions should be calculated, not reckless. There should be a fallback position in case subsequent information shows that some reversal is necessary.

Uncertainties that may turn into unpleasant surprises include technical innovations that do not work as expected; trials that fail; unanticipated by-products or side effects; an overriding patent application by a competitor; market research indicating lack of customer acceptance; escalating product development costs; or simply product reliability, quality, or producibility difficulties.

Another example of a minor risk event becoming a major amount at stake is the cumulative effect of a succession of relatively insignificant schedule delays resulting from a spate of untimely scope changes. The effect could be to miss a window of opportunity completely, such as reaching the market before a competitor does, forestalling technological obsolescence, or construction in the summer season rather than in winter.

Project Risk Identification

Risk identification begins with an understanding of the project itself. What are the project's deliverables? What are the real objectives? Answers to these questions will have a significant impact on the risks to be considered and the selection of possible alternative project strategies and workarounds. Clearly, these issues must be raised early in the project, even though the answers themselves will be associated with a high degree of uncertainty.

Risks can be classified in several different ways, and this is often necessary. For purposes of a project justification summary, they should be segregated into major and minor. For purposes of project reporting, they should be segregated into impacts on the project's management objectives:

- *Schedule risks.* Failure to complete tasks within the estimated time limits or risks associated with dependency network logic
- *Cost risks.* Failure to complete tasks within the estimated budget allowances
- *Scope risks.* Risks associated with changes of scope, or the subsequent need for fixes to achieve the required technical deliverables

- *Quality risks.* Failure to complete tasks to the required level of technical or quality performance or simply failure to meet the customer's reasonable expectations

Deliberately chosen risks, such as correctly identifying project objectives for a venture opportunity, may be distinguished from those that are latent. Latent risks are those that are inherent in the product, such as the result of an innovative solution or lack of product acceptance. Latent simply means that the risk event exists but is dormant, only to surface some time later in the project or product life cycle. Some risks must be considered beyond project management's responsibility such as a catastrophic event, financial collapse, or change in political direction.

For purposes of risk identification and response, the most useful approach is to classify project risk according to primary source (rather than effect)—for example:

- External but unpredictable
- External predictable but uncertain
- Internal nontechnical
- Technical
- Legal

This form of classification enables project management to rank the groups according to ability to influence and respond. Ability to respond is, of course, independent of probability, amount at stake, and therefore risk event status. Risk event status is a measure of the relative significance of the risk event.

Risk Assessment and Quantification

Perhaps the biggest impediment to conducting project risk management on a project is the intuitive sense that project risks are so many and varied. Attention to every possible risk might thwart the project at the outset. The real issue is which risks should receive attention.

Many lesser risks, such as typical probabilities of cost and schedule overrun, can be covered by conventional contingency allowance calculations. The risks that require special attention are those that produce medium and high project risk criterion values. To some extent, the selection of these particular risks is an iterative process in which preliminary analysis may suggest the need for further study.

Although various statistical methods can be used to identify degrees of risk, in most cases probability and impact are at best subjective judgments, and an elementary categorization is sufficient for the purpose. Simply ranking each as high, medium, or low and then multiplying them together will give a range of risk criterion values that can be described by the scale minimal, low, medium, high or extreme. Figure 9.3 shows a methodology flow diagram for arriving at the risk event status or priority ranking.

Conduct a simple project risk assessment by using the sequence described next. To ensure the best possible understanding of the results, however, first establish a risk baseline based on the organization's external status quo. This will establish the risks to the sponsoring organization of not carrying out the project at all.

FIGURE 9.3. RISK ASSESSMENT METHODOLOGY.

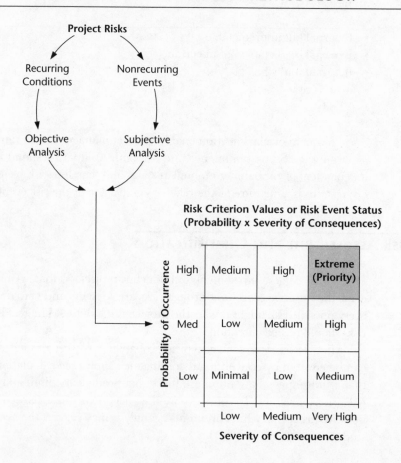

Step 1: Identify

Identify and list the possible risk events—for example, late delivery of critical materials, shortage of key skills, unanticipated increases in production workload, or functional failure with relatively untried technologies. Screen out any risk events that should properly be covered by corporate policy, such as resource conflicts in a matrix environment, changes in corporate policy, or those that are already covered by blanket corporate insurance, such as personal injury and property damage. Similarly, issues such as bankruptcy or other catastrophe should be part of the organization's overall business strategy and planning.

Step 2: Analyze Probability

Subjectively assess the probability associated with each risk event or analyze the probability using one of a number of more specialized techniques that can help: influence diagrams, risk contribution analysis, probability distribution, probability trees, risk modeling, and sensitivity profiles, for example. These are mathematical techniques that can become highly sophisticated. For the typical practitioner, however, the best estimates are those based on good experience and thoughtful opinion.

Step 3: Analyze Consequences

Determine the amount at stake and the criticality of each risk event by analyzing its consequences and severity. Note that the amount at stake and criticality may vary with time according to when the event takes place in the project life cycle. For example, a cold snap during excavation for a building project may be an advantage. The same cold snap occurring when the building is well advanced, but the heating system not yet activated, could be serious.

Usually consequences and severity can be arrived at by examining the data and using some subjective judgment. Also, there is always the possibility of risk events combining, such as a delay in activating the heating system and a cold snap. In more complex situations, it may be necessary to develop a mathematical model and conduct a series of computer runs.

In both Steps 2 and 3, the opinion of experts may be sought to advantage. For example, an expert could be asked to estimate the optimistic, most probable, and pessimistic values for a particular situation, with percentage chances of better-than-optimistic or worse-than-pessimistic outcomes. The amount at stake for each and the sensitivity of this amount to changes in related variables might also be sought.

Step 4: Respond

This is probably the most creative step of all. It entails trying to visualize each risk event as a potential opportunity and planning to respond to the consequences accordingly. Otherwise, the plan should be to mitigate each by avoidance through a workaround, contractual transfer if appropriate, a specific response plan, or assigning specific contingency funding.

A workaround is an alternative solution to a potential problem—for example:

Requirements: Provide airtight food container.

Solution: Sheet metal box with tight-fitting lid.

Risk: Nonavailability of suitable sheet metal.

Workaround: Substitute durable molded plastic container with self-sealing top.

Step 5: Document

Finally, assemble the results of the risk assessment in a documented set of project risk recommendations. Make sure that management and the project sponsor clearly understand the risks so that their decisions are well informed. Ultimately, management must either accept the risks and go ahead with the project, or abandon it.

By following these steps, one can incorporate uncertainty directly into early project planning and deal with any consequences expeditiously during project execution. The five steps are shown as a matrix in Figure 9.4.

This methodology offers a number of benefits—for example:

- It forces a clearer understanding of the project's overall goals, objectives, scope definition, and feasibility.
- It provides a means for incorporating uncertainties directly into the project management processes of formulating and implementing the project.
- It highlights the risks that are the most significant and therefore should receive attention.
- It may introduce models and techniques by which the variability and uncertainty of estimates can be conveyed quantitatively.
- It provides an information base of quantitative data to support trade-off decisions, such as choices between cost, schedule, and performance, or the comparison of different options, and an early warning for risk events.
- It produces a consistent and workable project plan, with a rational basis for contingency planning and evaluation.

FIGURE 9.4. RISK MANAGEMENT STEPS.

	Process			
	Identify	Analyze	Respond	Document
Event	Step 1			
Probability		2		
Consequence		3	4	Step 5

(Risk Factor labels the vertical axis. Arrows connect Step 1 → 2 → 3 → 4 → Step 5.)

When analyzing by modeling, as suggested in Step 3, three levels are typically required:

1. A detailed analysis of the joint impact of a few apparently critical risks within an activity
2. An examination of the joint effects of all risks within an activity
3. The broad overall impact of risks from several or all activities

In-depth project risk impact analyses are generally the purview of specialists who are familiar with both the technical aspects of the project and its management. Such analyses require a significant commitment of time and resources and are appropriate only when the amount at stake is high.

The Quality Risk

The risk to product quality requires special mention, if only because it tends to be subjugated to the objectives of scope, time, and cost. In practice, quality is the easiest to overlook during project implementation. The best way to express the risk to quality is by asking, "What if the project fails to perform as expected during its operational life because of poor project workmanship?"

Since the in-service life of the product is typically much longer than the period required to plan and produce that product, any quality shortcomings and their effects may surface over a long period. Of all the project objectives, conformance to quality requirements is the one most remembered long after cost and schedule performance have faded into history. Consequently, management of the project's product quality has the most impact on the long-term actual or perceived success of the project.

Quality risk impacts may remain hidden (that is, latent) and ignored, but they are not forgiven if the project fails to deliver on its long-term objectives. These risks deserve special attention.

Response Development

The first step in developing responses to the identified risks is to ensure the existence of a proactive attitude to risk within the project organization. Good policies and procedures can certainly help, but without orientation, training, and buy-in, little may be accomplished. In short, the need for risk management on the project must be firmly established. Project risk policies need to encourage the following:

- A positive environment in which approaches are deliberately sought to avoid or reduce risk events
- Defensive planning to reduce risk impacts
- Retention and allowance for residual risks
- Some flexibility in the use of contingency allowance for dealing with the unexpected and safeguarding against its improper use for scope changes
- The transfer of risks to those who have the best opportunity to control the risk or its impacts

Where appropriate, risk policies should be based on the principle of placing responsibility on the shoulders of those who represent the source of the risk and are in the best position to control it. Bear in mind that risks vary considerably through the project life cycle. Potential impacts increase as tasks with risk events of high probability are undertaken and then decrease as the bulk of the work is completed. They may also change considerably because of changes in the scope of the project or the method of working. Continuous review of the situation with appropriate adjustments is strongly recommended.

Risk Documentation

Project risk management, particularly risk evaluation and analysis, is data intensive. Reliable data sources, both historical and for the current project, are essential. If data are unavailable, other techniques have to be adopted to simulate a particular risk for consideration. And even when data are available, practical difficulties arise in correct interpretation for application to current work. As with cost estimating, for example, there is no better source of information than an organization's own historical database, which should consist of recorded risk events and comments from past projects, presented in a consistent format for retrieval.

If a project is already in the implementation phase, every effort should be made to collect appropriate ongoing data as the project proceeds to establish a current project database of frequently recurring risk. This will be particularly valuable for updating the assessment of overall project risk. For many projects, especially those in the formative phases, required data must be obtained through lessons learned by others or by careful questioning of experts or persons with relevant knowledge. It is necessarily subjective in nature. Whatever the source is, all risks identified, their assessment and quantification, and the recommended responses must be carefully documented. Properly assembled, this information will provide the baseline for risk management during project implementation.

The compilation of historical data during the project and on completion is a challenging task, and it is easily set aside unless its value is recognized and the data collected and organized as part of the project's ongoing management responsibility. The descriptions of risk assessments, events experienced, and their consequences should be recorded.

Risk Control

When the methodology outlined is followed, a picture of project risk will emerge that shows where, when, and to what extent exposure may be anticipated. One can then develop suitable risk management control strategies, whether by way of adjustment, deflection, or other form of contingent planning.

Possibly the most significant element of project risk is the extent to which its scope lacks definition at the time of project implementation. Figure 9.5 shows probability curve distributions for three projects, all with the same expected cost value of 100 percent. As the curves on the figure show, the probability of Project A's being completed for this value is the highest compared to Projects B and C because it has the best definition of its scope of work.

Risk control may simply involve the proper recognition of certain risks by clarifying the project's scope, grade of quality, schedule, budget, or all four. Identifying "nice to haves," as distinct from "must haves" in the project's scope will greatly help in scope management. Ensuring that the quality grade of the project's product is suited to its purpose, and maintained in that way, will greatly reduce quality risks.

How often the project initiation battle cry has gone up: "Our objective is to build the best there is!" Not surprisingly, such an unrealistic definition of quality

FIGURE 9.5. SCOPE DEFINITION, RISK, AND CONTRACT SELECTION.

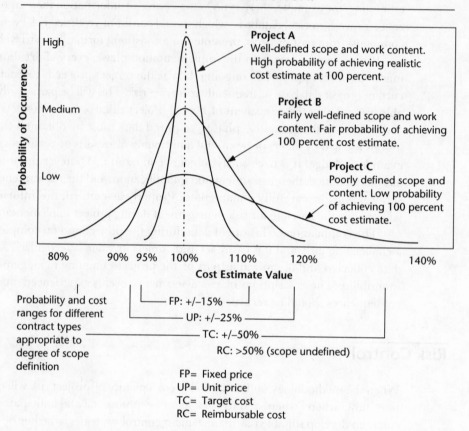

leads to a high risk of cost and schedule overrun. An adequate contingency allowance and good control, even on a tight budget, will reduce the chances of cost overrun. A logically developed schedule with attention to resource requirements and conflicts will reduce the probability of schedule overrun.

Deflection involves the transfer of risk by such means as insurance or bonding, recognizing it in a main contract, or contracting it out to a third party. Contracting out a risk inappropriately simply means paying for it whether or not the risk event takes place. Contracting out is cost-effective only if the contractor has proper and effective control over the source of the risk or risks concerned.

Figure 9.5 also suggests the type of contract appropriate to the range of uncertainty. Table 9.1 shows the impact of different issues on different types of contract[7] and how risk is distributed or handled in each case.

TABLE 9.1. RISK IMPLICATIONS OF DIFFERENT TYPES OF CONTRACTS, FROM THE CLIENT'S PERSPECTIVE.

Issue	Type of Contract			
	Fixed Price	Unit Price	Target Cost	Reimbursable Cost
Financial objectives of client and contractor	Different but reasonably independent	Different and in potential conflict	Considerable harmony. Reduction of actual cost is a common objective provided cost remains within the incentive region	Both based on actual cost but in potential conflict
Contractor's involvement in design	Excluded if competitive price based on full design and specifications	Usually excluded	Contractor encouraged to contribute ideas for reducing cost	Contractor may be appointed for design input prior to execution
Client involvement in management of execution	Excluded	Virtually excluded	Possible through joint planning	Should be active involvement
Claims resolution	Very difficult, no basis for monetary evaluation	Difficult, only limited basis for monetary evaluation	Potentially easy, based on actual costs. Contract needs careful drafting	Unnecessary except for fee adjustment. Usually relatively easy
Forecast final cost at time of bid	Known, except for unknown claims and changes	Uncertain, depending on quantity variations and unknown claims and changes	Uncertain. Target cost usually increased by changes, but effective joint management and efficient working can reduce final cost below an original realistic budget	Unknown
Payment for cost of risk events	Depending on contract terms, undisclosed contingency, if any, in contractor's bid. Otherwise by claim and negotiation	Depending on contract terms, undisclosed contingency, if any, in contractor's bid. Otherwise by claim and negotiation	Payment of actual cost of dealing with risks as they occur, and target adjusted accordingly	Payment of actual costs

Contingent planning includes the management of a contingency budget, the development of schedule alternatives and workarounds, complete emergency responses to deal with major specific areas of risk, and an assessment of liabilities in case of total project cancellation.

Unexpected Risks

Problems that are totally unexpected can occur. The difficulty is to distinguish between problems that are unexpected in the event but could and should have been foreseen, and those that could not have been foreseen in any way. The former may simply be a reflection of weaknesses in the original planning assumptions—for example:

- Predictions prove to be false or overstated.
- Timely information for project performance is missing.
- People are not available when required.
- Key individuals or members of the workforce lack competence.
- Disruption follows misunderstandings, personal conflicts, or internal politics.
- Burnout and sickness take their toll.
- There is a loss of control during project realization.

Only problems that could not have been foreseen are truly unexpected risks. The 1973 Arab oil embargo is a good example. Cost estimates prepared before the embargo contained no provisions for such increased fuel costs; no estimator could possibly have been expected to foresee that problem.

If weakness in any of the original planning assumptions surfaces, then it is time to examine all the planning assumptions. There may still be time to head off similar problems. If the impacts are greater than can be accommodated by the standard mitigation responses, it is time to get approval for major changes to the project. These may mean modifying the scope or quality of the work, taking more time, spending more money, or some of all four, to complete the project. If a situation develops that is beyond recall, then seek approval to abort the project as promptly as possible to minimize further wasted time and effort.

Application of Project Contingency Allowances

Contingency allowances are different, separate, and in addition to the schedule and financial resources determined by good estimating techniques. Good estimating requires stating the estimating strategy, the planning assumptions, and the typical risks. Estimates, whether of time or cost, are all based on the most likely values under normal or typical conditions. Any potential or anticipated variations from these conditions should be factored into contingency allowances.

For example, when using a probabilistic estimating technique, particularly when a range of any type is associated with a cost item, the given range is actually a basic contingency allowance, both positive and negative, for that cost item. These basic contingencies reflect the inherent variability of the various items. Consequently, given probabilistic estimates, no additional basic contingency should be added at the bottom of the estimate. That would be accounting for it twice.[8] However, there is usually a need to consider other types of uncertainties. Separate allowances may be required to cover potential scope changes or work not yet completely designed. One can then establish the total allowances required to bring the project's probability of overrun (or underrun) to an acceptable level. Show these allowances just once: as a summary at the bottom of the estimate. Carefully avoid contingency layering because of combining various estimate segments to form larger segments. Otherwise, one may find the accumulated total is excessive and the total project plan is too long, too costly, or both.[9]

The Project Environment

A discussion of project risk management would not be complete without considering the project environment: the social and cultural arena into which the product of the project will be launched rather than its natural physical habitat. In reality, project success is an elusive notion at best and is highly dependent on perception: the perception of satisfaction of the project's customers and stakeholders, which encompass just about anyone involved with the project. Collectively they establish the culture surrounding the project, that is, the project's environment.

The stakeholders within the project organization are self-evident. It is the external stakeholders who are more difficult to identify. Typically, that is many people, and today there is a rapidly growing awareness of and concern among them for the impacts on their physical environment. This is particularly true of commercial, industrial, and infrastructure projects. It is also often true of administrative, corporate projects, and the subsequent stress in the working environment.

The problem is that people are understandably resistant to change because the known is always more comfortable than the unknown. They may also have vested interests or an initial lack of understanding, as well as a perception that there will be winners and losers and that they might be the losers. These are major risks to be reckoned with, and it is essential that they are properly handled as part of project risk management strategies.

A good example of external stakeholder risk is public concern over safety or environmental damage. An organization may have a finely tuned project risk management program in place, and still find itself in the middle of a hysterical local community, distraught over public fears and media distortion of a risk issue. Effective public communication is the appropriate response. Public stakeholders are willing to take risks if they see a clear benefit. They are understandably opposed to risks that are not of their own choosing or for which they see no personal advantage.

Successful projects invariably reflect a healthy cooperative project team spirit and constructive attitudes toward project objectives. Appropriate procurement strategies, project organizational structure, responsibility distribution, and appropriate forms of contract are necessary to support this positive attitude. However, equitable handling of project risks is also a vital part of achieving success. Effective project risk management maintains these good relations and avoids the confrontations and frustrations that otherwise undermine initial enthusiasm and good intentions.

Anecdotes Worth Remembering

A Little Foresight Goes a Long Way

A well-established general contractor won a very competitive three-year contract for extending a public sewage treatment plant. Mechanical and electrical work were subcontracted and represented about 15 percent and 2 percent, respectively. Construction proceeded well until the electrical contractor suddenly went bankrupt. The cost of recovery added another 2 percent to the cost of the main contract, substantially eroding the general contractor's profit margin.

Investigation of the bankruptcy revealed that both the electrical and mechanical subcontractors were involved in another large contract that had apparently gone sour. This gave rise to a significant probability that the mechanical contractor might also find itself in trouble, although there was no such indication at the time. A two-pronged risk approach was adopted consisting of an early warning system and a response plan. The early warning system was established by subscribing to a credit bureau that would report confidentially on the financial condition of the mechanical contractor on a weekly basis. The response plan consisted of making the necessary union arrangements to enable the main contractor to protect all materials and equipment on site that would otherwise be sequestered by the bankruptcy receiver. The main contractor also made plans to take over the work instantly, should the mechanical contractor collapse.

About a year later, the mechanical contractor went under. The early warning paid off: work crews were immediately transferred to the main contractor's payroll, and work continued with less than an hour's interruption. To the relief of the main contractor's owners, the end of the contract even brought in a small profit.

It's Never Too Late to Change Strategy

A large consulting company was invited by a government to make a proposal on a project management assignment for a large airport extension. The consultant initially declined because key staff were on overseas assignments and figured that their chances of winning the award would not be high. However, the government department was persuasive because it needed a minimum of three proposals to be able to make any award. The consultant felt some obligation if it was to succeed in future opportunities.

Three of the four weeks of the proposal preparation time passed by, and the consultant's available staff were struggling to assemble a credible response. When it became apparent that they were unlikely to make the deadline, the consultant searched its staff database for a project manager with experience. No one was available with airport experience, but there was a project manager with considerable project management experience. He was flown in with only four days and a long weekend to assemble the necessary submission.

The new project manager changed the orientation of the proposal focusing on competent project management methodology rather than on airport technology. The proposal was duly completed and submitted on time. The consultant breathed a sigh of relief and moved on to other business. Several weeks later, and to everyone's surprise, the company was awarded the assignment though its total proposed fees were not the lowest. Government officials subsequently allowed that of the three submissions, the consultant's proposal had made the most sense.

Choosing the Right Response

Some years ago, a small but reputable canned food producer introduced a new product. Unfortunately, the risk of food poisoning was found to be higher than normal, though still slight, and the situation received media attention. Several times representatives of both the producer and the government inspectors attempted to allay public fears by quoting statistics to show that the risk to an individual was actually very low. Their efforts had little effect on sagging sales, and the product had to be abandoned.

What the official representatives failed to recognize was that the issue was the sanctity of food and trust in those that deliver it. The issue was that unexpected risk suddenly was being imposed without warning in a system and context assumed by the public to be a very low risk. The feeling of the public was one of surprise and loss of control.

Compare that with the response of Warren Anderson, chair of Union Carbide, when he stepped to the microphone for the first time after the terrible Bhopal accident in India. He did not talk about facts or statistics, but about how he and the other people at Union Carbide felt. What the cameras showed the world that night was a corporate executive sickened and saddened by tragedy. It was an honest response, spoken from the heart. More than anything else, this gave him considerable credibility in the weeks that followed.

Research shows that the perception of risk is more emotional than rational and that project risk communication must begin by recognizing the legitimacy of public emotion.

CHAPTER TEN

WORK BREAKDOWN STRUCTURES

Gene R. Simons, Christopher M. Lucarelli

The work breakdown structure (WBS) provides the framework for all planning, scheduling, estimating, budgeting, work authorization, and cost accumulation. This framework allows the project manager to translate the project plan, which has been developed by the manager and the project team, into the actions necessary to achieve the project objectives. It allows the project team to collect all the customer requirements—whether from the objectives, vision statement, statement of work, contract, memorandum of understanding, or any other document that may have initiated the project—into a single document that will guide the remainder of the project planning effort.

The WBS accomplishes six main functions:

1. It echoes the objectives. It indicates all the major work activities needed to accomplish the objectives of the project. If it is not stated in the WBS, then it may not be accomplished. For example, if meeting government regulations is a deliverable of the project but is not included in the WBS, then neither responsibility nor resources to accomplish this activity will be assigned.
2. It is the organization chart for the project. It indicates which internal departments, partners, and external suppliers are responsible for the delivery of each work package. This is especially important when the project crosses organizational boundaries; that is, the project organizational structure is different from the structure of the organization in which it resides.

3. It serves to track project costs, schedule, and performance for each element at every level. It is often the basis for the chart of accounts used to collect project costs under the project accounting system.

4. It may be used to communicate the project status, especially when it is used in conjunction with the responsibility assignment matrix, which will be described later in this chapter. The organizational responsibility for the delivery of each work package is documented in the WBS and the responsibility assignment matrix.

5. It may be used to identify communication issues and to allow the project team to budget properly for communication costs. The project team must plan for communication among the various organizations doing the work on the project. Investments may have to be made in formal linkages such as electronic communication. Without clearly defining the relationship among the resources executing the project, effective project tracking and control is impossible.

6. It represents how the project will be controlled. It dictates the general structure of the project and whether it will be controlled from a deliverable (engine, body, software) perspective or a functional (design, build, test) perspective. This choice depends on a number of factors, including the need for historical and real-time information as well as the relationship between the functional structure of the project and the organizational structure of the firm.

Project Planning

Project planning is part of the concept phase of the system development cycle and also includes the planning for the definition phase. A common definition of the system development cycle encompasses concept (including feasibility), definition, procurement (or acquisition), implementation (or operation), and turnover (or divestment).

The first task of the project team is to translate the vision provided by top management or the external customer into a set of objectives that will provide both direction to and limitations (constraints) on the project team. The starting point for this could be any document indicating the customer's requirements and expectations, such as a statement of work (SOW), a memorandum of understanding (MOU), or a contract.

Project objectives may be divided into four categories:

1. *Deliverables.* What will the customer receive at the end of the project: a report, a prototype, a product, a production facility, or something else? Deliverables include both the primary deliverable and the secondary deliverables

that should occur as a result of the project. For example, the primary deliverable of a new product development project could be achieving a particular cost target for the new product, while a secondary deliverable could be the date of market entry. It is essential that the project team and the customer agree on the priorities assigned to both the primary and the secondary deliverables. By definition, the primary deliverables would have higher priority.

2. *Benefits to the customer.* The direct and indirect value of the deliverables, these benefits should be put in the terms of and be related to the customer's objectives. If a product is being developed in a highly competitive environment, then time to market becomes a critical performance measurement from the company's perspective. Remember that it is not always the bottom line that is most important in a project.

3. *Resources or budget.* This is a general statement of the cost not to exceed or any other budget constraints. A summary of the major resources needed, including special facilities and personnel from other departments within the firm, as well as external resources (consultants), is also necessary.

4. *Schedule.* This refers to the major milestones of the project, including when the primary deliverables will occur. A measure of the rigidity of the milestone dates must also be included in the schedule. Is there a key date, such as a trade show, that must be met?

It is extremely important to identify the primary customer at this stage. The translation of the primary customer requirements into specific directions and constraints is done by the functional managers responsible for the contract. These managers become the secondary customers of the project.

If the project is internal, the primary and secondary customers may be the same people. It is critical that internal new product or process development (NPD) projects be treated in the same manner as external projects as far as the definition issues listed below are concerned.

The next step in the planning process is to translate the project objectives into a work plan designed to accomplish these objectives. This process will be guided by some form of top-down project plan. This is an explicit expansion of the vision statement that includes specific requirements and must be compared to the objectives to ensure they are in parallel.

Top-down planning includes (but is not limited to) such items as the following:

- NPD requirements: technical, cost, market, or something else for the product or process to be developed, that is, what it is supposed to do and how it will be integrated with existing systems

- Delivery date
- Major milestones for the project phases
- Budget and other cost limitations
- Reporting and organization structure, including the project champion
- Regulatory issues
- Resources to be used

The requirements must clearly show the relationship between this project and the strategic goals of the firm. In other words, they explain why the project is being done. Communication is essential to the planning of the project because it defines the boundaries for the project management teams.

An issue that often arises is the level of detail provided in the top-down plan by management. For example, should a project team be directed to develop an electric-powered vehicle, or should the choice of power system be one of the tasks they must accomplish? If the purpose of the project is to develop applications for the firm's new electric motor, then this restriction makes sense; this is a project deliverable. Otherwise, the project team should receive the broadest possible guidelines.

Case Example

To examine project planning and organization in the context of NPD in a medium-sized company, we will focus our attention on the Capital Electronics Company, which produces engineered products primarily for commercial rather than retail markets. It designs, develops, produces, and services these products in a highly regulated (government) environment.

The Detector Detector Case

Hap Arnold, a partner in Capital Electronics, came back from a conference of law enforcement agencies with an idea for a new product. Capital Electronics, which he and two college friends founded twenty years ago, is noted for developing a variety of devices in the security field, including wire-tapping, electronic surveillance, and electronic countersurveillance devices. Most of the products are sold directly through catalogues or by direct mail to law enforcement agencies. Last year, sales topped $100 million for the first time in the company's history.

Hap's idea is to design a device that can detect a radar detector; it would tell a traffic officer in the field if a particular automobile has a radar detector in use. Upon returning from the conference, Hap appointed Alice James, an electronics engineer who had joined Capital five years ago after she completed her master's degree, as project manager. He then contacted Dave Everest, owner of BUY-RITE, Inc. (a direct mail marketing firm), and offered a percentage interest in the yet-undeveloped product in return for Dave's marketing the device. Dave accepted the deal in principle but wanted to know more before he committed any funds.

Next, Hap, Alice, and Dave met to discuss the project, and Hap laid out the initial product specifications:

- Can detect a radar detector tuned to any of the bands currently in use
- Will not interfere with the police radar in the patrol vehicle
- Cannot be detected by a radar detector
- Can be recharged, with a twelve-hour battery life
- Can be plugged into a cigarette lighter in the patrol vehicle
- Weighs less than six ounces
- Meets government standards for emissions
- Meets government drop test standard (it must be virtually unbreakable)
- Target selling price of $350

Hap indicated to Alice that her first job was proof of concept, which focused on the first three specifications. Dave questioned the proposed selling price and suggested that a market study should be conducted to determine the size of the market and what similar devices were selling for. Alice felt that manufacturing should get into the project early to help determine the product cost as well as the ability to meet the weight specification and the government standards.

At the close of the meeting, Hap reiterated his concept, which was to design, develop, and market an affordable device that would allow traffic officers in the field to determine whether a vehicle had a radar detector in use. He charged Alice with the responsibility of bringing the product from proof of concept through to release to manufacturing. Hap also indicated that he wanted to launch the detector at the next national law enforcement conference and trade show, which would take place in eight months.

Hap pointed out that he had asked Dave to partner with him on this project because Capital did not have the funds to do this along with the other three product design and development projects that it had started this year: a new model of Capital's antibug detector for the Asian market, a new ultraminiature video camera, and an explosives sniffer. Finally, Hap and Dave agreed that they would negotiate their partnership in the venture after the concept had been proved.

Note that this case is concerned only with the concept, definition, and procurement phases of the system development cycle. This project will be complete with the delivery of complete manufacturing information to the shop as well as a market plan.

The vision statement is the starting point for the formal top-down planning of this project. A vision statement is an overview of the project and tends to describe a broad objective within a defined environment. It briefly summarizes the objectives of the project developed by top management as an attempt to relate the goals of the project to the strategic objectives of the firm, the customer, or both.

For Capital Electronics, the vision statement may be found in Hap Arnold's request to design, develop, and market an affordable device that would allow traffic officers in the field to determine whether a vehicle had a radar detector in use. It is also clear from Hap's statement that this device must be ready in eight months and be cost competitive.

It is very important as this stage for the project manager to identify the customers for the project, whether they be internal, external, or both. Hap Arnold is the internal customer for the detector, and Dave Everest is the external customer. As the project progresses, additional customers such as the Federal Communications Commission may be identified.

It is also desirable at this step to make some assessment of the risks associated with the project. Is Capital risking only time and money for the detector, or is it risking the company's reputation if the device is a fiasco at the law enforcement show? Customers are a vital part of this initial or strategic risk identification and review.

Project Planning

At this point, the project team must translate the vision statement into a set of objectives for the project. In the case example, Alice must translate Hap's wishes into a specific set of objectives that must then be reviewed and accepted by the customers. As mentioned previously, there are four categories of project objectives.

Deliverables

It is important at this stage to list the deliverables, both primary and secondary, so there is a clear understanding between the project team and the project customer as to what the project will produce. In many cases, secondary deliverables become as important as the primary deliverables. Unless they are explicitly stated and delivered, the customer will be dissatisfied. "I know what I *told* you I wanted, but this is what I *really* wanted" is one of the most dismaying statements that a project manager can hear from a customer.

In addition, the cost of all deliverables must be reflected in the project budget. The customer must know what is being paid for and why. This will allow the project team to determine what should be included in the project, as well as the contract negotiations, to proceed in a more open atmosphere. Hap did not indicate any cost restrictions on the development of the detector. It is therefore Alice's responsibility to come back to Hap with a project budget for his approval.

Although it is important that the customers agree with the objectives of the project, the objectives are an internal document meant to guide the project team. There may be objectives stated that are not shared with the customer, such as secondary deliverables that are internal, internal resource identification, and internal dates. In this case, there may be two sets of objectives: the first to be shared with the customer (public) and the second for internal control. It is critical that all the objectives stated in the public version be included in the internal version.

In the detector case, the primary deliverables were an operational prototype plus full manufacturing and marketing plans. An example of a secondary deliverable was presentation at the law enforcement show in eight months. The issue of primary and secondary deliverables—the required deliverables and the deliverables that may be modified—is up to the customers. For example, how important is the weight restriction of six ounces, and what impact on the success of the product would a heavier device have?

An example of an incorrect deliverable would be to develop a model of the detector for use in Asia. Hap Arnold did not ask for this, and so working on it would divert money and resources and add time to the project team's design effort.

Benefits to the Customer

An important reason for the translation of the primary and secondary objectives into performance metrics is that it reduces the ambiguity about the expectations of the project and develops goals for the project team that are realistic. In the detector case, the primary benefit of the project was market entry for the device with an expectation of sales and profits. A secondary benefit was to develop new technologies that may be applicable to other products.

An example of an incorrect benefit would be to match a similar project recently undertaken by a competitor. Although this may be a future objective of Capital Electronics, it is not a requirement of this project.

Resources or Budget

The focus here should be internal resources, external resources, and resources expected from the customers (internal and external). Since Hap gave Alice no guidance on how much she could spend to develop the detector, the development of a rough budget becomes an important part of the decision process. Alice must tell Hap how much this product development project will cost.

In the detector case, the following resources would be used:

- An as yet undefined amount of cash
- Internal engineering
- External consultants, including the marketing firm
- Fabrication and assembly facilities
- Test facilities

Schedule

The schedule must specify the major milestones of the project, including when the key deliverables will occur. Following are possible schedule milestones for the detector case:

1. Design and feasibility review in two months
2. Development and construction of the prototype completed in three months
3. Testing and analysis completed in five months
4. Revisions completed and prototype available in eight months for the law enforcement show
5. Manufacturing information, market plan, and cost estimates in ten months

The three major milestones are the design review and proof of concept, which should occur in two months; final testing, which should occur in five months (three months later); and the law enforcement show, which will occur in eight months. The project planner has to be careful not to start at the law enforcement show (eight months) and work backward to fit all the required activities into the available time. In developing the final schedule, the planner must work forward to ensure that the proposed milestones can be met.

Constructing the Work Breakdown Structure

Once the project objectives have been reviewed and accepted by the customers, the project planner must translate them into a list of the activities that must be performed in order to achieve these objectives. The project planner must be careful to include everything that must be done in order to be successful. Failure to address required activities will destroy both the schedule and the budget of the project, as well as the credibility of the planner. A simple listing of activities is not sufficient. The planner needs a structured approach to laying out the required activities that minimizes the chance of forgetting a critical activity. The WBS offers such an approach.

The development of a WBS for a project requires some rules to allow the project manager to communicate the structure to the project team and the customer. A number of authors provide the standard Department of Defense (DOD) structure as the model to be followed in defining the levels in the WBS. The DOD structure usually contains five levels. However, there is often an optional sixth level included:

Level	Element Name
1	Program
2	Project
3	Task
4	Subtask
5	Work Package
6 (Optional)	Level of Effort

The number of levels and the name of the levels are somewhat arbitrary as long as enough detail is provided.

Level 1 is the complete program that is going to be achieved and is divided into several projects. The program must be equal to the sum of all the costs and activities of all the projects in Level 2. Each project can be broken down into tasks in Level 3, the sum of which comprise the effort in the project. Each task can be further divided.

The top three levels are often used as summary levels for reporting progress to the customer, while the lower levels of used for internal control. Level 1 is used for authorization of work, Level 2 provides detailed information to prepare budgets, and schedules are completed at level 3.

There are two problems with the DOD structure. First, it is designed to be used for immense projects, such as the development of a new weapons system or building a power plant. In a large project, the work package (which appears at the fourth or fifth level) can easily have a budget of millions of dollars. However, most projects are under $1 million, and many project managers do not need to develop this elaborate structure, which is both time-consuming and difficult to follow. The key to project management success is simplicity.

The second problem is that the DOD structure focuses on one large project, ignoring the interrelationships with other projects in the organization. It assumes that a separate and distinct organization with its own resources will be conducting the program. The smaller project, on the other hand, must compete for limited resources with the other projects in the organization. In addition, smaller projects tend to be composed of temporary project teams made up of personnel borrowed from other groups within the firm. The lack of authority over personnel resources is the most common complaint of the manager of this type of project.

There is an alternative structure, designed for project managers who are developing project plans for a smaller project (one less than $1 million). In order to do this, we must modify the definitions from the DOD structure. The structure of the alternative WBS is much flatter than the DOD model:

Level	Element Name
1	Project
2	Work Package
3	Task
4	Subtask, if necessary

We will define a program as a set of projects with a common strategic goal. A manufacturing firm may have a very broad new product development program that includes a set of projects, each focused on a different product. Therefore, the program is not necessarily part of the WBS structure but the guiding vision of multiple projects, each with its own WBS, established to achieve the objectives of the program. In the detector case example, the program would include all new product development projects (antibug, camera, sniffer, detector), while the project of interest is the detection device that Capital plans to develop.

As an example, a consumer product manufacturer recently launched a program with the strategic goal of increasing sales by $20 million per year from six product development projects, each with a sales potential of $5 million per year. It is obvious that only four of the six projects need to succeed for the program goal to be realized. Therefore, the projects are in competition with each other, not only for the limited resources within the firm but from the standpoint of measuring success by comparing them to each other. If an executive review determined that there were enough successful projects to meet the program goal, a project that was a technical success could be canceled because its marketing plan was not as good as the marketing plans of the other projects in that program. An interesting strategic issue would arise if only three of the six projects succeeded. In that case, the program goal would be partially fulfilled, but the program would not be considered a failure.

The work package definition also needs to be expanded. A work package is a portion of the project that may be assigned to an organization, functional discipline, or individual for completion. It may be further divided into tasks and subtasks. This gives the project manager an organization chart to work with and defines how he or she will delegate authority and responsibility. In smaller projects, it is not unusual to develop the work packages at Level 2. By defining the work packages at this level, the project manager can take immediate advantage of the six functions of a WBS.

During the teaching of seminars to junior managers of technical projects, we found that many of these engineer-managers thought they were managing a project but were in fact managing a work package. This was most common in an environment with a number of major projects. An engineer-manager at an auto manufacturer who is in charge of designing a new door locking system may define his or her work as a project, whereas in reality it is a work package that is part of a project to produce a new model of an existing automobile by 1999, which in turn is part of the 1999 fleet development program.

The failure of a project in a program may not prevent the program from achieving its objectives if the rest of the projects are successful. If a work package fails, however, it is likely that the project will fail with it. In the case of the detector project, the failure to achieve cost feasibility could end the project.

Work packages should be divided at natural subdivisions of the work according to the way the work will be completed. Arbitrary cutoff points should be avoided. Keeping the work packages small minimizes the effort required to assess work in process because the status of the project is measured on the basis of completed work packages. If the work packages are large, assessment is more difficult and subjective.

Work packages should include these components:

- Clearly defined ownership
- Clearly defined start and end dates that are representative of physical accomplishments
- Results that can be compared with expectations
- A specific budget in terms of dollars, hours to completion, or other measurable units
- A structure that minimizes the required documentation

WBS Organization

The WBS may be organized in several ways.

Product-Oriented Organization

Level 2 would be each major system, while Level 3 would be the subsystems. This is sometimes called the deliverables approach, flow approach, or hardware approach because it focuses on the product components. One of the main advantages to this approach is that it collects costs on a product basis, which allows tracking the cost of each component and developing estimates for the actual production of that component. It facilitates design to cost by isolating the costs associated with designing, developing, and building each component in the system.

The detector could be organized into Level 2 work packages such as software, electronics, or packaging.

Phase-Oriented Organization

Level 2 indicates the sequence of life cycle of the product, while Level 3 is the systems and Level 4 is the subsystems. This approach is seldom used because contracts are usually for each phase, and the project work is usually not divided organizationally into such phases.

Function-Oriented Organization

Level 2 would be the departments performing the work, and Level 3 would be the components and subsystems. This is also called the organizational approach. It is best suited for smaller projects, where functional integration is a key need for the project. The detector could be organized into Level 2 work packages such as design, development and testing, manufacturing specifications, or marketing plan.

Examples of the product-oriented WBS and function-oriented WBS for the detector project are shown in Figures 10.1 and 10.2.

There is no standard numbering system for work packages in WBSs. Numbers are assigned to the different levels of the work package. In the example in Figure 10.1, the first number corresponds to the project level, the second number corresponds to the work package level, the third number corresponds to the task level, and so on. In the detector example, the number 2.4.3 represents task 3 of work package 4 in project 2, which is the competitive analysis task in the project.

The WBS can also become a template for the development of future project plans. A well-documented WBS that has been updated and corrected after completion of the project should be the starting point for detailed planning of a future project with similar requirements. The template ensures that the scope of the project is complete and acts as a checklist for the assignment of project activities. It also provides the planner with a historical reference for the cost and schedule of a similar project.

The WBS is an excellent visual aid for the project manager to use in informing the customer and the team about the project. It may help the work package

FIGURE 10.1. DETECTOR DETECTOR WORK BREAKDOWN STRUCTURE: FUNCTIONAL ORIENTATION.

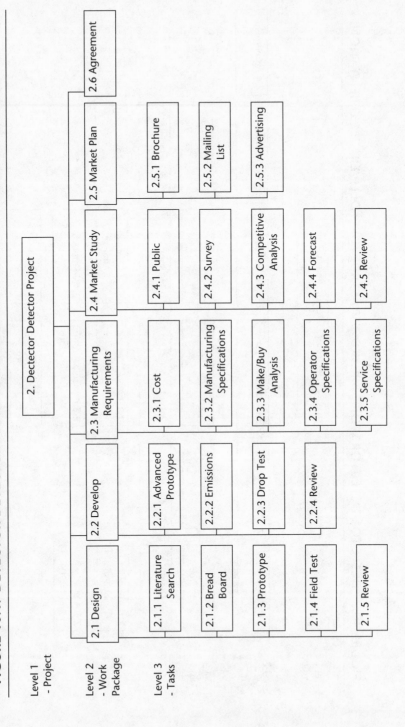

FIGURE 10.2. DETECTOR DETECTOR WORK BREAKDOWN STRUCTURE: DELIVERABLE ORIENTATION.

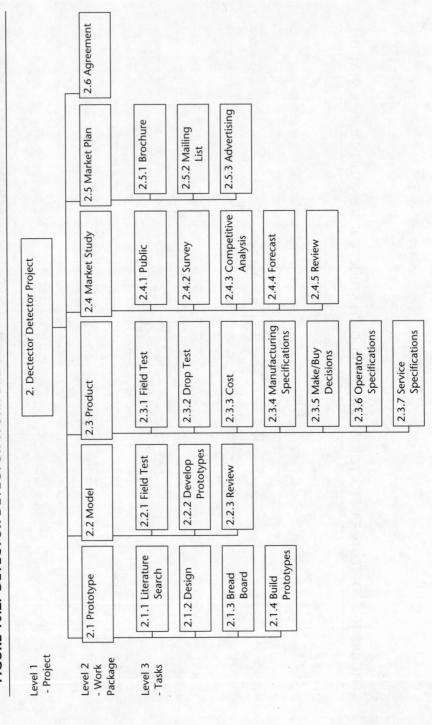

managers clearly see the relationship between their responsibilities and the other work packages that make up the project.

After the form and content of the WBS have been decided by the project team, there is one important step that must be taken before they move on to more detailed planning. Sometimes described as the requirements interface, this is the formal review of the WBS against the requirements of the project: the objectives, vision statement, statement of work, contract, memorandum of understanding, or any other document that may have initiated the project. Are all the requirements defined by the customer for the project accounted for in the WBS? For example, if there are plans to adopt any new technologies developed for the detector into other Capital Electronics products, is there a technology transfer work package? Similarly, nothing should be in the WBS that was not defined previously as part of the scope or vision statement.

Organizational Breakdown Structure

The WBS allows the display of the tasks required to accomplish the objectives. These tasks, however, must be clearly related to the responsible organization. The organizational breakdown chart represents this structure.

The organizational breakdown structure (OBS) is the representation of the management hierarchy of the company down to the functional departments assigned to the work packages. Planners need the OBS because organizations are dynamic and may change during the conduct of the project. In addition, the current organization may be poorly defined and not up to date.

Visualize the work packages along the x-axis and the departments along the y-axis of a matrix. The intersections between the two sets would indicate the department or departments that were assigned to perform a specific set of tasks (work packages). This matrix provides the structure for developing a bottom-up project budget after the level of effort is determined for department $y1$ on task $x1$.

This matrix also serves as the basis for the responsibility assignment matrix (RAM), also called the linear responsibility matrix or the responsibility matrix, which indicates the level of responsibility for each department. One possible division of these levels is:

1. Responsibility
2. Support
3. Notification
4. Approval

Thus, the WBS and the OBS intersect to form the RAM. Figure 10.3 illustrates an OBS for the detector detector project. The RAM shows everyone involved with the project who is responsible for each work package, who will be doing the actual work, who will be providing the support, and who will approve of the work.

The matrix of the WBS and the OBS provides a relatively complete picture of the task requirements and organizational interfaces associated with the project. The next step in the planning process is to verify that the project can be accomplished within the desired time frame through an overview approach known as schedule integration.

Project Schedule and Schedule Integration

Some additional steps are needed in the planning phase to ensure a reasonable fit between the activities that have to be accomplished and the milestones defined in the top-down plan. It forces the planners to step back and determine if the approach makes sense from the dual standpoints of time and resources.

FIGURE 10.3. ORGANIZATIONAL BREAKDOWN STRUCTURE.

	Design	Develop	Manufacturing Requirements	Market Study	Market Plan	Agreement
Electronics	R	R	R			
Software	S	S	S			
Mechanical	S	S	S			
Model shop	S	S				
Manufacturing	N	S	S			
Sales	N			S	S	
Technical writing			S			
Legal						R
BUY-RITE	S	N	N	R	R	
Executive committee	A	A			A	A

R = Responsible
S = Support
N = Notification
A = Approval

When Hap Arnold was developing the initial schedule under the objectives for the detector detector project, he started with the date of the National Law Enforcement Conference and worked backward to establish milestones for when each phase of the new product development *had to be completed* in order to have the prototype at the conference in eight months. He did not qualify whether that milestone date was feasible in the context of the work that has to be accomplished and the time and resources available.

Now that he has some idea of who will be doing the work along with some detail on the work that has to be accomplished, he should take time to test the feasibility of the proposed schedule. This is a high-level, yardstick-type of approach at this point in the development of the project plan. But he is better off knowing now if he cannot meet the commitments.

If these commitments cannot be kept, then the following trade-offs must be considered:

- Can the scope of the project be reduced? In other words, can he get rid of some of the lesser deliverables?
- Can he get more time from the customer, and thus extend the schedule?
- Can he add resources to expedite the work, that is, increase the project budget?

Clearly the customer would be more receptive to this discussion now than waiting until he is six months into the project and then surprise the customer with these problems.

The approach to schedule integration is to take each one of the major activities (Level 2 on the WBS) and determine if the proposed Level 3 activities fit into the time allowed for the Level 2 activity. For example, Hap estimated that developing the battery power system for the detector had to be accomplished in twelve weeks from design through acquisition in order for the prototype to be tested and available for the conference in eight months. But when he examined the Level 2 activities, he found the following sequence:

Design	2 weeks
Design review	1 week
Feasibility study	2 weeks
Acquisition of components	3 weeks
Build system	4 weeks
Test system	2 weeks
Install system	1 week

These estimates add up to fifteen weeks, not the twelve weeks planned. Discussion with the design team resulted in three alternatives:

1. Use an existing power system, which will save five weeks of design and development. Although this satisfies the schedule issue, it constrains the design process and could result in a prototype that is not considered innovative by the marketplace.
2. Miss the conference in eight months but aim to have the prototype ready for the next conference, six months later. Although this satisfies the deliverables, it will result in a higher budget (due to fixed costs) and delay in coming to market. Time is a competitive weapon.
3. Subcontract the acquisition and development work, which will save three weeks but double the cost of the subsystem. This satisfies the deliverables and the schedule but sharply increases the budget.

In evaluating these alternatives, the project team must recognize the objectives of the project customers, especially the perceived benefits; alternatives that may be suggested by the customers; and the need to get agreement between the internal and external customers.

Conclusions

In this chapter, we have translated the vision statement of the customer into a series of deliverables and responsibilities. At each step of the translation process, we returned to the customer's objectives to make sure that we were providing the desired results. If we failed to do our homework at this stage, we could pay for it later in terms of project delays due to misunderstandings of objectives and gaps in authority. Although the activities described in this chapter will not provide complete protection from project failure, experience has shown that they will minimize failure stemming from lack of understanding of the project's objectives.

Next, the tasks on the WBS will have to be organized into logical sequences before a schedule can be developed. This sequencing or precedence definition involves both physical and informational flows and is best defined in a network diagram. Network planning takes the project team into a high level of detail and requires definitions of methodologies and technical precedence. The team must develop time and recourse estimates and then evaluate the ability to deliver the project within the desired time frame with the resources available. The schedule that comes out of this process must be resource feasible and provide the project team with a road map to project success. The WBS is an indispensable link between the project objectives and the project plan. It defines how you plan to execute the project and who will do the work.[1]

CHAPTER ELEVEN

NETWORK PLANNING AND SCHEDULING

Jack Gido, James P. Clements

Planning and scheduling determine what needs to be done, who will do it, and how long it will take. Taking the time to develop a well-thought-out plan is critical to the successful accomplishment of the project objective. Developing a detailed plan and schedule encompasses (1) defining the specific activities needed to perform the project and assigning responsibility for each, (2) determining the sequence in which those activities must be accomplished, (3) estimating the time needed for each activity, and (4) preparing a project schedule. Many projects have missed their completion dates because no viable plan was created before the project was started. To avoid this, you must *plan the work, then work the plan*.

Planning is the systematic arrangement of tasks to accomplish an objective that is represented by the plan. The plan becomes a benchmark against which actual progress can be compared; if deviations occur, corrective action can be taken.

It is important that the people who will perform the work participate in planning it. They are usually the most knowledgeable about what detailed activities need to be done and how long each should take. By participating in the planning of the work, they become committed to accomplishing it according to the plan and within the schedule and budget. Participation builds commitment. In large, multiyear projects involving hundreds or even thousands of people, it is not possible to include everyone in the initial planning. But as the

Note: Adapted from Jack Gido and James P. Clements, *Successful Project Management*, South-Western College Publishing, 1999.

project progresses, many of these individuals can be involved in developing more detailed plans.

This chapter describes techniques used to plan and schedule the activities that must be carried out in accomplishing a project. (Numerous project management software packages are available to help plan and schedule projects in a completely interactive way.)

Project Objective

The first step in the planning process is to define the project objective: the expected result or end product. The objective must be clearly defined and agreed on by the customer and the organization or contractor that will perform the project. The objective must be clear, attainable, specific, and measurable. Achievement of the project objective must be easily recognizable by both the customer and the contractor. The objective is the target: the tangible end product that the project team must deliver.

For a project, the objective is usually defined in terms of scope, schedule, and cost; in other words, it requires completing the work within budget by a certain time. For example, the objective of a project might be to "introduce to the market in ten months and within a budget of $2 million a new electronic household cooking product that meets certain predefined performance specifications." Another example is to "produce a four-color, sixteen-page, back-to-school merchandise catalog and mail it by July 31 to all targeted potential customers in the county, within a budget of $40,000."

A project objective such as "complete the house" is too ambiguous, since the customer and the contractor may have different views of what is meant by "complete." A better objective is, "Complete the house by May 31 in accordance with the floor plans and specifications dated October 15 and within a budget of $150,000." The specifications and floor plans provide the details as to the scope of the work that the contractor agreed to perform. Therefore, no arguments should arise about whether the landscaping and carpeting were to be included or about the size of the entrance door, the color of paint in the bedrooms, or the style of lighting fixtures. All of these items should have been spelled out in the specifications.

Ideally, the project objective should be clear and concise at the beginning of the project. However, sometimes the project objective needs to be modified as the project proceeds. The project manager and the client must agree on all changes to the initial project objective because any changes might affect the work scope, completion date, and final cost.

Work Breakdown Structure

Once the project objective has been defined, the next step is to determine what work elements, or activities, need to be performed to accomplish it. This requires developing a list of all the activities using one of two approaches. One is to have the project team brainstorm the list of activities. This approach is suitable for small projects. For larger, more complex projects, it is difficult to develop a comprehensive list of activities without forgetting some items. For such projects, creating a work breakdown structure (WBS) is a better approach.

The WBS breaks a project down into manageable pieces, or items, to help ensure that all of the work elements needed to complete the project work scope are identified. The WBS is a hierarchical tree of end items that will be accomplished or produced by the project team during the project. The accomplishment or production of all these items constitutes completion of the project work scope.

An example of a WBS for a consumer market study project is shown in Figure 11.1. The graphic structure subdivides the project into smaller pieces called *work items.* Not all branches of the WBS have to be broken down to the same level. The lowest-level item of any one branch is called a *work package.* The WBS usually indicates the organization or individual responsible for each work item.

The criteria for deciding how much detail or how many levels to put in the WBS are (1) the level at which a single individual or organization can be assigned responsibility and accountability for accomplishing the work package and (2) the level at which the project manager wants to control the budget and monitor and collect cost data during the project. There is not a single correct WBS for any project. Two different project teams might well develop somewhat different WBSs for the same project.

Defining Activities

A list of specific, detailed activities necessary to accomplish the overall project can be generated through team brainstorming, especially for small projects. However, for projects in which a WBS is used, individual activities can be defined by the person or team responsible for each work package. An *activity* is defined as a piece of work that consumes time. It does not necessarily require the expenditure of effort by people; for example, waiting for concrete to harden can take several days but does not require any human effort.

For work package 1.1 in Figure 11.1 design, the following five detailed activities may be identified:

FIGURE 11.1. WORK BREAKDOWN STRUCTURE FOR A CONSUMER MARKET STUDY.

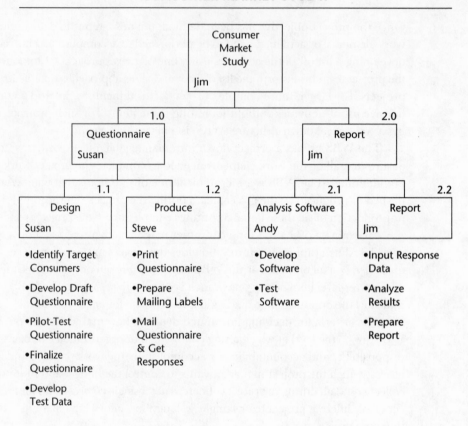

1. Identify target consumers.
2. Develop the draft questionnaire.
3. Pilot-test the questionnaire.
4. Finalize the questionnaire.
5. Develop test data.

Developing the Network Plan

When all the detailed activities have been defined, the next step is to portray them graphically in a network diagram that shows the appropriate sequence and inter-relationships to accomplish the overall project work scope.

Network planning is a technique that is helpful in planning, scheduling, and controlling projects that consist of many interrelated activities. Two network planning techniques, program evaluation and review technique (PERT) and the critical path method (CPM), were developed in the 1950s. Since that time, other forms of network planning, such as the precedence diagramming method (PDM) and the graphical evaluation and review technique (GERT), have been developed. All of these fall under the general category of network planning techniques because they all make use of a network diagram to show the sequential flow and interrelationships of activities. In the past, there were distinguishable methodological differences between PERT and CPM. Today, however, when most people refer to a CPM diagram or PERT chart, they mean a generic network diagram.

Network planning techniques are often compared with a somewhat more familiar tool known as a Gantt chart, sometimes called a bar chart. This older planning and scheduling tool, developed in the early 1900s, remains very popular today, mainly because of its simplicity.

The Gantt chart combines the two functions of planning and scheduling. Figure 11.2 shows a Gantt chart for a consumer market study. Activities are listed down the left-hand side, and a time scale is shown along the bottom. The estimated duration for each activity is indicated by a line or bar spanning the period during which the activity is expected to be accomplished. Columns that indicate who is responsible for each task can be added to the chart.

With Gantt charts, the scheduling of activities occurs simultaneously with their planning. The person drawing the activity lines or bars must be aware of the interrelationships of the activities—that is, which activities must be finished before others can start and which activities can be performed concurrently. One of the major drawbacks to the traditional Gantt chart is that it does not graphically display the interrelationships of activities. Therefore, it is not obvious which other activities will be affected if one activity is delayed. However, most project management software packages can produce Gantt charts that display the interdependencies among tasks by using connecting arrows.

Because planning and scheduling are done simultaneously with a traditional Gantt chart, it is cumbersome to make changes to the plan manually, especially if an activity at the beginning of the project is delayed and many of the remaining lines or bars have to be redrawn as a result. Network techniques, on the other hand, separate the planning and scheduling functions. A network diagram is the result, or output, of the planning function and is not drawn to a time scale. A schedule is developed from the diagram. Separating the two functions makes it much easier to revise a plan and calculate an updated schedule.

FIGURE 11.2. GANTT CHART FOR CONSUMER MARKET STUDY.

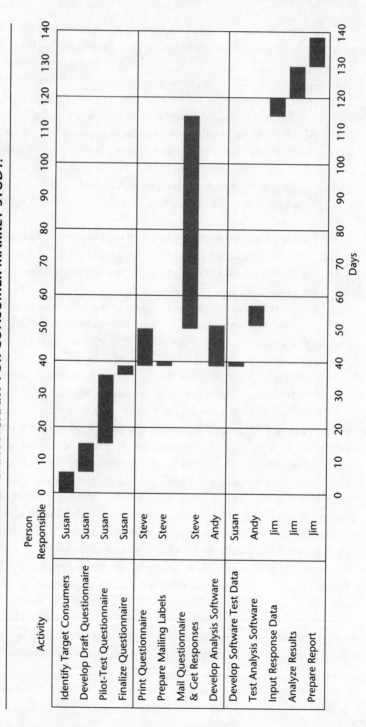

Network Principles

There are a few basic principles that must be understood and followed in preparing a network diagram. In a network diagram, each activity is represented by a box, and the description of the activity is written within the box, as shown in Figure 11.3. Activities consume time, and their description usually starts with a verb. Each activity is represented by one, and only one, box. In addition, each box is assigned a unique activity number. In Figure 11.3, the activity "Develop Draft Questionnaire" has been given activity number 2.

Activities have a precedential relationship—that is, they are linked in a precedential order to show which activities must be finished before others can start. Arrows linking the activity boxes show the direction of precedence. An activity cannot start until all of the preceding activities linked to it by arrows have been finished.

Certain activities have to be done in a serial order. For example, in Figure 11.3, only after "Develop Questionnaire" is finished can "Pilot-Test Questionnaire" start.

Some activities may be done concurrently. In Figure 11.3, "Prepare Mailing Labels" and "Print Questionnaire" can be done concurrently; when they are *both* finished, "Mail Questionnaire and Get Responses" can start. Similarly, when "Review Comments and Finalize Questionnaire" is finished, all four activities ("Prepare Mailing Labels," "Print Questionnaire," "Develop Data Analysis Software," and "Develop Software Test Data") can start and be worked on concurrently.

Loops of activities, that is, a path of activities that perpetually repeats itself, cannot be part of a network diagram. In addition, some projects have a set of activities that are repeated several times. For example, consider a project involving the painting of two rooms. Painting each room requires (1) preparing the room to be painted, (2) painting the ceiling and walls, and (3) painting the trim. Assume that three experts will be available: one to do the preparation, one to paint the ceilings and walls, and one to do the trim.

It may seem logical to draw a network diagram for the project as shown in Figure 11.4 or 11.5. However, Figure 11.4 indicates that all the activities must be done in serial order, which means that at any one time, only one person is working while the two other people are waiting. Figure 11.5, on the other hand, indicates that both rooms can be done concurrently, which is not possible because only one expert is available for each type of activity.

Figure 11.6 shows a technique known as *laddering*, which can be used to diagram this project. It indicates that each expert, after finishing one room, can start working on the next room. This approach will allow the project to be completed in the shortest possible time while making the best use of available resources (the experts).

FIGURE 11.3. NETWORK DIAGRAM FOR CONSUMER MARKET STUDY.

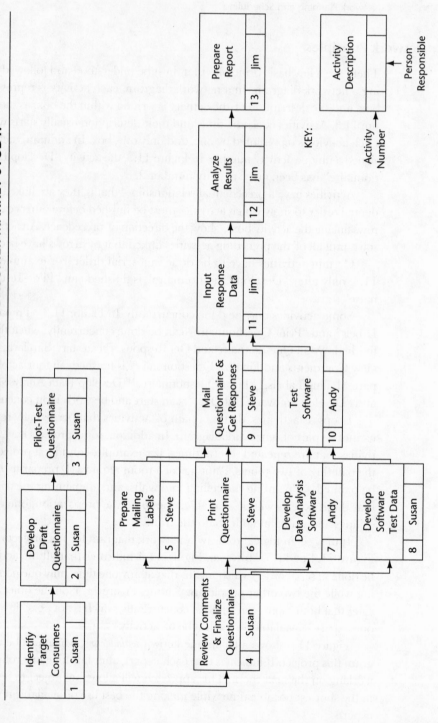

FIGURE 11.4. ACTIVITIES PERFORMED SERIALLY.

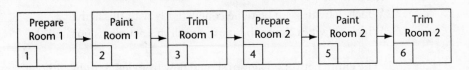

FIGURE 11.5. ACTIVITIES PERFORMED CONCURRENTLY.

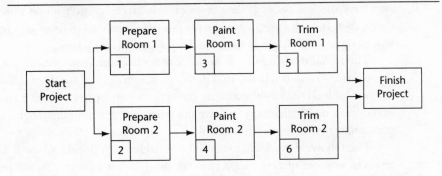

FIGURE 11.6. LADDERING ACTIVITIES.

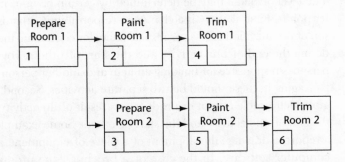

Preparing the Network Diagram

Given a list of activities and a knowledge of network principles, you can begin to prepare a network diagram by drawing the activities in their logical precedential order, as the project should progress from its beginning to its completion. When deciding on the sequence in which the activities should be drawn, consider the following three questions about each activity:

1. Which activities must be finished immediately before this activity can be started?
2. Which activities can be done concurrently with this activity?
3. Which activities cannot be started until this activity is finished?

The entire network diagram should flow from left to right, although some arrows may flow from right to left to prevent the overall diagram from becoming too long. Unlike the Gantt chart, the network diagram is not drawn to a time scale. It is easier to visualize the entire project if the network diagram can be drawn to fit on a large sheet of paper. If the network is very large, however, it may require multiple pages. In such cases, it may be necessary to create a "to-from" reference system to show the linkages between activities on different pages.

The initial drawing of the network diagram for a project does not have to be excessively neat. It is better to sketch out a rough draft of the diagram and make sure the logical relationships among the activities are correct. Then go back later and draw a neater diagram (or have the computer generate the diagram if project management software is available).

The following guidelines should be considered in deciding how detailed (in terms of number of activities) a network diagram for a project should be:

- If a WBS has been prepared for the project, activities should be identified for each work package.
- The level of detail may be determined by certain obvious interface or transfer points. First, if there is a change in responsibility—that is, a different person or organization takes over responsibility for continuing the work—it should define the end of one activity and the start of others. For example, if one person is responsible for building an item and another person is responsible for packaging it, these should be two separate activities. Second, if there is a tangible, deliverable output or product as a result of an activity, it should define the end of one activity and the start of others. Some examples of outputs are a report, a drawing, the shipment of a piece of equipment, and the design of computer software. In the case of a brochure, the production of a draft brochure should be defined as the end of one activity; another activity, perhaps "Approve Draft Brochure," would follow.
- Activities should not be longer in estimated duration than the time intervals at which actual project progress will be reviewed and compared to planned progress. For example, if the project is a three-year endeavor and the project team plans to review progress monthly, then the network should contain no activities with estimated durations greater than thirty days. If there are activities with longer estimated durations, they should be broken up into more detailed activities with durations of thirty days or fewer.

Whatever the level of detail used in the initial network diagram, some activities may be broken down further as the project progresses. It is always easier to identify activities that need to be done in the near term (during the next several weeks or months) than those that are a year in the future. It is not unusual to add more detail to a network diagram as the project moves forward.

In some cases, an organization may do similar projects for different customers, and certain portions of these projects may include the same types of activities in the same logical precedential relationships. For example, in the construction of new office building, the design and installation of a certain type of heating, ventilating, and air-conditioning system may follow a standard sequence. If so, it may be worthwhile to develop standard subnetworks for these portions of the projects, to save effort and time when a network diagram is developed for an overall project. Standard subnetworks should be developed for those portions of projects for which the logical relationships among the activities have been well established through historical practice. These subnetworks may be modified as necessary for a particular project.

Finally, when the entire network diagram has been drawn, each activity box is assigned a unique activity number. Figure 11.3 shows a complete network diagram for a consumer market study project. Notice the inclusion of the person responsible on this diagram.

The network is a road map that displays how all the activities fit together to accomplish the project work scope. It also is a communication tool for the project team because it shows who is responsible for each activity and how their work ties into the overall project.

Developing the Schedule

Planning deals with determining what activities need to be done and in what sequence in order to accomplish a project objective. The result is a plan in the form of a network diagram that graphically portrays activities in the appropriate interdependent sequence to accomplish the project work scope. When network planning techniques are used, the scheduling function depends on the planning function. A schedule is a timetable for a plan and therefore cannot be established until the plan has been developed.

Duration Estimates

The first step in establishing a project schedule is to estimate how long each activity will take, from the time it is started until the time it is finished. This duration estimate for each activity must be the total elapsed time—the time for the work to be done plus any associated waiting time. In Figure 11.7 the duration estimate for Activity 9 is sixty-five days, which includes both the time to mail the questionnaires and the waiting time to get the responses back. The activity's duration estimate is usually shown in the lower right-hand corner of the box.

A good practice is to have the person who will be responsible for performing a particular activity make the duration estimate. This generates a commitment from that person and avoids any bias that may be introduced by having one person make the duration estimates for all of the activities. In some cases, though—such as for large projects with several hundred people performing various activities over several years—it may not be practical to have each person provide activity duration estimates at the outset. Rather, each organization or subcontractor responsible for a group or type of activities may designate an experienced individual to make the duration estimates for all the activities for which they are responsible. If an organization or subcontractor has performed similar projects in the past and has kept records of how long specific activities actually took, these historical data can be used as a guide in estimating activity durations for future projects.

An activity's duration estimate must be based on the quantity of resources expected to be used on it. The estimate should be aggressive yet realistic. It should not include time for a lot of things that could possibly go wrong, nor should it be too optimistically short. It is generally better to be somewhat aggressive and estimate a duration for an activity at five days, say, and then actually finish it in six days, than to be overly conservative and estimate a duration at ten days and then actually take ten days. People sometimes perform to expectations; if an activity is estimated to take ten days, their effort will expand to fill the whole ten days allotted, even if the activity could have been performed more quickly.

Inflating duration estimates in anticipation of the project manager's negotiating shorter durations is not a good practice. Nor is padding estimates with the vision of becoming a hero when the activities are completed in less time than estimated.

Throughout the performance of the project, some activities will take longer than their estimated duration, others will be done in less time, and a few may conform to the estimates exactly. Over the life of a project that has many activities, however, delays and accelerations tend to cancel one another out. For example, one activity may take two weeks longer than estimated, but this delay may be offset by two other activities that are each done a week sooner than originally estimated.

Figure 11.7 shows the network diagram for a consumer market study with the duration estimates in days for each activity indicated in the lower right-hand box. A consistent time base, such as hours or days or weeks, should be used for all the activity duration estimates in a network diagram.

FIGURE 11.7. NETWORK DIAGRAM SHOWING ESTIMATED DURATIONS FOR THE CONSUMER MARKET STUDY.

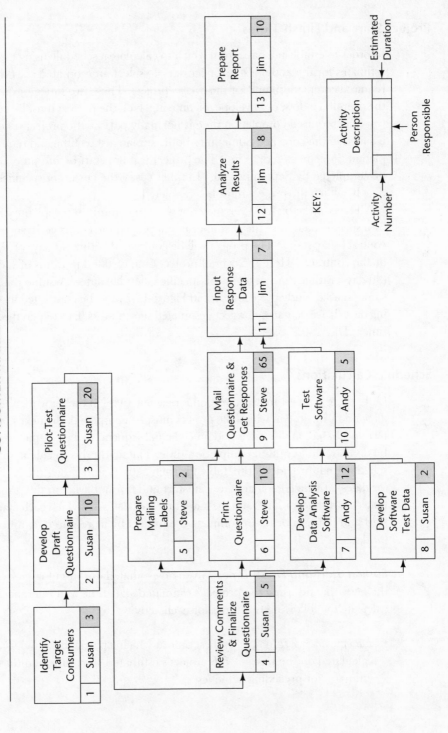

Project Start and Finish Times

In order to establish a basis from which to calculate a schedule using the duration estimates for the activities, it is necessary to select an estimated start time and a required completion time for the overall project. These two times (or dates) define the overall window, or envelope, of time in which the project must be completed.

The required completion time is normally part of the project objective and is stated in the contract. Sometimes both estimated start time and required completion time are stated, as in, "The project will not start before June 1 and must be completed by September 30." In other cases, the customer specifies only the date by which the project must be completed.

The contractor, however, may not want to commit to completing the project by a specific date until the customer has approved the contract. In such cases the contract may state, "The project will be completed within 90 days of the signing of the contract." Here the overall project time is stated in terms of a cycle time (90 days) rather than in terms of specific calendar dates. Assume that the consumer market study project shown in Figure 11.7 must be completed in 130 working days. If we define the project's estimated start time as 0, its required completion time is Day 130.

Schedule Calculations

Once there is an estimated duration for each activity in the network and an overall window of time in which the project must be completed, the next step is to determine (based on durations and precedential sequence) whether the activities can be done by the required completion time. The method is to calculate a project schedule that provides a timetable for each activity and shows the earliest times (or dates) at which each activity can start and finish, based on the project's estimated start time (or date) and the latest times (or dates) by which each activity must start and finish in order to complete the project by its required completion time (or date)

Earliest Start and Finish Times Given an estimated duration for each activity in the network and using the project's estimated start time as a reference, you can calculate the following two times for each activity:

- *Earliest start time (ES):* The earliest time at which a particular activity can begin, calculated on the basis of the project's estimated start time and the duration estimates for preceding activities

- *Earliest finish time (EF):* The earliest time by which a particular activity can be completed, calculated by adding the activity's duration estimate to the activity's earliest start time: $EF = ES$ + duration estimate.

The ES and EF times are determined by calculating forward—that is, by working through the network diagram from the beginning of the project to the end of the project. Rule 1 must be followed:

Rule 1: The earliest start time (ES) for a particular activity must be the same as or later than the latest of all the earliest finish times (EF) of all the activities leading directly into that particular activity.

Figure 11.8 shows three activities leading directly into "Dress Rehearsal." "Practice Skit" has an EF of Day 5, "Make Costumes" has an EF of Day 10, and "Make Props" has an EF of Day 4. "Dress Rehearsal" cannot start until all three of these activities are finished, so the latest of the EFs for these three activities determines the ES for "Dress Rehearsal." The latest of the three EFs is Day 10—the earliest finish time for "Make Costumes." Therefore, "Dress Rehearsal" cannot start any earlier than Day 10. That is, its ES must be Day 10 or later. Although "Practice Skit" and "Make Props" may finish sooner than "Make Costumes," "Dress Rehearsal" cannot start because the network logic indicates that all three activities must be finished before "Dress Rehearsal" can start.

Figure 11.9 shows the forward calculations for the consumer market study project. The project's estimated start time is 0. Therefore, the earliest "Identify Target Consumers" can start is Time 0, and the earliest it can finish is three days later (since its estimated duration is three days). When "Identify Target Consumers" is finished on Day 3, "Develop Draft Questionnaire" can start. It has a duration of ten days, so its ES is Day 3 and its EF is Day 13. The calculations of ES and EF for subsequent activities are done similarly, continuing forward through the network diagram.

"Test Software" in Figure 11.9 has an ES of Day 50 because, according to Rule 1, it cannot start until the two activities leading directly into it are finished. "Develop Data Analysis Software" does not finish until Day 50, and "Develop Software Test Data" does not finish until Day 40. Since "Test Software" cannot start until both of these are finished, "Test Software" cannot start until Day 50.

As a further illustration of Rule 1, refer once more to Figure 11.9. In order to start "Mail Questionnaire & Get Responses," the two activities immediately preceding it, "Prepare Mailing Labels" and "Print Questionnaire" must be finished. The EF of "Prepare Mailing Labels" is Day 40, and the EF of "Print

FIGURE 11.8. EARLIEST START TIMES.

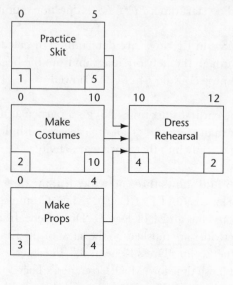

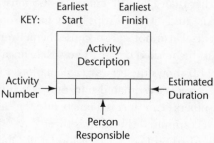

Questionnaire" is Day 48. According to Rule 1, it is the later of the two EFs, which is Day 48, that determines the ES of "Mail Questionnaire & Get Responses."

If you continue calculating the ES and EF for each remaining activity in the network diagram in Figure 11.9, you will see that the last activity, "Prepare Final Report," has an EF of Day 138. That is 8 days beyond the project's required completion time of 130 days. At this point, there is a problem.

Although the ES and EF times for each activity are shown on the network diagram in Figure 11.9, this is not normally the case. Rather, the ES and EF times are listed in a separate schedule table, like the one in Figure 11.13. Separating the schedule table from the network logic diagram makes it easier to generate revised

FIGURE 11.9. NETWORK DIAGRAM WITH EARLIEST START AND FINISH TIMES FOR CONSUMER MARKET STUDY.

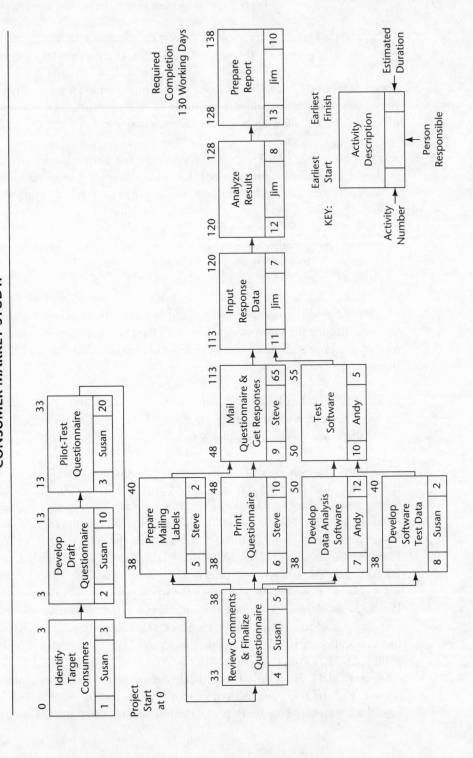

and updated schedules (perhaps using project management software), without continually making changes to the start and finish times on the network diagram itself.

Latest Start and Finish Times Given a duration estimate for each activity in the network and using the project's required completion time as a reference, you can calculate the following two times for each activity:

- *Latest finish time (LF):* The latest time by which a particular activity must be finished in order for the entire project to be completed by its required completion time, calculated on the basis of the project's required completion time and the duration estimates for succeeding activities
- *Latest start time (LS):* The latest time by which a particular activity must be started in order for the entire project to be completed by its required completion time, calculated by subtracting the activity's duration estimate from the activity's latest finish time: $LS = LF$ duration estimate.

The LF and LS times are determined by calculating backward—that is, by working through the network diagram from the end of the project to the beginning of the project. Rule 2 must be followed in making these backward calculations:

Rule 2: The latest finish time (LF) for a particular activity must be the same as or earlier than the earliest of all the latest start (LS) times of all the activities emerging directly from that particular activity.

Figure 11.10 shows two activities emerging directly from "Print Posters & Brochures." This project is required to be completed by Day 30. Therefore, "Distribute Posters" must be started by Day 20, since it has a duration of ten days, and "Mail Brochures" must be started by Day 25, since it has a duration of five days. The earlier of these two LSs is Day 20. Therefore, the latest that "Print Posters & Brochures" can finish is Day 20, so that "Distribute Posters" can start by Day 20. Although "Mail Brochures" does not have to start until Day 25, "Print Posters & Brochures" must finish by Day 20, or the whole project will be delayed. If "Print Posters & Brochures" does not finish until Day 25, then "Distribute Brochures" will not be able to start until Day 25. Since "Distribute Brochures" has an estimated duration of ten days, it will not finish until Day 35, which is five days beyond the project's required completion time.

Figure 11.11 shows the backward calculations on the consumer market study project. The required completion time for the project is 130 working days. Therefore, the latest that "Prepare Report," the last activity, can finish is Day 130, and

FIGURE 11.10. LATEST FINISH TIMES.

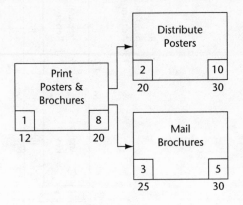

KEY:

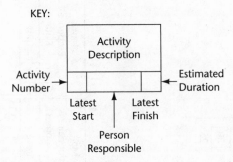

the latest that it can start is Day 120, since its estimated duration is 10 days. In order for "Prepare Report" to start on Day 120, the latest that "Analyze Results" can finish is Day 120. If the LF for "Analyze Results" is Day 120, then its LS is Day 112, since its estimated duration is 8 days. The calculations of LF and LS for prior activities are done similarly, continuing backward through the network diagram.

In order for the four activities emerging from "Review Comments & Finalize Questionnaire" to start by their LS times (so that the project can finish by its required completion time of 130 days), "Review Comments & Finalize Questionnaire" must be finished by the earliest LS of all four activities, according to Rule 2. The earliest of the four LSs is Day 30, the latest time by which "Print Questionnaire" must start. Therefore, the latest that "Review Comments & Finalize Questionnaire" can finish is Day 30.

If you continue calculating the LF and LS for each activity in the network diagram, you will see that the first activity, "Identify Target Consumers," has an LS of −8. This means that in order to complete the entire project by its required completion time of 130 days, the project must start 8 days earlier than it is estimated

FIGURE 11.11. NETWORK DIAGRAM WITH LATEST START AND FINISH TIMES FOR CONSUMER MARKET STUDY.

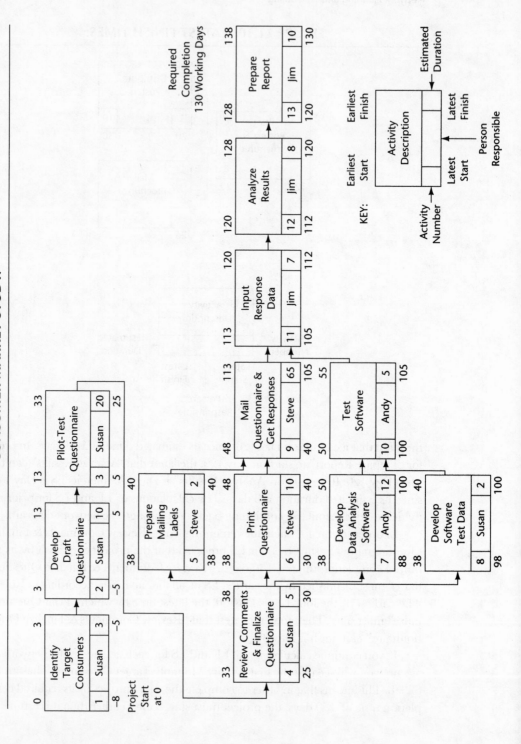

to start. Note that this difference of 8 days is equal to the difference obtained when calculating forward through the network diagram to obtain the ES and EF times. In essence, what we have found is that this project may take 138 days to complete, even though its required completion time is 130 days.

Like the earliest start and earliest finish times, the latest start and latest finish times are usually not shown on the network diagram itself, but rather in a separate schedule table (see Figure 11.13).

Total Slack In the consumer market study project, there is a difference of 8 days between the calculated earliest finish time of the very last activity ("Prepare Report") and the project's required completion time. This difference is the total slack (TS), sometimes called float. A negative number for total slack indicates a lack of slack over the entire project.

If positive total slack represents the maximum amount of time that the activities on a particular path can be delayed without jeopardizing completion of the project by its required completion time. If total slack is negative, it represents the amount of time that the activities on a particular path must be accelerated in order to complete the project by its required completion time. If total slack is zero, the activities on the path do not need to be accelerated but cannot be delayed.

The total slack for a particular path of activities is common to and shared among all the activities on that path. Consider the project shown in Figure 11.12. The earliest the project can finish is Day 15 (the sum of the durations of the three activities: 7 + 5 + 3). However, the required completion time for the project is twenty days. The three activities on this path can therefore be delayed up to five days without jeopardizing completion of the project by its required completion time. This does not mean that each activity on the path can be delayed five days (because this would create a total delay of fifteen days); rather, it means that all the activities that make up the path can have a total delay of five days among them. For example, if "Remove Old Wallpaper" actually takes ten days (three days longer than the estimated seven days), then it will use up three of the five days of total slack, and only two days of total slack will remain.

FIGURE 11.12. TOTAL SLACK EXAMPLE.

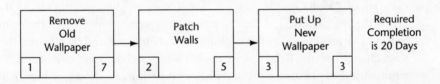

Total slack is calculated by subtracting the activity's earliest finish (or start) time from its latest finish (or start) time. That is, the slack is equal to either the latest finish time (LF) minus the earliest finish time (EF) for the activity, or the latest start time (LS) minus the earliest start time (ES) for that activity. The two calculations are equivalent: Total slack $= LF - EF$ or $LS - ES$.

Critical Path   Not all networks are as simple as the three-activity one just used to illustrate total slack. In large network diagrams, there may be many paths of activities from the project start to the project completion, just as there are many routes you can follow to get from New York City to Los Angeles. If twenty friends were going to leave at the same time and each was going to drive a different route, they could not get together for a party in Los Angeles until the last person had arrived—that is, the one who took the longest (or most time-consuming) route. Similarly, a project cannot be completed until the longest (or most time-consuming) path of activities is finished. This longest path in the overall network diagram is called the *critical path*.

One way to determine which activities make up the critical path is to find which have the least slack. Subtract the earliest finish time from the latest finish time for each activity (or subtract the earliest start time from the latest start time—both calculations will result in the same value). For example, refer to the activity, "Analyze Results," in the schedule in Figure 11.13. Its $LF - EF$ is $120 - 128 = -8$ days, which is the same as its $LS - ES$, $112 - 120$ days $= -8$ days. Then look for all the activities that have the lowest value (either least positive or most negative). All the activities with this value are on the critical path of activities.

The values of total slack for the consumer market study project are shown in Figure 11.12. The lowest value is -8 days. The activities that have this same value of total slack make up the path 1–2–3–4–6–9–11–12–13. These nine activities constitute the critical, or most time-consuming, path. The estimated durations of the activities on this path add up to 138 days ($3 + 10 + 20 + 5 + 10 + 65 + 7 + 8 + 10$). Among them, these activities need to be accelerated 8 days in order to complete the project within the required 130 days. Figure 11.14 highlights the activities that make up the critical path.

To eliminate the -8 days of slack, the estimated durations of one or more activities on this critical path need to be reduced. Suppose we reduce the estimated duration of "Mail Questionnaire & Get Responses" from 65 days to 55 days by giving the respondents less time to return the questionnaire. Since the estimated duration of an activity on the critical path is being reduced by 10 days, the total slack changes from -8 days to $+2$ days. The revised duration estimate of 55 days can be used to prepare a revised project schedule, as shown in Figure 11.15.

FIGURE 11.13. SCHEDULE FOR THE CONSUMER MARKET STUDY PROJECT: TOTAL SLACK.

	Activity	Responsible	Estimated Duration	Earliest		Latest		Total Slack
				Start	Finish	Start	Finish	
1	Identify Target Consumers	Susan	3	0	3	-8	-5	-8
2	Develop Draft Questionnaire	Susan	10	3	13	-5	5	-8
3	Pilot-Test Questionnaire	Susan	20	13	33	5	25	-8
4	Review Comments & Finalize Questionnaire	Susan	5	33	38	25	30	-8
5	Prepare Mailing Labels	Steve	2	38	40	38	40	0
6	Print Questionnaire	Steve	10	38	48	30	40	-8
7	Develop Data Analysis Software	Andy	12	38	50	88	100	50
8	Develop Software Test Data	Susan	2	38	40	98	100	60
9	Mail Questionnaire & Get Responses	Steve	65	48	113	40	105	-8
10	Test Software	Andy	5	50	55	100	105	50
11	Input Response Data	Jim	7	113	120	105	112	-8
12	Analyze Results	Jim	8	120	128	112	120	-8
13	Prepare Report	Jim	10	128	138	120	130	-8

FIGURE 11.14. CRITICAL PATH FOR THE CONSUMER MARKET SURVEY.

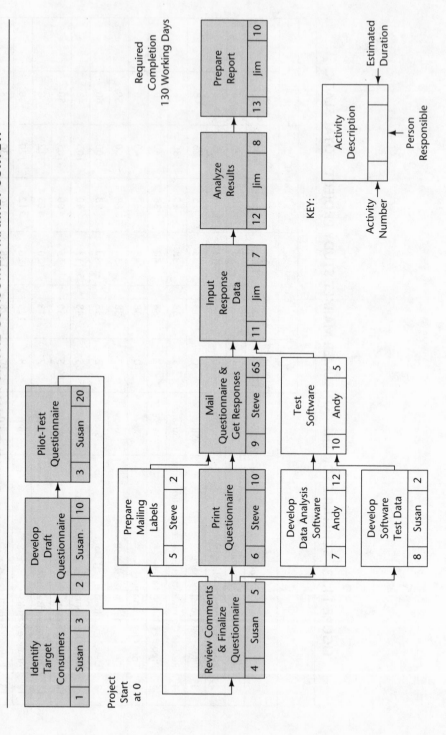

Required Completion
130 Working Days

KEY:

Activity Description

Estimated Duration

Person Responsible

Activity Number

Project Start at 0

FIGURE 11.15. REVISED SCHEDULE FOR THE CONSUMER MARKET STUDY.

	Activity	Responsible	Estimated Duration	Earliest		Latest		Total Slack
				Start	Finish	Start	Finish	
1	Identify Target Consumers	Susan	3	0	3	2	5	2
2	Develop Draft Questionnaire	Susan	10	3	13	5	15	2
3	Pilot-Test Questionnaire	Susan	20	13	33	15	35	2
4	Review Comments & Finalize Questionnaire	Susan	5	33	38	35	40	2
5	Prepare Mailing Labels	Steve	2	38	40	48	50	10
6	Print Questionnaire	Steve	10	38	48	40	50	2
7	Develop Data Analysis Software	Andy	12	38	50	88	100	50
8	Develop Software Test Data	Susan	2	38	40	98	100	60
9	Mail Questionnaire & Get Responses	Steve	55	48	103	50	105	2
10	Test Software	Andy	5	50	55	100	105	50
11	Input Response Data	Jim	7	103	110	105	112	2
12	Analyze Results	Jim	8	110	118	112	120	2
13	Prepare Report	Jim	10	118	128	120	130	2

This schedule shows that the critical path now has a total slack of +2 days, and the project is now estimated to finish in 128 days, 2 days earlier than the required completion time of 130 days.

A large network diagram can have many paths or routes from its beginning to its end. Some of the paths may have positive values of total slack, and others may have negative values of total slack. Paths with positive values of total slack are sometimes referred to as *noncritical paths,* and paths with zero or negative values of total slack are referred to as *critical paths.* In this case, the longest path is often referred to as the *most critical path.*

Free Slack Another type of slack that is sometimes calculated is free slack: the amount of time a particular activity can be delayed without delaying the earliest start time of the activities that immediately follow it. It is the relative difference between the amounts of total slack for activities entering into the same activity. Free slack is calculated by finding the lowest of the values of total slack for all the activities entering into a particular activity and then subtracting it from the values of total slack for the other activities also entering into that same activity. Since free slack is the relative difference between values of total slack for activities entering into the same activity, it will exist only when two or more activities enter into the same activity. Also, since free slack is a relative difference between values of total slack, it is always a positive value.

For an illustration of free slack, consider Figures 11.13 and 11.14. In the network diagram (Figure 11.14), there are three instances where a particular activity has more than one activity entering into it:

- Activity 9, "Mail Questionnaire & Get Responses," has Activities 5 and 6 entering into it.
- Activity 10, "Test Software," has Activities 7 and 8 entering into it.
- Activity 11, "Input Response Data," has Activities 9 and 10 entering into it.

In the schedule (Figure 11.13), the values of total slack for activities 5 and 6 are 0 and −8 days, respectively. The lesser of these two values is −8 days for Activity 6. The free slack for Activity 5 is the relative difference between its total slack, 0, and −8. This relative difference is 8 days: 0 − (−8) = 8 days. This means that Activity 5, "Prepare Mailing Labels," already has a free slack of 8 days and can slip by up to that amount without delaying the earliest start time of Activity 9, "Mail Questionnaire & Get Responses."

Similarly, the values of total slack for Activities 7 and 8 are 50 and 60 days, respectively. The lesser of these two values is 50 days. Therefore, Activity 8, "Develop Software Test Data," has a free slack of 10 days (60 − 50 = 10) and can slip by up to that amount without delaying the earliest start time of Activity 10, "Test Software."

Summary

Planning is the systematic arrangement of tasks to accomplish an objective. Because the plan lays out what needs to be done and how it is to be accomplished, it becomes a benchmark against which actual progress can be compared; if deviations occur, corrective action can be taken.

The first step in the planning process is to define the project objective: the expected result or end product. The project objective is usually defined in terms of scope, schedule, and cost. The objective must be clearly defined and agreed to by the customer and the organization or contractor that will perform the project.

Once the project objective has been defined, the next step is to determine what work elements, or activities, need to be performed to accomplish it. This requires a listing of all the activities.

The work breakdown structure (WBS) breaks a project down into manageable pieces, or items, to help ensure that all of the work elements needed to complete the project work scope are identified. It is a hierarchical tree of end items that will be accomplished or produced by the project team during the project. It usually indicates the organization or individual responsible for each work item.

Network planning is helpful in planning, scheduling, and controlling projects that consist of many interrelated activities. In addition, it is useful for communicating information about projects. Each activity is represented by a box in the network diagram, and the description of the activity is written within the box. After a list of activities has been created, a network diagram can be prepared. When deciding on the sequence in which the activities should be drawn to show their logical precedential relationship to one another, you must determine (1) which activities must be finished immediately before each activity can be started, (2) which activities can be done concurrently, and (3) which activities cannot be started until prior activities are finished.

After a plan is developed, the next step is to develop a project schedule. The first step in this process is to estimate how long each activity will take, from the time it is started until the time it is finished. A good practice if possible is to have the person who will be responsible for an activity estimate its duration.

An activity's duration estimate must be based on the quantity of resources expected to be used and should be aggressive yet realistic. A consistent time base—such as hours or days or weeks—should be used for all the activity duration estimates.

The earliest start and earliest finish (ES and EF) times and the latest start and latest finish (LS and LF) times can be calculated for each activity. The ES and EF times are calculated by working forward through the network, using the project's estimated start time and the duration estimates for activities as a basis. The earliest finish time for an activity is calculated by adding the activity's duration estimate to the activity's earliest start time. The earliest start time for a particular activity must be the same as or later than the latest of all the earliest finish times of all the activities leading directly into that particular activity.

The LS and LF times are calculated by working backward through the network. The latest finish time for an activity is calculated on the basis of the project's required completion time and the duration estimates for succeeding activities. The latest start time is calculated by subtracting the activity's duration estimate from the activity's latest finish time. The latest finish time for a particular activity must be the same as or earlier than the earliest of all the latest start times of all the activities emerging directly from that particular activity.

The total slack for a particular path through the network is common to and shared among all activities on that path. If it is positive, it represents the maximum amount of time that the activities on a path can be delayed without jeopardizing completion of the project by its required completion time. If total slack is negative, it represents the amount of time that the activities on that path must be accelerated in order to complete the project by its required completion time. If it is zero, the activities on that path do not need to be accelerated but cannot be delayed. The critical path is the longest (or most time-consuming) path of activities in the network diagram and represents a series of activities that cannot be delayed without delaying the entire project.

CHAPTER TWELVE

SCHEDULE CONTROL

Jack Gido, James P. Clements

Once a project plan has been established, it must be implemented. This means performing the work according to the plan and controlling the work so that the project scope is accomplished within budget and on schedule. Once the project starts, it is necessary to monitor its progress to ensure that everything is going according to the plan. This involves measuring actual progress and comparing it to planned progress. If at any time the project is not proceeding according to plan, corrective action must be taken and replanning must be done.

Chapter Eleven showed how to establish a baseline plan and a schedule. Once a project actually starts, it is necessary to monitor the progress to ensure that everything is going according to schedule. This involves measuring actual progress and comparing it to the schedule. If the project appears to be behind schedule, corrective action must be taken. A project that is too far behind schedule may be difficult to get back on track.

The key to effective project control is to measure actual progress and compare it to planned progress on a timely and regular basis and to take necessary corrective action immediately. Problems will not go away without corrective intervention. Based on actual progress and consideration of other changes that may occur, it is possible to calculate an updated project schedule regularly and forecast whether the project will finish ahead of or behind its required completion time.

Note: Adapted from Jack Gido and James P. Clements, *Successful Project Management*, South-Western College Publishing, 1999.

This chapter covers the details of controlling a project, focusing mainly on the critical role of controlling the scheduling to ensure that the work gets done on time.

Project Control Process

The project control process requires regularly gathering data on project performance, comparing actual performance to planned performance, and taking corrective actions if actual performance falls behind planned performance. This process must occur regularly throughout the project.

Figure 12.1 illustrates the steps in the project control process. It starts with establishing a baseline plan that shows how the project scope (tasks) will be accomplished on time (schedule) and within budget (resources, costs). Once this baseline plan is agreed to by the customer and the contractor or project team, the project can start.

A regular reporting period should be established for comparing actual with planned progress. Reporting may be daily, weekly, biweekly, or monthly, depending on the complexity or overall duration of the project. If a project is expected to last a month, the reporting period might be as short as a day. On the other hand, if it is expected to run five years, the reporting period might be a month.

During each reporting period two kinds of data or information need to be collected:

1. *Data on actual performance.* This includes the actual time that activities were started or finished, or both, and the actual costs expended and committed.
2. *Information on any changes to the project scope, schedule, and budget.* These changes could be initiated by the customer or the project team, or they could be the result of an unanticipated occurrence such as a natural disaster, a labor strike, or the resignation of a key project team member.

Once changes are incorporated into the plan and agreed to by the customer, a new baseline plan has to be established. The scope, schedule, and budget of the new plan may be different from those of the original one.

The data and information must be collected in a timely manner and used to calculate an updated project schedule and budget. For example, if project reporting is done monthly, data and information should be obtained as late as possible in that monthly period so that when an updated schedule and budget are calculated, they are based on the latest information. If the project manager gathers

FIGURE 12.1. PROJECT CONTROL PROCESS.

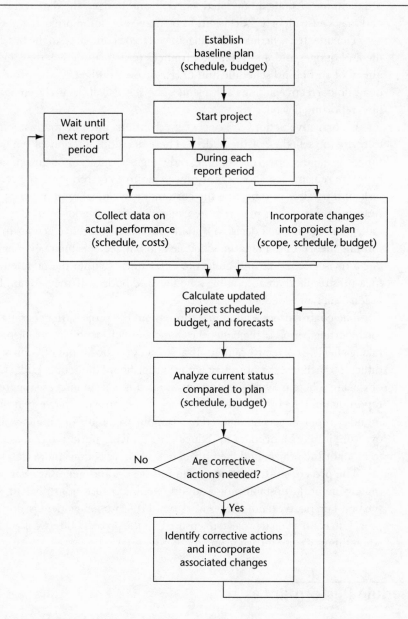

data at the beginning of the month and then waits until the end of the month to use them to calculate an updated schedule and budget, the data will be outdated and may cause incorrect decisions to be made about the project.

The updated schedule and budget need to be compared to the baseline schedule and budget and analyzed for variances to determine whether the project is ahead of or behind schedule and under or over budget. If the project status is okay, no corrective actions are needed; the status will be analyzed again for the next reporting period.

If corrective actions are necessary, decisions must be made regarding how to revise the schedule or the budget. These decisions often involve a trade-off of time, cost, and scope. For example, reducing the duration of an activity may require increasing costs to pay for more resources or reducing the scope of the task (and possibly not meeting the customer's technical requirements). Similarly, reducing project costs may require using materials of a lower quality than originally planned. Once a decision is made on which corrective actions to take, they must be incorporated into the schedule and budget. It is then necessary to calculate a revised schedule and budget to determine whether the planned corrective measures result in an acceptable schedule and budget. If they do not, further revisions will be needed.

The control process continues throughout the project. In general, the shorter the reporting period is, the better the chances are of identifying problems early and taking effective corrective actions. If a project gets too far out of control, it may be difficult to achieve the objective without sacrificing the scope, budget, schedule, or quality. There may be situations in which it is wise to increase the frequency of reporting until the project is back on track. For example, if a five-year project with monthly reporting is endangered by a slipping schedule or an increasing budget overrun, it may be prudent to reduce the reporting period to one week in order to monitor the project and the impact of corrective actions more closely.

The project control process is an important and necessary part of project management. Just establishing a sound baseline plan is not sufficient, since even the best-laid plans do not always work out. Project management is a proactive approach to controlling a project, to ensure that the project objective is achieved even when things do not go according to plan.

Schedule Performance

Throughout a project, some activities will be completed on time, some will be finished ahead of schedule, and others will be finished later than scheduled. Actual progress—whether faster or slower than planned—will have an effect on the schedule of the remaining, uncompleted activities of the project. Specifically, the actual finish times (AF) of completed activities will determine the earliest start and earliest finish times for the remaining activities in the network diagram, as well as the total slack.

Figure 12.2 is a network diagram for a simple project of wallpapering a room. It shows that the earliest the project can finish is Day 15 (the sum of the durations of the three activities: 7 + 5 + 3). Since the required completion time is Day 20, the project has a total slack of five days.

Suppose that activity 1, "Remove Old Wallpaper," is actually finished on Day 10 rather than on Day 7 as planned, because it turns out to be more difficult than anticipated. (See the bottom row of Figure 12.2.) This means that the earliest start and finish times for activities 2 and 3 will be three days later than on the original schedule. Because "Remove Old Wallpaper" is actually finished on Day 10, the estimated start (ES) for "Patch Walls" will be Day 10, and its estimated finish (EF) will be Day 15. Following through with the forward calculations, we find that "Put Up New Wallpaper" will have an ES of Day 15 and an EF of Day 18. Comparing this new EF of the last activity to the required completion time of Day 20, we find a difference of two days. The total slack got worse; it changed in a negative direction, from +5 days to +2 days. This example illustrates how the actual finish times of activities have a ripple effect, altering the remaining activities' earliest start and finish times and the total slack.

It is helpful to indicate on the network diagram which activities have been completed. One method is to crosshatch or shade the activity box, as was done in the second row of Figure 12.2.

FIGURE 12.2. EFFECT OF ACTUAL FINISH TIMES.

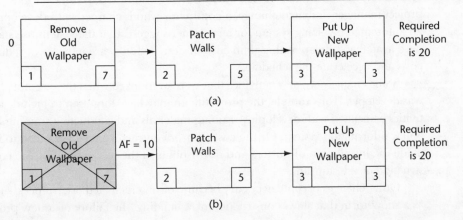

(a)

(b)

Incorporating Project Changes into the Schedule

Throughout a project, changes may occur that have an impact on the schedule. These changes might be initiated by the customer or the project team, or they might be the result of something unanticipated. For example, a home buyer tells the builder that the family room should be larger and the bedroom windows should be relocated. Or a customer tells the project team developing an information system that the company has just decided that the system must have the capability to produce a previously unmentioned set of reports and graphics.

These types of changes represent revisions to the original project scope and will have an impact on the schedule and cost, with the degree of impact depending on when the changes are requested. If they are requested early in the project, they may have a smaller impact on cost and schedule than if the request comes later in the project. For example, changing the size of the family room and relocating the bedroom windows would be relatively easy if the house were still being designed and the drawings being prepared. If the changes were requested after the framing was put up and the windows were installed, the impact on costs and schedule would be far greater.

When the customer requests a change, the contractor or project team should estimate the impact on the project budget and schedule and then obtain customer approval before proceeding. If the customer approves the proposed revisions to the project schedule and budget, any additional tasks, revised duration estimates, and material and labor costs should be incorporated.

An example of a change initiated by a project team is the decision by a team that is planning a town fair to eliminate all amusement rides for adults because of space limitations and insurance costs. The project plan would then have to be revised to delete or modify all activities involving adult rides. As an example of a project manager–initiated change, a contractor who is charged with developing an automated invoicing system for a customer suggests that the system use standard available software rather than custom-designed software in order to reduce costs and accelerate the schedule.

Some changes are new activities that were overlooked when the original plan was developed. For example, the project team may have forgotten to include activities associated with developing training materials and conducting training for a new information system. Or the customer or contractor may have failed to include the installation of gutters and downspouts in the work scope for the construction of a restaurant.

Other changes become necessary because of unanticipated occurrences, such as a snowstorm that slows construction of a building, the failure of a new product to pass quality tests, or the untimely death or resignation of a key member of a project team.

Still other changes can result from adding detail to the network diagram as the project moves forward. No matter what level of detail is used in the initial network diagram, there will be some activities that can be broken down further as the project progresses.

Any type of change—whether initiated by the customer, contractor, project manager, a team member, or an unanticipated event—will require a modification to the plan in terms of scope, budget, and/or schedule. When such changes are agreed on, a new baseline plan is established and used as the benchmark against which actual project performance will be compared.

With respect to the project schedule, changes can result in the addition or deletion of activities, the resequencing of activities, the changing of activities' duration estimates, or a new required completion time for the project.

Updating the Project Schedule

Network-based planning and scheduling allows project schedules to be dynamic. Because the network plan (diagram) and schedule (tabulation) are separate, they are much easier to update manually than a traditional Gantt chart is. Project management software packages are available to assist with the automated generation of schedules, network diagrams, budgets, and even network-to-Gantt-chart conversions.

Once data have been collected on the actual finish times of completed activities and the effects of any project changes, an updated project schedule can be calculated. (These calculations are based on the methodology explained in Chapter Eleven.) The earliest start and finish times for the remaining activities are calculated by working forward through the network, but they are based on the actual finish times of completed activities and the estimated durations of the uncompleted activities. The latest start and finish times for the uncompleted activities are calculated by working backward through the network.

As an illustration of the calculation of an updated schedule, consider the network diagram shown in Figure 12.3 for the consumer market study project outlined in Chapter Eleven. Assume the following completed activities:

- Activity 1, "Identify Target Consumers," actually finished on Day 2.
- Activity 2, "Develop Draft Questionnaire," actually finished on Day 11.
- Activity 3, "Pilot-Test Questionnaire," actually finished on Day 30.

FIGURE 12.3. NETWORK DIAGRAM FOR CONSUMER MARKET STUDY PROJECT SHOWING ACTUAL PROGRESS AND CHANGES.

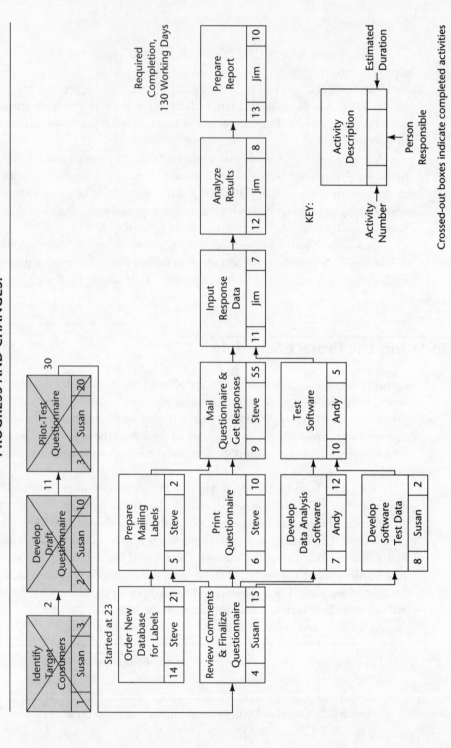

In addition, there were two project changes. First, it was discovered that the database to be used to prepare the mailing labels was not up to date, so a new database needs to be purchased before the mailing labels can be prepared. This new database was ordered on Day 23. It will take twenty-one days to get it from the supplier. Second, a preliminary review of comments from the pilot test of the questionnaire indicated that substantial revisions to the questionnaire were required. Therefore, the duration estimate for activity 4 needs to be increased from five days to fifteen days.

The network diagram in Figure 12.3 incorporates the information on completed activities and project changes. Figure 12.4 shows the updated schedule. Note that the total slack for the critical path is now −5 days, instead of the +2 days in the baseline schedule in Figure 11.15 in Chapter Eleven. The anticipated project completion time is now Day 135, which is beyond the required completion time of 130 days.

Approaches to Schedule Control

Schedule control has four steps:

1. Analyzing the schedule to determine which areas may need corrective action
2. Deciding what specific corrective actions should be taken
3. Revising the plan to incorporate the chosen corrective actions
4. Recalculating the schedule to evaluate the effects of the planned corrective actions

If the planned corrective actions do not result in an acceptable schedule, these steps need to be repeated.

Throughout a project, each time a schedule is recalculated—whether it is after actual data or project changes are incorporated or after corrective actions are planned—it is necessary to analyze the newly calculated schedule to determine whether it needs further attention. The analysis should include identifying the critical path and any paths of activities that have a negative slack, as well as paths where slippages have occurred (the slack got worse) compared with the previously calculated schedule.

A concentrated effort to accelerate project progress must be applied to the paths with negative slack. The amount of slack should determine the priority with which these concentrated efforts are applied. For example, the path with the most negative slack should be given top priority.

FIGURE 12.4. UPDATED SCHEDULE FOR THE CONSUMER MARKET STUDY PROJECT.

	Activity	Responsible	Estimated Duration	Earliest		Latest		Total Slack	Actual Finish
				Start	Finish	Start	Finish		
1	Identify Target Consumers	Susan							2
2	Develop Draft Questionnaire	Susan							11
3	Pilot-Test Questionnaire	Susan							30
4	Review Comments & Finalize Questionnaire	Susan	15	30	45	25	40	−5	
5	Prepare Mailing Labels	Steve	2	45	47	48	50	3	
6	Print Questionnaire	Steve	10	45	55	40	50	−5	
7	Develop Data Analysis Software	Andy	12	45	57	88	100	43	
8	Develop Software Test Data	Susan	2	45	47	98	100	53	
9	Mail Questionnaire & Get Responses	Steve	55	55	110	50	105	−5	
10	Test Software	Andy	5	57	62	100	105	43	
11	Input Response Data	Jim	7	110	117	105	112	−5	
12	Analyze Results	Jim	8	117	125	112	120	−5	
13	Prepare Report	Jim	10	125	135	120	130	−5	
14	Order New Database for Labels	Steve	21	23	44	27	48	4	

Corrective actions that will eliminate the negative slack from the project schedule must be identified. These corrective actions must reduce the duration estimates for activities on the negative-slack paths. Remember that the slack for a path of activities is shared among all the activities on that path. Therefore, a change in the estimated duration of any activity on that path will cause a corresponding change in the slack for that path.

An analysis of a path of activities that has negative slack should focus on two kinds of activities. First are activities that are near term (that is, in progress or to be started in the immediate future). It is much wiser to take aggressive corrective action to reduce the durations of activities that will be done in the near term than to plan to reduce the durations of activities that are scheduled sometime in the future. If you postpone until the distant future taking corrective action that will reduce the durations of activities, you may find that the negative slack has steadily deteriorated. As the project progresses, there is always less time remaining in which corrective action can be taken.

From Figure 12.4, we can see that it would be better to try to reduce the durations of the near-term activities on the critical path, such as "Review Comments and Finalize Questionnaire" or "Print Questionnaire," than to put off corrective action until the last activity, "Prepare Report."

The second kind of activities to focus on are those that have long duration estimates. Taking corrective measures that will reduce a twenty-day activity by 20 percent—that is, by four days—has a larger impact than totally eliminating a one-day activity. Usually longer-duration activities present the opportunity for larger reductions.

Look again at Figure 12.4. There may be more opportunity to reduce the fifty-five-day duration estimate for "Mail Questionnaire and Get Responses" by five days (9 percent) than to reduce the shorter duration estimates of other activities on the critical path.

There are various approaches to reducing the duration estimates of activities. One obvious way is to apply more resources to speed up an activity, perhaps by assigning more people to work on the activity or asking the people already working on it to put in more hours per day or more days per week. Additional appropriate resources might be transferred from concurrent activities that have positive slack. Sometimes, however, adding people to an activity may in fact result in the activity's taking longer, because the people already assigned to the activity are diverted from their work in order to help the newcomers get up to speed. Another approach is to assign a person with greater expertise or more experience to perform or help with the activity, so as to get it done in a shorter time than was possible with the less experienced people originally assigned to it.

Reducing the scope or requirements for an activity is another way to reduce its duration estimates. For example, it might be acceptable to put only one coat of paint on a room rather than two coats, as originally planned. In an extreme case, the decision may be to eliminate some activities, deleting them and their durations from the schedule.

Increasing productivity through improved methods or technology is yet another approach to reducing activities' durations. For example, instead of having people keyboard data from a customer survey into a computer database, optical scanning equipment might be used.

Once specific corrective actions to reduce the negative slack have been decided on, the duration estimates for the appropriate activities must be revised in the network plan. Then a revised schedule is calculated to evaluate whether the planned corrective actions reduce the negative slack as anticipated.

In most cases, eliminating negative slack by reducing durations of activities will involve a trade-off in the form of an increase in costs or a reduction in scope. If the project is way behind schedule (it has substantial negative slack), a substantial increase in costs or reduction in work scope or quality (or both) may be required to get it back on schedule. This decision could jeopardize elements of the overall project objective: scope, budget, schedule, or quality. In some cases, the customer and contractor or project team may have to acknowledge that one or more of these elements cannot be achieved. For example, the customer may have to extend the required completion time for the entire project, or there may be a dispute over who should absorb any increased cost to accelerate the schedule: the contractor or the customer.

Some contracts include a provision whereby the customer pays the contractor a bonus if the project is completed ahead of schedule. Conversely, some contracts include a penalty provision: the customer can reduce the final payment to the contractor if the project is not completed on time. Some of these penalties can be substantial. In either of these situations, effective schedule control is crucial.

The key to effective schedule control is to address aggressively any paths with negative or deteriorating slack values as soon as they are identified rather than hoping that the situation will improve as the project goes on. Addressing schedule problems early will minimize the negative impact on cost and scope. If a project falls too far behind, getting back on schedule becomes more difficult, and it comes at the cost of spending more money or reducing the scope or quality.

Projects that do not have negative slack need attention too; it is important not to let the slack deteriorate by accepting delays and slippages. If a project is ahead of schedule, a concentrated effort should be made to *keep* it ahead of schedule. Project meetings are a good forum for addressing schedule control issues.

Time-Cost Trade-Off

The time-cost trade-off methodology is used to reduce the project duration incrementally with the smallest associated increase in incremental cost. It is based on the following assumptions:

1. Each activity has two pairs of duration and cost estimates: normal and crash. The *normal time* is the estimated length of time required to perform the activity under normal conditions, according to the plan. The *normal cost* is the estimated cost to complete the activity in the normal time. The *crash time* is the shortest estimated length of time in which the activity can be completed. The *crash cost* is the estimated cost to complete the activity in the crash time. In Figure 12.5, each of the four activities has a pair of normal (N) time and cost estimates and a pair of crash (C) time and cost estimates. The estimated normal time to perform activity A is seven weeks, and its estimated normal cost is $50,000. The crash time for this activity is five weeks, and the cost to complete the activity in this duration is $62,000.

2. An activity's duration can be incrementally accelerated from its normal time to its crash time by applying more resources: assigning more people, working overtime, using more equipment, and so on. Increased costs will be associated with expediting the activity.

3. An activity cannot be completed in less than its crash time, no matter how many additional resources are applied. For example, activity A cannot be completed in less than five weeks, no matter how many more resources are used or how much money is spent.

4. The resources necessary to reduce an activity's estimated duration from its normal time to its crash time will be available when needed.

FIGURE 12.5. NETWORK WITH NORMAL CRASH TIMES AND THEIR COSTS.

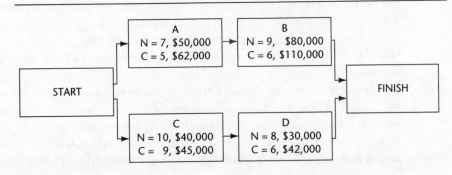

5. Within the range between an activity's normal and crash points, the relationship between time and cost is linear. Each activity has its own cost per time period for accelerating the activity's duration from its normal time to its crash time. This acceleration cost per time period is calculated as follows:

$$\frac{\text{Crash Cost} - \text{Normal Cost}}{\text{Normal Time} - \text{Crash Time}} \qquad (12.1)$$

For example, in Figure 12.5, the cost per week to accelerate activity A from its normal time to its crash time is

$$\frac{\$62,000 - \$50,000}{7 \text{ weeks} - 5 \text{ weeks}} = \frac{\$12,000}{2 \text{ weeks}} = \$6,000 \text{ per week} \qquad (12.2)$$

The network diagram in Figure 12.5 has two paths from start to finish: path A-B and path C-D. If we consider only the normal duration estimates, path A-B will take sixteen weeks to complete, and path C-D will take eighteen weeks to complete. Therefore, the earliest the project can be finished based on these time estimates is eighteen weeks: the length of its critical path, made up of activities C and D. The total project cost, based on the cost associated with performing each activity in its normal time, is:

$$\$50,000 + \$80,000 + \$40,000 + \$30,000 = \$200,000.$$

If all the activities were performed in their respective crash times, path A-B would take eleven weeks, and path C-D would take fifteen weeks. The earliest the project can be finished based on the crash time estimates is fifteen weeks, which is three weeks earlier than if the activities were performed in their normal times.

It is usually not necessary or even constructive to crash all the activities. For example, in Figure 12.5, we want to crash only the appropriate activities by the amount necessary to accelerate project completion from eighteen weeks to fifteen weeks. Any additional crashing of activities will merely increase total project cost; it will not reduce the total project duration any further because that is determined by the length of the critical path. In other words, expediting activities not on the critical path will not reduce the project completion time but will increase total project cost.

The objective of the time-cost trade-off method is to determine the shortest project completion time based on crashing the activities that result in the smallest increase in total project cost. To accomplish this, it is necessary to shorten the total project duration, one time period at a time, crashing only activities on the critical path(s) and with the lowest acceleration cost per time period. From Figure 12.5, we determined that based on normal time and cost estimates, the earliest the project could be completed is eighteen weeks (as determined by the critical path C-D), at a total project cost of $200,000. The cost per week of accelerating each of the activities is as follows:

Activity A, $6,000 per week

Activity B, $10,000 per week

Activity C, $5,000 per week

Activity D, $6,000 per week

To reduce the total project duration from eighteen to seventeen weeks requires first identifying the critical path, which is C-D, and then determining which activity on the critical path can be accelerated at the lowest cost per week. Activity C costs $5,000 per week to accelerate, and activity D costs $6,000 per week to accelerate. Therefore, expediting activity C is less expensive. If activity C is crashed one week (from ten weeks to nine weeks), the total project duration is shortened from eighteen weeks to seventeen weeks, but the total project cost increases by $5,000, to $205,000.

To shorten the total project duration one more time period, from seventeen weeks to sixteen weeks, we must again identify the critical path. The durations of the two paths are sixteen weeks for A-B and seventeen weeks for C-D. Therefore, the critical path is still C-D, and it must be reduced again. Looking at path C-D, we see that although activity C has a lower acceleration cost per week than activity D, we cannot accelerate activity C any further since we reached its crash time of nine weeks when the project was reduced from eighteen to seventeen weeks. Therefore, the only choice is to accelerate activity D by one week, moving it from eight weeks to seven weeks. This reduces the duration of critical path C-D to sixteen weeks, but the total project cost increases by $6,000 (the cost per week for accelerating activity D), from $205,000 to $211,000.

Once again, let us reduce the project duration another week, from sixteen to fifteen weeks. If we look at our two paths, we see that they are now of equal duration, sixteen weeks, so we now have two critical paths. To reduce the total project duration from sixteen to fifteen weeks, it is necessary to accelerate each path by one week. In looking at path C-D, we see that the only activity with any remaining time to be crashed is activity D. It can be crashed one more week, from seven to six weeks, at an additional cost of $6,000. To accelerate path A-B by one week, we have a choice of crashing activity A or B. Activity A has a $6,000 cost per week to accelerate, compared with a $10,000 per week rate for activity B. Therefore, to reduce the total project duration from sixteen to fifteen weeks, we need to crash activities D and A one week each. This increases the total project cost by $12,000 ($6,000 + $6,000), from $211,000 to $223,000.

Let us try again to shorten the total project duration by one week, this time from fifteen to fourteen weeks. We again have two critical paths with the same duration of fifteen weeks. Therefore, both must be accelerated by one week. However, in looking at path C-D, we see that both activities are already at their crash time—nine weeks and six weeks, respectively—and therefore cannot be expedited any further. Accelerating path A-B would be of no value, because it would increase the total project cost but not reduce the total project duration. Our ability to reduce the total project duration is limited by the fact that path C-D cannot be reduced any further.

Figure 12.6 displays the incremental acceleration in total project completion and the associated incremental increase in total project cost. It indicates that reducing the total project duration by one week would increase the total project cost by $5,000. To reduce it by two weeks would cost $11,000, and to reduce it by three weeks would cost $23,000.

If all four activities were crashed, the total cost of the project would be $259,000, but it would still not be completed any earlier than fifteen weeks. Using the time-cost trade-off method, we were able to reduce the project duration from eighteen weeks to fifteen weeks at an additional cost of $23,000 by selectively crashing the critical activities with the lowest acceleration cost per time period. Crashing *all* the activities would have resulted in a waste of $36,000 because no reduction in total project duration beyond fifteen weeks could be achieved.

Summary

Once a project starts, it is necessary to monitor the progress to ensure that everything is going according to schedule. This involves measuring actual progress and comparing it to the schedule. If at any time the project falls behind schedule, cor-

FIGURE 12.6. TIME-COST TRADE-OFF.

Project Duration (Weeks)	Critical Path(s)	Total Project Cost
18	C-D	**$200,000**
17	C-D	$200,000 + $5,000 = **$205,000**
16	C-D	$205,000 + $6,000 = **$211,000**
15	C-D, A-B	$211,000 + $6,000 + $6,000 = **$223,000**

rective action must be taken. The key to effective project control is to measure actual progress and compare it to planned progress on a timely and regular basis and to take necessary corrective action immediately. Based on actual progress and on consideration of other changes that may occur, it is possible to calculate an updated project schedule regularly and forecast whether the project will finish ahead of or behind its required completion time.

Schedule control involves four steps: analyzing the schedule to determine which areas may need corrective action, deciding which specific corrective actions should be taken, revising the plan to incorporate the chosen corrective actions, and recalculating the schedule to evaluate the effects of the planned corrective actions. Corrective actions that will eliminate the negative slack from the project schedule must be identified. These corrective actions must reduce the duration estimates for activities on the negative-slack paths. When analyzing a path of activities that has negative slack, you should focus on two kinds of activities: activities that are near term and activities that have long duration estimates.

There are various approaches to reducing the duration estimates of activities. These include applying more resources to speed up activity, assigning individuals with greater expertise or more experience to work on the activity, reducing the scope or requirements for the activity, and increasing productivity through improved methods or technology.

The time-cost trade-off methodology is used to incrementally reduce the project duration with the smallest associated increase in incremental cost. It is based on the assumptions that each activity has a normal and a crash duration and cost estimate, that an activity's duration can be incrementally accelerated by applying more resources, and that the relationship between time and cost is linear.

CHAPTER THIRTEEN

PROJECT RESOURCE PLANNING

Marie Scotto

There is a terrific Dilbert cartoon about resource planning that goes something like this:

Director: I need an estimate of your project resource needs for the coming year.

Manager: But I don't know what projects I will be working on yet.

Director: Oh, I just need a ballpark figure. Don't worry; you don't have to be too specific.

Manager: I'm not falling for that one again! If I give you a figure, you'll remember it as a commitment, and you'll expect me to hit it on the nose at the end of the year.

Director: Oh, don't be silly. I just need a figure.

Manager: Okay: twenty thousand man-hours.

Director: That's too much. I'll make it ten thousand.

(One year later)

Director: Can you explain why you overran your ten thousand-man-hour budget?

Manager: (with head in hands) Do you see an image when you look in the mirror?

We laugh at such spoofs because they hit a nerve: we recognize in the characters either ourselves or someone we know very well. This particular cartoon makes three quite significant points about project resource planning:

1. We are asked to determine resource needs before we have a clear idea of the size of the workload.
2. Business managers are suspicious of work estimates and have a tendency to believe they are excessive (even though for years, business projects have overrun both their effort and duration estimates).
3. Project estimates, even when they are ballpark figures, are treated as commitments.

The truth about project resource planning is that no one knows exactly the extent of the resources needed for business projects, which are unique on-time work efforts. The truth about such statements is that no one wants to hear them. However, resource planning for business projects is one of the most serious project management problems, so it is time to take a long, hard look at exactly this issue.

Why Are We So Often Understaffed for Project Work?

Ask any project manager what his or her main problem is and the reply is likely to be "insufficient staff." But the main purpose of project planning is to ensure that commitments can be met with the amount of staff one has available or, at the very least, identify the staff required to do the job. So assuming project planning is being done effectively, why would any project ever run short of resources? Or is the planning ineffective, and is that the problem? What is being done wrong? Why do projects so often miss delivery dates, overrun budgets, and lament the lack of staff?

The answer is that there are a lot of reasons, most of them having to do with the fact that business organizations were not designed to handle projects, so project management techniques are misapplied. Over the past fifteen years or so, as the business world has experimented using project management for projects, we have bemoaned the failure of business projects to meet our expectations. Some published statistics claim that more than 80 percent of all business projects overrun both their resource and calendar time budgets. So companies invested in project management software, spent millions on project management training, joined the Project Management Institute in droves, and worked on building high-performance teams, but we still have not found a way to make it work, especially as it relates to resource planning.

The plain truth is that the fit is bad. Project management concepts do not fit the average business organization. Project management was designed for a highly structured industry (construction) with both performance and cost standards and enforcement agencies to require compliance to industry-approved guidelines.

The formal project world is very different from the world of business. Except for production lines and some clerical areas, the average business area that works in project mode is relatively unstructured, with few documented procedures, no performance history, few work standards, and fewer agents to enforce what standards there are. If businesses want to use project management techniques effectively, they must first make some substantive changes to the way they operate and then learn about project management itself. They must learn how to adapt those concepts that do not fit their environments well, and how to apply other concepts (that do fit) from a mode of project management designed especially for nonstandard work.

Business Versus Project Organizations

Business organizations were designed for mass production: for repetitive work that could be broken into small tasks. As long as the consumer environment was relatively predictable and stable, the hierarchical business structure worked well. Businesses knew well in advance what they were going to produce, designed efficient processes to create and distribute the product, planned to produce it for a number of years, organized in support of that process, and since the market was hungry, customers were generally happy to have whatever they produced.

The hierarchy provided the answer to efficient mass production, and therefore affordable products. As long as there was a scarcity of product on the market, the producers could call the shots. As long as the producers were calling the shots, deciding what they would produce and how they would produce it, the hierarchy worked. Even in today's fast-paced, changing business environment, there is still a need for hierarchy for work that is relatively stable and highly repetitive (though some management thinkers have suggested otherwise).

But increasingly companies must be able to improve products or create totally new products and services with great frequency. Some industry leaders have designed methods to "mass customize" their products as a competitive edge. Such agility and responsiveness takes an ability to work in a much less predictable mode, which itself calls for a far more structured environment than the average business area employs. Just as the hierarchy imposed structure and served mass production well, the environment that has served project management also imposes structure, in both similar and different ways:

- The project world, which very successfully serves construction projects, is engaged in highly structured work for which there are industry-accepted cost standards. Project estimators do not guess at the probable cost of specific jobs; they refer to industry standards, which are used as the base for all estimating.

- The project world is staffed with day workers on an as-needed basis.
- The project world uses professional craftspeople who are normally licensed to perform specific types of work. If the project runs short of resources, there is a large community of licensed, union crafts workers available to hire.
- Individual jobs are standard, which means tasks are also standard. Workers therefore can go from project to project and be productive almost immediately.
- The project world accepts the concept of contingency budgets to buffer expected unknowns. All fixed-price bids include "unallocated" budget for contingency.
- In the project world, fixed-price bids are not requested until complete job specifications have been drafted.

It is important to understand that the same attention to standards, details, and data that supported the industrial world for mass production must now be applied to the project world for rapid project performance. Although there has been a recent emphasis on flat organizations, empowered teams, less structure, and the need to push authority down to lower levels of the hierarchy, we are now witnessing the chaos that results in organizations' having too few designed processes.

"Structure follows strategy," or so Peter Drucker believes. So do systems. The environments we work in and the systems that support them must be designed to fit the strategic directions the organization is going in. Environments must be designed to support the kinds of work the organization expects to do. Projects are much different from repetitive functional work. They do not produce mirror image products. They are one-time efforts, usually unique and rarely repeated. The biggest difference between the project organization and the hierarchy is that the hierarchy is rigidly structured to produce one and only one product, while the project organization must be structured to produce a variety of products. One-time, unique efforts require a flexible environment. The well-structured environment with documented process choices supports flexibility better than an unstructured environment that depends on the creativity of individuals. But the structure must be project focused. Existing hierarchies are not well suited for project work.

Projects usually have an urgency: the required deliverable is needed as soon as possible. That means the business needs access to the most expert workers in the organization. Where the hierarchy required separation between functions, projects often require functional experts to work together. Projects also need at least a core of workers who are able to focus on the work of the project until it is completed. Workers within the hierarchy generally have ongoing functional responsibilities that can distract them, sometimes totally, from the project. Even if project resource needs were understood perfectly at the planning stage, the business would experience shortfalls as functional employees are pulled off projects to focus on day-to-day problems.

Because the business environment or our expectations have not yet adjusted properly to support project work, we have not yet developed a methodology for project success that can be repeated and improved. Businesses experience resource shortages because they are still using too many planning approaches that, while effective in the production hierarchy, are not appropriate in the project organization.

This is true of both types of business organization that engage in project work: the organization that does project work for internal clients and the organization that is in the business of doing project work for outside clients. For the sake of clarity within the rest of this chapter, I shall call these, respectively, internal project organizations and consultant shops.

Defining Resource Needs: Issues

A number of issues cause problems in defining business project resource needs.

Business Versus Project Planning

Few business managers appreciate the extent to which working in project mode differs from normal functional operations. Project management was never designed to work properly in the average business organization. It was designed for a community of day workers who are assigned as needed, not for staff workers who are paid whether the business needs them or not. For that reason, business projects are hampered by the fact that their organizations rarely, if ever, staff up to peak requirements. And they never hire more staff than they can justify with known facts. In other words, the concept of contingency planning is not easily accepted within the business organization, though it has always been an integral part of formal project planning. This is true for both internal and consultant project organizations.

When business managers plan project requirements, they are pressured to plan for minimum, not maximum, resources. Although each manager would like to own as many resources as she thinks she will need, the organization challenges her to justify each resource. Unless her justification is strong, management cuts budget allotments to the lowest possible level. The business community believes in understaffing, which it can prove is generally good business most of the time.

When workers have to be paid whether they work or not, good business practice is to understaff. The value of this strategy is so generally accepted that the stock market has been known to respond to an announcement of significant staff reductions by immediately increasing the price of that company's stock. Many industry leading companies boast of being "lean and mean." Running a business organization on the lean side makes good sense. At least, it made perfectly good sense for the mass production hierarchy that knew well in advance the work it would have to do. If and when the business required more resources for known peaks, such as Christmastime in the retail industry or even unexpected peaks, it was always possible to add overtime hours for hourly paid workers. Beyond that, they could hire temporary or part-time employees to fill in. In other words, first the need had to be experienced; then the staff was expanded.

For salaried employees, business organizations were even more tempted to underplan. Since salaried workers are neither limited in the amount of time they can work nor paid for extra hours, underplanning ensures an economic use of corporate resources. The salaried employee's workweek expands with pressure and shrinks as pressure is reduced, while payroll remains static. Of course, when workloads are too heavy for staff employees to handle, even with expanded workweeks, or when staff lacks the required skills, businesses turn to contract workers. Recently both consultant shops and internal shops have been leaning more heavily on contracted resources to augment tight project schedules.

Unlike the construction industry, which uses skilled crafts workers, the business organization, especially when in project mode, needs skills that are not readily available in the outside world. Except at the very lowest task levels or as strategic advisers, contracted resources are rarely as productive as internal staff who know the company and its processes well. And they are very much more expensive. One company I know uses a contract labor posting charge of $19,000 a month for computer programmers, a fairly common amount. Yet even with such enormous costs, there are some companies that have had contract workers on premises for five, seven, and even ten years. How many staff could a company hire for $228,000 a year, even with benefits? Contract labor is used liberally because staff budgets are historically underplanned and therefore too limited to accommodate the workload.

Underplanning should not be confused with empire building. Due to the penchant of functional managers' using last year's budget to build on and the fact that functional managers were often paid relative to the size of their staff, some functional areas have wound up with much larger staffs than required. The result was the birth of the downsizing phenomenon. But simply because the hierarchy unwittingly bred empire building and unnecessarily fat areas, it does not change the fact that business has always attempted to underplan and highly values this ability. This is especially true since the downsizing phenomenon.

In contrast, in the world of formal project management, like the construction industry, underplanning is not very useful. Contractors need to plan for unknowns and unknowables. This means there must be excess in the plan to accommodate things they cannot know at the planning stage. This concept is quite repulsive to business planners, but it makes absolute sense for project planners, especially those who work in the fixed-price world, where both the price and the delivery date are fixed. In such cases, regardless of how seriously anyone might underestimate the job, the contractor must deliver as promised. To be able to survive in such a world, there must be an accommodation of risk in all estimates. The formal project world historically allows contingency in all project plans. *Contingency* is budget for things we cannot identify but know will show up as the project proceeds.

For instance, if the estimated cost for a particular job at $100,000 with a duration of three months and an allowable profit of 10 percent, the effective project manager would never price the job at $110,000 with a promise to deliver within thirteen weeks. Recognizing that he will probably run into a number of unknowables within the job, he wisely inserts the cost of such risk into the bid. This is especially true if the contract carries liquidated damages: penalties that the contractor must pay for not delivering within the terms of the contract. Taking all issues into consideration, a more appropriate estimate for this job might be $127,000 (15 percent above cost plus profit), to be delivered within fifteen weeks. In the formal project world, contingencies of between 10 and 15 percent are common. In some areas, another 10 to 15 percent is kept in management reserve for possible additional needs not accommodated by normal contingency. So it is possible that even in this highly structured industry, some projects will come in 30 percent over original cost estimate and still be considered successful.

On the other hand are cases where the project manager bids especially low in order to get a particular job. When this happens, you may be sure he does so in the strong belief that the contract will require many in-progress changes to the original scope of work. It is often easier to inflate the cost of each change to accommodate extra work after one has the contract than to bid appropriately in the first place and chance losing the bid. One thing is certain: contractors who do not include enough contingency within their plans, either originally or for changes, will lose rather than profit on each job.

What, then, does this mean for the business manager? What seems immediately obvious is that project resource planning and business resource planning are quite different efforts, and we must use a sensible approach to minimize the differences.

First, since businesses pay people whether they work, they cannot hire people they are not sure will be needed. They must therefore plan to hire contract labor should the need arise. That is, when they plan projects, they need to give the more strategic tasks to employees who know the company and its products well, leaving tasks that are skills rather than information based for contract workers.

Second, businesses must ensure that all skills-based tasks and process steps are well documented. Contract workers can be productive only if there is enough documented instruction supporting the work they are asked to do. If they require too much mentoring, their use will greatly inflate the price of the job.

Third, businesses must introduce the concept of contingency into all project plans. Microsoft uses a "milestone" approach to managing its projects, with each milestone incorporating a 20 percent contingency. But although Microsoft sometimes misses published deadlines, it is much better than most other companies at managing large, complex projects. So if it uses 20 percent, I believe the average business organization should consider at least 30 percent until it is as structured as Microsoft.

The Need for a Standard Development Methodology

Basic to the construction industry's ability to use project management concepts so successfully is a standard methodology approved by the industry. The methodology is not so much a set of process steps as a standard set of small line-item jobs. Such work as "sandblast surface," "wash surface with acid," and "trowling floor, sidewalks" is identified by both crew size and cost per square foot. The business area that uses project management needs to identify the work required to create all project deliverables. At the very least, there should be a documented set of steps available to all projects. The deliverables from each step should be demonstrated in the form of exhibits within the process.

Naturally, the smaller the job step is, the more accurate both the estimating and the execution can be. However, the smaller the job steps, the more management attention will be needed. There is a system of measuring project accomplishment, known as *earned value,* that uses a set of rules for reporting progress that businesses could learn from. The most accurate way of reporting progress is on completed tasks. Earned value requires that tasks be small enough to be completed frequently enough to maintain control. The most common task size for business projects is less than one week. Microsoft sizes tasks at one day, and each developer must produce a deliverable every day. I believe that when tasks are much larger than one week's duration, projects can more easily run out of control.

There are two significant issues here: having small tasks improves the ability to maintain control during work in progress, and having standard tasks serves a number of purposes:

- A well-documented and -exhibited methodology imposes a standard project approach on all teams.

- It forms the basis of an ability to continually improve the development process
- It reduces planning time since teams no longer have to identify tasks for themselves.
- It supports improved resource planning by forming the basis of a performance database that could collect actual effort data for use in estimating on future projects

An Appropriate Estimating System

Before we can discuss the problems with estimating resource needs and how to overcome them, we need to recognize that there is a mode of project management designed specifically to address the special issues of high-risk, nonstandard work.

Since the early 1960s, when the U.S. Navy designed the project evaluation and review technique (PERT) system, there have been the two modes of project management, PERT and critical path management (CPM), that have been accepted and respected within the project community. CPM is the mode that supports the fixed-price world, using recognized cost standards. PERT is the mode that supports projects that must estimate costs without the benefit of accepted cost standards and often without even the benefit of performance history. Such projects are far riskier than are CPM projects. For that reason, CPM projects are said to operate in the "deterministic" mode, and PERT projects operate in the "probabilistic" mode. The deterministic mode supports fixed-price contracts, and the probabilistic mode supports cost-plus contracts. The problem is that the business world believes it can use a fixed approach, that is, being told before time what the cost will be and when delivery will be. In order to use such a mechanism, we would need far more information than we currently have or are ever likely to have.

CPM, for instance, is a system that analyzes the critical path of a project to determine the least costly, least time-consuming way to run the project. We know, for instance, that the direct costs of doing a specific task tend to increase as time is decreased, while indirect costs, those associated with the entire project, tend to decrease as time is decreased. The point, then, is to identify those tasks along the critical path whose costs will increase less per time period than the indirect project costs will decrease for the same time period. In that way, we both shorten the critical path and decrease the total project costs. The process of shortening task time by increasing the number of resources working on it is called crashing the task. (See also Chapter Twelve.) In order to do a proper job of crashing, one needs access to a number of data items—for instance, the standard task or job cost, the standard crew size, the standard duration, the cost of crashing per time period, and the minimum acceptable duration.

In the fixed-price world, computer programs help do the CPM analysis. In the business world, few of us have enough structure to employ standard task names on all projects. It is important to understand that project management functions very well in a highly structured, standardized environment. It cannot be expected to function the same way in a loose, "every team do its own thing" environment.

Rather than attempt to identify exactly the cost and time of business projects, businesses would be better served to use the PERT approach, which was designed to serve industries that lack the heavy structure of the construction industry. In the PERT approach, estimators attempt to identify the range of probable costs for each specific task. In the formal application of PERT, they even try to estimate the probable most likely point on the range to use. There is a calculation that adjusts the most likely estimate based on the size of the range. This sometimes leads to skewed task estimates, that is, a most likely estimate that is closer to one end of the range than the other. The interesting fact is that even when specific task estimates are skewed, when we calculate the critical path, the most likely for the entire path tends to follow normal distribution.

Those in the business world would certainly improve their performance by using normal distribution in estimating. In normal distribution, the most likely single probability occurs at the midpoint of the range and does not need to be estimated.

Figure 13.1 is a display of the type of cost range used in PERT estimating, with normal distribution imposed. In this example, the range of resources required is from 10 hours to 70 hours, with 40 hours, or the midpoint of the range, identified as the most likely number of resources needed. However, using the most likely would give only a 50 percent probability of success, since 40 hours represents only half the area under the curve. The lines on each side of the midpoint represent the standard deviations from the norm. We know a lot about standard distribution. We identify the size of each standard deviation by taking the entire range and dividing it into six equal parts. In our example, the range is 70 minus 10, or 60; 60 divided by 6 is 10, so each standard deviation is 10 hours distance from the midpoint and each other.

Another thing we know about standard deviation is that within the first standard deviation on each side of the midpoint, we have approximately 68 percent of all probabilities. This means that if we decide not to use the most likely estimate but increase the resource requirement by one standard distribution to the right, we increase our probabilities from 50 percent to 84 percent since half of the 68 percent lies between the midpoint and the first positive standard deviation. We would then use an estimate of 50 resource hours for this particular task.

We know so much about normal distribution that assuming the range is anywhere near reasonable, we can identify every probability within the range. The probability of meeting either the effort estimates or duration estimates depends

FIGURE 13.1

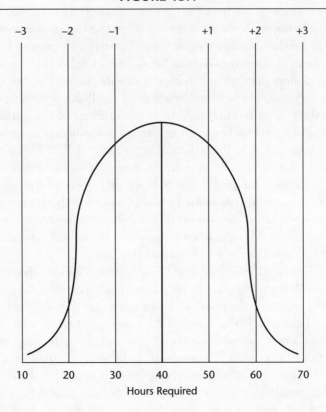

on the number of standard deviations by which the proposed project budgets exceeds the mean or midpoint. Table 13.1 identifies the probabilities of every other whole point along the range from -1 standard deviation to $+3$, or the end of the range. According to these statistics, we achieve close to an 85 percent probability by using the estimate that falls at the first positive standard deviation, or 50 hours. We achieve close to a 90 percent probability at $+1.3$ or 53 hours and a 95 percent probability at about $+1.7$ or 57 hours in the example.

   In addition to using a systematic method for estimating task size, the business needs to ensure the ability to improve the method as it gains experience. For that reason, it must document the items it is questioning in the search for both the most optimistic and the most pessimistic estimate. Many companies are now using computer systems to capture the questions used in estimating. They form the basis for future analysis when estimates deviate significantly from actuals. This brings us to another recommendation critical to the ability to improve resource estimates: that of collecting actuals to compare against estimates.

TABLE 13.1. PROBABILITY TABLE.

Number of Standard Deviations from the Midpoint	Probability of Meeting the Budget Estimates
3.0	.999
2.8	.997
2.6	.995
2.4	.993
2.2	.986
2.0	.977
1.8	.964
1.6	.945
1.4	.919
1.2	.885
1.0	.841
.8	.788
.6	.726
.4	.655
.2	.579
0	.50
2.2	.421
2.4	.345
2.6	.274
2.8	.212
−1.0	.159

The ability to improve resource estimates is paramount to good resource planning. But implementing a system to collect actuals that are honest and accurate ranges from difficult to impossible in the average business environment. Here is a situation where the business depends on workers to tell it the truth, whether it is a truth managers are comfortable with or not. Managers who question the fact that the worker took longer—sometimes much longer—than the estimate allowed are sending the message loud and clear that it is not in workers' best interest to tell the truth when that truth is unpleasant. Data collection systems that cannot collect accurate data are worthless. This is perhaps the single most difficult issue for many business managers.

The fact is that regardless of whether the worker could work within the estimate or not, it is the actual number of effort hours, not the estimate, that are real. A business that wishes to implement a project management system that can be improved and eventually help it achieve more and more project successes must be brutal in accepting reality and trying to determine objectively how to improve performance. While we may occasionally have workers who need educating in good production practices, more often than not, the reason for the failure is either that the estimate is woefully inadequate because it is not based on any tested data, or the systems that support project work are unsuitable and need to be improved.

Project Estimating with Insufficient Knowledge

It is difficult enough to design and implement an estimating system that gives the ability to predict resource requirements more accurately; that we are asked to do it before we have a clear idea of the work involved is counterproductive to any efforts made to improve resource planning. It is understandable that business managers want to know the approximate cost of future work so they can make a decision as to whether the payback is sufficient, but to expect accurate estimates before the details have been worked out is not realistic. Perhaps the reason they expect such an unreasonable capability from project organizations is that they have assumed business projects can work in CPM mode, and they have limited understanding about the way CPM projects are approached.

In the construction world, only that phase of the project called construction is done in a fixed-price mode. All other phases are done by other companies and are usually either cost-plus contracts or time and material contracts. Furthermore, by the time the contractor is asked to estimate the fixed price of the job, blueprints specifying in exact detail how the job is to be done are available. Not only does he know at what time that the walls must be painted; he is usually told what kind of paint to use. Table 13.2 compares the way the construction world implements CPM and the way the business world attempts to.

A far more reasonable way to work would be for the project client to request a ballpark figure at the study stage. That figure should be revisited and adjusted at the end of the study stage and again at the end of the design stage. In that way, resources would be planned only for the next phase, not necessarily for the entire project. Resource requirements must be reevaluated as more is learned about the work. We get more information as we work through the project. This methodology should allow businesses to use that information for the good of the project.

The Need for Commitment Management

Another issue that highlights the difference between the project organization and the hierarchy is the need for all levels of the organization to be committed to success. To paraphrase Vidal Sassoon, "If they don't work good, you won't look good." The need for successful projects is growing by the day. No one cannot af-

TABLE 13.2. CPM THE BUSINESS WORLD WAY AND THE CONSTRUCTION WORLD WAY OF IMPLEMENTING CPM.

Phases of Construction or Development	Formal Project Management	Business Project Management
Problem identification	Performed by the client	Performed by the client
Feasibility, environmental impact, and other studies	Performed by a company that specializes in such studies—usually a cost-plus or time and material contract; produces a report with recommended alternatives	Often not done, but many companies require a fixed estimate of project costs and duration at this time
Macro- and microdesign specifications	Performed by an architectural firm—usually a cost-plus or time and material contract; produces blueprints for the building contractor	Performed by the project team—usually in fixed-price mode
Construction, development, build, create, deliver	Performed by a construction contractor—usually a fixed-price contract; (building, bridge, road, etc.)	Performed by the project team—usually in fixed-price mode

ford to allow project teams to perform badly. Businesses must make a commitment to succeed. The commitment must begin at the top and be communicated all the way down to the lowest worker on the project totem pole. They will succeed. And they will all work together to succeed. One of the most important rules to impose is that once the project plan has been approved, no single person, department, or division can change it. That means all affected members must be involved in and approve of the change. When everyone works together, there are no failures, only disappointments.

Improving Resource Planning for Projects: A Restatement

- Projects need access to the most expert staff within the organization.
- There should be a core of project workers who will be able to focus on the work of the project until it is complete.

- Project planners must learn to expect more work than they can identify when they do their estimates. Hard as it may seem at first, they must not underplan project resources.
- All projects must use contingency, of both resources and calendar time.
- Projects should be planned so that internal staff is used on all tasks requiring knowledge of the company.
- As much project work as possible should be structured and documented with examples of required deliverables to allow for the hiring of outside personnel when necessary.
- Businesses must develop a standard methodology with standard, well-defined tasks for all project work.
- Businesses must define small enough tasks to ensure project control. One-week tasks or even smaller are recommended.
- Businesses must implement a performance database to collect actual hours worked for comparison against estimates.
- The system used to collect actuals must be entirely nonthreatening to the workers.
- A systematic approach to estimating must be used—one that documents the issues considered in arriving at the estimate.
- The PERT estimating approach identifies the probability of successfully meeting the estimate. Anyone using PERT should incorporate at least an 85 percent probability into the estimates.
- Businesses must implement a phased project approach that allows them to revisit estimates as they gain more information about the remaining work.
- Businesses must make a commitment to success and ensure that every project organization has the support in resources, tools, methods, and management that it needs.

In Conclusion

A good plan is the best road map available at the time. As we travel, especially through new experiences, as we add to our knowledge about specific efforts, we need to change the map, adding to it, adjusting it, and generally making it more useful for the next time. At the end of every project, the team should evaluate how well the plan predicted reality and suggest improvements that can help future projects. However, appropriate project resource planning recognizes the fact that no organization can hire enough resources to cover every eventuality and includes mechanisms to add temporary and part-time personnel as needed.

CHAPTER FOURTEEN

CLOSING OUT THE PROJECT

J. Davidson Frame

The most common formulation of the project life cycle is to posit it as a four-phase affair:

Phase 1: Project initiation
Phase 2: Project planning and development
Phase 3: Project implementation
Phase 4: Project closeout

Anyone who has read a project management textbook or sat through a project management course recognizes that phases 2 (planning and development) and 3 (implementation) get the lion's share of attention, phase 1 (initiation) gets a cursory mention, and phase 4 (closeout) may be overlooked entirely.

The same phenomenon is mirrored in the interest that project team members invest in their projects. Most of the team's interest and energy focus on phases 2 and 3, which entail the planning and execution of project work. Their involvement in phase 1 is superficial, since in most organizations project selection and launch decisions are made before a team is even created. Their interest in phase 4, the closeout phase, is practically nonexistent. By this point in the project, all the interesting work has been done; furthermore, they may be tired of the project and want to move on to new challenges.

In fact, closing out the project merits close attention. A key premise of this chapter is that the inattention given to closing out projects properly is an important contributing factor to project failure. Consequently, rather than treat project closeout as a poor relation in the project family, we should deal with it consciously and energetically.

What Customers Care About

It has become an article of faith in management that a central goal of business activity must be to satisfy customers, and this reality certainly holds true in the project management arena. Not long ago, project success was defined in terms of getting the job done (on time, within budget, and according to specifications). Today we recognize that this is too narrow a perspective. It does not take a great imagination to visualize a situation where a project is achieved on time, within budget, and according to specs, but it is nonetheless deemed a failure because its customers do not feel it addresses their needs and wants adequately.

If the traditional four-phased project life cycle is viewed from a customer perspective, we encounter a dramatic revelation. The phases that customers care most about are the very ones that have been downplayed in the theory and practice of project management. Customers care most about phases 1 and 4. With respect to phase 1, their concern is: "Did you get my needs and requirements right?" If not, then the planning and implementation activities of phases 2 and 3 are a waste of time. With respect to phase 4, their concern is: "Are you about to hand me a deliverable that meets my needs and is operable and maintainable? If not, then what have you been doing on the project these past few months?"

The link between project closeout and the level of customer satisfaction with a project effort should be obvious. As the project is drawing to a conclusion, customers are usually quite anxious. They are asking themselves a stream of questions along the following lines: "At last, we are near to having what we have been waiting for. Will the project team really meet its deadline? Are they going to tack on extra costs? Will the deliverable work properly? Can we employ it properly ourselves once it has been handed over to us?"

A Typical Project Closeout Scenario

Ideally, everything is under control as projects close out. The project team is achieving all the desired specifications, deadline dates are being met, and the budget is on target. Furthermore, customers express delight at how things are going and eagerly await their deliverable. Upon receiving it, their delight continues, and to show their appreciation for a job well done, they pay all their bills promptly and send a letter of thanks to the project manager.

Regrettably, what actually happens at closeout is quite different. Anyone preparing to close out a project should be prepared to deal with the following realities:

Team members are concerned about future jobs. On most projects, team members are borrowed resources. They come from different functional areas (such as marketing, information technology, and operations), do their jobs, and then return to their functional homes. As projects wrap up, core team members who have been assigned to the project for most of its life may wonder: "What's next? Is there life after the project? If so, is it an interesting life?" Given these concerns, team members may not be fully focused on doing what it takes to close out a project properly.

Bugs still exist. As projects come to closure, tests often show that problems exist that need to be resolved. This holds true on a wide range of projects, from developing a software system, to writing a manual, to building a home, to testing a new drug for Food and Drug Administration approval. The surfacing of such problems at this time can be a major source of frustration for both team members and customers.

Resources are running out. Throughout its life, resources are being expended on a project. Toward the end, the resources are nearly depleted. If unanticipated problems arise (and they often do), then the team may find that there are insufficient resources to tackle the difficulties effectively. Today the resource shortage is exacerbated by the tendency of organizations to tighten the resources that it gives to projects owing to competitive pressures.

Documentation attains paramount importance. Projects are filled with documentation requirements: project documentation (such as budgets, schedules, time sheets), technical documentation (such as specifications, systems topologies, test results), change management documentation (such as change request forms, change control board dispositions, traceability documentation), and user documentation (user manuals, training syllabi, training workbooks). Ideally, documentation requirements are handled effectively from the start of the project. Regrettably, what typically happens is that documentation efforts are put off until the end of the project, an unfortunate turn of events for a number of reasons. First, the team may experience loss of institutional memory. That is, players who made key decisions earlier on the project are no longer available to document their actions. Second, individual team members cannot remember how and why they carried out their efforts, so they are unable to supply quality documentation. Third, schedule pressures common at the end of projects, coupled with lack of resources, create an environment that encourages shortcuts in documentation.

Promised delivery dates may not be met. Research I have recently carried out suggests that the majority of projects in knowledge-based industries face problems of schedule slippage. Often the slippage is not a consequence of poor project implementation, but rather a result of excessively optimistic promises made at the outset of the project. When an account executive promises a customer that a ten-month job will be done in six months, schedule slippage is built into the project before any work has begun.

The players may possess a sense of panic. As schedule slippage looms and resources are running out, a wide range of players may experience a sense of panic. The account executive who launched the project may be nervous that project problems will harm relations with the customer. The customer may become alarmed at the possibility of not receiving the deliverable on time in order to meet business requirements. The project manager and team may grow worried that they will be blamed for slippages and cost overruns. If panic takes over, then the prospects for an orderly project closeout grow slim.

Good Closeouts

Good closeouts are important for "aesthetic," administrative, and customer-relations reasons. Aesthetically, good closeouts enable the team to wrap up projects in a clean, pleasing fashion. Loose ends are tied up. Psychologically, team members, customers, and management walk away from the effort with a sense that the project was under control to the end.

Administratively, good closeouts contribute to an environment of efficient organizational operations. When checklists are reviewed systematically, paperwork is properly filled out and filed, contractual obligations are fulfilled, and so on, the likelihood of committing mistakes is reduced and maintenance of good records is ensured.

From the perspective of customer relations, good closeouts maximize customer satisfaction and increase customer confidence that the project has been implemented with care. Messy closeouts can cause customers to question the competence of the project team and may lead to delays in customer acceptance of the deliverable.

What to Account for at Closeout

A checklist of a standard project closeout contains a number of standard items.

Preparation and Collation of Project Documentation

The preparation and collation of documentation assume growing importance as projects wind down. Systems documentation, user manuals, training material, maintenance documents, and budget reports are examples of the kinds of documentation that must be prepared before the project is complete. For documentation to be handled properly, projects should have documentation plans. Documentation milestones should be factored into project schedules to identify document-related actions and deliverables that should be produced at different times during the life of the project. Certainly every attempt should be made to avoid postponing documentation to the last minute.

Preparation for the Handover

Once a deliverable has been produced, it is handed over to the customer. Smooth handovers do not occur by accident. To see this, consider a project whose deliverable is an electronic box. Arrangements must be made with the customer to receive the box. The box must be fully tested before delivery to make sure it functions properly. Once it is on the customer's premises, it should be tested again to see that it is performing according to specifications. All pertinent documentation and peripheral equipment must be delivered with the box (no item should be forgotten). For handovers to occur properly, they must be carefully planned, with checklists created to make sure that the proper steps are taken.

Preparation for Operations and Maintenance

Once a deliverable is handed over to the customer, the operations and maintenance (O&M) phase begins. Since O&M occurs after the project is over, it is tempting for project staff to think, "What happens after I've done my job is none of my concern." Such a view reflects an insensitivity to customer sensibilities.

Clearly when customers undertake a project, it is with a view to obtaining deliverables that are operable and maintainable. To increase the likelihood of a smooth transition from the project to the O&M phase, the project team must make a conscious effort to work with the customer staff charged with operating and maintaining the deliverable. They may play an active role in the earliest stages of implementing their solution (for example, they can help install equipment). They should also make themselves available to answer whatever questions the customer may have.

Preparation for Customer Training

To the extent that the deliverable emerging from a project is something new to the customer, it is likely that the customer will need some training on how to employ and maintain it effectively. Steps must be taken to arrange for such an effort. Responsibility for developing and delivering the material may lie with the human resource management department or an outside party. It is likely that project team members will have to work with the training people to help them put together the courseware and test it for accuracy.

The Checklist of Work

A detailed checklist should be maintained describing all the work that was supposed to be done on the project. The project team should systematically go through this checklist before turning the deliverable over to the customer for customer acceptance testing. By doing this, they reduce the likelihood of leaving things out that should have been done. Also, a careful review of the items on the checklist against the deliverable may uncover hitherto unseen quality problems.

The Customer Acceptance Test

Before signing off on the deliverable, customers will want to perform tests on it to make sure it performs the way it is supposed to. The tests may entail nothing more than a simple checklist review of the deliverable to ascertain whether it contains all the promised components, or they can be complex affairs, extending over weeks or months. Once the deliverable has passed the acceptance test, customers take it over, and the key responsibilities of the project team have ended.

An important customer relations point should be raised here. If during closeout customers see that the project is out of control—perhaps test results are disappointing, people are scrambling to put together the documentation, and the team expresses a sense of panic—they will approach the customer acceptance effort with a great deal of caution. They may be suspicious that hidden problems lurk in the deliverable. Consequently, the customer acceptance tests may drag on. In contrast, a well-executed closeout increases customer confidence in the deliverable and leads to speedier customer acceptance testing.

Reassignment of Resources

On most projects, the majority of resources are borrowed. For example, during the design phase, design personnel show up from the design shop, do their work, and then return home to the design shop. Occasionally testing personnel show up with their testing equipment, perform their tests, and then return home. And so on. However, there is often a core group of people who stick with the project for much of its life, and as the project winds down they wonder, "What's next?" Clearly they need to be reassigned to other undertakings. If this reassignment is not carried out effectively, team members may grow distracted, and this can lead to a messy closeout. Similarly, the equipment and materials that were provided to the project need to be reassigned properly.

Review of Contract Performance

Beyond conducting a customer acceptance test, customers will want to review project performance on a broader level. In particular, on contracted projects they will assess project performance against the promises contained in the contract. Have all the tasks been carried out in conformance with the contract? Did the deliverable achieve the specified requirements (this can be determined during the acceptance test)? Was work done on time and within budget? During the closeout phase, the project team has a responsibility to prepare for the final contract review. They can do this by going through a checklist to see whether any undone work remains. Also, they can supply cost and schedule data that may need to be examined during the contract performance review.

Collection of Final Payments

Project closeout includes dealing with the final disposition of project-related payments. For example, if project work is paid for periodically by means of progress payments, the last payment should be collected once the work is done. On some contracts, a certain portion of payments may be held back until several months after project work has been completed as an insurance policy of sorts to make sure the deliverable functions as promised. The matter of final payments is a management-level issue and lies outside the realm of project team responsibilities.

Conduct of Lessons-Learned Exercise

When the project work is done, the project team should carry out a lessons-learned exercise (sometimes called the postmortem). This exercise should highlight the strengths and weaknesses associated with the project effort. Typical questions addressed include: What did we do right? What did we do wrong? How can we do better the next time? Although there may be a temptation to restrict the lessons-learned exercise to technical issues, it should in fact be broad based and examine management- and customer-related issues as well.

The lessons-learned exercise can be conducted in various ways. For example, it can be an elaborate affair or a rather perfunctory one. It can be based entirely on a self-assessment by the project team, or can include evaluations by independent outsiders.

Conveying Lessons Learned

Winston Churchill noted that those who do not study history are condemned to repeat its mistakes. Churchill's observation certainly applies to project management. Organizations that do not learn from their experiences absolutely *will* repeat blunders that they have made before.

The lessons gained are not all rooted in bad experiences. In projects, some actions may lead to great results. These positive experiences must not be forgotten, so that they can be repeated in the future.

Merely capturing lessons in a document is not too helpful. Typically such documents wind up gathering dust on a shelf or being tossed into a trash bin. If the project lessons are to be learned truly, then they must be conveyed effectively to others in the organization. Some typical approaches to conveying project lessons follow.

Distributing Written Lessons to Pertinent Players

The most common approach to capturing and conveying lessons—writing them up and distributing them to pertinent players—has a number of problems. For example, who precisely are the "pertinent" players? Senior management? Resource managers? Other project managers? Technicians? Another problem is that few recipients of lessons-learned documents have the time and inclination to review them seriously. Most likely, the documents will be unread.

In one company, senior management have instituted a policy of highlighting key lessons learned on various projects, and all project managers are expected to master them. To make sure the lessons are properly studied, they are discussed at senior-level meetings, and individuals who have not learned their lessons will realize that their lack of preparation is embarrassingly obvious.

Embedding Lessons in Revised Project Methods and Procedures

One sure way to ensure that lessons are conveyed throughout the organization is to revise the organization's way of doing business by incorporating the lessons into the organization's business processes. For example, if project staff often forget to include important items in making cost estimates, procedures can be revised to require them to employ standard checklists when making estimates. Care must be taken not to create too many rules, which may ultimately lead to a fatal clogging of the organization's information arteries. Methods and procedures included in the organization's business processes must be regularly reviewed to see which are still relevant and which have grown obsolete and should be discarded.

Creating a Lessons-Learned Data Bank

Some organizations create central data banks to hold their lessons-learned experiences. With well-constructed data banks, project staff can query them on special topics and be directed to appropriate real-world responses. For example, query topics along the following lines can be created: "Problems with equipment installation," "customer complaints," "scope creep," "schedule slippages," and so on.

One organization encourages project staff to review learned lessons in the central data bank by punishing people who repeat mistakes covered in the data bank.

Sharing Lessons Learned in Meetings

Project workers from different parts of the organization can be encouraged to get together periodically to discuss both the good and bad experiences they have had on their projects. In some organizations, this has been institutionalized in monthly lunches.

Maintaining a Stable, Experienced Workforce

All of us carry our life's lessons with us in our heads. When we make mistakes, hopefully we learn from them and avoid them in the future. One approach to ensuring that lessons have been conveyed effectively is to maintain a stable, experienced workforce. When there is a churning in the makeup of the workforce (a common experience in this era of business process reengineering) important lessons are lost each time an experienced worker is reassigned to a different job.

Highlighting Important Lessons at Project Kickoff Meetings

In some organizations, lessons-learned experiences are shared at the outset of new projects during the kickoff meeting. Occasionally people who have experienced relevant lessons on other projects are brought in to share their insights.

Conclusion

The importance of the project closeout phase of the project life cycle is often over-looked. As projects wrap up, most of the interesting work has been completed. The excitement felt during the start-up days is long gone. Test results on the deliverable may show that problems still exist. Staff are concerned about future job assignments. Resources may be running low, and schedule slippages may loom. Finally, a bevy of documentation requirements must be addressed. Given these realities of the last moments of a typical project, it is no wonder that project close-out is not approached with eagerness and diligence.

Yet effective project closeouts are essential for project success. An otherwise successful or uneventful project may turn into a disaster if the closeout effort is botched. Months of good customer rapport may go out the window if a product with missing components is delivered to the customer, poor user documentation is supplied to the customer, or contractual obligations have been overlooked. Beyond these customer-related issues, poor closeouts introduce inefficiencies into an organization's operations, possibly leading to rework, lost files, and incomplete records. Such sloppiness drives up the cost of operations and tarnishes an organization's reputation.

The steps that organizations and project teams should take to bring projects to closure in an organized way are rather humdrum, yet they are vital to project success.

PART THREE

HUMAN RESOURCE MANAGEMENT

CHAPTER FIFTEEN

THE PROJECT MANAGER

Barry Z. Posner
James M. Kouzes

Successful project management is essentially about dealing effectively with people. The ability of the project manager has been likened to that of bandleaders "who pull together their players, each a specialist with individual score and internal rhythm," so that "they all respond to the same beat."[1]

A review of the project management literature will reveal a vast array of ideas about what characteristics may be needed for project success, and even some consensus (as indicated by the chapters that follow dealing with team building, leadership skills, motivation, power and politics, conflict and negotiations, and cross-functional cooperation), but there is absolutely no agreement—actually very little discussion even—about how an individual acquires these competencies.[2] Without being glib, it is easy to say that project managers—both the good ones and the not-so-good ones—come in a rainbow of shapes and sizes, backgrounds and beliefs, interests and proclivities.

The interpersonal competencies required to be successful as a project manager obviously can be learned, but it is also true that some people seem more natural and comfortable at it than others. Moreover, every project manager is capable of learning to be a *better* project manager.

Learning to be a Better Project Manager

Results from an extensive six-year-long research study at the Honeywell Corporation about how managers learned to manage revealed these clusterings: job experiences and assignments, relationships, formal education, and training.[3] After interviewing thousands of managers across a variety of industries, the Center for Creative Leadership categorized the experiences and events that managers considered important in their development as job assignments, other people with whom they had come into contact, hardships that they had endured, and formal training.[4]

In our own studies, we have found that experience is by far the most important opportunity for learning; this can be personal experience, reflecting on the experience of interacting with others, or formal studying (learning about and from experiences of people outside one's interpersonal or organizational existence).[5] The results of all these studies are so similar that we can conclude that experience is the best teacher. Other people rank a close second in importance, and formal education and training are also significant contributors.

Trial and Error

There is no suitable surrogate for learning by doing. Whether it is facilitating a team's meetings, leading a special task force at work, heading a charity's fundraising drive, or chairing a professional association's annual conference, the more chances that people have to serve in leadership roles, the more likely it is that they will develop the skills to lead—and the more likely that they will learn those important leadership lessons that come only from the failures and successes of live action.

Just any experience does not by itself support individual development. Boring, routine jobs do not help anyone improve their skills and abilities or move forward in their career. People must be stretched with opportunities to test themselves against new and difficult tasks. Challenge and change are essential for learning to do one's best. Seeing change as a challenge is important to psychological hardiness, and challenge is also the key ingredient in people's enjoying what they do. Now it turns out that challenge is also crucial to learning and career enhancement. So experience can indeed be the best teacher, if it contains the element of personal challenge.

There are other ingredients in the recipe of job assignments that advances careers and learning. Researchers from the Center for Creative Leadership, in their review of developmental experiences in managerial work, found that managers must be given broader and broader responsibility if they are to blossom into senior executives—for example: switching from line to staff and vice versa; experiencing changes in job content, status, or location; making radical job moves; taking on assignments dealing with the implementation of change, including starting something from scratch or fixing a troubled operation or program; and being given vast resources in scope of responsibility.[6] Staff assignments at corporate headquarters that give high visibility are useful and personally empowering. Staff jobs that have low visibility tend not to be stepping-stones to advancement (or more challenging learning opportunities). Project teams and task forces obviously can add to the ability to work with diverse groups inside and outside the company. Hardships and business crises can be especially powerful triggers for self-insight and lessons in handling loss.

The first prescription, then, for becoming a better project manager is to broaden one's base of experience. People are more likely to follow someone if they have confidence that the person understands the area, the technology, the organization, and the industry. Job rotation is one way of broadening experience, but we suggest going beyond that. Volunteering for leadership roles in professional associations and community groups is a great way to develop skills in working with people, and such organizations are always in need of good people. We advise seeking new project assignments early in one's career and not hesitating to ask for a new assignment within two years. Anyone who is in the same job longer than that is out of the learning curve. Also, the tougher assignments, with higher risk and greater payoff, are typically the most beneficial to careers.

Yet even the most venturesome jobs will not help anyone grow if they do not take the time to reflect on what they have learned from life's trials and errors. When we do recall, in vivid detail, the people, the places, the events, the struggles, the victories—the very smell and texture of the action—we discover lasting lessons about how to lead others more effectively. We find embedded in experience the grains of truth about ourselves, others, our organizations, and life itself.

Unexamined experiences do not produce the rich insights that come with reflection and analysis. Proceeding from observations based on experience to principles and applications (that is, inductive learning) is a preferable process for learning how to be a better project manager than beginning with an a priori "truth." Learning from experience is much like watching the game films after an athletic event. These documentaries show players how they executed their plan, what they did well, and where they need to improve. Athletic teams make extensive use of postgame review, and so do successful project managers.

Observing Others

Other people have always been essential sources of guidance. Of all the potential relationships at work, the three most important for learning are mentors, immediate supervisors, and peers.

Mentors are particularly valuable as informal sponsors and coaches. They show how to navigate the system, make important introductions, and point others in the right direction.

Immediate supervisors (managers) are obviously important to careers. They can help staff to advance—or slow their progress. They serve as extremely important sources of performance feedback and modeling. The best ones are those who challenge, trust, are willing to spend time with staff, and are consistent in their behavior. They must most certainly be credible if others are to learn and develop.

Chances are that most people have had good and bad managers in their careers. Good ones naturally are preferable. Bad ones are not necessarily roadblocks to development, but they can create unwanted stress in employees' lives. The best bet for anyone who gets stuck with a bad boss—whether a tyrant or a weakling, uninvolved or meddlesome—is to learn to manage amid that behavior. Because it is unlikely that anyone will change that person, the best growth strategy in this position is to treat this person as you wish to be treated, remaining positive about yourself, and interacting in an assertive but nonconfrontational manner. Bad managers may not be pleasant to work with, but they can be great examples of what *not* to do. And in some companies, surviving an unbearable manager can even earn one a badge of courage.

All project managers are in a network of relationships. Not only must they influence managers and team members; they must also influence peers and important constituents, both internal and external, even when they lack formal authority. However, developing effective lateral relationships, which may be a perplexing demand, turns out to be a key predictor of job success.[7] Peers are valuable sources of information; they can tell us what is happening in other parts of the organization. Trusted peers can also serve as advisers and counselors, giving others feedback on their personal style and also helping others to test out alternative ways of dealing with problems.

Finally, everyone can learn from people without having a relationship with them. As often as people mention learning from mentors, managers, or peers, they mention outside role models. Many of us look to historical figures or to well-known contemporaries for inspiration and learning. In fact, we are just as likely to look to great men and women of the past for guidance as we are to look to those with whom we work today.

Too little has been said of the influence of historical role models. Biographies have always been a rich source of information on the great military, governmental, religious, community, and business leaders of the past. The popularity of biographies of modern business executives, and their books about management, is evidence of a keen interest in discovering the secrets of others' successes. Advancements in video technology and CD-ROM make contemporary leaders even more accessible as exemplars. To gain access to the wealth of knowledge others have, we recommend interviewing, observing, reading about, or studying admired project managers.

Mentors are difficult to find; many of us will never have the experience of being the protégé of an influential project manager. However, anyone can still learn firsthand from those they think are masters of the craft. Ask to interview a project manager you respect. Usually this person will be flattered and agree to meet. It is tougher to get busy project managers to allow you to follow them through a typical day, but if you ever have that opportunity, take it.

Education and Training

Formal leadership education and training represent a third way to become a better project manager. Every large company, and most medium-sized ones, have some type of internal training department. Most also send their employees to external programs for further development.

Although less important as a source of learning than either experience or other people, formal training and education can be of importance in developing project manager skills. Training is a high-leverage way of improving one's chances of success. Research studies, reports the American Society for Training and Development, illustrate clearly that "learning on the job accounted for more than half of the productivity increases in the United States between 1929 and 1989. . . . Additional research shows that people who are trained formally in the workplace have a 30 percent higher productivity rate after one year than those who are not formally trained."[8]

Our advice is to spend a minimum of fifty hours annually on personal and professional development. At Malcolm Baldrige National Quality Award-winning companies, it is one hundred hours. Training does not need to be learning that takes place in a classroom for several days in a row. It might be one day every other month or one morning each month. Or a group might get together for this purpose. Everyone reads a magazine, article, or book (chapter by chapter) and then, at a brown-bag discussion at lunchtime, discusses how the ideas might be used, adapted, or modified in their department, work group, or function. For·a relatively small investment of time, each group member gets two to four times the educational value from the hours they spend in training than they do from the hours spent on the job. Training and education are vastly underdeveloped and underused opportunities for creating a personal edge in learning to be a better project manager.

No project manager should wait for others to point out what he or she needs to do to improve. They should make a list of developmental needs, beginning with their own strengths and weaknesses in managing projects and people. They can ask for feedback from people they know or human resource professionals in their company, or ask colleagues if they can recommend any useful diagnostic questionnaires.

Once they initiate their own learning agenda, they will find the opportunities to build on strengths and overcome weaknesses. Charting career success in the next century, say experts, is predicated on being self-reliant (think about yourself as a business of one), being connected (you must be a team player), being specialized (you must have a deep understanding of something); and being a generalist (you must know enough of different disciplines and functions to be able to mediate among them).[9]

Those who are developing their project management capabilities can take courses in functional areas about which they know little. It is important to stay up to date in the field, but the most effective project managers are generalists. We advise getting as much breadth as early as possible and taking advantage of educational programs offered by the organization. External training and developmental programs provide good perspective, stimulation from other sources, and networking opportunities.

Continuing Learning by Looking Within

We all face uncertain and ambiguous career paths, with little job security. The most critical requirement for being successful will turn out to be learning how to learn, for knowledge and skill, like any other asset, depreciates in value overtime. Continuous process improvement has to apply to each of us individually, as well as to organizational products and services.

The skill needed in this fast-moving "New Economy" exclaims *Fortune* magazine's editors is "*reflection*: To the degree that individuals are successful at plumbing their depths, these people should be better off, and the companies that employ them may gain competitive advantage. In fast-shifting markets, the unexamined life becomes a liability."[10] Learning, including knowing how to and realizing the importance of, is the sine qua non for both personal and organizational vitality.

This advantage is evident from studies about people who are able to be introspective or are afforded the opportunity to be reflective. People who lose their jobs, for example, and are able to put their stress into words by writing down their deepest thoughts and feelings, including anger and hostility at being laid off, are able to stay healthier and more productive and get on with their lives (and find new jobs) more quickly than people who do not face their feelings or are unable or unwilling to give personal meaning to what is happening in their lives.[11]

Lessons Learned

There are plenty of opportunities to develop, practice, and sharpen project management skills and talents. Here are some areas to consider:

- Evaluate your own experiences after each project. Determine the lessons learned for the next project.
- Meet with admired and successful project managers in your organization. Talk with those in other firms to find out about their lessons learned.
- Read (and study) the lessons learned from histories of previous projects and participate in classes and workshops based on these best practices.

Everyone in today's workforce is a project manager regardless of title, function, or discipline. That is the nature of today's increasingly complex and interconnected workplace.[12] Success demands that each of us be learners, always on the lookout for learning opportunities and taking the time to make learning from experience the equivalent of enjoying running a race where there is no finish line.

CHAPTER SIXTEEN

POWER, POLITICS, AND
PROJECT MANAGEMENT

Jeffrey K. Pinto

One of the truly fascinating aspects of the corporate environment is the role that power and political behavior play in successful project management. Most of us tend to regard political activity with a sort of repugnance, finding the conduct of politics to be both personally distasteful and organizationally damaging. There is an interesting paradox at work here, however. Common experience will demonstrate to both practitioners and neutral observers that for all our often-expressed personal disdain for the exercise of politics, we readily acknowledge that this process is often one of the prime moving forces within any organization, for better or worse.

Political behavior, sometimes defined as any process by which individuals and groups seek, acquire, and maintain power, is pervasive in modern corporations. Examples include activities as significant as negotiating for a multimillion dollar commitment of money for a new project and as mundane as determining who will attain a corner office; as predatory as the willful attempt to derail another's career to as benign as deciding where the yearly office party will be held. The key underlying feature of each of these and countless other examples is that the processes by which we make decisions and seek power, the issues we deem power

Note: Portions of this chapter were excerpted from Pinto, J. K. (1996). *Power and politics in project management.* Upper Darby, PA: PMI Publications.

laden, and the steps we go to maintain our position are often an emotionally charged sequence having important personal and corporate ramifications.

The field of project management is particularly fraught with political processes, for several unique reasons. First, because project managers in many companies do not have a stable base of power (either high status or overriding authority), they must learn to cultivate other methods of influence in order to secure the resources from other departments necessary to attain project success. Second, and closely related to the first reason, projects often exist outside the traditional line (functional) structure, relegating project managers to the role of supernumerary. Almost all resources (among them, financial, human, and informational) must be negotiated and bargained for. Finally, many project managers are not given the authority to conduct formal performance evaluations on their project team subordinates, denying the managers an important base of hierarchical power. Without the authority to reward or punish, they are placed in the position of having to influence subordinates behavior to engage in appropriate behaviors. Consequently, they must learn important human skills such as bargaining and influence, conflict management, and negotiation.

Senior and successful project managers have long known the importance of maintaining strong political ties throughout their organizations as a method for achieving project success. Indeed, it is the rare successful project manager who is not conversant in and knowledgeable of the importance of politics for effectively performing the job. That point illustrates an important underlying aspect of the characteristics of political behavior: it can be the project manager's firm friend or most remorseless foe. In other words, whatever decision one comes to regarding the use of politics in the quest for project success, it cannot be ignored.

No one would argue that project managers must become immersed in the brutal, self-serving side of corporate political life. Clearly there are so many examples of predatory behavior that most of us are leery of being considered "politically adept." Nevertheless, the key point is that project management and politics are inextricably linked. Successful project managers are usually those who intuitively understand that their job consists of more than simply being technically and managerially competent.

In my research and consulting experience, I have found that most companies spend thousands of hours planning and implementing a multimillion or even multibillion dollar investment, developing intricate plans and schedules, forming a cohesive team, and maintaining realistic specification and time targets, all to have the project derailed by political processes. This is a pity, particularly because the end result is often foreseeable early in the development of the project—usually as the result of a project manager's refusal to acknowledge and cultivate political ties, both internal to the organization and externally with the clients.

At some point, almost every project manager has faced the difficulties involved in managing a project in the face of corporate politics.[1] Recalcitrant functional managers, unclear lines of authority, tentative resource commitments, lukewarm upper management support, and hard lessons in negotiation are all characteristics of many project managers' daily lives. Set within this all-too-familiar framework, it is a wonder that most projects ever get completed.

Although project management theory has sought for years to find new and better methods for improving the discipline, it is ironic that power and political behavior, one of the most pervasive and frequently pernicious elements affecting project implementation, has rarely been addressed. Even when it has been examined, the discussion is often so cursory or theory driven that it offers little in the way of useful advice for practicing project managers. Whatever our current level of understanding of power and politics in organizations, we must all come to the realization that its presence is ubiquitous and its impact significant. With this acceptance as a starting point, we can begin to address power and politics as a necessary part of project management and learn to use it to advantage through increasing the likelihood of successfully managing projects.

Modes of Power: Authority, Status, and Influence

Among the sorts of options that project managers are able to use in furthering their goals, it is useful to consider their alternatives in terms of three modes of power: authority, status, and influence (see Figure 16.1). This authority, status, and influence model has been proposed by Robert Graham as a way to make clear the methods by which project managers can achieve their desired ends.[2] The model is valuable because it illustrates clearly one of the key problems that most project managers have in attempting to develop and implement their projects in corporations.

Much has been written on the sorts of power that individuals have. One framework suggests that each of us has available two distinct types of power: power that derives from our personality (personal power) and power that comes from the position or title we hold.[3] Let us define authority as this latter type of power: one that accrues from the position we occupy in the organization (positional power). In other words, the positional power base derives solely from the position that managers occupy in the corporate hierarchy. Unfortunately, the nature of positional, or formal, power is extremely problematic within project management situations due to the temporary and detached nature of most projects regarding the rest of the formal organizational structure.[4] Project teams sit outside the normal vertical hierarchy, usually employing personnel who are on loan from their

FIGURE 16.1. THE AUTHORITY, STATUS, INFLUENCE MODEL.

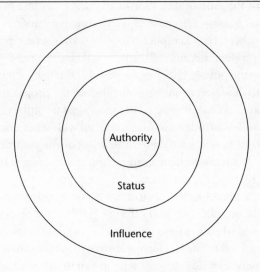

functional departments. As a result, project managers have a tenuous degree of positional power within the organization. Other than the nominal control they have over their own team, they may not have a corporatewide base of positional power through which they can get resources, issue directives, or enforce their will. In most organizations project managers cannot rely on authority as a power base with any degree of certainty.

The second mode of power, status, is often problematic for most project managers. Status implies that the project manager, due to the nature, importance, or visibility of his or her project, can exert power and control over others in the corporate hierarchy as needed. Certainly some projects and project managers do possess an enormous degree of status due to the importance of their projects (examples are the project manager for the Boeing 757 program and the project manager for the recently completed "Chunnel," the tunnel under the English Channel connecting England and France), the vast majority of project managers toil in relative obscurity, working to bring their projects to fruition while receiving little public recognition for their work. Although it would be nice to think that most project managers can rely on status as a form of power and control over resources to improve their projects' likelihood of success, the reality is that very few projects or project managers can depend on their status as a persuasive form of power.

This, then, leads us to the final form of power or control that project managers may possess: influence. Influence is a form of power that is usually highly individualized; some individuals are better able to use influence to achieve their desired ends than are others. One of the best examples of influence is the power an individual possesses because of a dynamic personality or personal charisma that attracts others. For example, well-known athletes are popular choices for endorsing new products because of the personal charisma and "referent" appeal that they hold with the public. Other examples of influence include informational or expert power. To illustrate, if only one member of the project team has the programming or computer skills that are vital to the successful completion of the project, that person, regardless of title or managerial level within the organization, has a solid base of influence in relation to other members of the project team.

The key point to bear in mind about influence is that it is often an informal method of power and control.[5] Project managers who use influence well in furthering the goals of their project usually work behind the scenes, negotiating, cutting deals, or collecting and offering IOUs. As a power tactic, influence is most readily used when managers have no formal positional authority to rely on. Hence, they are forced to use less formal means to achieve their desired ends. Influence is most widely seen as a power tactic in situations in which there is no obvious difference in authority levels among organizational members.

What is the implication of the authority, status, and influence model? Graham notes that the nature of project management work, the manner by which project managers and their teams are selected, and the relationship of projects to the formal organizational hierarchy force project managers to rely to far greater degrees on their ability to cultivate and effectively use influence as a negotiating and power tactic than either of the other two forms of power.[6] Formal, broad-based authority rarely exists for project managers to use in furthering their project's ends. And while some projects and project managers have the status to gain the resources they need, it is much less likely that the typical project manager can learn to develop the skills to use influence as a power tactic. The key is realizing that influence is a form of corporate political behavior that can be used for the benefit of the project, and ultimately of the organization. In order to understand the relationship better between the use of informal influence tactics and political behavior, we need to explore in some detail exactly what organizational politics implies.

Building Awareness of Power and Politics in Project Management

An understanding of the political side of organizations and the often intensely political nature of project implementation gives rise to the need to develop appropriate attitudes and strategies that help project managers operate effectively within the system. What are some of the steps that project managers can take to become politically astute, if this approach is so necessary to effective project implementation?

Understand and acknowledge the political nature of most organizations. Research on politics and organizational life demonstrates an interesting paradox at work: the vast majority of managers hate engaging in political activities, believing that they waste time and detract from the more important aspects of their jobs. On the other hand, these same managers acknowledge that although they do not like politics, politicking is an important requirement for business and personal success.[7] The underlying point is important: we have to acknowledge politics as a fact of organizational and project life. Denying the political nature of organizations does not make that phenomenon any less potent. I realize that, in offering this view, I run the risk of offending some readers who are uncomfortable with the idea of politics and believe that, somehow, through the combined efforts of all organizational actors, it is possible to eradicate the political nature of companies or governmental agencies. Unfortunately, practical experience does not bear out this view; politics is too deeply rooted within organizational operations to be treated as some aberrant form of bacteria or diseased tissue that can be excised from the organization's body.

Before managers are able to learn to use politics in a manner that is supportive of project implementation, they must first acknowledge its existence and its impact on project success. Once we have created a collective basis of understanding regarding the political nature of organizations, it is possible to begin to develop some action steps that will aid in project implementation.

Learn appropriate political tactics. This principle reinforces the argument that although politics exists, the manner in which organizational actors use it determines whether the political arena is a healthy or unhealthy one. There are appropriate and inappropriate methods for using politics. Since the purpose of all political behavior is to develop and keep power, both the politically naive and shark personalities are equally misguided and equally damaging to the likelihood of project implementation success. A project manager who through either naiveté or stubbornness refuses to exploit the political arena is destined to be not nearly as effective in introducing the project as is a project team leader who knows how to use politics effectively. On the other hand, project managers who are so politicized as to appear predatory and aggressive to their colleagues are doomed to create an atmosphere of such distrust and personal animus that there is also little chance for successful project adoption.

Pursuing the middle ground of political sensibility is the key to project implementation success. The process of developing and applying appropriate political tactics means using politics as it can most effectively be used: as a basis for negotiation and bargaining. Politically sensible managers understand that initiating any sort of organizational disruption or change due to developing a new project is bound to reshuffle the distribution of power within the organization. That effect is likely to make many departments and managers very nervous as they begin to wonder how the future power relationships will be rearranged. "Politically sensible" implies being politically sensitive to the concerns (real or imagined) of powerful stakeholder groups. Legitimate or not, their concerns about the new project are real and must be addressed. Appropriate political tactics and behavior include making alliances with powerful members of other stakeholder departments, networking, negotiating mutually acceptable solutions to seemingly insoluble problems, and recognizing that most organizational activities are predicated on the give and take of negotiation and compromise. It is through these uses of political behavior that managers of project implementation efforts put themselves in the position to influence the successful introduction of their projects most effectively.

In writing on project management and the nature of power, Lovell makes a similar point in arguing that effective project managers must work to maintain constructive political alliances with powerful senior management and influential department managers.[8] He notes that the persuasive skills and political acumen of a seasoned project manager will allow him or her to understand and make use of the organization's power environment, the positions of the various stakeholders, the times and means to develop and maintain alliances, and how to move around political roadblocks. All of these are skills that require objectivity and sensitivity in order to be done successfully.

Understand and accept WIIFM. One of the hardest lessons for newcomers to organizations to internalize is the primacy of departmental loyalties and self-interest over organizationwide concerns. There are many times when novice managers will feel frustrated at the foot dragging of other departments and individuals to accept new ideas or systems that are "good for them." It is vital that these managers understand that the beauty of a new project is truly in the eyes of the beholder. One may be absolutely convinced that a project will be beneficial to the organization; convincing members of other departments of this truth is a different matter altogether.

Other departments, including project stakeholders, are not likely to offer their help and support of the project unless they perceive that it is in their interests to do so. Simply assuming that these departments understand the value of a project is simplistic and usually wrong. One of my colleagues, Bob Graham, likes to refer to the WIIFM principle when describing the reactions of stakeholder groups to new innovations. "WIIFM" is an acronym for "What's In It For Me?" This is the question most often asked by individuals and departments when presented with requests for their aid. They are asking why they should support the process of implementing a new project. The worst response project managers can make is to assume that the stakeholders will automatically appreciate and value the project as much as they themselves do. Graham's point is that time and care must be taken to use politics effectively, cultivate a relationship with power holders, and make the deals that need to be made to bring the system on-line. This is the essence of political sensibility: being level-headed enough to have few illusions about the difficulties one is likely to encounter in attempting to develop and implement a new project.

Try to level the playing field. Functional line managers often view the initiation of a new project with suspicion because of its potential to upset the power balance and reduce the amount of authority a line manager has with his or her staff. To a point, these concerns are understandable. A project team does in fact create an artificial hierarchy that could compete with the traditional line managers for resources, support, status, talented personnel, and other scarce commodities. However, it is also clear that organizational realities that mandate the need for project managers and teams also need to set these individuals up with some degree of authority or status to do their job most effectively.

I have previously suggested that authority and status typically do not accrue to project managers in most organizations. One approach to giving project managers a measure of status in the formal functional hierarchy is to give them the ability to conduct performance appraisals on their project team subordinates. On the surface, this suggestion seems to be simple common sense, and yet it is often resisted in organizations. Line managers want to maintain their control over subordinates through keeping sole right to this evaluation process; hence, they may resist allowing project managers this measure of equal footing. Nevertheless, it is a powerful tool because it sends the clear message throughout the company that projects are valuable and project contributions among team members will be remembered and rewarded.[9]

Learn the fine art of influencing. How does a project manager succeed in establishing the sort of sustained influence throughout the organization that is useful in the pursuit of project-related goals? Keys and Case highlight five methods managers can use for strengthening their level of influence with superiors, clients, team members, and other stakeholders (Table 16.1 summarizes the methods).[10] They suggest that one powerful method for creating a base of influence is to establish a reputation as an expert in the project that is being undertaken. This finding was borne out in research on project manager influence styles.[11] A project manager who is widely perceived as lacking any sort of technical skill or competency cannot command the same ability to use influence as a power mechanism to secure the support of other important stakeholders or be perceived as a true leader of

TABLE 16.1. FIVE KEYS TO ESTABLISHING SUSTAINED INFLUENCE.

- Develop a reputation as an expert
- Prioritize social relationships on the basis of work needs rather than on the basis of habit or social preference
- Develop a network of other experts or resource persons who can be called upon for assistance
- Choose the correct combination of influence tactics for the objective and the target to be influenced
- Influence with sensitivity, flexibility, and solid communication

Source: Keys and Case (1990).

the project team. One important caveat to bear in mind about this point, however, is that the label of "expert" is typically a perceptual one. That is, it may or may not be based in fact. Many of us are aware of project managers who cultivate the reputation as technical experts. Unfortunately, in many of these cases, when they are faced with a true technical problem, the "expertise" that they have taken such pains to promote is shown to be woefully inadequate, perhaps even obsolete. A reputation as an expert is useful for gaining influence: truly being an expert helps immeasurably with a project manager's credibility.

A second technique for establishing greater influence is to make a distinction between the types of relationships that we encounter on the job. Specifically, managers need to make conscious decisions to prioritize their relationships in terms of establishing close ties and contacts with those around the company who can help them accomplish their goals rather than on the basis of social preference.[12] Certainly there are personality types and interest groups toward whom each of us is prone to gravitate. However, from the perspective of seeking to broaden their influence ability, project managers need to break the ties of habit and expand their social networks, particularly with regard to those who can be of future material aid to the project.

The third tactic for strengthening influence is to network. As part of creating a wider social set composed of organizational members with the power or status to aid in the project's development, canny project managers will establish ties to acknowledged experts or those with the ability to provide scarce resources the project may need during times of crisis. It is always helpful to have a few experts or resource providers handy during times of munificence. We never know when we may need to call on them, especially when resources are lean.

A fourth technique for expanding influence is based on the fact that it works only when it is done well. In other words, project managers seeking to use influence on others must carefully select the tactic they intend to employ. For example, many people who consider themselves adept at influencing others prefer face-to-face settings rather than using the telephone or leaving messages to request support. They know intuitively that it is far harder to refuse such requests than when they are made through an impersonal medium. If the tactics that have been selected are not appropriate to the individual and the situation, influence will not work.

Finally, and closely related to the fourth point, successful influencers are socially sensitive, articulate, and flexible in their tactics. For example, in attempting to influence another manager through a face-to-face meeting, a clever influencer seems to know intuitively how best to balance the alternative methods for attaining the other manager's cooperation and help. The adept influencer can often read the body language and reactions of the target manager and may instinctively shift the approach in order to find the argument or influence style that appears to have the best chance of succeeding. Whether the approach selected employs pure persuasion, flattery and cajolery, or use of guilt appeals, successful influencers are often those people who can articulate their arguments well, read the nonverbal signals given off by the other person, and tailor their arguments and influence style appropriately to take best advantage of the situation.

Develop negotiating skills. An often neglected aspect of the project manager's job involves negotiation. They are forced to negotiate on a daily basis with a variety of organizational members and external groups. Nevertheless, with the exception of some seasoned project managers who have developed their skills through trial and error, most project managers are inherently uncomfortable with the process. Further, because they find it distasteful, they have never sought to improve their negotiation skills or learn new techniques and approaches.

All project managers must hone their negotiation skills in order to improve their influence abilities. As part of this task, we need to learn to recognize the tricks and ploys of our opponents who sit across the table from us. Once we learn to anticipate and recognize their techniques, it becomes easier for us to develop appropriate responses—that is, those with the greatest likelihood of succeeding. The key is to use a form of principled negotiation in which you search for fairness, win-win outcomes, and mutually acceptable solutions.[13] A negotiation is not an opportunity to take advantage of the other party. It is a chance to gain the best terms possible for your side while seeking to address the other party's interests as well. As such, all negotiations should be treated as long-term deals, whether or not this is the case. When we recast a negotiation as a bargaining session between long-time colleagues, it changes the dynamic from one of manipulation and coercion to one of mutual problem solving.

Recognize that conflict is a natural side effect of project management. Many managers react to conflict with panic. They view any squabbling among team members as the first step toward team disintegration and ultimate project failure. This response is natural and understandable; after all, it is their responsibility if the project fails.

As a result, the most common reactions to intrateam conflicts are to do everything possible to suppress or minimize the conflict, hoping that if it is ignored, it will go away. But it almost never does. Conflict that is left to fester beneath the surface is a ticking time bomb and will almost always go off at the worst possible time later in the development process. If willful ignorance does not work with conflict, what does?

Project managers need to understand the dynamics of the conflict process better. In fact, we need to recognize conflict *as* progress.[14] The natural results of individuals from different functional backgrounds working together are professional tension and personality friction. In suggesting that project managers adopt a more sanguine attitude about conflict, I am not arguing that all conflict should be ignored. Nor do I suggest that all conflict must be either immediately suppressed or addressed. Instead, project managers need to use discretion in determining how best to handle these problems. There is no one best method for dealing with conflict. Each situation must be dealt with as a unique and separate event.

Conclusion

Politics and project management are two processes that are very different yet inextricably linked. No one can go far in project management without understanding just how far politics will take them in their organization. It is in confronting their frequent failures at getting their projects successfully implemented through traditional power means that most managers are forced through expedience to adopt methods for influence and politics. These are not "bad" terms, in spite of the fact that the majority of managers in organizations do not enjoy employing political means to their ends and do not understand the political processes very well. Too many have learned about politics the hard way, through being victimized by someone who was cannier, more experienced, or more ruthless. Given that our first experiences with politics were often unpleasant, it is hardly surprising that many of us swore off political behavior.

For better of worse, project managers do not have the luxury of turning their backs on organizational politics. Too much of what they do depends on their ability to manage not only the technical realm of their job but also the behavioral side. Politics constitutes one organizational process that is ubiquitous; it operates across organizations and functional boundaries. Politics should not be viewed as inherently evil or vicious; rather, it is only in how these techniques are employed that they have earned so much animus. All of us, bearing the scars of past experiences, understand the potential for misuse that comes from organizational politics.

CHAPTER SEVENTEEN

TEAM BUILDING

Hans J. Thamhain

All projects require effective teamwork for successful integration of their multidisciplinary activities. At one time, project leaders could ensure such integration through defining the project, organizing its team properly, and following established procedures for project tracking and control. That is no longer true. Today's challenging business climate requires project teams that can dynamically and creatively work toward established objective in a changing environment.[1] It requires effective teamwork among people and organizations from different support groups, subcontractors, vendors, government agencies, and customer communities. Uncertainties and risks are introduced by technological, economic, political, social, and regulatory factors.

These factors create enormous challenges to project leaders who have to organize and manage their teams across organizational lines and must often work with resource personnel over whom they have little or no formal authority, and deal effectively with resource sharing, multiple reporting relationships, and accountabilities.[2] Managing projects effectively in such a dynamic environment requires task leaders to understand the interaction of organizational and behavioral variables. They must develop their multidisciplinary work group into a unified team and foster a climate conducive to involvement, commitment, and conflict resolution. Because of these complexities, traditional forms of hierarchical team structure and leadership are often not effective and are being replaced by more network-based or self-directed team processes.[3]

Team Building: Concepts, Developments, and Research

Team building is the process of taking a collection of individuals with different needs, backgrounds, and expertise and transforming them into an integrated, effective work unit. In this transformation process, the goals and energies of individual contributors merge and focus on specific objectives. Team building is an ongoing process that requires leadership skills and an understanding of the organization, its interfaces, authority, power structures, and motivational factors. This process is particularly crucial in environments where complex multidisciplinary or transnational activities require the skillful integration of many functional specialties and support groups with diverse organizational cultures, values, and intricacies.[4] Following are some typical examples of multidisciplinary activities that require unified teamwork for successful integration:

Establishing a new program

Transferring technology

Improving project-client relationships

Organizing for a bid proposal

Integrating new project personnel

Resolving interfunctional problems

Working toward major milestones

Reorganizing mergers and acquisitions

Moving the project into a new activity phase

Revitalizing an organization

Because of their potential for producing economic advantages, there has been a great deal of research on work teams and their development. Starting with the evolution of formal project organizations in the 1960s, managers in various organizational settings have expressed increasing concern with and interest in the concepts and practices of multidisciplinary team building. As a result, many field studies have been conducted to investigate work group dynamics and criteria for building effective, high-performing project teams. These studies have contributed to the theoretical and practical understanding of team building and form the fundamental concepts discussed in this chapter..

Prior to 1980, most of these studies focused solely on the behavior of the team members, with limited attention given to the organizational environment and team leadership. Although the qualities of the individuals and their interaction within the team are crucial elements in the teamwork process, they represent only part of the overall organization and management system that influences team performance and that was recognized by Bennis and Shepard as early as 1956.[5]

Since 1980 an increasing number of studies have broadened the understanding of the team work process.[6] These more recent studies show the enormous breadth and depth of subsystems and variables involved in the organization, development, and management of a high-performing work team.[7] These variables include planning, organizing, training, organizational structure, the nature and complexity of tasks, senior management support, leadership, and socioeconomic variables, to name just the most popular ones.[8] Even further, researchers such as Dumaine, Drucker, Peters and Waterman, Moss Kanter, and Thamhain have emphasized the nonlinear, intricate, often chaotic, and random nature of teamwork, which involves all facets of the organization, its members, and environment.[9]

What We Know About Team Building

The basic concepts of organizing and managing teams go back to biblical times. In fact, work teams have long been considered an effective device to strengthen organizational effectiveness. Since the discovery of the importance of social phenomena in the classic Hawthorne studies, management theorists and practitioners have tried to foster group identity and cohesion in the workplace.[10] Indeed, much of the human relations movement that occurred in the decades following Hawthorne is based on a group concept. McGregor's theory Y, for example, spells out the criteria for an effective work group, and Likert called his highest form of management the participating group or system 4.[11]

In today's more complex multinational and technologically sophisticated environment, the group has reemerged in importance as the project team.[12] Especially with the evolution of contemporary organizations, such as the matrix, traditional bureaucratic hierarchies declined, and horizontally oriented teams and work units became increasingly important to effective project management.[13] These teams became the conduit for transferring information, technology, and work concepts across functional lines quickly, predictably, and within resource restraints.

Typical examples of such contemporary teams range from dedicated venture groups, often called skunk works, to product development teams, process action teams, and focus groups. These team concepts are being applied to different forms of project activities in areas of products, services, acquisition efforts, political election campaigns, and foreign assistance programs. For these kinds of highly multifunctional and nonlinear processes, researchers stress the need for strong integration and orchestration of cross-functional activities, linking the various work groups into a unified project team that focuses energy and integrates all subtasks toward desired results. These realities hold for most team efforts in today's work environment, and they are especially pronounced for efforts associated with risk, uncertainty, creativity, and team diversity such as high-technology and multinational projects. These are also the work environments that first departed from traditional hierarchical team structures and tried more self-directed and network-based concepts.[14]

The life cycle of these teams often spans the complete project, not just the phase of primary engagement. For example, the primary mission of the product development team may focus on the engineering phase, but the team also supports activities ranging from recognition of an opportunity, to feasibility analysis, bid proposals, licensing, subcontracting, transferring technology to manufacturing, distribution, and field service.

Given the enormous challenges, scope, and complexities of teamwork in today's project environment, it is not surprising that managers are greatly concerned about their ability to transform an ad hoc collection of people assigned to a particular task into a coherent, integrated work team.[15]

Characteristics of High-Performing Project Teams

The characteristics of a project team and its ultimate performance depend on many factors related to people, task, and organizational issues. Obviously each organization has its own way to measure and express performance of a project team. Nevertheless, in spite of the existing cultural and philosophical differences, there seems to be a general agreement on the characteristics of a successful project team:[16]

- Technical project success according to agreed-on plans
- On-time performance
- On-budget performance
- Responsiveness and flexibility to customer requirements and changes
- Strategic position of the project for future business
- Ability to stretch beyond planned goals
- Organizational learning benefiting future projects

When describing an effective project team, managers stress consistently that high performance, although ultimately reflected by desired results and adherence to schedule and budget, derives from many factors that can be grouped into two broad categories:

- People-oriented characteristics: Involvement and energy, capacity to resolve conflict, effective communication, team spirit, mutual trust, effective interface, high achievement needs, and ability to achieve continuous improvement
- Project result–oriented characteristics: Technical and project success, on-time and on-budget performance, commitment and result orientation, innovation and creativity, concern for quality, flexibility and willingness to change, and ability to predict trends

The significance of these factors has been tested in field research studies, which verify the strong association between these team qualities and project performance at a confidence level of 95 percent or better.[17]

The managerial value of a high-performance team model lies in two areas. First, it offers some clues as to what an effective team environment looks like. This can stimulate management thinking, resource allocations, and activities for effective team building, as well as benchmarking for further research on organization development. Second, the results allow managers to investigate and manage the drivers and barriers toward an effective team environment, and ultimately manage toward high team performance.

Figure 17.1 provides a simple model for organizing and analyzing team performance. It defines four sets of variables, which themselves are intricately interrelated, that influence the team's characteristics and its ultimate performance: (1) drivers and barriers toward high team performance (defined later in this chapter); (2) managerial leadership style, including components of authority, motivation, autonomy, trust, respect, credibility, and friendship; (3) the organizational environment, such as working conditions, job content, resources, and organizational support factors; and (4) social, political, and economic factors of the firm's business environment. Using a systems approach allows researchers and management practitioners to break down the complexity of analyses of team performance and define managerial strategies for transforming resources into desired results.

Drivers and Barriers to High Team Performance

Using the team performance model of Figure 17.1 as a framework, additional insight into team performance can be gained by investigating the drivers and barriers toward effective teamwork. Drivers are factors that influence the project environment favorably, such as interesting work and good project leadership, and that are perceived as contributing to team effectiveness, thus correlating positively with team performance. Barriers are factors that have an unfavorable influence,

FIGURE 17.1. VARIABLES FOR ANALYZING PROJECT TEAM PERFORMANCE.

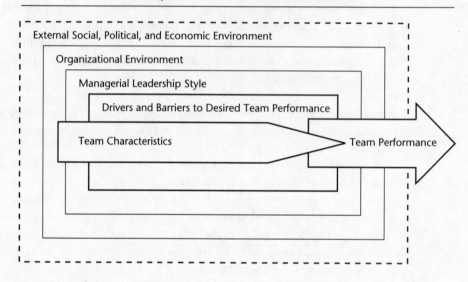

such as unclear objectives and insufficient resources, therefore impeding team performance.[18] The following six drivers have the strongest positive association to project team performance:

- Professionally interesting and stimulating work
- Recognition of accomplishment
- Good interpersonal relations
- Proper technical direction and team leadership
- Qualified project team personnel
- Professional growth potential

These are the strongest barriers to high team performance:

- Unclear project objectives and directions
- Insufficient resources
- Power struggle and conflict
- Uninvolved, disintegrated upper management
- Poor job security
- Shifting goals and priorities

The six drivers not only correlate favorably with the direct measures of high project team performance, such as technical success and on-time and on-budget performance, but also are associated positively with thirteen indirect measures of team performance: commitment, effective communication, innovative performance, mutual trust, high response rate, willingness to change, team spirit, personal involvement, work interest and ownership, high morale and team spirit, minimum reliance on top-down directions and procedures, team self-development, ability to resolve conflict, and needs for achievement. The six barriers have exactly the opposite effect. These findings provide some focus and support to the broad range of field research observations and criteria for effective team management discussed throughout this chapter.[19]

An important lesson follows from the analysis of the field data. The strong and statistically significant correlation of the drivers and barriers to high team performance suggests that managers must foster a work environment supportive to their team members. Creating such a climate and culture involves multifaceted management challenges that increase with the complexities of the project and its organizational environment. No longer will technical expertise or good leadership alone be sufficient; excellence across a broad range of skills and sophisticated organizational support systems will be required to manage these project teams effectively.

Many management practitioners and researchers consider team building to be one of the most critical leadership qualities that determine the performance and success of multidisciplinary efforts, and the organization's ability to learn from its experiences and position itself for future growth.[20] The outcome of these projects critically depends on carefully orchestrated group efforts, requiring the coordination and integration of many task specialists in a dynamic work environment with complex organizational interfaces. Therefore, it is not surprising to find a strong emphasis on teamwork and team-building practice among today's managers, a trend that is expected to continue, and most likely to intensify, for years to come.

Recommendations for Building High-Performing Teams

With increasing technical complexities, cross-functional dependencies, and the need for innovative performance, project leaders are experiencing great difficulties in managing the team from the top down. More and more, managers have to rely on information and judgments by their team members for developing solutions to complex problems. With decision processes distributed throughout the team and solutions often evolving incrementally and iteratively, power and responsibilities are shifting away from management toward the project team members. Individually and collectively, team members are taking higher levels of responsibility, authority, and control for project results. Teams thus become self-directed, gradually replacing the more traditional, hierarchically structured project team. These emerging team processes are a significant development for orchestrating the multifunctional activities that come into play during the execution of complex projects. These processes rely strongly on group interaction, resource and power sharing, group decision making, accountability, self-direction, and control. Leading such self-directed teams also requires a great deal of team management skills and overall guidance by senior management.

A number of specific recommendations may help managers in cultivating productive working conditions for multidisciplinary task integration and in building high-performing project teams.

Negotiate the work assignment. At the outset of any project, team leaders should discuss with their team members the overall task, its scope, and the team objectives. Involvement of the team members during the early phases of the assignment, such as bid proposals and project and product planning, can produce great benefits toward plan acceptance, realism, buy-in, personnel matching, and unification of the task team. A thorough understanding of the task requirements usually comes with intense personal involvement, which can be stimulated through participation in project planning, requirements analysis, interface definition, or a producibility study. In addition, any committee-type activity, presentation, or data gathering will help to involve team members, especially new ones, and facilitate integration. It also will enable people to understand their specific tasks and roles in the overall team effort better. Senior management can help develop a priority image and communicate the basic project parameter and management guidelines.

Communicate organizational goals and objectives. Management must communicate and update the organizational goals and project objectives. The relationship and contribution of individual work to overall business plans and their goals, as well as of individual project objectives and their importance to the organizational mission, must be clear to all team personnel.

Plan the project effectively. An effective project definition and involvement of potential team members early in the life cycle of a project or specific mission will have a favorable impact on the work environment, enthusiasm of the team toward the assignment, commitment toward the project objectives, team morale, and ultimately team effectiveness. Because project leaders have to integrate various tasks across many functional lines, proper planning requires the participation of all stakeholders, including support departments, subcontractors, and management. Modern project management techniques such as phased project planning and stage-gate concepts provide the conceptional framework and tools for effective cross-functional planning and organizing the work toward effective execution.

Staff and organize the project team. Project staffing is a major activity, usually conducted during the project formation phase. Because of the pressures on the project manager to produce, staffing is often done hastily and prior to adequate definition of the basic work to be performed. The results are often poor matches of personnel to job requirements, conflict, low morale, suboptimum decision making, and, in the end, poor project performance. For best results, project leaders should define the project organization, the tasks, and the work process before starting to interview candidates. These interviews should always be conducted one on one.

Define the project organization, interfaces, and reporting relations. The keys to building a successful project organization are clearly defined and communicated responsibilities and organizational relationships. The tools for systematically describing the project organization come, in fact, from conventional management practices: a charter of the program or project organization; a project organization chart, which defines the major reporting and authority relationships; a responsibility matrix or task roster; and the job description.

Build a high-performance image. Building a favorable image for an ongoing project, in terms of high priority, interesting work, importance to the organization, high visibility, and potential for professional rewards, is crucial for attracting and holding high-quality people. Senior management can help develop a priority image and communicate the key parameters and management guidelines for specific projects. Moreover, establishing and communicating clear and stable top-down objectives helps to build the desired image. Such a pervasive process fosters a climate of active participation at all levels and helps attract and hold quality people, unifies the team, and minimizes dysfunctional conflict.

Define the work process and team structure. Successful formation and development of a project team requires an infrastructure conducive to teamwork. The proper setup and communication of the operational transfer process, such as concurrent engineering, stage-gate process, and design-build, is important for establishing the cross-functional linkages necessary for successful project execution. Management must also define the basic team structure for each project early in its life cycle. The project plan, task matrix, project charter, and operating procedure are the principal management tools for defining organizational structure and business process.

Build enthusiasm and excitement. Whenever possible, managers should try to accommodate the professional interests and desires of their personnel. Interesting and challenging work is a perception that can be fostered by the visibility of the work, management attention and support, priority image, and the overlap of personnel values and perceived benefits with organizational objectives. Making work more interesting leads to increased involvement, better communication, lower conflict, higher commitment, stronger work effort, and higher levels of creativity.

Ensure senior management support. It is critically important that senior management provide the proper environment for a project team to function effectively. At the onset of a new development, the responsible manager needs to negotiate the needed resources with the sponsoring organization and obtain commitment from management that these resources will be available. An effective working relationship among resource managers, project leaders, and senior management critically affects the perceived credibility, visibility, and priority of the engineering team and their work.

Define effective communication channels and methods. Poor communication is a major barrier to teamwork and effective project performance. Management can facilitate the free flow of information, both horizontally and vertically, by good design of the work space, regular meetings, reviews, and information sessions. In addition, voice mail, e-mail, electronic bulletin boards, and conferencing can greatly improve communications, especially in complex organizational settings.

Build commitment. Managers should ensure team member commitment to their project plans, specific objectives, and results. If such commitments appear weak, managers should determine the reason and attempt to modify possibly negative views. Because insecurity is often a major reason for low commitment, managers should try to determine why insecurity exists, then work to reduce the team members' fears and anxieties. Conflict with other team members and lack of interest in the project may be other reasons for such lack of commitment.

Conduct team-building sessions. A mixture of focus team meetings, brainstorming sessions, experience exchanges, and social gatherings can be powerful tools for developing the work group into an effective, fully integrated, and unified project team. Such organized team-building efforts should be conducted throughout the project life cycle. An especially intensive team-building effort may be needed during the team formation stage. Although formally organized and managed, these team-building sessions are often conducted in an informal and relaxed atmosphere to discuss critical questions: How are we working as a team? What is our strength? How can we improve? What support do you need? What challenges and problems are we likely to face? What actions should we take? What process or procedural changes would be beneficial?

Ensure project leadership. The project management and team leadership positions should be carefully defined and staffed at all projects levels. To build and lead a project team, especially in a dynamic or self-directed work environment, requires a project leader who exudes credibility, trust, and respect, qualities that usually come from the image of a sound decision maker with a good track record.

Create proper reward systems. Personnel evaluation and reward systems should be designed to reflect the desired power equilibrium and authority and responsibility sharing of an organization. A QFD-philosophy helps to focus efforts toward desired results on company internal and external customers and to foster a work environment that is strong on self-direction and self-control.

Manage conflict and problems. Project managers should focus their efforts on problem avoidance. That is, through experience, they should recognize potential problems and conflicts at their onset, and deal with them before they become big and their resolutions consume large quantities of time and effort.

Ensure personal drive and leadership. Project managers and team leaders can influence the team environment by their own actions. Concern for their team members, the ability to integrate the personal needs of their staff with the goals of the organization, and the ability to create personal enthusiasm for a particular project can foster a climate of high motivation, work involvement, open communication, and ultimately high engineering performance.

A Final Note

The increasing complexities of project environments, both internally and externally, prompt enormous managerial challenges for directing, coordinating, and controlling teamwork. Especially with the expansion of self-directed team concepts, additional managerial tools and skills are required to handle the burgeoning dynamics and infrastructure. Effective teamwork is a critical determinant of project success. To be effective in organizing and directing a project team, the leader must not only recognize the potential drivers and barriers to high-performance teamwork, but also know when in the life cycle of the project they are most likely to occur. The effective project leader takes preventive actions early in the project life cycle and fosters a work environment that is conducive to team building as an ongoing process. The new business realities force managers to focus also on cross-boundary relations, delegation, and commitment, in addition to establishing the more traditional formal command-and-control systems.

The effective team leader is usually a social architect who understands the interaction of organizational and behavioral variables and can foster a climate of active participation and minimal dysfunctional conflict. This requires carefully developed skills in leadership, administration, organization, and technical expertise. It requires the ability to involve top management and ensure organizational visibility, resource availability, and overall support for the new project throughout its life cycle. Moreover, project leaders and their management must understand the interaction of organizational and behavioral variables, so they can facilitate a climate of active participation, minimal dysfunctional conflict, and effective communication. They must foster an ambiance conducive to change, commitment, and self-direction. Four major conditions must be present for building effective project teams: (1) professionally stimulating work environment, (2) good project leadership, (3) qualified personnel, and (4) a stable work environment.

Building effective project teams involves the whole spectrum of management skills and company resources, and is a shared responsibility between functional managers and the project leader. By understanding the criteria and organizational dynamics that drive people toward effective team performance, managers can examine and fine-tune their leadership style, actions, and resource allocations to achieve continuous organizational improvement.

CHAPTER EIGHTEEN

CROSS-FUNCTIONAL COOPERATION

David Wilemon

There is a growing interest in the use of cross-functional teams (CFTs) in managing important projects, for a number of reasons:

- Intensifying global competition, which requires companies to respond to opportunities and threats worldwide with intelligence and speed
- Increasing emphasis on delivering high quality and value to customers
- The importance of quick response capability, such as speed to market and meeting a variety of new and complex customer needs
- Changing organizations (through flattening, empowering, and power sharing, for example), changing reward systems, and deemphasis of command-and-control management
- The movement away from command-and-control, functionally based organizations toward team-based, highly entrepreneurial enterprises
- The increasing use of alliances, partnerships, and networks, which require entirely new ways of thinking and acting

In these new organizational designs, cross-functional teamwork may extend far beyond the boundaries of the traditional organization.

The material for this chapter stems from interviews conducted with project team leaders and team members in two technology-based organizations. The first organization, referred to here as Medtech, designs, develops, and manufactures various types of medical diagnostic equipment. The second company, referred to as Teletech, designs and manufactures telecommunications equipment. One project leader and five team members in each organization were interviewed. Both projects were approximately midway in their development and were considered successful in terms of development progress by their respective organizations.

The Medtech project leader had 15 years of organizational experience and had managed three successful medical technology projects. The mean organizational experience for the CFT members at Medtech was 10.5 years. The Teletech project leader had 12 years of experience, and each team member averaged 9.3 years of organizational experience. The team leaders and team members had all worked on at least two successful development projects. The development schedule for the Medtech project was 1.5 years, and for the Teletech project 2.3 years. A semistructured interview protocol was used to guide the interview process. The interviews focused on these questions:

- What is your function in this team?
- What factors, if any, have contributed to the success of this project?
- What factors, if any, have limited your team's performance?
- What steps, if any, were taken to help your team perform more effectively together?
- Were these activities useful? If yes, how so?
- What have been your major personal lessons learned from participating in this project?

During the interviews, additional probes were made regarding how the team set its goals; how roles were clarified; how the project planning process worked; and how the team developed and maintained its relationships with customers, senior management, suppliers, and functional departments. All interviews were recorded and transcribed. To help explain, clarify, and give contextual insights to the issues discussed in this chapter, examples and the voices of the interviewees will be used. Interviews conducted during the process of project completion have several advantages over retrospective interviews, such as potential memory loss in postproject interviews. In addition, the perspectives presented here are based on my own experiences working with various types of cross-functional teams for over twenty years.

Defining Cross-Functional Teams

Among the number of definitions for cross-functional teams, two are particularly relevant for the concepts developed in this chapter:

> A group of people with a clear purpose representing a variety of functions or disciplines in the organization whose combined efforts are necessary for achieving the team's purposes. The team may be permanent or ad hoc and may include vendors and customers, as appropriate.[1]

Another explanation of cross-functional teamwork emphasizes its benefits:

> Cross-functional teams have considerable currency now as a logical means to generate more creative, less problem-riddled solutions, faster. By cutting across functions and assembling all of the employees working on the same project onto a team, companies hope to reduce disputes among functions, preempt problems, and unleash the energy and effort that people give when contributing to a meaningful project they see as their own.[2]

Cross-functional teamwork is particularly important to project management in that so many projects require the careful, mindful contributions of several disciplines. In fact, many complex projects could not be accomplished without such teamwork. Among the companies that frequently rely on cross-functional teamwork are AT&T, Sun Microsystem, Hewlett-Packard, Black & Decker, 3M, and Xerox.

Traditional Organizational Integration Problems

Achieving effective cross-functional teamwork requires considerable thought, work, and planning. In fact, the way most organizations are structured and the way various cultures and subcultures exist within organizations makes achieving cross-functional teamwork a major challenge. Consider the following observation regarding how various functional groups and their "thought worlds" view reality as it applies to new product development projects:

> For new product development, one could infer that departmental thought worlds would selectively filter information and insights. Because of specialization, a certain thought world is likely to best understand certain issues, but also

to ignore information that may be equally essential to the total task. Their intrinsic harmony would also reduce the possibility for creative learning, since members of the department think they already know everything.[3]

In a detailed example Robert Lutz, president and chief operating officer of Chrysler, discusses the challenges his company faced achieving cross-functional teamwork:

> Chrysler's first turnaround, the company's storied come-back of the early- to mid-1980s, is a familiar story by now. But our most recent turnaround (which is still going on) is . . . an equally impressive story. What makes it impressive . . . is the degree to which we have been successful in implementing "teamwork" concepts into virtually everything we do—including research and development.
>
> Traditionally, Chrysler, like virtually all other western automakers, was organized around vertically oriented, "chimney-like" functional departments. Each department—Design, Engineering, Procurement and Supply, and so forth—was pretty much a world unto itself—a silo, if you will.
>
> The Design department, working more or less in a vacuum, would design a car and then . . . "shove it out the door" to the Engineering department. But, because Engineering hadn't been involved in the process, changes for feasibility would invariably be required—resulting in what I call "redo" loops.
>
> Then, Engineering, in a vacuum itself, would engineer the car and shove it out the door to Procurement & Supply to buy parts and components from suppliers. But again, there would be more redo loops, because our suppliers had been in a vacuum of their own.
>
> The same thing would happen all the way down the line until, finally, all of the redo loops started to look like a massive fur-ball!
>
> The results, sadly, were mammoth costs, uncompetitive product development times, and, last but not least "lowest common-denominator" cars and trucks. That's because even though there were intense turf battles all along the way, the sense of ownership for a complete vehicle was so diffuse it was almost as if nobody was responsible for it.[4]

There are several challenges most traditional organizations face when they attempt to achieve highly coordinated, multifunctional projects:

- Limited internal integration exists among various functional organizations, such as R&D, manufacturing, and marketing. As a consequence, that are numerous disconnects and dropped balls, missed handoffs, and unproductive surprises when they attempt to coordinate multidisciplinary efforts.

- Limited external integration exists of key stakeholders with the key processes of the organization: customers, suppliers, and partners.
- Cross-disciplinary business processes, such as project management, new product or process development, Total Quality Management, and management information system implementation, are poorly executed.
- Important up-front issues are often rushed, which eventually leads to serious technical performance problems, for example, serious technical problems found late in a project's development cycle or the inability to satisfy the customer's real needs.
- There is low sharing of information among organizational members.
- Responsibilities are both diffused and confused, resulting in a lack of focus.
- "Signal distortion" occurs when individuals and groups attempt to communicate.
- Change is resisted.
- Limited project and organizational learning occurs.

Fortunately, these problems and challenges can be minimized and in some cases eliminated by the use of cross-functional teams.

Factors Determining the Need for CFTs

As noted in Figure 18.1, the need for cross-functional teamwork in project management is largely determined by the complexity of a project. For our purposes, complexity is defined by how many different groups and organizations are involved in a project, the degree of project novelty, the length of a project, project size, and scope.

Benefits of Cross-Functional Teamwork

Glenn Parker notes that there are at least six potential benefits of cross-functional teamwork:[5]

1. *Speed.* Cross-functional teams help organizations reduce the time it takes to get things done. This is particularly important in project management where timely schedule accomplishment is a major determinant of project success.
2. *Complexity.* A CFT can bring together, integrate, and magnify the talents of several disciplinary experts who by working together minimize functional differences and barriers. Such interdisciplinary work can bring out the best of

FIGURE 18.1. FACTORS INFLUENCING THE NEED FOR CROSS-FUNCTIONAL TEAMWORK.

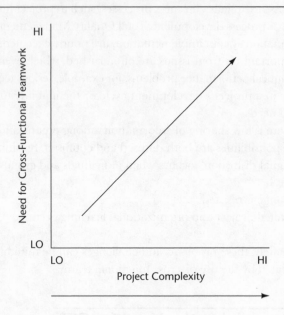

specialists and can focus this talent on solving complex, highly sophisticated problems.

3. *A customer focus.* This is achieved by assembling key organizational resources to solve specific important problems.

4. *Creativity.* Creativity is encouraged by bringing different people together and creating synergy from their different views, perspectives, expertise, and problem-solving approaches. Team members can hear the ideas of others and augment them with their own thoughts. The result is often better and more creative approaches than any one person could have done.

5. *Organizational learning.* CFTs can be useful for capturing and sharing the learning that occurs during a complex project. The likelihood that this will occur is far greater than from the compartmentalized, "hand-it-over-the-wall" approach to managing complex projects. Learning helps individuals, teams, and organizations avoid making the same mistakes by building a reservoir of experience and solutions in the management of projects.

6. *A single point of contact.* A CFT can be the single, identifiable point of contact for information and expertise regarding a project.

Activities Facilitating Cross-Functional Teamwork

There are a number of activities that can transform a group of people from different functional disciplines into a fully functioning CFT. I have found eight activities that are particularly helpful in building a highly effective CFT.

Team Visioning

There has been considerable discussion about the importance and function of having a team vision or team mission. There must be a compelling vision if energy from diverse individuals and groups is to be attracted to a project.[6] In some cases the vision will be straightforward—for example, to develop a heart pacemaker with the highest achievable quality standard, build an irrigation project that will significantly elevate the living standard of a developing economy, or safely send a team to Mars and back. The best vision statements are authentic and simple, and they provide a goal that team members want to achieve. Equally important, the project vision often has a direct connection to a person or group beyond the team, such as the customer. Some of the best vision statements consist of only a short sentence or two, and usually they are no longer than a paragraph. Keeping it simple and profound are good criteria for a great cross-functional team vision.

The project leader at Medtech made a point about the role of his cross-functional team's vision this way: "You must have a powerful, compelling vision to attract the energy and minds of the people you work with. Unless they identify with the vision, they will not give the project their best efforts. I would never lead an important project unless we had crafted a compelling vision."

Chartering

The charter for a team, which may actually exist before the team's vision is fully developed, is senior management's expectations for the team. The charter also may describe the authority of the project leader, the basic understandings and agreements between the project leader and senior management of the host organization(s), the customer, functional managers, and often details of the commitment of resources. The project leader at Medtech defined his team's project charter as follows: "My charter is really about the fundamental understanding I have with my bosses. It gives me legitimacy when I work with others. It also helps clarify the arena of expectations between me, my bosses, and the customer."

Often the internal sponsors of the project initiate and develop the charter, but the project leader can also do this work. The experiences of the Teletech project leader were noted this way: "I did not have my marching orders laid down before me on a silver platter. I had to take the initiative. I created the project goals with my team, we estimated the resource requirements, and considered other such pivotal issues. I then sold our plan to the people upstairs. If I had waited for my bosses to create the momentum for this project I would still be sitting here. Their plates are fuller than mine. I felt that I have to be the initiator to get things moving!"

This project leader makes a powerful point: if senior management does not take the initiative for forming a charter, then the project leader should. Many team leaders have learned midway in a project the dangers and disappointments of not being clear on what a project needs to be successful. A seasoned team member at Medtech with several projects under his belt made this comment: "I always want to know if our management is fully behind the project. Do they really understand what's required to be successful or not? If they don't know about the success requirements I know from experience that we will likely sail on some troubled waters. In fact, I've had enough experience to know to ask the project leader some very focused questions about the project charter. That's my number one concern and inquiry at the front end of a project."

Senior managers who sponsor projects are advised to discuss thoroughly with their project leader and, in some cases, the entire core team what the project team needs to do in order to meet expectations. The quality of this dialogue can be sharpened if everyone has a clear understanding of the project requirements. In an important sense, the project charter helps a team and the organization define the requirements for success.

Goal Clarification

Clarifying the goals of the project is another important early-on task of the team.[7] As Glenn Parker observes:

One of the most important roles that clear goals play on a cross-functional team is to reduce the potential for conflicts represented on the team. Even without any past differences, people often come to a team with a belief that the contribution of their function is the most important and should take precedence over the other areas, or have more clout in the decision-making process or in resource allocation. Sometimes the assumed rank order of the various disciplines is embedded in the existing culture of the organization.[8]

There are several dimensions of the goal clarification process. First, basic agreement must exist within the team regarding the goals of the project. What is this project supposed to accomplish? Why is it important? These are the more global project goals. What are the specific goals of each team member? For example, how does a software developer on the team define his or her goals as they relate to the overall project? After the team goals and individual team member goals (or functional goals) have been established, the team needs to examine where goals may conflict. One way to identify these conflicts is for each member of the CFT to discuss his or her goals and for the other members of the team to focus on where others' goals may affect them.

A project team member discussed the goal clarification process at Teletech as follows: "Gaining clarity around the goals of the project is essential to my success. We first make certain that everyone understands the project goals. Is the team clear? Is senior management clear? Is the customer clear? After this has been determined, we then look for conflicts over goals within the team itself. We try not to move forward until these internal conflicts and disagreements over our goals have been settled."

What frequently happens in goal clarification sessions is that conflicts are surfaced that people were not even aware of before. This early identification is beneficial in that the conflicts can be far more easily handled earlier than later in a project.

Role Clarification

Somewhat like the goal clarification process, role clarification essentially involves who does what and when. In some projects, the who and what are not major issues; they will be well known from almost the start. In other projects, team members (and functional organizations) may have overlapping capabilities and "get into each other's turf." Conflicts over roles may develop between R&D and engineering over design responsibilities, for example, or between R&D and marketing over contact with the customer.

One project team member at Teletech commented on role clarification this way: "You have to be real careful about roles and responsibilities in a cross-functional project team. People often can get agreement on what the goals are fairly quickly. Then they have to see who will perform critical project functions. There is where it can get sticky, particularly if people are territorial. My suggestion is to tackle these issues early; otherwise people will be both disappointed and surprised by the lack of performance."

One effective method for gaining clarity about roles within a CFT is to conduct a role clarification session early, with each group or each individual explaining his or her contribution to the group and what support is needed from each of the others. Another approach is to have various team members explain their responsibilities and tell each team member what is needed from him or her. An experienced project leader can avoid many role-related problems by carefully thinking through the requirements of a project and the needs of project contributors and their capabilities.

The Project Management Plan

One of the most important CFT tasks is the development of the project management plan. This is the road map the team will follow in executing the project. The team leader and usually the core team plan all the major activities of the project, determine performance requirements, estimate how long it will take, check for the interdependencies of tasks, and derive costs for subactivities and for the overall project. During the process of developing the project plan, some team building will likely occur in terms of how people learn to work with each other. And by the end of the project planning phase, team members should have a good idea of the teamwork requirements.

The Teletech project leader made this comment about the project management plan: "I personally enjoy project planning. It serves two critical purposes. First, it lays out what must be done and when. Second, it helps build your team. People must communicate, coordinate, and integrate their efforts in developing the project plan. They also must deal with all varieties of conflicts and disagreements. I know that the quality of our plan will largely determine how well the project will be executed. By the time the plan is developed we usually are starting to work fairly well as a team."

Implementation

The implementation phase is where the project is actually carried out. It also is a time of testing the team itself, the project management plan, and the team's ability to deal with contingencies. Implementation is complicated by its dependency on vendors, customers, and even partners. One project team member at Teletech described the project implementation process in his organization this way: "You can have the greatest plan in the world and everyone will say that they've bought into it. But the real test is when the project starts rolling. There are a lot of things which can go wrong and which demand attention and a lot of teamwork. Implementation is the real thing—it's not an academic exercise. You test everything you've planned for during project implementation."

What helps implementation is to have an effective project management plan, have the support of every involved group and person, be clear on the customer requirements, and have a team that is capable and trained in teamwork processes.

Learning

Project team learning is an important component of the process described here. What teams often experience, unfortunately, is that the project may be successful and that much was learned by the team during the planning and implementation phases but little was captured and stored for later use.[9] As a consequence, we often find the next generation of projects making similar mistakes. When this occurs, the project is likely to cost more, take longer, and result in lower customer satisfaction. One Medtech project team member explained his view of learning as follows:

> What happens around here is that everyone works real hard, very hard to achieve a successful project. Yes, we learn a great deal because we've never done these types of projects before. I learn, the guy in manufacturing learns, and the R&D people learn, but no one takes the time to reflect on the project, so there's no real discussion of what went right and where we screwed up. As soon as one project is completed, we scatter and are quickly assigned to the next one. Where's the knowledge gained? What's the retention factor? Where's the benefit to all the projects that will follow? Answers to these issues may or may not surface. My experience is that a lot of very useful learning simply evaporates at the conclusion of our projects.

In order to ensure that project leaders and team members do gain from their experiences and that project team knowledge is captured and stored, a few companies are conducting extensive postproject review sessions to capture the knowledge gained from each project experience. Usually these sessions are conducted using a multimethod approach. First, the entire team may be interviewed regarding their experiences, what they have learned, what they have experimented with, what they wished they had done differently, and what were the critical incidents in the project.

Equally important is the learning that goes on at the individual team member level. These contributors may be asked a similar set of questions—for example: What was your most significant learning? What do you wish you and the rest of the team had done differently? If you had this project to do over, what would you recommend? What was your greatest disappointment (if any) in this project? What were the two or three most important incidents in the life of this project? What did you learn from them?

A more effective approach is to conduct a learning assessment as the project progresses. This minimizes the memory loss problem and will capture the learning in real time. Such an assessment also can reduce mistakes and errors from being repeated on the same project in the future.

Cross-Functional Team Skills

The skills depicted in Figure 18.2 are beneficial in creating and maintaining effective cross-functional teamwork.

Interpersonal skills include such capabilities as communicating, listening, writing, helping skills, and dealing with the dysfunctional behaviors of others. Such skills are both teachable and learnable, and there are seminars and workshops that focus on most or all of these skills. Without some grounding in these skills, the best teams become bogged down in issues and problems that may become insurmountable.

Conflict management and negotiation skills help CFTs deal with their internal differences as well as differences with management, functional groups, customers, and suppliers. Examples of key knowledge areas here are understanding the fundamental causes of conflict in project-oriented work environments, the vari-

FIGURE 18.2. MAJOR CROSS-FUNCTIONAL TEAM SKILLS.

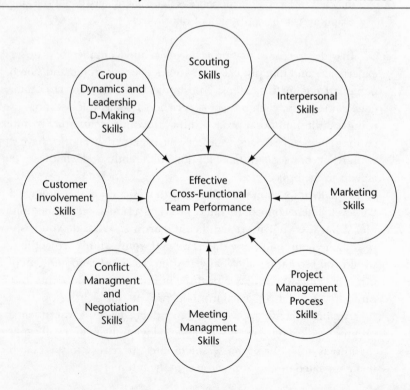

ous methods that can be used to solve conflicts, and how to negotiate effectively in order to arrive at win-win solutions to problems. Training in these areas may be sought through internal training capabilities or through a number of commercially available seminars and workshops.

Meeting management skills help a team maximize its time together. For many teams, teamwide information is both sought and shared through meetings. Examples of these skills are structuring a meeting, gaining clarity regarding its purpose, developing a consensus, sharing responsibilities for the success of a meeting, dealing with dysfunctional behaviors, and effective follow-up processes to ensure implementation of team decisions.

Increasingly teams must deal directly with customers. In fact, *customer involvement skills* are often needed even before a cross-functional team is officially formed. This involvement often continues until after product launch or project completion. Project teams are identifying a number of skills that can help build and maintain productive relationships with customers, among them, listening skills, negotiating skills, conflict management skills, creativity, and problem-solving skills. One large telecommunications company offers a course for its project teams entitled, "How to Communicate with Customers."

One of the project team members interviewed at Medtech commented about communicating with her customers as follows:

> You have to be real careful in terms of what you say to customers. We went to the customer's site, and our R&D people were promising the customers every feature imaginable. When the customer would ask about some feature being added, R&D would say, "no problem." What R&D didn't realize was that their promises were slowly killing the project because we were going to miss the market window and the cost of these features would price us out of the market. From this experience, I learned that the customer really needs to hear one clear voice. If everyone is promising the customer different features, it winds up as a chaotic, counterproductive exercise.

Group dynamics and leadership skills include understanding how groups develop and mature (or do not); how leadership roles may change in the group depending on the type of problems to be solved; the interactions between the leader and team members and between team members; group maturation affects problem-solving capabilities within the team; and how teams often develop defensive routines rather than facing the real issues that need addressing.

Scouting skills—gathering information and data from various support groups, suppliers, customers, and even competitors—are seldom discussed in the literature but can be highly important for a team. As one of the Teletech project team members remarked: "When we go to the customer's site, we all look and listen to what's going on. What does the customer think about this project? Who will use it? Who is their sponsor? Where is our customer's business headed? What trends do they see? What was mentioned about competitive projects? How satisfied does the customer appear with our efforts? What is it about the current project that excites the customer?"

Scouting can be equally useful dealing with suppliers because they often have a different knowledge base than the customers do. Finally, scouting skills can be critically important within a company in understanding project sponsors and various functional groups. Team members need to be aware that information derived from mindful scouting can pay handsome dividends when captured and shared.

A related set of skills are the team's *marketing skills*. Most effective project teams need to market themselves to various functional groups, customers, suppliers, senior management sponsors, and other groups and organizations. Unless this kind of marketing and information sharing goes on, the team may find that others are not aware of the team's capabilities or its progress or may have a distorted view of a team's goals and performance.

The project leader at Medtech made this comment: "We were making great progress on the patient monitoring instrument project. The entire team knew we were in good shape in terms of meeting our major project goals. I was taken back when one of our senior managers who I thought was totally on board asked if the project was underway yet. That comment blew me and the others on the team completely out of the water. I spent the next few days briefing several senior people on the project and how well we were doing." As experienced managers know, if there is a lack of information in an organization, people fill their knowledge gaps with rumors, projections, and assumptions.

Finally, project teams and their members need to understand their organization's *project management processes*. Too often, people on teams do not fully understand how project management works and what is required of everyone for the process to be useful. Examples of knowledge here include how schedules are established; how costs are managed and reported; how performance is tracked; project review processes; how interdependencies among tasks are identified, coordinated, and engaged; and how they affect the project.

Before a project is officially launched, the team must be instructed on project management processes and tools. On a critical, high-profile project, it is insufficient and too costly for teams to learn about project management in real time. One project member at Medtech commented on this point as follows: "On our last project we did some team building before the project actually got underway. That was very helpful to me and to the other less experienced team members. Equally important, our corporate project management group gave a three-day workshop on project management. We learned about project planning, scheduling, developing a critical path for the major project activities, costing, budgeting, customer-supplier involvement, and how to track performance. I found this workshop very useful."

Role of Senior Management

One of the most important roles that senior management can play is establishing the context and culture within which CFTs perform. This can be facilitated by promoting clear, compelling superordinate goals for the organization. The more that various organizational members can identify with the goals of the organization, the more likely it is that effective cross-functional teamwork can occur. Clear goals for the overall organization help focus the resources of the organization on performance and thereby reduce some of the conflict that can arise over interfunctional priorities and turf battles.

Another important action senior managers can take to promote cross-disciplinary teamwork is to provide training in many of the necessary skills, such as project management training, teamwork skills, group dynamic skills, communication, and conflict management. It is important for senior managers to note the effect of their own behavior. If they do not model and practice effective teamwork, it probably will not happen at the working levels of the organization. The project manager at Medtech discussed this point as follows: "The organization I worked in before I came here was full of conflict. The top people were always fighting, and it impacted the rest of us. In one case the senior marketing director refused to talk to the director of engineering. Did that affect us? You bet it did. We couldn't get anything done. What's interesting is that senior management had really been promoting teamwork for months. After that incident, I never took their initiatives seriously. I'm pretty sure that the others felt the same way."

Senior managers can facilitate cross-functional teamwork by actively encouraging the use of these teams, recognizing and rewarding teamwork, and creating a culture where teamwork is recognized as an effective management approach.

Impact of Cross-Functional Teams on Team Members

If an organization uses cross-functional teams extensively in carrying out its project management assignments, there are several potential impacts on team members. Some team members will have the opportunity to learn more. They will, for example, learn about other team member capabilities, as well as the capabilities of the functional groups within the organization. They also may feel greater pressure and stress, because project teams often are under considerable pressure to perform, yet they also may feel far more empowered than if they were working solely in their functional groups. One Teletech team member commented as follows: "I've had a wonderful experience on this project. We acted like a team from the start. I learned about other people's backgrounds, their strengths, and their limitations. I also felt stress because I was the only one from my functional group on the project. My boss empowered me to make virtually all the decisions that involved manufacturing. It was very stressful at times."

Another issue that frequently crops up is that team members experience divided loyalties. They feel ownership for the project, but they also are loyal to their functional home. This too can be stressful, as team members may get conflicting signals from the project and their functional boss. One team member with several years of project management experience made this comment: "The project manager once told me to do one thing, and my functional boss told me to do just the opposite. I was caught in the middle. I finally resolved it by calling a meeting and telling them how their conflicting directives affected my performance. After that incident, we all three agreed to meet on important decisions affecting me— a costly process in terms of time, but it reduced the conflicts I experienced."

Many organizations are finding that cross-functional teams are excellent training grounds for future project managers. Team members learn about project management, resolving conflict between functional groups, communicating, customer needs, supplier capabilities, and, of course, teamwork processes.

Functional Manager Responsibilities

Functional managers are often viewed as a barrier to highly effective cross-functional teamwork.[10] In some of the companies that carry out cross-functional teamwork well, we often see a different view of the functional manager's role in facilitating CFTs. Donnellon gives useful advice on the role of middle managers in facilitating teamwork. She found that the more effective middle managers (functional managers) think of themselves as resource providers rather than as resource controllers. She also notes that these managers can perform an important role in advising and mentoring team members and even teams, particularly helpful if the functional manager has had extensive teamwork experience.[11] The functional managers also are responsible for developing people technically in engineering, manufacturing, marketing, and similar other areas. The more proficient the functional manager is at keeping his or her staff at the state of the art, the more valued these people will be as team members. Another responsibility of functional managers is linking to their senior managers for resources, support, and advice. Finally, functional managers need to encourage, recognize, and reward risk taking and creative problem solving by those working on projects.

Gaining Team Member Commitment

One of the most important factors for gaining team member commitment within CFTs is having clear, compelling goals for the project. If these goals are not clear, there will be a lack of focus within the team. Clearly related to this point is a strong sense of connectedness to the organization's vision. Differently put, is this project aligned with the larger organization's vision? If it is not, there is likely to be considerable discussion around the issues of "Are we relevant?" and "Are we doing the right thing?" In some cases, however, the misalignment may be intentional, as in a new venture that will take the organization in an entirely different direction.

Commitment can be increased when there is a clear congruence between individual and team values, such as emphasis on customer satisfaction, quality, mutual respect, and information sharing. One of the most important factors in gaining commitment is to provide exciting, challenging work. The greater the job challenge is, the higher the commitment level many team members will experience. Similarly, the greater the perceived opportunities for growth and recognition, the higher the commitment that is likely to be experienced. One cross-functional team member at Teletech made this comment:

> What motivates me? I will tell you it is a challenging project where I can learn some new things technically and can learn more about our customers and our own organization. If I feel that I'm growing and gaining professionally I'm motivated—no question about it. What makes me dislike project work is when there is a feeling that no one really cares that much about the project. It's hard to commit my energies to those types of projects.

Another factor that helps with commitment is having a supportive environment for teams. An organization can create a supportive climate for teamwork by offering training for project team leaders, assisting middle managers to be aware of the needs of cross-functional teams, and providing the tools that facilitate teamwork, such as groupware software, space, and administrative and secretarial support. Moreover, providing rewards for effective team performance can encourage teamwork.[12] A final important factor that helps team members commit to a project is seeing that leadership is a shared responsibility. A feeling of shared leadership for the project's success can create high levels of commitment.

Indicators of Poorly Functioning CFTs

Achieving highly effective, authentic cross-functional teamwork can be challenging, and teams often struggle to do so. By identifying the causes of poor teamwork from indicators that signal when a team is not functioning well, approaches can be devised to get a team back on track.[13] Listed below are several characteristics of poorly functioning teams.

Lack of clear objectives. This is one of the most important characteristics of poorly functioning CFTs. When the objectives are not clear to participants, they often quit performing or engage in activities that do not promote the objectives of the project. One indicator of this problem is poor performance or loss of team energy.

Lack of alignment. "Buy-in" or alignment is one of the most important qualities of a high-performing team. When team members are "out of alignment," it means that they have not accepted the goals of the project. In some cases they actually understand the goals but do not agree with them or even may disagree with the goals and attempt to block their attainment. One of the major causes of this is the lack of careful team building and consensus building around goals early in the project. When people are not in alignment, it clearly can be frustrating, but it also can be a time of great creativity. A team member may not agree with a particular technological approach, and in the course of discussing the disagreement the group eventually reaches a better resolution.

Poor meetings. The lack of good meeting management processes can drain the energy from a team very quickly. Effective meetings are important for cross-functional teams because important information is shared at them. Meetings also are a source of a great deal of creativity if they are managed well. Finally, meetings help teams reach closure on important issues. The meeting management skills of CFT leaders are paramount. Another important factor is setting a climate where meetings are looked at as one of the most productive parts of the project.

Conflicts over roles. Different people on a team often perform highly diverse roles. If there is lack of agreement about these roles, then conflict will often develop between project participants, and work will not get done. Early in the life of a project, teams need to discuss who will do what and when they will be required to do it. Roles and responsibilities are seldom static; thus, individuals and teams need to think about how roles evolve over the life of a project. When conflict and disagreements over roles arise, people spend their energy in ways that do not contribute to project accomplishment.

Lack of follow-up. Almost all project participants have anecdotal stories of the great decision that was made but never implemented. It happens too frequently in project management. Simply stated, making a decision is clearly not the same as task accomplishment. The best teams develop a culture of follow-through on decisions. The key questions that need to be asked are: What is the decision? Who will carry it out? and How will we know when a successful conclusion is reached?

Lack of information sharing. A major problem often encountered in poorly functioning CFTs is a lack of information sharing among team members.[14] There are several reasons that this might occur. Team members, for example, might guard what they create and be reluctant to share it. On one team I worked with, the software engineers were reluctant to share information because each developer (there were three) wanted to come up with the brilliant idea and be recognized and rewarded for it. Another related reason is that if the trust level is low, people often wonder what will happen to their ideas if they share them. Great teams are usually built on the basis of intensive interaction and extensive information sharing among team members. Low levels of information sharing on a complex, multifunctional project is a certain recipe for disaster.

Poor leadership. The lack of effective leadership is a major cause of poor project performance. In some cases, CFTs have to be restarted due to the poor leadership being exercised within them. Leadership occurs not only with the project leader but throughout the team. The most effective teams I have seen have always had a designated leader, but various leadership functions were shared among the team members. In the best teams, everyone leads at some point. Other indicators of poor leadership are a lack of initiative within the team, a low team energy level, and a lack of accomplishment.

Lack of senior management support. The support of senior management is a major contributor to CFT success. Conversely, the lack of management support often leads to low performance levels. Support of senior management signals several factors to the organization: that they sanction the project, are knowledgeable about it, and want it to succeed. Experienced project leaders know that one of the best investments of their time is keeping senior management involved and enthused. As one project leader remarked, "If you have the full support of management, you have a partner." Solid management support also will lower the amount of detrimental conflict a team experiences with functional managers and within the team itself.

Ineffective team members. Poorly trained or ineffective team players are a cause of low team performance. Sometimes a team member is not a good performer because he or she lacks the right skills to do the job well. In other cases, members have the technical skills but are not capable of performing or able to do so in a team environment. Cross-functional team leaders often have to work with the teams they are given or inherit. However, when given the opportunity, the leaders may greatly influence the quality of their teams by carefully selecting the most appropriate team members for the project. Three important criteria for selecting team members are their expertise, the ability to work in a team environment, and the ability to work well with the organization, particularly its functional groups, and perhaps with customers, users, and suppliers. A leader who inherits a team or is assigned team members (a common practice) can try to improve areas of weakness by coaching, mentoring, and setting a good example.

There are, of course, other indicators of poorly functioning CFTs. One contributor to ineffective teams is the lack of an organizational culture that supports teamwork. If a company does not have a productive culture that promotes teamwork, it can take years to develop one. Too often projects are managed in organizational environments that are hostile to effective teamwork. The following questions can help to assess the organization's propensity to support teamwork:

- How do people in our organization view teams: as necessary to accomplishing the important goals of the organization or as another management fad?
- Where is the focus of power in our organization: in the functional organizations or with the various programs and projects the organization is trying to achieve? Is there a shift in power? If so, how and why?
- Do our senior people have teamwork experience?
- What is the track record of teams in our organization? Do they perform at high levels? Are they given the most complex jobs to do? Are some of the best people in the organization serving on teams?
- Does our organization have a supportive infrastructure and culture to support teams? Do we have the right facilities to encourage teamwork? Do teams have the right tools? Do important teams have access to the best people in the organization? Are effective cross-functional teams recognized and rewarded?

The Challenge to Organizations

In exploring the difficulties encountered by organizations as they attempt to achieve highly effective CFTs, Donnellon found that the transition to teams in most organizations requires considerable work, training, and the sustained support of senior managers. She also noted a common disparity between the ideal in teamwork and actual accomplishments of teams. Finally, she explained that there is often tension with individuals as they adjust to the requirements of teamwork.[15] Other observers of cross-functional teams have noted similar challenges.[16] For example, Henke, Krachenberg, and Lyons wrote, "In spite of these clear benefits, cross-functional teams are still looked on with suspicion in some firms. As a result cross-functional teams are in varying stages of development in many industries, including automotive, electronic, pharmaceutical, household appliance, and petro-chemical."[17]

These issues will not surprise astute managers who are fully aware that accomplishing high-performing cross-functional teamwork is often one of the most challenging tasks organizations face.[18] What is required is a vision for teamwork, patience, training, and the sustained support of senior management.

For companies considering the implementation of CFT, the following process can be helpful. First, select a demonstration project to initiate cross-functional teams. Staff the project with an experienced project leader and experienced team members. Second, determine early and jointly what the organization and the various functional groups need to do to support CFTs. If the organization has limited experience with multidisciplinary teams, the accurate forecasting of what is needed will be limited. As unexpected issues crop up, a record of them should be made so that subsequent implementation efforts will be much easier. Once the demonstration project is concluded, the project leader, team members, functional managers, and senior management need to capture the learning from this initial pilot project. This experience will yield many useful insights that can be used to facilitate future CFTs.

The major question that remains is not whether project-oriented organizations should use CFTs but how best to increase their efficiency and effectiveness.

CHAPTER NINETEEN

PROJECT LEADERSHIP

David F. Caldwell, Barry Z. Posner

What it takes to bring in a project on time, on budget, and on target has been addressed in scores, if not hundreds, of articles over the years. One of the more influential perspectives delineated the roles that had to be filled if projects were to be successful.[1] The authors argued that successfully completing technical projects required five work roles: *idea generating* (developing an idea for a new product or procedure), *project leading* (coordinating the activities and people necessary to develop the idea into a product), *championing* (gaining formal management support for the new idea), *gatekeeping* (collecting outside information regarding markets, technologies, and capabilities and channeling it into the team), and *sponsoring* (providing resources and support for the project). This schema helped crystallize research in two ways. First, it provided an organizing framework for understanding many of the factors that are necessary for a complex project to be successful. Second, it emphasized the importance of a multifaceted view of project leadership, the focus in this chapter. Specifically, we explore the things that project managers can do, particularly in dealing with others, to improve project teams' performance.

In the past few years, a number of studies have attempted to identify, in a more specific fashion, what project leaders do and how their actions affect the performance of projects. For example, Barczak and Wilemon suggest that the roles project leaders take relate to guiding and directing the team, fostering communication within the team, creating a climate in which members feel satisfied with their work, and acting as a liaison between the team and other groups.[2] Other studies have identified somewhat different roles. In fact, Chakrabarti and Hauschildt (1989) reviewed twenty studies investigating factors related to project management success and attempted to classify the wide variety of roles described by project type and stage.[3]

At times, it seems that the title of one intriguing article, "Technical Leadership: Much Discussed But Little Understood," summarizes the state of knowledge regarding project leadership.[4] This is no doubt in part because different researchers have approached the questions in separate ways (theoretical versus empirical), focused on different structural units (organization versus team), looked at various types of tasks (project management versus innovation), and have had different purposes (identifying what practices are actually used versus identifying what practices should be used).

Despite the different approaches to research, two things are clear from a review of the literature on leading project teams, particularly technical teams. First, effective project team leaders must fill many roles. Some of these roles are directly related to what goes on within the team. Although these activities have been given many names, they represent the things that a leader must do to create a shared vision among team members, motivate and inspire team members, establish and monitor goals, and ensure that the group is making effective decisions. Other roles relate to managing the relationships between the team and the environments in which it operates. Second, tensions exist between some of these roles. Actions a team leader takes to strengthen the internal processes of the team may influence how the team relates to external groups. And things a leader does to work with external groups will influence how the project team internally works together.

This chapter focuses primarily on the external leadership roles that project managers fill. There are a number of reasons for this emphasis on our part. First, a great deal has been written recently about how truly effective leaders inspire and energize their constituents.[5] In our view, these guidelines for practice are applicable whether the leader is responsible for a project team or a permanent part of the organization. Second, there is a great deal of evidence that, at least in project teams where technology is important, communication between team members and outsiders is critical for understanding the success of the team.[6] However, many of these observations have not been translated to specific guidelines for project team leaders. Finally, many of the structural approaches to improving the performance of project teams, such as parallel engineering or the use of specialized integrating groups designed to provide formal links between the team and other groups in the organization, have outpaced changes in management practices.[7]

Our intention is to present some broad propositions about how project managers can improve the performance of their teams by helping team members deal more effectively with the groups with which they must work if their project is to be successful. This is a key leadership responsibility of project managers. In order to understand more clearly why this leadership responsibility is so essential, we begin by outlining a model of the external activities of project teams.

How Project Teams Deal with Other Groups

The relationships between groups and individuals working on projects and how they contribute to project success were the focus of an extensive set of field investigations. Ancona and Caldwell conducted in-depth interviews with team leaders and executives within companies, surveyed all members of the company teams, and obtained measures of the teams' performance both while the teams were working and after their projects were completed.[8] These researchers were interested in two questions. The first was learning more, from a behavioral perspective, on how project teams interacted with other groups. They found that there were three dimensions of dealing with outside groups. That is, the activities that teams engaged in to work with outsiders—either people not on the team but inside the organization or people in other organizations—could be reliability grouped into three broad categories:

1. *Ambassador:* Activities aimed at representing the team to others and protecting the team from outside interference—for example, preventing outsiders from overwhelming the team with requests and persuading others that the teams' activities were important.
2. *Task coordinating:* Activities aimed at coordinating the team's efforts with others, which included obtaining feedback about the team's progress, negotiating with other groups, and integrating each other's efforts.
3. *Scouting:* Activities representing general scanning for ideas and information about the markets, trends, technologies, and competition. In contrast to the other two sets, these actions were less specifically focused and more directed to building a general awareness and knowledge base than addressing specific issues.

   The nature of these three activity sets represents the complexity of the boundary management tasks of technical teams. Scouting provides the team with broad technical and market information that is necessary for the project to be successful. These activities are primarily lateral and involve investigating markets, technologies, and competition—in short, bringing a great deal of data into the team. Task coordinating represents the lateral connections across functions that are necessary to ensure that the project meets the expectations of others. In contrast to the other activity sets, ambassador activities are primarily, although not exclusively, vertical; that is, they are aimed at securing effective support for the project, obtaining needed resources, and ensuring that the project is meeting strategic goals.

The second question these researchers attempted to answer was how these interactions with individuals outside the team (that is, teams' management of their boundaries) affect the performance of the project team. The short answer is that the ways project teams managed their boundaries were strongly related to the performance of the project teams. However, these relations were not simple; rather, they were dependent on both the frequency of specific activities and when performance was measured (that is, measured either as the team was working or after their project was fully completed).

The extent to which project team members engaged in task coordinating activities was directly related to top management's assessment of the project team's performance. And this result was much stronger when the evaluation was obtained after the team completed its project than if the evaluation was made while the team was still working. In other words, the frequency with which team members engaged in things such as problem solving with other groups was related to the ultimate success of the team's efforts more strongly than to interim evaluations of the team's progress.

There was a surprising relation between scouting activities and project team performance. Teams with high levels of scouting activities were rated substantially lower in performance at all points in time than those that engaged in fewer of these activities. At first glance, these results seem contrary to common sense. Why would teams that spend a great deal of effort understanding technical and mark trends have poorer performance than those that do not? Research results suggest that teams that engage in constant scouting, that is, continually searching for new external information, were frequently unable to go beyond looking at possibilities and commit to a particular project design. Teams that studied constantly shifted their strategy and direction based on any new external information they received. Any new information led the team to reconsider decisions that had already been made and kept them from being able to move ahead.

A different pattern emerged for the relation between ambassador activity and performance. Teams with high levels of ambassador activity received positive evaluations from executives during the team's operations. However, when performance was assessed after the project was completed, the relation between these activities and the success of the team was much lower. It seems that teams that devoted a great deal of effort to "managing upward" were initially viewed as successful by top management, but the impact of these activities declined over time.

Combining these results suggests that different boundary activities are important at different points of time in a project's life. Scouting, that is, developing a broad understanding of the project parameters, should be done very early, perhaps even before the full team has begun its work. Ambassador activities are most important early in the project team's life in order to ensure that the project has the support of important groups. Task coordinating is necessary throughout the life of the project team.

Ancona and Caldwell also asked team members to evaluate their team's performance and rate the effectiveness of the members in working together. Two findings are worth noting.[9] First, although how the team worked with outsiders was strongly related to management's evaluation of team performance, it was unrelated to the team's own evaluation of its performance. Second, when the team felt that it worked well together, the members believed their performance was high. These results have a relatively simple but powerful implication: team leaders must help team members understand the true levers for improving team performance.

What Project Leaders Can Do

A great deal of research shows the importance of the relations between the team and other groups. An obvious conclusion from this research is that successful project teams spend considerable time and effort in communicating and building good working relationships with other groups. An equally clear conclusion is that the project leader neither can nor should be responsible for doing all of these boundary management activities. There are too many activities with too many different groups for a single individual to do. However, it is the project leader's responsibility to ensure that the optimal levels of these activities are completed. For project leaders, the issue becomes one of how to create the conditions whereby team members effectively take on these responsibilities themselves. Following are six general propositions about what project leaders can do to reach this goal.

Develop a map of the environments in which the team operates. The success of projects is intimately related to the ability of team members to bring necessary information into the team and build relationships with external groups. Part of the role of the successful team leader is to develop an action plan for collecting information and enlisting the support of other groups. Although this seems like a simple requirement, it is frequently overlooked.

Too often project leaders fail to anticipate the information other groups can provide the team or the expectations that outsiders may have for the team. A simple example may illustrate this. Recently a group of our colleagues was responsible for developing an education program to be delivered overseas. The team members invested a great deal of effort over a very short period of time to design an immensely creative program. They worked extensively to ensure that the program would meet the expectations of potential students and worked closely with the academic departments that would deliver the various segments of the program. They also worked to build good relations with the international partners who would recruit students. In short, the team did an exemplary job of designing a program linking student requirements to the school's competencies. Unfortunately, the program was never delivered. The university did not give final approval to the program because a deadline for the program's review by an accrediting board was missed. The group would have had plenty of time to meet the deadline had they only known of it.

This example represents a sad story of wasted efforts and missed opportunities. The team worked hard to collect information from outside groups, and it devoted itself to meeting the requirements of the outside groups as it learned of them. What the team failed to do was anticipate all of the relevant groups with a stake in the project. Is it always possible to anticipate external requirements? Probably not. However, the team leader can ensure that the project team starts its work by attempting to understand all the potential groups that could affect the team's efforts and developing plans for learning about the specific information or concerns the outside groups might possess. Identifying the external groups with which the team must interact and establishing what roles these groups will have in relation to the project team is essential.

Ensure that external actions of team members are related to project needs. Different types of external activities are related to the performance of the project team. In addition, research shows that different types of activities are most consequential at different times in the life of the project. Scouting is best done early in the life of the project; ambassador activities are most critical early in the life of the project; and task coordinating is important throughout the life of the project. The most obvious result of this finding is that project leaders should work with team members to ensure that external activities are focused on areas that have the greatest potential for improving performance.

There is a less obvious implication of this finding. Since the project team must work with different groups at different times, coordination and joint problem solving with outsiders is important early in the life of the project. With other outside groups, such work is not required until late in the project team's efforts. The dilemma that project teams frequently face is that joint problem solving between groups is most efficient if those groups have a good relationship; however, building good relationships is difficult if teams meet only to solve specific problems.

One team came to a creative resolution to this dilemma. The project team leader identified the outside groups the team would have to deal with and some indication of when issues would arise that would require the groups to coordinate with one another. The leader then designed a plan to ensure that the project team members had established personal relationships with members of outside groups before the groups needed to work together to solve problems. During slack times in the project, the leader saw to it that her team members made contacts with members of other groups. The goal of establishing these contacts was twofold. First, the team leader felt it was important that coordination take place between "people," not between "groups." Therefore, part of the goal was simply to establish the types of personal relationships that can allow for effective communication. More important, the leader believed that true problem solving could take place only if team members understood the perspectives and concerns of the outside groups. Creating opportunities for relationship building allowed members of the project team and outside groups to learn about one another without the tension of having to solve specific problems. When the groups actually needed to address issues, a basis for mutual problem solving already existed.

Foster collaboration across teams. As Ancona and Caldwell showed, high-performing project teams spent a great deal of effort attempting to coordinate their actions with other groups.[10] Project leaders can take a number of actions to create a climate in which those efforts are likely to take place in a spirit of cooperation rather than competition.[11] For one thing, they can be diligent in quickly establishing norms of reciprocity across groups and partners, to give all those involved a sense of mutuality and to work toward predictability and stability in relationships. Sustaining ongoing interactions and creating both the expectations and conditions for durable and frequent interactions encourage people to cooperate in the present because they know they will have to deal with this person (or people or groups) again in the future.

Project leaders can successfully foster collaboration by seeking integrative solutions. They often accomplish this by framing differences and problems so that external participants focus on what is to be gained rather than what is to be lost. For example, researchers have found that people are more willing to make concessions when negotiators focus on the benefits to be achieved rather than on the possible costs. Integrative solutions are also more likely to emerge when project leaders share information and resources outside their own domains. This collaboration increases the involvement of others and thus the likelihood of their feeling some ownership and responsibility for making things work well. Although seeking broad-based support seems enticing to project managers, this is actually easier to revoke than specific support; its very breadth creates ambiguity and accommodates ready excuses for torpedoing a range of specific proposals. More effective project leaders enlist support and backing for a concrete idea than garnering general endorsements (for one reason, because supporting a specific proposal reduces others' level of risk taking).

The simplest way to understand why competition does not promote excellence is to realize that trying to do well and trying to beat others are two different things.[12] Indeed, competition actually works at cross-purposes with success because it demands more resources than cooperation.

Tjosvold describes the differences in behavior and results between people working cooperatively and those working competitively:

> In cooperation, people realize that they are successful when others succeed and are oriented toward aiding each other to perform effectively. They encourage each other because they understand the other's priorities help them to be successful. Compatible goals promote trust. People expect help and assistance from others and are confident that they can rely on others; it is, after all, in others' self-interests to help. Expecting to get and give assistance, they accurately disclose their intentions and feelings, offer ideas and resources, and request aid. They are able to work out arrangements of exchange that leave all better off. These interactions result in friendliness, cohesion, and high morale.

He contrasts this with people who view others as competitors. These people

> recognize that others' success threatens and frustrates their own aspirations. They are closer to reaching their goals when others perform ineffectively and fail to reach theirs. They suspect that others will not help them, for to do so would only harm their own chances of goal attainment. Indeed, they may be tempted to try to mislead and interfere in order to better reach their own goals. They are reluctant to discuss their needs and feelings or to ask for or offer assistance. Closed to being influenced by the other for fear of being exploited, they doubt that they can influence others, except by coercion and threat. These interactions result in frustration, hostility, and low productivity, especially in joint tasks.[13]

Help team members develop the skills for working with other groups. Getting project team members to focus their efforts on working with outside groups is often not easy. Team members are frequently selected for technical expertise alone, not for their abilities to work with others. In many organizations, team members continue to report to and be evaluated by their functional managers as opposed to project team managers. Thus, the composition and structure of project teams sometimes make it difficult for team managers to motivate members to work with external groups. In addition, the nature of project work, with its tight time lines and specific deliverables, can focus team members on internal issues, not what is happening in the external groups with which the teams must ultimately work.

Given these circumstances, it is frequently up to the project team leader to help team members develop the skills to work effectively with outside groups and motivate them to focus their efforts in those areas. The first step is helping individuals understand the relationship between these external activities and performance. Providing training and feedback in order to help individual team members improve their capabilities for dealing with outsiders is one enabling strategy. Examples include briefing team members on the roles of other groups, describing how other groups contribute to the project success, and coaching team members on techniques for building links with others.

We observed the leader of one highly successful team, responsible for developing a specialized computer-aided design tool, apply some of these ideas. The team leader believed that he would need to teach members of his team how to work effectively with others. Part of his plan for doing that involved inviting three people from the manufacturing function to team meetings on a regular basis. These three individuals not only provided the team with valuable information about manufacturing issues but also allowed the team leader to demonstrate problem-solving skills with other groups. Over time, the team leader was able to provide coaching and feedback to his team members on techniques for working with others. As the team moved forward with its project, the leader began inviting other outsiders to meetings. By this time, team members were both comfortable and skilled at dealing with others. Not surprisingly, the team made phenomenal progress in gaining commitment from other functional areas for supporting the new product.

Set a positive example. Project team leaders must model the actions they seek, along with encouraging and supporting other team members involved in these activities. The behaviors of project leaders, especially in their relations with members outside the project team and in the manner in which they speak about "outsiders," establishes the standard for the other members of the team. When team leaders belittle the contributions of other teams (departments or functions), this action sets in rapid motion similar behaviors from other team members. Of course, the opposite is also true. It is imperative that project leaders have a high level of consciousness about the symbolic impact of their actions on the behavior of the project team.

Similarly, by encouraging and recognizing the external actions of their team members, project leaders ensure that everyone on the team realizes the importance of these actions. Behaviors that are neither recognized nor reinforced are not likely to continue, so project leaders need to be vigilant in being on the lookout for these behaviors and make certain that team members' behaviors in these areas are not overlooked or taken for granted.[14] To the extent that project managers can identify how these actions have helped the team and single out those responsible, they can both elevate the status of these activities and establish peer-level role models.

Build credibility with people both in the group and outside. A great deal of research has shown that credibility is the foundation of leadership.[15] For the project manager, credibility takes on many forms. Previous research has consistently shown that the technical expertise of a leader is an important part of the project team's performance. For example, Clark and Wheelwright identify direct engineering management as an important role of the project team leader.[16] They believe that project team leaders must work directly with technical specialists on the project team to maintain the project plan integrity and ensure that pieces of the project are effectively integrated. For the project manager, credibility about technical issues and credibility within the team is not enough. Since the project manager will largely be responsible for bringing information to the team and for representing the team to outsiders, successful leaders must establish credibility with others outside the group.

Kouzes and Posner note that building credibility requires many actions but that much of the process is summed up in the phrase "doing what you say you will do."[17] People observe the actions of the leaders and draw conclusions about priorities from those actions, not from the statements the leader makes. What this means is that building credibility is based on being predictable, communicating clearly, following through on commitments, and being forthright and honest.

Credibility is critical, particularly when the team leader needs to fill the ambassador activities so necessary for the project's success. When it is absent, success is difficult to obtain. In the course of doing some work with a company a few years ago, we followed the progress of a project team's effort to develop a new computer system. Ultimately the project was only marginally successful. As we talked with executives in the company over time, it became clear that the reason the project suffered was that the team was never able to develop support from the functional groups that would have to market, manufacture, sell, and service the new product. The lack of support came in good part from the team leader's failure to develop credibility with other groups. When we talked to the project leader, he said that he preferred working on technical issues and did not really like spending time working with other groups that did not understand all the technical challenges his team was resolving. When we asked him how the team would coordinate with manufacturing and marketing, he replied, "Have common goal statements. In other words, we have goals around time to market, we have goals about product cost, we have goals around product functionality, we have goals around product quality."

The leader's preference for working only with his technical equals and his reliance on impersonal ways of coordinating made it impossible for him to develop personal credibility with those outside the group. No one ever saw him. When goal statements were changed or schedules slipped, the team leader would escalate the dispute to the vice president. Ultimately the company replaced the team leader, and the project was salvaged, although it missed a very real window of opportunity in the market. After all this had taken place, we talked to the project leader one last time. He was bitter about his experiences and blamed others in the organization for not meeting their commitments. It seemed that nothing in his experience had taught him that people will be committed to those they trust and that in organizations, trust comes through interactions.

Some Further Considerations

Although our focus has been primarily on external factors and their impact on the leadership efforts of project managers, we should also note several ongoing dilemmas. For instance, external factors often interact with internal team characteristics and dynamics to create problematic tensions. Team members often have different "models" than do external raters of what causes performance. For example, team members frequently believe that the team's success is exclusively a function of how the team members work with one another, yet others understand that the success of the team depends on both how the team works together and how successful the team is in getting support from other parts of the organization. Therefore, project managers need to be vigilant as to how their group members work with one another and with outsiders. Also, bringing in lots of external information, particularly if outside groups have different expectations, can lead to conflict within the group, and project leaders must help develop the capabilities to deal with these conflicts as they arise. Group members may resist building external links (for example, because doing so may slow things down, create conflicts, force members to work with people they do not know, and the like). Project leaders must help team members understand why external relationships are critical to their success and provide support and encouragement when these efforts seem difficult. Finally, some tactics for enhancing internal team operations (for example, setting up operations separate from others) can inhibit external relationships. Successful project leaders will be able to balance efforts directed at creating internal cohesion, especially if it creates a we-they attitude, with the need to find common ground with those outside the immediate team.

Project Leadership: Working Effectively Externally

There is some truth to the statement that leadership is much discussed but little understood. However, by adopting a multifaceted perspective on leadership and being more cognizant about the external relationships required to lead project teams successfully, we have been able to shed considerable insight into this discussion. Successful project managers meet their leadership challenges in large part through unraveling the complexity and uncertainties of their situations by focusing on key principles and actions. In the technical arena, it is especially true that most people who know how end up working for those who know why.

CHAPTER TWENTY

PROJECT TEAM MOTIVATION

Peg Thoms

We are all motivated. However, we are not all motivated to do the same things. The job of the manager is to see that employees do the work that the organization needs to have done. Motivation can be defined as the direction and the intensity of effort that an individual exerts on any particular task. Managers, of course, want workers to do the assigned tasks with maximum effort. Over the years, there has been much debate about whether managers can influence the motivation of subordinates. When we talk about project teams, the issue becomes even more complicated since so much of project work is self-directed. Despite the complexity of human motivation, it appears that project managers can and do influence the motivation of project team members in a positive direction.

Motivation to perform appropriate activities well is particularly important when working on projects, for three primary reasons. First, projects typically have specific time frames during which the entire project must be completed. Because other departments are often dependent on project completion, a lack of direction and effort can negatively affect other areas of the organization. Second, projects tend to be costly due to the high labor cost of the professionals who usually work on projects, the special materials used on product development and design projects, and the high priority given to project work. Low levels of motivation can lead to wasted resources and money. Third, projects are often related to corporate strategy—responses to either anticipated trends in an organization's market or to potential or real problems. A lack of motivation by project team members can literally spell doom for an organization that is operating in a dynamic environment.

Project managers with a good understanding of human motivation can make a tremendous difference in the amount of effort that team members exert. When effort is high, the quality of work performed by project teams will also go up, and the possibility of meeting project deadlines improves. Sometimes project managers assume that individual motivation will naturally be high, since project teams are typically made up of professionals. Although we expect that because professionals have a high level of interest in their area of expertise, the amount of effort exerted is still a wild card. It is safe to say that most of us will give more of ourselves and our talents in work environments that provide effective rewards and clear direction, and draw us into the organization's goals.

This chapter explores some of the leading theories of motivation with applications to project teams, explains several problems that can affect the effort and direction of project team work, and points out how to make rewards more effective. Finally, it explains strategies that have been proven to boost motivation.

Leading Theories of Motivation and Project Management

Although most managers have no doubt read or studied theories of motivation at some time during their academic or professional careers, it is rare for those theories to be explained in the context of project team management. Nevertheless, many practical implications can be drawn from the theories. Here we review equity, expectancy, reinforcement, goal setting, and control theories and the job characteristics model. Each has practical implications for project managers. Those who understand and use these basic principles will find that they can increase the quality of the projects they manage, and attract and retain the best professionals.

Equity Theory

Equity theory suggests that we all think about the time and effort that we put into our work (including our education), and we compare that with outcomes of the work: recognition, pay, benefits, opportunities to develop our technical expertise, collegiality, a good work environment, job (and thereby, financial) security, and job satisfaction, for example.[1] When we think that the comparison is equal, we will continue to exert the same effort. If we decide that we are giving more than we are getting, we will slack off. If we decide that we are getting more than we are giving, we might try harder. (Managers who are curious about whether people see the equation as equal can ask around. Probably most people will say that they see themselves as underrewarded. Think about the implications of that.)

Equity theory, however, is a bit more complex. It predicts that we will also look at other people with similar training who do similar work and compare our inputs and outcomes with theirs. Again, when we perceive an imbalance, equity theory predicts that we will make an adjustment to our effort. Practicing managers already know that project team members are continuously comparing themselves with other team members and external professionals who work in their fields. Usually when the manager hears about it, it is because the team member feels underpaid and is complaining. The importance of perceptions of pay fairness cannot be overstated when dealing with professionals.

What are the implications for project managers? First, managers should know the trends in compensation and benefits for professionals in the fields that they supervise. Sometimes workers' perceptions of what others are making, both inside and outside the organization, are correct, and sometimes they are incorrect. Managers should be careful to do a reality check on their own perceptions; managers in professions often have unrealistic perceptions of their own worth on the job market. This information can be obtained from professional associations, compensation consulting firms, and human resource professionals. Share this information and, whenever possible, pay industry rates with the team.

Second, take a look at all of the outcomes for workers. Maybe pay is low, but the organization provides the best laboratory, working conditions, benefits, or training. Barring excessive pay inequality, most people will sacrifice some money for better work environments. Talk up the positives. Do not highlight the negatives. Project managers are often technical professionals who have been trained to be critical and are sometimes more loyal to their profession than they are to their employers. It is not uncommon for these managers to join or lead discussions about negative aspects of an organization. Later, these same managers wonder why their team members are not putting forth more effort.

Expectancy Theory

Expectancy theory suggests that our effort will be greatest when we expect that we can perform a task.[2] Research has shown that when people feel that they have control and are capable of doing something, they will perform better. This self-efficacy comes from past work experiences, observing others, and verbal encouragement from managers and coworkers.

In addition, expectancy theory tells us that our effort will be greatest when we believe that we will obtain rewards when we perform. If we believe that no matter how productive we are, we will not be able to obtain desired outcomes, we will not put forth much effort. Since many project team rewards are related to group performance, it can be problematic when a team member does not have confidence in the rest of the team. Suppose that a team member who is an excellent performer with a high level of technical expertise has worked on past projects where the team did not meet the organization's expectations and did not get the entire bonus for which they were eligible. The excellent performer may consider it unlikely that she will receive the bonus on a current project and may adjust her individual effort downward.

Finally, this theory proposes that we will try harder when we value the reward. Often managers assume that all team members will respond to group incentives, but because we all value different rewards and different levels of rewards, that may not be true. In fact, some of us may place higher value on recognition or personal professional growth than money. One example of a lack of understanding about rewards would be a situation where a manager holds a dinner dance at a country club to reward a project team. The team members who do not enjoy dancing will not feel good about this event and might even reduce effort in the future so that they do not get "rewarded" again.

The implications for project managers are clear. First, build self-efficacy. Give team members small assignments that build up to projects, thereby building skills and efficacy. Remind team members about past successes and times when they overcame obstacles. Share the experiences of others who have been in similar situations as examples of persistence, learning, and performance. Provide lots of encouragement when you sense that team members lack confidence in their ability to perform. This may be a simple pep talk, but a personal note that can be reread will probably work better.

Second, check to make sure that team members who perform well receive promised rewards. A review of the past experiences of team members would be helpful. In the past, a manager may have promised a team member a special project if he or she performed well, but later was not able to make that assignment. Failed promises may affect the effort of the team member on current projects, so never promise rewards that cannot be delivered. Hold the organization accountable for outcomes (such as promotions and raises) that it promises to team members.

Third, find out what individual team members value and provide rewards that are important to each. Some place a high value on feedback, and others care about money. A savvy manager knows, and can find and provide rewards that will lead to increased effort. How do project managers find out this information? They ask, listen, and observe.

Reinforcement Theory

Reinforcement theory teaches that reinforcement must be ongoing.[3] It tells us that when performance becomes punishing, effort will stop. It also tells us that the fixed-interval, fixed-schedule type of reinforcing performance (for example, the biweekly paycheck) is not as effective as variable pay on variable schedules.

Although food pellets do not have to be dropped to most team members every time they perform well, humans do need to have their performance reinforced regularly. People tend to repeat behavior for which they are rewarded and stop behavior for which they are not rewarded. A manager who has been relying on money as the only reward for project teams cannot afford to reinforce as often as may be needed to encourage peak effort. This means that additional types of reinforcement will have to be found.

How often a manager should reinforce team members depends on each team member. Do an analysis to try to determine the needs of each team member. At what point is there a drop in effort or performance? Who asks for feedback frequently? Who complains about the formal reward system and is never satisfied with pay? Once the manager determines which team members need more reinforcement, he or she can take a more informed approach.

Reinforcement theory tells us that variable pay is more motivating than fixed pay. Recent research indicates that variable pay programs like profit sharing (based on company earnings) and gain sharing (based on company cost savings) can lead to increased corporate performance. As reinforcement theory predicts, compensation strategies that put some pay at risk have a positive impact on performance. Changing the schedule by which team members are paid will be a bit more difficult since monthly billing cycles drive corporate pay schedules. In other words, it is unlikely that people who cannot make their mortgage payment will perform well. However, project managers can use other rewards on a variable schedule. For example, a manager can give the company credit card for dinner out with the family at the time it is earned. A long weekend can be given after a project team makes a breakthrough or meets a goal. People like pleasant surprises, and reinforcement theory suggests that rewards given on a variable schedule will lead to continuing effort.

Goal Setting Theory

Goal setting is one of the best proved of the many theories of motivation. It works, and managers who are not currently using it should start. Basically, this theory says that when a manager sets clear, specific, and challenging goals, performance will increase.[4] Setting a challenging goal is more effective than saying to project team members, "Do your best." Even if the goal is not fully achieved, the team and individual team members will do more. Surprisingly, research indicates that people do not have to participate in goal setting for it to work.

An effective goal identifies exactly what will be done, what standards will be used to evaluate how well it was done, and when it must be accomplished. The goal should make the team stretch. If it is too easy, there will be a tendency to stall, members will become bored, and some may even be insulted. Base the goals on past experience and performance. If a similar project was completed in three months, a schedule of two and a half months may be appropriate this time. If sales or production goals were met on schedule on a previous project, set higher goals this time.

Recent studies[5] have shown that the effectiveness of goal setting may be diminished when a task is complex and novel, as is true of many projects. When a project is very complex or new or requires the development of new skills, short-term, less difficult goals should be used to break it into what team members will see as achievable pieces. A project manager may need to involve project teams in goal setting in these situations.

Goal setting as it is used in many organizations has one major problem. Most reward programs, both merit pay increases and bonuses, are tied to the accomplishment of goals. In other words, most organizations make attaining the written goal a requirement in order to get the reward. As a result, most rational people will set easily attainable goals. Managers, whose own incentive pay is tied to accomplishment of department goals, will support less challenging goals too. What happens is that low goals are set, met, and rewarded. The organization loses the peak performance that it could have attained with challenging goals.

To use goal setting effectively, project managers must change the way most incentive pay is determined. A variety of approaches can be used. For example, goals can be weighted depending on how challenging they are, pay can be based on actual performance levels rather than accomplishment of specified goals, or companies can use profit-sharing plans that encourage peak performance. If you use challenging goals, you must reward the increased performance that will probably result even if the goals are not fully achieved.

Control Theory

Control theory is a metacognitive theory of motivation. In other words, it is an extremely complex process that is hard to understand and predict. Control theory extends goal setting by explaining how humans process information and make decisions about how much effort to put forth.[6] This theory suggests that we are continuously comparing our performance against standards (usually goals). We seek feedback from managers, coworkers, and the work itself that will allow us to make these comparisons. When we find an error or an inconsistency between our work and the standard, we try to find out why, and then decide what to do about it. This process is frequently compared to how a thermostat works. If a thermostat detects a discrepancy between the temperature setting and the temperature in the room, it signals the furnace to produce more hot air or the air-conditioner to produce more cool air until the error is corrected.

Project managers can have a positive impact on this ongoing process in a number of ways. First, and most important, managers need to provide feedback or find ways for teams to get it themselves. Both positive and negative feedback help teams correct errors. It has been suggested that the more errors made early in a project, the better for the project in the long term. As the team finds and corrects early problems, they are less likely to find a fatal flaw near the end. Detecting and correcting errors also builds confidence.

Managers may need to help team members process errors. One reaction to an error can be decreased commitment to a goal if the team or individual feels helpless to prevent or correct the error. A project manager can encourage commitment to goals and help in the problem-solving process. Managers can also assist the team in making correct attributions about what went wrong. For example, was the error a result of team carelessness, a mistake by another department, or a lack of information? Each of those attributions has a different impact on the future motivation of the team. The manager can help the team make the correct attribution and implement the appropriate response.

Job Characteristics Model

The job characteristics model has been useful in guiding the redesign and enrichment of jobs. This theory predicts that when people can use a variety of skills on their job, when the job requires completion of a task that has a visible outcome, and when the work is perceived as important, workers will feel good about their jobs.[7] In addition, the theory predicts that there will be positive outcomes when workers have some autonomy and receive feedback about their performance. Extensive research has shown that when the job characteristics described above exist, workers will feel more satisfied with their jobs. That job satisfaction will probably be associated with low rates of turnover, absenteeism, and job accidents. When a job provides autonomy and feedback, productivity will probably increase as well.

Project team work, by its nature, already provides some of these job characteristics. However, this theory addresses the needs of individuals. Although it appears that many of us like working in groups, we all need to feel that the work we do as individuals is important. This theory suggests that project managers need to assign projects in ways that will allow members to use a variety of skills. Team members should be involved in and have some responsibility for the whole project rather than just one small piece of it. Managers should provide feedback to individuals, as well as to the team, regarding their performance. Although often project teams have autonomy as a unit, team members may not. Project managers should find ways to give some autonomy to each team member. One way is to make one individual primarily responsible for one aspect of the overall project and let team members make some decisions independently.

Problems with Group Work Related to Motivation

It has been noted over the years that there are problems relating to motivation that are peculiar to group work. These problems can have a devastating effect on individual motivation and project outcomes. Most of us are familiar with well-known projects that went sour like the Bay of Pigs invasion and the *Challenger* disaster. Similar smaller-scale situations occur on a regular basis in many organizations. Project managers can limit project disasters by understanding the cause of the problems and taking some preventive measures. The three common problems that will be addressed here are free riding, groupthink, and social loafing. These are problems common to group work that can have significant impact on the motivation of project teams. The key is retaining individual responsibility while encouraging teamwork.

Free Riding

"Free riding" means that one or more project team members does less work than others.[8] Typically free riding infers a malicious intent on the part of the "hitchhikers" to take advantage of the other team members and the organization. Particularly when project team rewards are group incentives, free riding can have devastating effects on team motivation. Some victims of free riding will take matters into their own hands, censoring the perpetrator and even taking their own action (appropriate or otherwise). Other members may buy into excuses that the free rider has given (usually personal problems) and cover the individual, enabling this type of behavior to continue. Still other team members will simply keep quiet, all the while growing increasingly dissatisfied with the manager and the organization. Team members usually feel very uncomfortable about disciplining other team members. They expect "management" to do that.

Project managers can detect free riding by monitoring assignment reports and project schedule accomplishments, and by observing project team interactions. In addition, talking to team members can be enlightening. Most of us have been taught not to tattle on others, but when we feel used, we usually find ways to let our bosses know. A general sense of dissatisfaction on a project team might be another indication of free riding.

A project manager who detects a free rider should investigate the situation immediately. When the other team members see that the manager is getting to the bottom of the situation, they realize that the manager cares about them and will not tolerate this type of behavior in the future. If a project manager finds that the situation is short term, perhaps related to a personal problem, it might be corrected quickly and easily using organizational resources outside the department. For example, if a team member is going through a divorce, the person may be referred to the company's employee assistance counseling program. On the other hand, if the problem is an insidious attempt to take advantage of other team members and the company, prompt disciplinary action is called for. It is not unheard of for a member of a highly technical team to use company resources for lucrative private consulting work, ignoring or sidelining project assignments. Besides the negative impact that such behavior has on project team motivation, it can have major financial implications for organizations.

Groupthink

The term *groupthink* refers to the process whereby all members of a group begin to think alike or to pretend that they think alike.[9] When groupthink has occurred, no member of a project team would raise objections or concerns about a project, even when those concerns were legitimate and based on hard data.

Groupthink inhibits team members from doing their best as they try to conform to what they think the group wants and needs. They may put quality behind collegiality. Some professionals, uncomfortable with group decisions, may leave if they feel that they cannot do their best work.

Groupthink occurs for several reasons. First, it is likely to arise in highly cohesive groups where team members are personal and professional friends. Many people hesitate to challenge a buddy. Second, if a project leader is highly directive, letting the team know exactly what the leader's preferences are, groupthink is more likely to occur. It is threatening to disagree with a boss; dissenters may be concerned about being seen as a troublemaker. Third, if members of a project team do not feel personally vulnerable, they may do things that they would not do as an individual. In general, people tend to make riskier decisions in groups than they would ever make as individuals. Fourth, groupthink is more likely to occur in a group that has a "mindguard": an individual who monitors and censors those who disagree with either the leader or the group decisions, or who presents contrary information.

A number of strategies are available for preventing groupthink. On any project that requires innovation and creativity, try to use a heterogeneous team. Do not ask for volunteers; assign project team members because they are different and sometimes disagree. Be careful about good friends' working together too often on projects. We sometimes assign people to teams because we want to reduce the possibility of conflict. This may not be a wise strategy.

Appoint one team member to play the role of devil's advocate. Make that individual accountable for raising and investigating every potential pitfall. The manager should withhold opinions on decisions until the group has had a chance to express its views. Reward team members who disagree and express their opinions. Discourage mindguards and regularly remind team members of the project's primary objectives. If meeting a deadline is more important than quality, groupthink may actually be helpful. If quality is more important, groupthink will be deadly. Be particularly cautious as the project nears completion. As deadlines draw near, it becomes more tempting to ignore difficult questions and concerns than in the early stages. All project managers should routinely use strategies to prevent groupthink.

Social Loafing

Social loafing occurs when individuals who are working on a project team fail to take initiative because they believe that someone else will do it or should do it.[10] Much research has explored social loafing in situations where another person is attacked or is hurt while others are present. Scientists have learned that if we believe that other people know about a problem, whether that is true or not, we are less likely to act. We feel less personally responsible.

On project teams, it is important that individual team members feel responsible for the success of the project and take the initiative to solve problems. Social loafing is a tough problem to prevent unless it is done on an ongoing basis. Specifically discuss this issue with project teams when projects are initiated. Tell team members that they will be held personally responsible for taking action even if others know about a situation. And then do it. "But John knew about it too!" should never be a legitimate excuse when something goes wrong. Encourage team members to find and investigate unusual situations. Reward people who take initiative every time it occurs, even if the action they take is not exactly right.

Remember also that we all learn through vicarious experiences. Use storytelling to teach people how you want them to behave. Nothing beats a good story about the project team member who realized too late that no one else had reported the missing piece of equipment.

Effective Rewards

There is an old cliché in management that what gets rewarded gets done. That cliché is true to a certain extent. However, what is rewarding to one person is not rewarding to another. Many managers, especially those hung up on mistaken notions of "fairness," tend to reward all project team members with the same thing (usually money). They are then a bit baffled when some team members perform well and others do not. The most frequent explanation for such seemingly irrational behavior is that "some people are not motivated." In addition, some rewards are inherently better than others, some do not motivate anyone, and some may even reward behavior that is undesirable. An effective reward is one that is likely to lead to continuing and additional good performance or other desirable behavior.

Characteristics of Effective Rewards

Certain characteristics make for an effective reward. First, an effective reward is one that is available to use whenever the project manager wants to reinforce behavior or performance. If money is available, then it might be an effective reward. Typically, however, money is not readily available, and managers must learn to use other rewards, like recognition and feedback, that are relatively free and easy to use.

Next, it should be possible to take back a reward if the team member or team stops performing. Merit increases, although technically reversible, are rarely taken back after being added to base salary. Incentive bonuses, commissions, profit sharing, gain sharing, and recognition are given only in subsequent years when the performance is high. Today, many organizations give cost-of-living increases annually to employees, in order to keep their pay competitive, but use incentive bonuses to motivate workers.

Third, an effective reward should be tied to work performance. Any reward that is not related to a team's or a team member's work behavior is at best wasted and at worst sends the wrong message. The Thanksgiving turkey given to all employees does not do anything to improve performance and may make the vegetarians angry. The beautiful watch given for twenty-five years of service has less positive impact on performance than a handwritten note that praises a job well done. Rewards should be given as close to the time of the performance as possible. Profit sharing and gain sharing, two effective group incentives, are most motivating when paid out quarterly rather than annually. Recognition and feedback can be given to a team or team member within minutes of the performance or behavior.

Finally, a reward is more effective when given publicly than privately. Most of us like to be rewarded in front of our peers. In addition, seeing others receive rewards helps to build a belief that good performance will be recognized by this manager. It also makes the manager more accountable for accurately tracking performance and rewarding the appropriate teams and individuals. The project manager who publicly rewards teams and team members will find that these actions pay off in terms of project quality and meeting deadlines in the future.

Many project managers rely too heavily on money as a reward, yet there are a number of rewards that are relatively inexpensive but can be highly effective. Handwritten letters, verbal recognition given during a team meeting, incentive bonuses tied to meeting deadlines that are tracked on a large public bulletin board, or special plaques given to each member of a project team that delivered under budget are all examples of effective rewards.

Making Current Rewards More Effective

Project managers who want their teams to give a high level of effort can assess the rewards on which they currently rely and make the necessary changes. Let us look at a few examples.

A manager uses merit increases and incentive bonuses tied to meeting project deadlines. This manager could give only cost-of-living increases and use the leftover money to increase the bonuses, and then add quality conditions to the bonuses. The bonus payouts could be tracked on a bulletin board in the department and handed out at a semiannual party at her home, to which she invites significant others in the organization. That makes the reward even more public and garners support from people who can choose to support team members when they have to work extra hours to meet project schedules. The project manager can also write letters of recognition acknowledging exemplary performance.

The organization has a profit-sharing plan with an annual distribution. The manager can try to arrange for the payouts to be quarterly. If that cannot be done, the manager could distribute letters quarterly that indicate how the plan is doing and indicate what sort of payout might be expected at the end of the year. The project manager can also write letters of recognition acknowledging exemplary performance.

The company has lost money during both of the past two years and cannot afford any raises this year. A manager in this company can increase personal contact with team members, providing feedback and verbal recognition. The manager can invite team members to a cookout to reward completion of project deadlines and write letters of recognition acknowledging exemplary performance.

The company gives cost-of-living raises, a turkey to each employee at Thanksgiving, and expensive gifts for every five years of service. Managers with the nerve can replace all three of these rewards and instead give raises based on performance. Better yet, they can keep a small cost-of-living increase and use the rest of the money on performance bonuses given as the performance occurs. Instead of the turkey and service awards, they can hand out movie passes and restaurant gift certificates to team members who perform well or complete project deadlines ahead of schedule. They must be sure to reward support staff members who work with the teams as well. They are the most likely to be upset about losing the turkey and service awards and are often overlooked when project team members are rewarded.

These are the keys to improving a reward system:

- Make rewards performance contingent.
- Reward at irregular time periods as the performance occurs.
- Use a variety of rewards.
- Make the rewards public.
- Use rewards that stop if the desired performance is discontinued.

Project teams are frequently rewarded with group incentive programs, and these rules apply to group rewards as well. In addition, project managers need to design group rewards that reinforce team cooperation and meeting deadlines, as well as performance quality. If a reward program reinforces behaviors like working outside the team, undercutting other team members, and playing political games in order to obtain personal rewards, that is the behavior that will be elicited.

Project bonuses (for example, for a new patent), gain sharing, and profit sharing are some of the approaches used in organizations that have project teams. Profit sharing is an important group incentive that rewards the right thing—the impact of the project on the company's profitability—and has been shown to have a positive effect on an organization's performance. Project team members are well known for getting angry when an organization makes money off a project and does not share the profits. They also tend to forget about the projects that lose money. Profit sharing reinforces the organization's priorities. In the public sector where cost savings may be the objective of the project, a short-term gain sharing approach might be a better group incentive.

Motivation and the Stage of the Project

Motivational strategies should vary depending on the stage of the project because different stages have different problems. The three stages addressed here are getting the project started, project development, and wrapping up the project. Each presents a unique challenge for project managers.

Getting Started

The goal of the first stage is to get the team and each individual member moving and motivated. Part of the process of motivating the project team is explaining the project, yet many managers fail to tell their team members why the project matters. How does it fit into the big picture? Who cares? What will it do for the organization? Why were they chosen to work on the project? What is in it for them?

The method used to kick off the project is also extremely important. Gathering everyone together into a crowded conference room and passing out assignments is unlikely to encourage anyone to bounce out of bed early the next day to work on the project. Holding the meeting in a comfortable location, serving special refreshments, creating a project theme, allowing plenty of time to answer questions, and inviting senior executives to explain the project's importance will generate some excitement and energy that might make starting the project more motivating.

In addition, it is important to discuss the reward program for the team and individual members before the project work begins. It might be a good idea to involve team members in the development of the incentive package. Project deadlines and requirements also need to be specifically and carefully outlined. Allow time for people to express concerns and raise questions. This will be an appropriate time for the project manager who has set challenging goals to emphasize confidence in the team's ability to meet the goals.

Project Development

In the next stage, the day-to-day work on the project proceeds, and the project develops. A project manager who provides an exciting launch for a project needs to keep the energy flowing when the team gets bogged down in details and runs into problems. The excitement of a new project can wear thin rather quickly when the difficult work is underway. At this stage, the best rewards are feedback, recognition as short-term goals are met, and surprises for the teams and team members who are performing well.

It is difficult to provide too much feedback. If a manager is directly supervising a project team, it is appropriate to monitor work progress and give both negative and positive feedback on a daily to weekly basis. The frequency of the feedback should depend on the team and team members. If they are working on a new or complex task, more frequent feedback is best. If they are experienced with project work or with the technical aspects of the project, less feedback is acceptable. If the team is self-managed, the manager needs to help the team find ways to get feedback directly, perhaps by setting up systems to assist the team in self-monitoring their progress and performance quality. These systems may be complex information systems or simple time lines posted on the department bulletin board. Feedback allows teams to adjust their behavior and better meet goals, focuses attention on priorities, and reminds them that the project manager cares about their work.

Recognition of meeting short-term goals and exceptional performance is critical to keeping morale high. This recognition can take the form of verbal congratulations at project team meetings, a plaque that publicly recognizes the completion of each goal with a new metal plate, or a dozen pizzas delivered at lunchtime. It is important to acknowledge both the team and the individuals who have made contributions. Handwritten notes of congratulations are highly effective and will often be kept and displayed for months. For unusual performance, it is appropriate to copy the note, send it to the department head, and let the team member know what was done. Project managers need to watch for signs that energy is running low—absenteeism, a lack of communication among team members, increased conflict when discussing project problems—and intervene with encouragement.

Surprises can brighten a tough day of dealing with project snags and create a positive mood that will jump-start a dragging project. Motivational surprises might be a flower on each team member's desk, a T-shirt with the company logo and project name printed on the back, or an invitation to dinner at a good restaurant. These relatively simple motivational tools can be planned when the original project budget is developed. Create a series of surprises and rewards as part of the project planning. Managers who spend as much time thinking about how to keep the team energized as they do thinking about the equipment requirements of the project will see increased motivation and performance.

Wrapping Up the Project

The final stage of a project can sometimes be the most difficult. Often teams are tired of the work, bored with the technical details, and anxious about the next project. This stage varies with the length of the project and the attention span of each individual. The project manager must keep the team focused and bring the project to closure. The key is directing the team's attention to the outcomes for the organization, the team, and team members.

Get the team members involved with planning the implementation and evaluation of the project with end users or customers. Plan a celebration to bring closure to the project and give the project team the rewards that were promised when the project was initiated. Provide honest, thorough feedback to each team member regarding individual performance on the project.

Motivational Strategies

At the departmental level, two strategies can boost motivation: creating and communicating a positive vision of the future and selecting team members who are motivated to do the type of project work required.

Creating and Communicating Vision

The word *vision* is regularly (and sometimes excessively) used by political leaders and the media, and overuse and inappropriate use of the term have created confusion about what a vision is and how it works. Some people think that only charismatic world leaders can create and manage a vision. That is not correct. New research[11] indicates that an organizational vision leads to improved performance, increases job satisfaction, and can help transform organizations. Ideally, every organization would have a vision that guides its day-to-day work, but even if the company does not, a manager can create one for a department or project team.

Consider the unit and the work the teams do:

- What would the ideal work environment be like?
- What quality of work should be seen consistently?
- How will all team members perform on the job and behave toward each other?
- What will completed projects look like, and how will they be received by the end users?
- What is important to the departmental boss, the customers, and the team members?
- What are the values of the various constituents?
- What kinds of people should be working on the project teams?

Pull this information together into an image of the department in the future. Do not try to summarize the image into one concise, general statement. If a written version is desired, a project manager can write a movie script about someone walking into the department five months from now. Describe in detail what it will be like.

Begin to communicate this positive image to teams and individuals. Introduce it in parts as appropriate. Include a discussion, or at least a mention, of the vision at every meeting. Set goals that will help the department achieve the vision. Provide feedback that tells team members if the work they do and the way they behave is consistent with the vision of the future. Reward and encourage people and teams that demonstrate consistent behavior and performance.

Recruiting and Selecting Motivated People

The most important thing that a manager does is recruiting and selecting motivated people. (Many project managers, however, spend more time selecting a computer than selecting an employee.) There are a number of ways to improve selection practices so that motivated people are on the project teams. I assume that project managers have some input into who serves on the project teams that they manage. This may not be true for all, but when it is, making the right choices is critical.

First, decide what technical skills are critical for the team being formed. Are these skills that could be easily and quickly taught to a motivated person? If not, the manager will have to screen candidates for these critical technical skills. If so, focus on selecting a person with the desired attitudes rather than all of the desired skills. Be very careful to identify only the technical skills absolutely required to do the job.

Second, identify the performance skills needed to work on a project team successfully. For example, most project managers probably need people who take initiative, have a high level of energy, have a customer orientation, and are self-motivated. Develop a structured interview that will determine which candidates have the desired performance skills. Ask questions that get candidates to talk about past experiences and predict how they will behave in the future. To get at self-motivation, a manager might ask, "Tell me about a time when you were very frustrated about a problem with an assigned project. How did you handle it?" or "Suppose that you feel discouraged about a project because another team member criticized your work. How would you deal with this?" The candidates who described how they successfully dealt with frustration and problems using appropriate methods are the ones who might work best on the team. The ones who say they argued with their coworkers or have to have a drink are the ones the manager might want to pass over.

Third, a manager may want to recruit people who love to do the kind of work that needs to be done. Ask them about what kind of work energizes them. Have them describe situations when they have felt highly motivated. If those situations are similar to the work environment and the types of projects done in the department, these people are likely to make the best team members. If the situations are completely different, do not hire the person.

The key in recruiting and selecting motivated people is to look at the whole package, not just the technical skills of the candidates. It is significantly easier to train a motivated person than to motivate a highly skilled person. Each manager has to determine the balance that is appropriate for each project team.

Conclusion

Motivation is an extremely complex process that varies among individuals. Project managers cannot motivate everyone to do everything that they desire, but they can create a motivating and exciting work environment—one that offers a range of rewards, provides adequate performance feedback, and allows some autonomy in decision making.

In addition, managers need to monitor project work to detect problems common to group work that can interfere with motivation. Preventive strategies can be implemented that will limit the possibility that problems will occur. Some problems are related to the stage of the project. These can be anticipated and controlled with careful planning. Other strategies should be ongoing. Creating and communicating a positive vision of the future will provide guidance for teams and team members. That will make it more likely that their efforts will be focused in the right direction. Managers should also try to recruit and select highly motivated individuals by using selection standards and techniques that will predict attitude as well as technical abilities.

Developing and maintaining a motivating work environment for project teams is time-consuming and can be frustrating. However, it is an investment that will produce a tremendous return for the project managers who make the effort.

CHAPTER TWENTY-ONE

NEGOTIATION SKILLS

John M. Magenau

Negotiation skills are vital to the success of all project managers. In fact, this
job requires negotiating more than most others. In many situations, project managers lack the power to order people to do things and therefore must
negotiate agreements to accomplish their objectives. For example, they negotiate
with department managers in the organization to release the people needed for
their project; with suppliers to obtain the materials and services needed to complete the project on schedule; with team members and upper management about
project responsibilities, task completion dates, and budgets; and with customers
about costs, project completion dates, and project changes.

Because of the different circumstances, each of these situations may require a different negotiation strategy. A project manager who is negotiating with
suppliers might negotiate more competitively if he or she believes several sources
can provide equally good materials or services. On the other hand, if there is only
one good supplier, the manager will probably develop a cooperative approach. In
other negotiations, where maintaining good relationships with team members or
customers is considered important to future project success or repeat business,
they may choose a more cooperative approach. In this chapter we discuss the characteristics of negotiation, conditions under which negotiation is appropriate,

Note: I acknowledge the contribution of David R. Gustafson in providing the negotiation scenario
used in this chapter.

the basic steps of preparation for negotiations, negotiating strategies, and how to choose a strategy of negotiation.

What Is Negotiation?

Negotiation is a process by which two or more people who begin with conflicting positions attempt to reach an agreement by modifying their original positions or developing new proposals that reconcile the interests underlying them. Several aspects of this definition are useful for orienting us to what negotiation is and the circumstances in which it is used.

Negotiation is a process. Negotiations take place over time. The time might be very brief, involving an exchange that takes place over a few seconds, or it may be lengthy and involve discussions that take place over several months or even years. In order for negotiation to take place, there must be sufficient time available. People sometimes avoid negotiating because they do not want to spend the time dickering.

Negotiation involves two or more people. The simplest negotiations take place between two people. More typically, however, negotiations involve more than two individuals—for example, a multiparty negotiation between a consortium of companies that are working on the same large project. In many negotiations, the project manager will be part of a team of negotiators and representing the interests of others (other constituents such as higher-level management, say, or project team members) who are not present at the negotiation table.

The social structure of negotiation can become quite complicated. In addition to the negotiations taking place between the parties, there also may be negotiations within one's own team or constituents. As more people become involved, the negotiations are likely to become more complex. The addition of more people will probably bring more, and possibly conflicting, interests to the negotiation table. This will make it more difficult to find options that are satisfactory to everyone concerned.

Negotiators have conflicting positions. If there were no conflict, there would be no need to negotiate. Negotiators start with positions that at least appear to be incompatible. For example, the head of the engineering department may not want to give a project manager the engineer he wants for his team when and for as long as he wants her.

Negotiators attempt to reach agreement. Usually the purpose of negotiation is to reach agreement about something. (This goal is not always accomplished.) Because neither party has the power (or if they have the power, they decide not to use it) to make decisions unilaterally, they must reach a voluntary agreement with the other side. Neither side feels compelled to accept what the other side initially presents to it, and both sides believe they can get a better offer by trying to influence the other side in their own direction. The parties will continue trying to reach agreement as long as they believe an agreement is preferable to the alternatives of not reaching agreement. The alternatives might include doing business with someone else, seeking intervention by higher authority, going to an arbitrator or to court, or simply doing without what the other side has to offer.

Negotiators modify their original positions. During the course of negotiation, the parties usually modify their original proposals by making concessions toward some middle-ground position. Consequently negotiators have an expectation of give and take during the negotiation process. Sometimes negotiators are able to invent or discover options that reconcile or integrate their underlying interests in such a way that everyone is well satisfied. This allows both parties to satisfy their interests to a greater extent than would have been possible if they had simply conceded to some middle-ground position.

A Project Management Scenario

In order to put the discussion in a more concrete context, I will introduce two sides of a project management negotiation scenario between Zeus Energy Division (ZED) and Corn Products Industries (CPI).

ZED's Perspective

You are the project manager for a new cogeneration boiler construction project being built by Zeus Energy Division (ZED). Your client is Corn Products Industries (CPI). Your timetable calls for completion of the project in fourteen months, and you have a budget of $3 million. During the past few weeks, it has been increasingly difficult dealing with on-site demands from your client. CPI has insisted on a list of change orders to suit its immediate concerns. Your counterpart says that because CPI is paying millions for the plant, they are entitled to make appropriate changes to the project for as long as is necessary to "get it right." You are concerned that every day spent in processing change orders adds further delay to your targeted completion date because engineering must approve the changes, design must alter the plans, and fabrication must change the structure.

ZED is already in trouble on this project; its budget and schedule are being stretched to the limit. You are under increasing pressure from upper management to complete the job with the expected profit margin. You have $25,000 to work with and still meet your goals. Upper management is giving close scrutiny to your performance on this project because your last three jobs came in well over budget and yielded little profit to the company. You have been told in no uncertain terms that a similar performance on this project could cost you your job.

Because you view CPI as a potential long-term customer, you are reluctant to refuse their demands. CPI has indicated that there may be several future projects if this one is completed to their satisfaction. Since the sales department got wind of this, they have been pressuring your team mercilessly to keep CPI happy. Sales feels that ZED will be in a prime position to win the contract for another corn products boiler in the next four months if everything goes smoothly. On the other hand, you believe ZED's bid for the project was too low, and that is why every change you agree to is threatening your profit margin.

When you arrived at work this morning, a fax for the latest change order from CPI was sitting on your desk. They want major changes to accommodate enhanced boiler capacity and higher operating temperatures. You think these changes are unnecessary. Worst of all, you found out from your engineers and estimators that the proposed changes would add $75,000 to the cost of the project and add four weeks to the schedule. Meanwhile, you have been told that it is imperative that CPI maintain existing steam production schedules. You have heard from ZED's local sales representative that CPI may be willing to spend some money for the changes, but he was not sure how much.

You have scheduled a meeting for later this week to negotiate an agreement on the requested changes. You are under strong pressure to reach a settlement that preserves ZED's profit margin, but at the same time you must keep CPI happy. As you sit at your desk, you are staring out the window thinking about how you should approach the upcoming negotiations.

CPI's Perspective

You are a manager with Corn Products Industries (CPI) responsible for constructing a cogeneration plant. Recently your engineers developed new final steam conditions that will optimize efficiency of the boiler. Because this project represents a large investment for CPI, you firmly believe that you are entitled to make the changes you feel are necessary to maximize the performance of the completed facility. From your perspective, the changes are logical and not excessively expensive. However, you have been encountering increasing resistance from the ZED project manager on your change requests. Her approach has been to stall or try to talk you out of making the changes. Because of her reluctance, you are becoming suspicious that the ZED project manager has no intention of making the changes you have requested. As a result, your attitude toward her and Zeus has begun to sour.

You have previously told the ZED sales representative that this is first in a series of such plants that will be constructed over the next ten years. Although you have not made any commitment to do future business with ZED, you have made it clear that if ZED performs to CPI's satisfaction, it will get preferential consideration when future contracts are awarded.

Your greatest concern now is completing this plant on time. CPI has entered into negotiations with a major soft drink producer for corn syrup, and your ability to meet your commitments for that contract is contingent on having the new plant on-line and producing reliably by the scheduled completion date. Failure to have the plant operating on schedule would void any contract with the soft drink producer and result in the loss of hundreds of plant jobs. Because the company's negotiations with the soft drink manufacturer are at a preliminary stage, you are required to keep this information confidential to avoid attracting the attention of your competitors.

There is $100,000 in your budget to spend on additional change order costs if necessary. You cannot agree to schedule extensions, however, because of your secret negotiations with your soft drink client. Sources in the industry have given you information that ZED is experiencing financial difficulty and needs future boiler orders.

Your engineers have revised the burning capacity requirements for the cogeneration plant, with the figures based on the information that the soft drink company has supplied you. The changes will require more boiler capacity and hotter operating temperatures. You faxed a list of the requested changes to the ZED project manager earlier this morning. She has just called you back and set up a meeting later in the week to "resolve various issues." You are sure that change orders will be at the top of her list, and you are now planning for the negotiation and trying to decide on what type of strategy to use.

Preparation for Negotiation

Thorough preparation is essential to successful negotiation. Those who have not prepared properly prior to negotiation are likely to find themselves reacting to events rather than influencing them. The chances that they will conclude an agreement that will satisfy their reasons for negotiating in the first place will be reduced if they have not thought things through ahead of time. In highly competitive situations, they will be on the defensive if the opponent senses a lack of preparation. The opponent's confidence and commitment to their position will increase if they think the other side is unprepared. This section looks at the basic steps of preparation for negotiation.[1]

Consult with Others on Your Side

You need to talk to various groups or individuals on your side who will be affected by the negotiations. For example, both negotiators need to learn about any parameters upper management will place on the negotiations with regard to the costs and time involved. Both ZED and CPI should have received information from their engineers on the feasibility, costs, and time required to make the changes. Conversations with subcontractors, suppliers, and customers may also be necessary if the results of the negotiations will affect them or they will be implementing the agreement. After collecting this information, you will be in a position to identify your side's interests, frame issues, prioritize issues, and develop positions on the issues along with arguments to support them.

Identify Interests

Next you need to think about why you are negotiating with the other side. You should ask yourself about the basic wants or concerns your side is trying to satisfy with an agreement. In our example, the ZED project manager wants to complete the project within budget and on schedule. She also wants to avoid making unnecessary changes, but at the same time she wants to keep her client happy in order to increase the chances that ZED will get future business. The CPI project manager's primary interests are securing ZED's cooperation in making changes as needed and keeping the project on schedule so CPI can satisfy its potential soft drink client. CPI's project manager also has a budget, but he appears to have more flexibility here than ZED's project manager does.

Interests are different from the specific concrete proposals that will be discussed at the negotiating table. Interests are the concerns underlying the proposals, and proposals are intended to satisfy the interests underlying them. During negotiations, proposals can be evaluated in terms of how well they satisfy interests. Similarly, the success of the negotiations can be evaluated in terms of how well interests have been satisfied by any agreements reached.

Another important aspect of interests is that they are not limited to the obvious or tangible substantive matters, such as project cost or completion date. There often are less obvious interests in a negotiation that nevertheless can have an important effect on the outcome of negotiations. These interests include the process of negotiation, the relationship with the other side, and principles.[2] Interests can be classified as instrumental or intrinsic for each of these three categories.

Interests are *instrumental* if favorable terms are valued because of their impact on future dealings. Interests are *intrinsic* if favorable terms are valued regardless of their effect on future dealings. Thus, ZED's concern about possible future business is an instrumental interest, as is CPI's concern about the impact of the negotiations on its ability to honor a possible contract with its soft drink client. On the other hand, staying within a budget is an intrinsic interest for ZED.

Aside from the outcomes of negotiation, the parties may have an interest in the process of negotiation. Some of us may prefer to conduct business in a smooth, harmonious fashion that is characterized by honesty and openness. Others may enjoy a more aggressive and competitive process and the feeling that they have extracted as many concessions as possible from the other side. When it comes to relationships, most of us want to be treated with respect by the other side. Having the other's respect makes us feel better while we are negotiating (intrinsic interest), and it also may have important implications for our treatment in future negotiations (instrumental interest). Although ZED wants to keep the relationship positive because of its implication for future business, there also are negotiations in which the primary interest is in terminating the relationship so that the need for future interaction is eliminated. For example, if ZED refused CPI's change order requests, CPI might decide to complete the project with another contractor. This would require negotiations to terminate the agreement.

Negotiators also may have interests in principles that they wish to establish or have honored in their negotiations. These principles may assume great importance because they can have precedent-setting implications in future negotiations. In our scenario, the parties might negotiate principles that govern when changes can be made, how many changes can be made, and who pays for the cost of changes.

An awareness of these different types of interests is valuable because it serves as a reminder that there may be nonobvious but important immediate and longer-term interests at stake in a negotiation. When preparing for negotiation, it is important to consider the intrinsic and extrinsic interests related to process, relationship, and principle in addition to the substantive interests involved.

Identify Issues

An issue is a continuum on which negotiators can take different positions. The interests of the two sides will define the issues to be negotiated. For example, in our scenario, both negotiators have an interest in minimizing the cost of the change orders to themselves, establishing deadlines for completion of the project, being treated fairly by the other side, and perhaps establishing principles for allocating the costs of changes on this and future projects. ZED also has an interest in future business with CPI. These interests will lead to the issues on which the two sides will take different positions.

In the ZED-CPI negotiations the interests of the two sides might lead to the following issues: the allocation of the cost of the changes between ZED and CPI; the number of days or weeks the completion date for the project will be extended; the ground rules for conducting the negotiations; principles or procedures to be used in allocating the cost of future change orders; and the nature of any special considerations CPI will grant ZED in bidding on future projects. On each of these issues, each side can take different positions. For example, ZED might take the position that CPI should bear all of the cost of changes and extend the project completion dates by four weeks. CPI might propose that ZED make the changes without any additional charges or delays in completing the project.

On some issues, positions on both sides may be in agreement. For example, both sides might agree that they should develop shared principles for allocating the cost of future change orders. This would eliminate the need to negotiate every time a change occurs. However, they may disagree on the principle or principles to be used. Other matters may be issues for one side but not for the other. For example, a commitment from CPI on future projects would be an issue ZED might bring to the negotiation, but CPI would be less likely to introduce this issue. On the other hand, CPI might introduce the issue of penalties for not completing the project on time. ZED would prefer to avoid this issue.

The complete set of issues on both sides constitutes the bargaining mix or agenda of issues that need to be discussed during negotiations.[3] Although having many issues in the bargaining mix can complicate and lengthen negotiations because there are more issues that must be decided, having multiple issues also can facilitate negotiations by creating the possibility of trade-offs. For example, ZED might agree to a penalty clause if it does not complete the project on time if CPI agrees to pay 100 percent of the cost of overtime associated with any project changes.

Prioritize Issues

Once the mix of issues is identified, the next step is to evaluate their relative importance. In most negotiations, you will find yourself in a position of having to make concessions on one issue in order to gain on another. You also may wonder how much you should trade on one issue in exchange for concessions on another. The relative importance of the issues is a function of the value you place on the interests underlying them. In order to maximize their outcomes, negotiators should make larger and more frequent concessions on less important issues than they should make on more important ones. For example, avoiding additional cost due to changes is more important to the ZED project manager than keeping the project on schedule. For ZED's sales department, keeping CPI happy is more important than keeping the project within budget. The most important issues for CPI are getting the requested changes incorporated into the project and keeping to the original schedule. Relative to these two issues, the additional cost of the changes is a less important issue.

Develop Proposals

Developing proposals usually involves preparing an initial offer, target point, and resistance point on each issue. The resistance point represents the lowest outcome you are willing to accept for the foreseeable future; the target point represents your goal, or the outcome you would like to achieve as a result of the negotiation. It is generally more favorable to you than your resistance point.

The initial offer represents your first proposal or the first counterproposal you plan to make on an issue. It is generally more favorable to you than your target point.

Studies of negotiation summarized by Pruitt and Carnevale indicate that initial offers and subsequent proposals change more often during negotiation than do target points.[4] And target points are more subject to change than resistance points. These changes can be either upward or downward. For example, a target point might be revised downward if your opponent shows more resistance to your proposals than you anticipated. Or your target might be revised upward if the other side's initial offer is more generous than you expected. Your resistance point also could be revised if alternatives outside the negotiation improve or deteriorate during negotiation. Because resistance points are subjective, different negotiators may establish different resistance points, target points, and initial offers, even when they are provided with identical information.

Sometimes a resistance point is based on what Fisher, Ury, and Patton call a BATNA: the *best* *a*lternative *t*o a *n*egotiated *a*greement, which represents the best option outside the current relationship.[5] When you negotiate with suppliers, your BATNA might be what another vendor would charge you for a product or service. In the ZED-CPI scenario, the best alternative might be using an arbitrator or courts to settle the matter of change orders. Perhaps CPI could bring in another contractor to complete the project if they are unable to reach agreement with ZED. Establishing your BATNA before you negotiate will help you avoid agreeing to less favorable terms than you could get elsewhere, and it will prevent you from rejecting an agreement that is better than other alternatives. If you are able to improve your BATNA, you will strengthen your negotiation position.

In some cases, your resistance point may be identical to your BATNA. In others, your resistance point may be more favorable to you than your BATNA. Resistance points can be established on the basis of other considerations, such as budget limits set by a higher authority, costs you wish to recover, instructions from your constituents, and so on. Assume, for example, on the issue of paying for the cost of the changes that the ZED project manager sets her resistance point at $25,000, and the CPI project manager sets his resistance point at $100,000 on the basis of their respective budget requirements. If the BATNA for both negotiators is settling their dispute in court, the cost to both negotiators could be a much higher than the amount of money represented by their current resistance points.

In setting your target point and initial offer, it is useful to consider objective standards or standards of fairness that may apply to the situation. There are an number of principles that negotiators can use to support their demands in a negotiation.[6] Perhaps there is an industry standard, practice, or custom that one or both project managers might use to support their position regarding the change orders. If there is no industry norm to rely on, perhaps the project managers might adopt an equality norm, which would support a fifty–fifty division of the cost. An equity norm would favor allocation of cost to the manager who is requesting the changes from the original project specifications. Under a needs rule, the greatest portion of the cost would be assumed by the party with the greatest capacity to pay (least needy). In other situations, market value, scientific judgment, efficiency, costs, what a court would decide, or moral standards may be used as possible objective criteria.[7]

If they can be identified, objective standards or positions that are supported by norms of fairness provide good reference points for establishing your resistance point, target point, and initial offer. The chances that you will be asked to explain how you arrived at your proposals during the course of negotiation are good. Using these reference points will help ensure that your proposals fall within the realm of reality. If you are unable to provide any supporting rationale for your proposals, they are likely to be dismissed without serious consideration, and you are likely to loose credibility as a negotiator. Serious negotiation is unlikely to occur until a more realistic position is adopted, or you may eventually convince the other side that further negotiation with you is a waste of time.

There may be several standards that could be applied in a negotiation, and some of them will be more favorable to you than others. A good place to set an initial offer is at the point most favorable to you that is still supported by an objective standard or norm. A target point can be set at a point less favorable to you, but at one supported by a norm or standard that you are better able to defend than the one underlying your initial offer. This will allow you to make concessions from your initial proposal and still permit you to achieve your target.

For example, the ZED project manager might set her resistance point at $25,000, an amount supported by her need to meet her budget goals and earnest desire to keep her job. Her target point might be that CPI pay the full $75,000 cost of the changes based on both the equity and needs principles. Specifically, CPI should pay for the changes because it is requesting them, will benefit from them, and can better afford to pay for them. ZED's initial offer might be that CPI pay $75,000 plus a 20 percent surcharge for making changes to the original specifications. The surcharge would cover additional administrative expenses associated with the changes and serve as a deterrent to making frivolous changes.

Prior to the negotiations, CPI's project manager might set his resistance point at $100,000 on the basis of his need to stay within his budget. However, his resistance point is likely to drop to $75,000 as soon as he learns that this is the estimated cost of the changes. His target point might be set at $37,500 supported by the equality norm (fifty–fifty split of the $75,000 cost of the changes). And his initial position might be that ZED should absorb all of the cost because it is trivial in relationship to the total budget for the project. Furthermore, CPI is potentially an important customer.

The respective positions of ZED and CPI regarding the issue of who pays for the changes are shown in Figure 21.1. There is a positive settlement range for this issue because the resistance points of both companies overlap. Recall that the cost of the changes is estimated at $75,000. Because CPI can spend up to $100,000 on changes and ZED could spend an additional $25,000, together they can more than cover the additional cost. If for some reason CPI was willing to pay only $25,000 for changes, or the total cost of the changes was estimated to be $150,000, there would be a negative settlement range. This would make agreement impossible to reach unless either or both parties decided to change their resistance points.

In highly competitive bargaining situations, each party will try to estimate the other's resistance point and reach an agreement as close to it as possible. A very

FIGURE 21.1. NEGOTIATION POSITIONS ON THE ISSUE OF THE ALLOCATION OF THE COST OF CHANGE ORDERS, ZED VERSUS CPI.

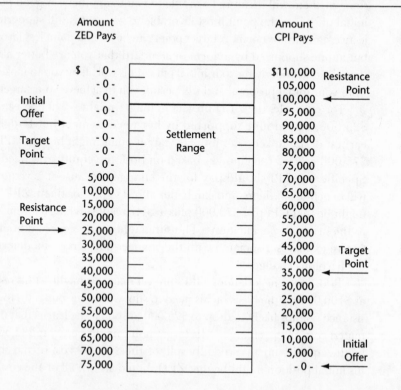

aggressive negotiator may even try to modify the other's resistance point so that a settlement can be reached that is even more favorable to him or her.

Negotiators are more likely to reach agreements, and reach them quickly, when there is a larger settlement range than when there is a smaller one.[8] Presumably this occurs because a wider settlement range provides more places where acceptable agreements can be reached.

Linking offers, target point, and resistance point to principles can be a double-edged sword and should be done with caution. On the one hand, this tactic may make proposals more rational, defensible, and likely to prevail. On the other hand, adopting positions linked to principles may lead to rigidity that makes reaching agreement more difficult.[9] That is, opposing negotiators may adopt different positions favoring their own interests, each supported by competing principles. If this occurs, the danger arises that one or both negotiators may become so committed to their respective positions that they are psychologically unable to make the concessions necessary to reach agreement.

To avoid the psychological trap of becoming too committed to positions based on principles, Fisher, Ury, and Patton advise negotiators to "frame each issue as a joint search for objective criteria," "reason and be open to reason," and "never yield to pressure, only to principle."[10] In other words, negotiators should be firm about reaching an agreement based on principles of fairness but remain flexible enough to consider different principles that may legitimately apply to a situation.

Negotiators should prepare for negotiation by developing a series of positions on the issues that are supportable by objective criteria. At the same time, they should be flexible enough to acknowledge the validity of other legitimate principles that may apply to the situation. This flexibility may motivate a search of innovative solutions that reconcile or integrate various principles previously thought to be contradictory. Or it may lead to a compromise solution that incorporates some elements of various principles. One side may even adopt the position of the other side if, after discussion, it proves to be fairer and easier to implement.

Learn About the Other Side

Negotiators should not only be thinking about their own interests, priorities, alternatives, and positions. They also should consider the same items for the other side. Any pertinent information they can learn about the other side prior to negotiation will help them anticipate the other side's behavior during the negotiations.

In the ZED-CPI negotiations, the ZED project manager has learned though her sales force that the CPI project manager may be willing to spend some money for the requested changes. She also knows that CPI plans to build several other boilers over the next several years. And if CPI is satisfied with ZED's performance on the current project, CPI is willing to give preferential consideration to ZED on future projects. For its part, CPI has learned from industry sources that ZED is experiencing financial difficulty and needs future boiler orders. These are valuable items of information for both negotiators to have as they prepare to negotiate. If other information is unknown prior to negotiation, many times it can be obtained through careful observation and listening as negotiations progress.

Archival data can be used to learn more about the other party. These include publicly available information from sources such as Dun and Bradstreet, financial statements, newspaper articles, stock reports, and legal judgments.[11] Other ways of obtaining useful information about the other side may be by visiting the other side's place of business, having preliminary discussions with them about what they would like to achieve in the forthcoming negotiations, trying to anticipate their interests by role playing with others on your side, and talking to people who know or who have previously negotiated with the other side. If you have had previous negotiations with the other side, your own notes and experience also should be useful.

Organize Your Team

In important or complex negotiations, typically each side is represented by a team instead of a single individual. You should carefully select the members of your negotiating team and brief them on their responsibilities. Certainly it is difficult for a single individual to talk, listen, think, write, observe, and plan simultaneously. For this reason, Kennedy, Benson, and McMillan recommend organizing a negotiation team into three roles: leader, summarizer, and recorder.[12]

The *leader*, usually the senior member of the bargaining team, serves as the team coordinator and spokesperson, and generally leads the team's effort. The leader usually does most of the talking at the negotiation table. In the ZED-CPI negotiations, the leaders are likely to be the respective project managers.

The *summarizer* listens carefully to the arguments of the other side and gives thinking time to the leader by intervening when appropriate, for example, by asking the other side for clarification of a point or summarizing the other side's position or arguments on some issue. The summarizer should be someone who is trusted and can work closely with the leader.

The *recorder* remains silent during the negotiation unless called on to speak about a particular issue. The recorder in the ZED-CPI negotiations might be a lawyer, engineer, or some other technical specialist knowledgeable about some critical aspects of the project. The responsibilities of this position also include watching the other team for verbal and nonverbal clues that might reveal something about their interests, priorities, or points of disagreement within their team. The recorder can also speak on matters related to his or her technical expertise.

The recorder takes notes on offers and counteroffers during the negotiations and may be called on to report to the team during private meetings away from the negotiating table. If the negotiations are complex, several team members may be assigned to the role of recorder.

Negotiating Strategies

The two project managers could adopt several different strategies in the forthcoming negotiations: concession making, contending, compromising, problem solving, inaction, and withdrawal.[13]

Concession Making

This strategy involves changing your proposal so that it provides less benefit to you and more benefit to the other side. The ZED project manager could engage in concession making by agreeing to the changes requested by CPI without any additional charges or extensions to the project completion date.

Contending

Contending involves trying to persuade the other side to make a proposal more favorable to you but less favorable to them. Commonly used contentious tactics include threats, arguments, and trying to convince the other side that you are unwilling to make any additional concessions. The CPI project manager could engage in contentious tactics by threatening not to award ZED future business if the changes are not made to his satisfaction.

Compromising

Compromising is a strategy that is intermediate between concession making and contending. A middle ground is sought that involves some degree of sacrifice for both sides. For example, the two project managers might agree to share the costs of the changes equally and also agree to a two-week extension of the project completion date. Some scholars view compromising not as a distinct strategy but as simple concession making by both parties or lazy problem solving.[14]

Problem Solving

Problem solving refers to efforts to find agreements that are highly beneficial to both parties. If they are successful, they can avoid the deep concessions that may be necessary under a concession-making or compromising strategy.

Sometimes problem solving is a joint effort in which the two sides work together by openly sharing information about interests and priorities and discussing the pros and cons of various proposals. At other times problem-solving efforts are more one-sided and less open and involve more of a trial-and-error approach.

A problem-solving effort in the ZED-CPI negotiations might involve the two project managers' exchanging honest information about their underlying interests as they relate to making the proposed changes, a discussion of the relative importance they attach to the issues of increased costs and time delays, and possibly sharing budget information. By exchanging this information, the two project managers would learn that avoiding increased cost is the greatest concern for ZED, and keeping the project on schedule is of highest priority for CPI. If CPI were willing to pick up most or all of the increased cost of the changes and ZED agreed to find a way to keep the project on schedule by adding staff, overtime, or outsourcing, perhaps an agreement could be reached that satisfied both project managers. Because CPI cannot tolerate delays in the completion of the project and ZED has a severely limited budget to pay for changes, such an agreement may be more beneficial for both parties than the simple compromise described above.

Inaction or Withdrawal

Inaction involves attempts to delay or avoid serious negotiations. Withdrawal involves terminating negotiations without an agreement. If they choose withdrawal, both parties might adopt their BATNAs. ZED could implement an inaction strategy by ignoring CPI's change orders, refusing to discuss changes with CPI, or talking about other issues when they do meet. An inaction strategy would not work as well for CPI because it is a strategy designed to maintain the status quo and CPI is the party seeking changes.

Choosing a Strategy

How should you choose between the strategies described above? Pruitt proposed the dual concern model to explain how negotiators choose strategies in negotiation.[15] The model is descriptive in nature rather than prescriptive because it seeks to explain how negotiators choose a strategy rather than to provide advice about how they should choose a strategy. However, what the model says about how negotiators actually choose a negotiation strategy also provides a good practical guide for choosing a strategy.

The dual concern model says that the choice of a negotiating strategy is primarily influenced by two key concerns: your level of concern for your own outcomes and your level of concern for the outcomes of the other side. A third consideration Pruitt added is the feasibility of the strategy under consideration. The relationship between the first two variables, or the dual concerns, and the choice of a strategy are shown in Figure 21.2.

The model indicates that negotiators choose contending or problem solving when they have a high level of concern for their own outcomes. This makes sense, because most people are less willing to sacrifice their own interests when they place great value on them. Thus, we are less likely to engage in concession making or compromise when important interests are at stake, and we are unlikely to choose inaction or withdrawal if we believe these interests can be satisfied in the current relationship. The choice between the remaining strategies of contending and problem solving depends on your level of concern with the other party's outcomes. If you have a high level of concern for the outcomes of the other side, you will choose problem solving because this is a strategy designed to satisfy the needs of both sides. If there is little concern for the other side's outcomes, contending is the strategy of choice because it seeks to satisfy your own interests at the expense of the other side. If your concern for your own outcomes is low but your concern with the other's outcomes is high, you are likely to choose concession making in

FIGURE 21.2. THE DUAL CONCERN MODEL.

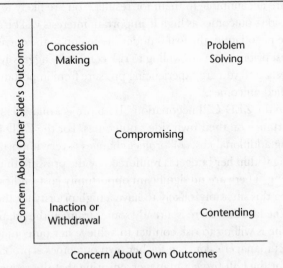

Source: Adapted from Pruitt, D. G. (1983). Strategic choice in negotiation. *American Behavioral Scientist, 27,* 167–194.

order to satisfy the other side. When both concerns are low, there is little interest in negotiation, and inaction and withdrawal are probable strategy choices.

The importance that negotiators place on these concerns and the feasibility of various strategies can change over the course of negotiations and across various issues under discussion. As a result, the choice of a strategy can vary over the course of negotiation and with different issues.

The dual concern model can be used as a guide to preparation for negotiation if negotiators ask themselves the following questions:

- What is my level of concern for my own outcomes?
- What is my level of concern for the other side's outcomes?
- What is the feasibility of the strategy suggested by my level of these two concerns?

Determining Your Level of Concern for Your Side's Outcomes

In thinking about your level of concern for your side's outcomes, it is useful to ask yourself about the importance of the interests that will be affected by the outcomes of negotiation, the opportunity costs associated with the negotiation, and extent to which you are willing to risk conflict with the other side in order to achieve your own outcomes. The importance that others place on the outcomes you achieve also will influence your calculations, especially if they are your constituents and you are accountable to them for results. You are likely to rate the importance of your side's outcomes as high if important interests will be affected by the outcome of the negotiation, the issues under discussion in the current negotiation are your highest priority, you are willing to risk conflict by aggressively pursuing your side's interests, and you are experiencing pressure from important constituents to achieve specified outcomes.

In the ZED-CPI negotiations, both project managers are likely to place high importance on their own side's outcomes. For the ZED project manager, minimizing additional costs of project changes is very important. The importance of staying within her budget is reinforced by the pressure that upper management is exerting. There are no significant opportunity costs indicated in the case, and resolving this situation is likely to have a high priority for the manager of this project. The fact that there is already some strain on the relationship is an indication that she is willing to risk conflict to achieve her outcomes. As a result, the ZED project manager's concern for her own outcomes is probably high.

For the CPI project manager, ensuring that the requested changes are made and keeping the project on schedule are very important. CPI has a big investment in the project, and a failure to have the changes completed on time will mean a loss of business and result in the loss of many jobs. There is no indication of opportunity costs, willingness to risk conflict, or constituent pressures in the case. Given the stakes, it is a safe bet that resolving this issue is the primary focus for the CPI project manager, that he is willing to risk conflict to accomplish his objectives and that there is substantial pressure from his managers to have the project completed on time. As a consequence, the CPI project manager's concern for his outcomes probably is high.

Determining Your Concern for the Other Side's Outcomes

In thinking about your level of concern for the other side's outcomes, you should ask yourself if there are interpersonal bonds of friendship with the other side that already exist or that you would like to establish. Your concern for the other side's outcomes also will be greater if you are dependent on them to achieve your outcomes or if you will you be dependent on them in future negotiations. It is important to keep such future dependencies in mind because negotiators sometimes become so caught up in their current conflict that they forget about the impact of their behavior on their long-term relationship with the other side.

If there are bonds of friendship or you perceive yourself to be dependent on the other side now or in the future, you are likely to have a high level of concern for the other side's outcomes. Although there is no indication that she has any type of interpersonal bond with the other project manager, the ZED project manager's concern for CPI's outcomes is likely to be high because of the good prospect of much-needed future business. The CPI manager probably would have less concern with CPI's outcomes because he is not dependent on ZED for future business. However, CPI is under a great deal of pressure to complete this project on time, so CPI is dependent on ZED because resolving the issues with ZED probably provides the only hope of completing the project on schedule. CPI is therefore also likely to have a high level of concern for ZED's outcomes.

The Feasibility of Problem Solving

This analysis suggests that both negotiators probably have a high level of concern with their own outcomes, as well as a high level of concern for the other side's outcomes. The dual concern model suggests that both project managers should adopt a problem-solving approach to the negotiation. However, both managers may wonder whether a problem-solving approach is feasible under the circumstances.

Problem solving becomes more feasible as the perception of common ground on the part of the negotiators increases.[16] This occurs because greater common ground makes the likelihood of finding alternatives that satisfy the interests of both parties more promising. Common ground on an issue increases as the size of the settlement range between the negotiator's resistance points becomes larger and to the extent that the parties believe that alternatives favorable to both sides exist or can be invented.

Negotiators are likely to believe there is integrative potential in a situation when they are confident in their own problem-solving ability, they have a track record of solving problems in the current negotiation, they have access to third parties who can assist them with locating or devising integrative alternatives, and they believe that the other side is ready to problem-solve too.

Your belief that the other side is ready to problem-solve depends on your trust in them, which is determined by your belief that they are concerned about your interests. The relationship between trust and problem solving is likely to occur as long as trust is coupled with the belief that the other side also has firm aspirations. Absent firm aspirations, trust can encourage contending rather than problem solving. This can occur because when we believe someone is concerned about us, but at the same time has a weak commitment to his own goals, we are likely to conclude that he will concede easily.

Your trust in the other side is likely to increase when you believe the other negotiator has a positive attitude toward you, is similar to you, or is dependent on you. Trust is more likely to exist when the other side has been helpful to you in the past, especially if the help has been voluntary.

Ways to Encourage Problem Solving

If your level of concern for your own and the other side's outcomes motivates you to problem-solve, what does this discussion suggest you should do to improve the chances that problem solving will be successful?

Explore for the possibility of common ground. Many negotiators have a "fixed-pie" bias.[17] They assume, many times incorrectly, that there is a fixed amount of what is being negotiated and that one side can benefit only if the other side loses. Instead, you should approach negotiations with an open mind and try to explore areas of common ground. For example, the ZED project manager might probe the CPI project manager's flexibility on paying for some of CPI's requested changes by asking, "What flexibility do you have to pay for the changes you are requesting?"

Build confidence in problem-solving ability. Although it is a longer-term process, negotiators can boost their own confidence in their problem-solving ability by improving their communication skills. They can try to build the other side's confidence in their own problem-solving ability by verbally reinforcing the other's problem-solving efforts or by encouraging them by saying things such as, "I know we can solve this problem if we put our heads together."

Tackle easier issues first. If easier-to-solve issues are scheduled first on the agenda, success in solving them may lead to the belief that more difficult issues can be solved later on in negotiations.

Identify third parties. Try to identify trusted and respected neutral third parties who you may be able to rely on to facilitate your problem solving efforts. Perhaps the ZED and CPI project managers know a trusted engineering consultant who could propose a solution that will meet all of CPI's needs without making all the changes.

Explore and convey readiness for problem solving. An indication of the other's readiness for problem solving can be gained through careful observation of clues in their behavior, by direct questioning, or by analyzing the factors relevant to their dual concerns.

The ZED project manager could attempt to build the CPI project manager's trust in her by actively listening to his concerns about needed changes, commiserating about the problems they have in common as project managers, and trying to be helpful in other situations outside the negotiation. So that she does not encourage contending from CPI's project manager, the ZED project manager also should stress the firmness of her need to stay within her budget and her concerns about the possible delays caused by the changes. The ZED project manager's trust in the CPI project manager should be enhanced by her knowledge that CPI is dependent on ZED for the completion of the project in a timely fashion.

The Feasibility of Contending

Contending is more feasible when the other side has low concern for its own outcomes, you have the capacity to employ contentious tactics effectively, the other side has little capacity to counter your tactics, and there is little risk of alienating the other side by using such tactics. Before deciding to use contentious tactics, you should attempt to evaluate the other side's level of concern for its own outcomes, consider what contentious tactics you have at your disposal as well as those available to the other side, and the risks you run in alienating the other side by contending.

Although the two project managers may initially be unaware of each other's level of concern for their own outcomes, it probably would not take long for them to discover that they both are highly resistant to yielding on the issues that are important to them. Because her job is on the line, the ZED project manager can make a very strong commitment to not contributing more than $25,000 toward the cost of the changes. Similarly, because an important contract with a customer and many jobs are at stake, the CPI manager can make a strong commitment to completing the needed changes within the schedule for the project. Both managers probably perceive a high degree of risk in alienating the other side. ZED runs the risk of the loss of future projects with CPI. CPI risks jeopardizing its contracts with its customers if the needed changes are not made in a timely fashion. Under the circumstances, both project managers are likely to conclude that contending is not a feasible strategy.

The Feasibility of Inaction and Withdrawing

The feasibility of inaction depends on the degree of time pressure each side is experiencing. There are two sources of time pressure: the cost per unit of time of continued negotiations and the necessity of meeting deadlines. Time pressure due to the continued cost of negotiation might result from lost opportunities incurred as a result of the controversy, the expenses associated with supporting a negotiation team away from home, or deterioration of the object of negotiation, as in the case of perishable items. Deadlines represent times in the future when significant costs will be incurred if the controversy is not settled. In considering the feasibility of inaction as a strategy, ask yourself what costs are associated with delaying the conclusion of negotiation and whether significant costs will result if you fail to meet specific deadlines.

There is some indication that the ZED project manager has been using inaction in response to the CPI manager's request for change orders. However, the cost of this inaction is beginning to show up in a souring relationship, which may put future business in jeopardy. The CPI project manager cannot use inaction as a strategy because postponing the resolution of the conflict would risk his company's contract with an important customer. Inaction is not a feasible strategy for either project manager.

The feasibility of withdrawing depends on the attractiveness of one's BATNA. Neither side has very attractive alternatives outside of their relationship with the other project manager. Going to court or to an arbitrator to settle the dispute or bringing in another contractor to finish the work is likely to be more costly in terms of time and money than trying to resolve the dispute through direct negotiation with the other side. Consequently withdrawal is not a feasible strategy at this stage of the negotiation.

The Feasibility of Concession Making

Concession making is a feasible strategy as long as one has the capacity to make concessions. It is a strategy favored under heavy time pressure because it provides a way of reaching agreement quickly. The capacity to concede depends on how close you are to your resistance point. The closer you are to your resistance point, the more difficult concession making becomes.

The ZED project manager, with $25,000 left in her budget, has less capacity to concede with regard to paying for the cost or the proposed changes than the CPI project manager does with $100,000 available in his budget. On the other hand, CPI has no room for concession making on extending the completion date for the project. It is uncertain whether the ZED project manager can agree to the proposed changes and still meet the original completion date, but she probably has greater flexibility on this issue than the CPI project manager does.

The circumstances of our case suggest that concession making is a feasible strategy for the CPI manager on the issue of the cost of the changes, but not on the project completion date. For the ZED project manager, concession making is less feasible on the issue of the cost of the changes than it is with regard to the project completion date.

The Feasibility of Compromising

Compromising is a less intense form of concession making or lazy problem solving. The conditions making a compromise strategy feasible are therefore similar to those underlying the feasibility of concession making and problem solving.

In our project management scenario, a simple compromise involving an equal division of the cost of the changes and an extension of the completion date for the project is not a feasible strategy. The ZED project manager has little capacity for concession making on paying for the cost of the changes, and the CPI project manager has no ability to concede on extending the completion date of the project.

Conclusion

The previous analysis of the ZED-CPI project management scenario indicates that both project managers have a high concern for their own outcomes and each other's outcomes. Both managers therefore are motivated for problem solving. In addition, problem solving is a more feasible strategy under the circumstances described than the other strategies we considered. Our application of the dual concern model therefore suggests that both managers should adopt a problem-solving approach.

Pruitt and Carnevale[18] describe several specific ways to develop win-win, or integrative agreements through problem solving in negotiations. One that might be used in the ZED-CPI scenario is an exchange of concessions. Because minimizing the cost of changes is the highest-priority issue for the ZED project manager and completing the project on schedule is the highest-priority issue for the CPI manager, the two managers can achieve a problem-solving agreement by exchanging concessions on these two issues. That is, ZED agrees to make the changes and still complete the project according to the original schedule if CPI agrees to pay most of the cost of the changes.

A major theme of this chapter is that the choice of an appropriate negotiation strategy is contingent on the specific situation faced by the negotiator. I described the key variables used to analyze the situation in connection with the dual concern model. Although problem solving was the most appropriate strategy in the ZED-CPI scenario, it is important to remember that other negotiation strategies might be more appropriate under different circumstances. Some complex negotiations may even call for the use of different strategies at different phases or on different issues of the same negotiation. Negotiators must then implement their chosen strategies by adopting the appropriate tactics. There is insufficient space in this chapter to discuss these tactics, but they are described in detail elsewhere.[19] Finally, a second key theme of this chapter is that careful planning and preparation are required to choose a strategy and to obtain successful negotiation outcomes.

CHAPTER TWENTY-TWO

CONFLICT MANAGEMENT

Vijay K. Verma

Conflict is the gadfly of thought. It stirs us to observation and memory. It instigates invention. It shocks us out of sheeplike passivity, and sets us at noting and contriving. . . . Conflict is a "sine qua non" of reflection and ingenuity.

JOHN DEWEY

Conflict is as inevitable in a project environment as change seems to be. When project team members interact during the course of completing their tasks and responsibilities, there is always a potential for conflict. In fact, it is virtually impossible for people with diverse background skills and norms to work together, make decisions, and try to meet project goals and objectives without conflict.

Project managers must identify, analyze, and evaluate both positive and negative values of conflict and their effect on performance. They must learn how and when to stimulate conflict and how to use it to increase the performance of project team members. Conflict need not have destructive consequences. Attitudes and conflict management styles play an important role in determining whether such conflict will lead to destructive or mutually beneficial outcomes.[1]

Views of Conflict

Over the years three distinct views have evolved about conflict in projects and organizations.[2] The traditional view (dominant from the late nineteenth century

Note: Portions of this chapter are adapted from Verma, V. K. (1996). *Human resource skills for the project manager.* Upper Darby, PA: Project Management Institute.

until the mid–1940s) assumes that conflict is bad, always has a negative impact, and leads to declines in performance as the level of conflict increases. Conflict must therefore always be avoided. In this view, conflict is closely associated with such terms as *violence, destruction,* and *irrationality.*

The response to conflict in the traditional view is to reduce, suppress, or eliminate it. The manager was responsible for freeing the project of any conflict, often using an authoritarian approach. Although that approach worked sometimes, it was not generally effective; when they are suppressed, the root causes cannot be identified, and the potentially positive aspects of conflict cannot emerge.

This traditional view of conflict is still widely held because industrial and business institutions that have a strong influence on our society concur with it. This negative view of conflict played a role in the development of labor unions. Violent or disruptive confrontations between workers and management led people to conclude that conflict was always detrimental and should therefore be avoided.

The behavioral or contemporary view, also known as the human relations view, emerged in the late 1940s and held sway through the 1970s. It argues that conflict is natural and inevitable in all organizations and that it may have either a positive or a negative effect, depending on how the conflict is handled. Performance may increase with conflict, but only up to a certain level, and then decline if conflict is allowed to increase further or is left unresolved. This approach advocates acceptance of conflict and rationalizes its existence. Because of the potential benefits from conflict, project managers should focus on managing it effectively rather than suppressing or eliminating it.

The newest perspective, the interactionist view, assumes that conflict is necessary to increase performance. While the behavioral approach accepts conflict, the interactionist view encourages conflict based on the belief that a harmonious, peaceful, tranquil, too-cooperative project organization is likely to become static, apathetic, stagnant, and unable to respond to change and innovation. This approach encourages managers to maintain an appropriate level of conflict—enough to keep projects self-critical, viable, creative, and innovative.

Using these three views of conflict, the managerial actions to be taken can be decided by comparing the actual level of conflict (a) and desired levels of conflict (d).[3] According to the traditional view, the desired level of conflict is always zero. If $a = 0$, do nothing, and if actual conflict rises above zero, it should be resolved. But the behavioral and interactionist views differ only in terms of the desired level of conflict, which could be equal to or above zero in the contemporary view and is always above zero in the interactionist view. If the desired level of conflict is above zero, then there are three possible outcomes depending on whether a is more than d or a is less than d. (See Table 22.1 for a summary of the three views of conflict, their effect on performance, and the recommended managerial actions.)

TABLE 22.1. A COMPARISON OF CONFLICT VIEWS.

	Traditional View	Contemporary View	Interactionist View
Main Points	Caused by troublemakers Bad Should be avoided Should be suppressed	Inevitable between humans Not always bad Natural result of change Can be managed	Results from commitment to goals Often beneficial Should be stimulated Should aim to foster creativity
Effect on Performance	Performance declines as the level of conflict increases	Performance mainly depends on how effectively the conflict is handled. Generally performance increases to a certain level as conflict level increases, then declines if conflict is allowed to increase further or left unresolved	Certain level of conflict is necessary to increase performance. Performance increases with conflict up to a certain level, then declines if conflict increases further or remains unresolved
Recommended Actions	Do nothing if $a = d$ Resolve conflict if $a > d$ (Where $d = 0$)	Do nothing if $a = d$ Resolve conflict if $a > d$ (Where $d \geq 0$)	Do nothing if $a = d$ Resolve conflict if $a > d$ Stimulate conflict if $a < d$ (Where $d > 0$)

Note: a = actual level of conflict among team members; d = desired level of conflict that team members are comfortable with.

When *a* is less than *d*, conflict management implies not only conflict resolution but also conflict stimulation. According to the behavioral and interactionist views, there is an optimal level of conflict that maximizes project and organizational performance. A project with no conflict whatsoever has little incentive for innovation, creativity, or change because its participants are comfortable with the status quo and are not concerned about improving their performance.

Conflict in Projects

Breakdown in communication is the overarching, most common, and most obvious source of conflict in projects. A lack of trust, respect, effective listening skills, and perceptual differences can lead to serious communication problems. Misinterpretation of a design drawing, a misunderstood change order, delays in delivery of critical components, and failure to execute instructions are all results of some type of communication breakdown. The communication skills of project managers are often put to the test by overlapping areas of responsibility, gray lines of authority, delegation problems, complex project organizational structures, and conflicts among participants. That is why communication is too important to be fully covered by administrative procedures alone. Project managers and their teams must also develop effective communication skills (especially listening skills) to resolve project conflicts. They must learn to create an atmosphere that encourages open communication in order to deal with conflict and gain team members' acceptance of and commitment to project goals.

In general, all potential conflict fits one of three categories, although a particular conflict situation may be based on two or more of the categories:

1. Goal-oriented conflicts are associated with end results, performance specifications and criteria, priorities, and objectives.
2. Administrative conflicts refer to the management structure and philosophy and are mainly based on definition of roles and reporting relationships and on responsibilities and authority for tasks, functions, and decisions.
3. Interpersonal conflicts result from differences in work ethics, styles, egos, and personalities of the participants.[4]

Project environments are particularly vulnerable to generating conflict. Thamhain and Wilemon have identified seven major sources of conflict in project management based on their research conducted in a private manufacturing company.[5] Table 22.2 shows a comparison between the rankings of intensity of conflict, as suggested by Thamhain and Wilemon and by Posner, and Table 22.3 shows sources of conflict and recommended solutions.

TABLE 22.2. SOURCES OF CONFLICT AND THEIR RANKING BY CONFLICT INTENSITY.

Sources of Conflict	Conflict Intensity Ranking	
	Thamhain and Wilemon	Posner
Conflict over project priorities	2	3
Conflict over administration procedures	5	7
Conflict over technical opinions and performance trade-offs	4	5
Conflict over human resources	3	4
Conflict over cost and budget	7	2
Conflict over schedules	1	1
Personality conflict	6	6

Sources: Thamhain, W. J., & Wilemon, D. L. (1975). Conflict management in project life cycles. *Sloan Management Review, 16*(3), 31–50. Posner, B. (1986). What's all the fighting about? Conflicts in project management. *IEEE Transactions on Engineering Management, EM-33*(4), 207–211.

The major difference in Posner's study, clear from Table 22.2, is the pattern of conflict over costs, changing from seventh to second place. Conflict over administrative procedures dropped from fifth to last position. These differences can be explained by a variety of changes in circumstances and ways of managing business, programs, and projects. Differences over cost can be attributed to tough global competition. Also, a shift in government contract pricing strategy (from a more flexible cost-plus basis to more rigorous fixed-price approach) has increased emphasis on cost issues. The decreased intensity of conflict over procedures can be explained by wider acceptance of project management concepts, strategies, and techniques.[6]

Managing Conflict in Projects

Because of the significant impact that conflict can have on project success, managing it well is one of the most important skills a project manager must possess. An American Management Association study of middle- and top-level executives revealed that the average manager spends approximately 20 percent of his or her time dealing with conflict.[7] The importance of conflict management is also

TABLE 22.3. PROJECT CONFLICTS AND RECOMMENDED SOLUTIONS.

Sources of Conflict	Definitions	Suggested Solutions
Conflict over project priorities	Views of project participants differ over sequence of activities and tasks. Includes goals incompatibility and differences in long-term versus short-term perspectives.	Develop a master plan compatible with long-term strategies.
Conflict over administration procedures	Conflicts over managerial and administrative issues of how the project will be organized and managed.	Clarify roles, responsibilities, and reporting relationships at the beginning of the project.
Conflict over technical opinions and performance trade-offs	Disagreements over technical issues, performance specifications, and technical trade-offs.	Use peer review and steering committees to review specifications and design.
Conflict over human resources	Conflicts concerning staffing and allocation of project personnel and where to get them and how.	Develop a work breakdown structure and a corresponding responsibility matrix.
Conflict over cost and budget	Conflict over cost estimates from support areas regarding work breakdown structures and estimating techniques.	Develop overall budgets supported by detailed budget and cost estimates of subproject tasks and activities
Conflict over schedules	Disagreements about the timing, sequencing, and scheduling of project-related tasks and information system to prepare and monitor project schedules.	Develop an overall schedule that integrates schedules for subprojects with staffing and other life constraints.
Personality conflict	Disagreements on interpersonal issues.	Emphasize team building and create an environment that emphasizes respect, diversity, and equality.

reinforced by a research study of managers that analyzed twenty-five skills and personality factors to determine which, if any, were related to managerial success. Of the twenty-five factors, the ability to handle conflict was most positively related to managerial success.[8]

Project managers must not only be aware of various interpersonal conflict resolution modes and their strengths and weaknesses in order to choose an appropriate approach but must also manage conflict using some practical guidelines that involve preparing for the conflict, facing it, and then resolving it by developing win-win strategies. They must also recognize that it is sometimes good to stimulate conflict in order to encourage self-evaluation, creativity, and innovation.

Stimulating Conflict

The whole notion of stimulating conflict is difficult to accept because conflict traditionally has a negative connotation. There is evidence, however, that in some situations, an increase in conflict actually improves performance.[9] Stimulating conflict is considered a proactive approach that requires up-front initiative aimed at minimizing the impact of potential negative conflict and avoiding costly patching-up operations later in the project life cycle. For example, certain policies regarding negotiating contracts and resolving disputes should be developed and agreed on at the beginning of the project. Generally management and project managers can stimulate conflict in the following ways.[10]

Accept conflict as desirable on certain occasions. Conflict may result as the project manager insists on developing sufficient front-end planning and a basic framework with clear project priorities, scope definition, and administrative procedures. To a degree, conflicts at the front end should be viewed positively, since a project manager's opportunity to participate in setting the project's budget and schedule (including arguing for objectives that may cause conflict) is likely to decrease conflicts down the road.

Bring new individuals into an existing situation. Thoughtful questions and comments from newcomers or outsiders may provide a different, fresh perspective. They may encourage long-time team members to remove their blinders and think of new ways of doing things. For example, a project manager may bring in an outside expert to increase team effectiveness by introducing team partnering and a win-win conflict resolution strategy.

Restructure the project organization. The project organization structure may have to be changed to suit the circumstances. For example, freeform structure is good during planning to allow active participation and creative expression, whereas strong matrix forms work better during the execution and termination phases.

New reporting relationships may create uncertainty, but they may also motivate project participants to discover innovative and creative ways to get work done.

Introduce programs designed to increase competition. A manager of projects may introduce competition to encourage task managers to accomplish their work packages ahead of schedule and under budget without compromising quality. Project managers must understand the difference between competition and conflict in order to get positive results. Competition may cause a conflict among task managers as they try to win against each other, but overall organizational output will probably increase.

Introduce programmed conflict. Some project participants may be keen in pushing their ideas. Project managers should play devil's advocate and use dialectical inquiry to develop and clarify opposing points of view. These approaches are designed to program conflict into processes of planning, decision making, and risk analysis, and thus make conflict legitimate and acceptable.[11]

Resolving Structural Conflicts

Structural conflict resolution techniques focus on the structural aspects of the project organization (such as procedures, personnel, resources, and reporting relationships) that may be causing the conflict. These techniques emphasize that certain structural features can cause conflict even if the project team members behave (as individuals) in a reasonable manner.[12]

Procedural changes mainly refer to changing work procedures to avoid conflict. For instance, a project manager or technical expert on the team may evaluate and select a vendor for a technical contract. The purchasing department may then follow traditional departmental procedures, causing delays that may lead to conflict. Such disputes can be avoided by involving the purchasing department in the process of evaluating bids for complex technical contracts and thereby ensuring purchasing's cooperation and prompt service when needed to expedite the contract.

Personnel changes involve transferring individuals into or out of the project in order to resolve personality conflicts. For example, a personality conflict between two high-performing technical experts may be reducing overall project output. If one of the experts is transferred to another project, both people are then able to make a significant and positive contribution to their projects and to the organization as a whole.

Authority changes clarify or alter lines of authority and responsibility to reduce conflict. Such situations usually arise in matrix structures, where functional managers may exert their authority over personnel who have been assigned to a specific project manager for the duration of the project. Clarifying or changing authority lines or reporting relationships in such circumstances will reduce typical structural conflicts between the project manager and the functional manager.

Layout changes rearrange work space to resolve conflict. This becomes essential when two project teams harass or disturb each other continually. It may be effective to build a physical separation between them to eliminate interaction.

Resource changes involve increasing resources so that the disputing parties can each have what they need. For example, a conflict may develop between two project managers (each handling a large but tight project) over the priorities for purchasing and accounting personnel. A manager of projects can resolve the conflicts by getting an authorization to hire separate accounting and purchasing personnel for each project so that both project managers get what they need.

Interpersonal Conflict Resolution Techniques

Interpersonal conflict resolution techniques are based on the recognition that the choice of a conflict management strategy depends on the intensity of the conflict and the relative importance people place on maintaining good relationships versus achieving goals. Like a leadership style, the specific method of resolving conflict also depends on a number of situational variables. The best approach will be the one that minimizes the obstacles to project completion and helps to develop cohesive and effective project teams.

Individuals attempt to manage interpersonal conflict in a variety of ways, depending on the relative importance and intensity of the conflict, the time pressure for resolving the conflict, the position taken by the players involved, and the motivation to resolve conflict on a long-term or a short-term basis.[13]

Conflict management possibilities also depend on the ratio of assertiveness to cooperation among the parties involved in the conflict, as well as on the type of conflict. Conflict resolution techniques range from the power-based steamroller approach to a more defensive, diplomatic, and tactical approach. Intermediate views suggest variations of avoidance, give-and-take negotiation, collaboration, and problem solving.

Blake and Mouton presented five general techniques for resolving conflict: withdrawing, smoothing, forcing, compromising, and collaborating/confronting/problem solving (also referred to as negotiating).[14] Project managers must analyze the situation and select the appropriate mode for managing conflict within their project organizations in order to create a climate conducive to achieving a constructive outcome. (See Figure 22.1.)

FIGURE 22.1. CHOOSING THE BEST CONFLICT RESOLUTION MODE.

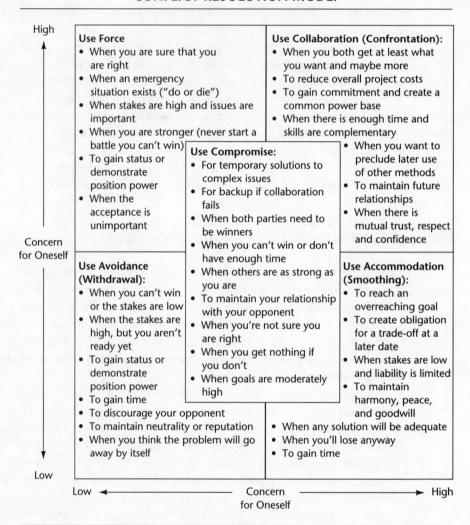

High

Use Force
- When you are sure that you are right
- When an emergency situation exists ("do or die")
- When stakes are high and issues are important
- When you are stronger (never start a battle you can't win)
- To gain status or demonstrate position power
- When the acceptance is unimportant

Use Collaboration (Confrontation):
- When you both get at least what you want and maybe more
- To reduce overall project costs
- To gain commitment and create a common power base
- When there is enough time and skills are complementary
- When you want to preclude later use of other methods
- To maintain future relationships
- When there is mutual trust, respect and confidence

Use Compromise:
- For temporary solutions to complex issues
- For backup if collaboration fails
- When both parties need to be winners
- When you can't win or don't have enough time
- When others are as strong as you are
- To maintain your relationship with your opponent
- When you're not sure you are right
- When you get nothing if you don't
- When goals are moderately high

Concern for Oneself

Use Avoidance (Withdrawal):
- When you can't win or the stakes are low
- When the stakes are high, but you aren't ready yet
- To gain status or demonstrate position power
- To gain time
- To discourage your opponent
- To maintain neutrality or reputation
- When you think the problem will go away by itself

Use Accommodation (Smoothing):
- To reach an overreaching goal
- To create obligation for a trade-off at a later date
- When stakes are low and liability is limited
- To maintain harmony, peace, and goodwill
- When any solution will be adequate
- When you'll lose anyway
- To gain time

Low

Low ◄——————— Concern ———————► High
for Oneself

Source: Verma, V. K. (1996). *Human resource skills for the project manager.* Upper Darby, PA: Project Management Institute, p. 122.

Withdrawing involves avoiding, denying, giving up, pulling out, or retreating and as such constitutes a refusal to deal with the conflict by ignoring it as much as possible. This style is appropriate when a cooling-off period is needed to gain better understanding of the conflict situation and also when the other party is both unassertive and uncooperative. Withdrawal, a passive, stopgap way of handling conflict, generally fails to solve the problem. Therefore, this style should not be used if the conflict deals with an issue that is of immediate concern or is important to the successful completion of the project.

Smoothing, or accommodating, is an appeasing approach of emphasizing areas of agreement while avoiding points of disagreement. It is appropriate to keep harmony and avoid outwardly conflictive situations. It works when the issues are more important than the personal positions and aspirations of the parties involved. Since smoothing tends to keep peace only in the short term, it fails to provide a permanent long-term solution to the underlying conflict. Generally conflict reappears again in another form.

Both smoothing and withdrawing incline toward ignoring or delaying tactics, which do not resolve conflict but will temporarily slow down the situation. Project managers must remember that if the conflict is not handled and resolved in a timely manner, it will likely lead to more severe and intense conflict in the future.

Forcing implies the use of position power and dominance to resolve the conflict. It involves imposing one viewpoint at the expense of another and is characterized by a win-lose outcome in which one party overwhelms the other. Forcing is used when there is no common ground on which to bargain or negotiate and when both parties are uncooperative and strong-willed. Project managers may use it when time is of the essence, an issue is vital to the well-being of the project, and they believe they are right based on the information available. Under such circumstances, project managers take the risk and simply dictate the action in order to move things forward. This approach is appropriate when quick decisions are required or when unpopular issues such as budget cuts, fast-tracking, or staff cutbacks are essential in a project.

Forcing usually takes less time than compromise and negotiation, but it leaves hard feelings because people dislike having others' views imposed on them. Conflict resolved by force may develop again and haunt the enforcer at a later date. Although forcing definitely resolves the conflict quickly, it should be used only as a last resort.

Compromising is primarily bargaining: receiving something in exchange for something else. It involves considering various issues, bargaining, using trade-off negotiations, and searching for solutions that bring some degree of satisfaction to both parties. Neither party wins, but both get some satisfaction out of the situation. Both may temporarily feel hurt because they had to give up something that was important to them, but compromising usually provides acceptable solutions. A definitive resolution to the conflict is achieved when a compromise is reached and accepted as a just solution by both parties. The only problem with compromising in a project situation is that sometimes important aspects of the project might be compromised in order to achieve short-term objectives (an example is compromising on safety issues to reduce costs).

Collaborating is an effective technique to manage conflict when a project situation is too important to be compromised. It involves incorporating multiple ideas and viewpoints from people with different perspectives. It offers a good opportunity to learn from others. Active collaboration by both parties in contributing to the resolution makes it easier to get their consensus and commitment. Collaboration is not very effective when more than a few players are involved and their viewpoints are mutually exclusive.

Confronting or problem solving implies a direct confrontation, with disagreement addressed directly. Conflict is treated as a problem for which both parties are interested in finding a mutually acceptable solution. This approach requires a give-and-take attitude between the parties, meaning that both are somewhat assertive and somewhat cooperative. It involves pinpointing the issue and resolving it objectively by defining the problem, gathering necessary information, generating and analyzing alternatives, and selecting the best alternative under the circumstances. Confrontation requires open dialogue between participants, who must be mature, understanding, and technically and managerially competent.

In most cases, confronting or problem solving may take longer than other techniques, but they provide final solutions by ultimately resolving the underlying problems. Table 22.4 summarizes these six interpersonal conflict resolution techniques.

Finding the Best Conflict Resolution Approach

Since each conflict situation is unique and dynamic, it is difficult to recommend the best conflict resolution approach. Choice of approach depends on these factors:

- Type and relative importance of conflict
- Time pressure
- Position of the players involved
- Relative emphasis on goals versus relationships

Forcing, smoothing, and withdrawing techniques are generally not effective in resolving conflicts because they fail to deal with the real cause of the conflict. They may be appropriate when it is important to create a period of peace and harmony while the parties think about their next move.

TABLE 22.4. CONFLICT MANAGEMENT SYLE.

Style	Description	Effect
Withdrawing/avoiding	Retreats from an actual or potential conflict situation	Does not solve the problem
Smoothing/accommodating	Emphasizes areas of agreement rather than areas of difference	Provides only short-term solution
Compromising	Searches for and bargains for solutions that bring some degree of satisfaction to all parties	Provides definitive resolution
Forcing	Pushes one's viewpoint at the expense of others; offers only win-lose situations	Hard feelings may come back in other forms
Collaborating	Incorporates multiple viewpoints and insights from differing perspectives; leads to consensus and commitment	Provides long-term resolution
Confronting/problem solving	Treats conflict as a problem to be solved by examining alternatives; requires give-and-take attitude and open dialogue	Provides ultimate resolution

Techniques involving compromise are usually used in labor-management disputes, but they have some potential problems. For example, in compromising, each party gives up something, and neither gets exactly what it wants. Consequently, both parties may be unhappy with the final decision.

Under some circumstances, the best solution for managing project conflicts is the confronting/problem solving, or negotiation, mode. Since project management involves solving problems as the project progresses through its life cycle, this type of conflict management is very practical. This approach aims for a win-win strategy, which is best for both the project and the parties involved. Project managers should acquire proper training in the procedures, nuances, and skills of professional negotiation. It is important to bear in mind, however, that negotiation and confrontation take time. They simply cannot be managed in a cursory or rapid manner, but instead require a significant commitment from the project manager in terms of time and willingness to allow all parties to air their grievances.

Conflicts are managed effectively if they are resolved on a permanent basis. The relationship between the desire for achieving goals and the desire for maintaining good long-term relationships has a significant impact on the choice of a conflict resolution style.

Strategies for Managing Conflict in a Project

Identification, analysis, and evaluation before taking action are the keys to effective management of conflict. Project managers must use practical strategies that involve following three steps: preparing for conflict, facing conflict, and then resolving conflict. Also essential are interpersonal skills, including effective communication, negotiation, and appreciation of cultural differences.[15]

Preparing for Conflict

Realistic project managers know that conflict is a normal—and in some cases necessary—part of working in groups and teams. The art of preparing for conflict thus involves both expecting that it will occur and having a plan for handling it.

Expecting Conflict. The sources of conflict (schedules, priorities, human resources, technical issues, administration, personality, and cost) will vary with the phases of the project. Moreover, the focus of conflict will vary with the attributes of the team and the project goals. With an experienced team, the focus of conflict is within the team itself. If the project goals are vague and loosely defined, the focus of the conflict will likely be between the team and upper management or between the project team and the client, or both. The project manager should analyze the reasons or sources of conflict and how they vary with the phases of the project cycle before taking any action.

Planning Ahead to Handle Conflict. After analyzing the sources, intensity, and focus of conflict, project managers should plan how to deal with conflict. One of the planning tools is to develop a framework within which to view conflicts objectively. Conflicts that arise as the project teams progress through stages of team development come from each person's need to answer questions that establish his or her position clearly:[16]

- Am I in or out? In this type of conflict, people are likely to ask themselves whether they belong to the team. They raise issues that are unimportant in themselves just to break the ice and initiate communication.

- Where do I stand? (Am I up or down?) Are people at the top or at the bottom of a hierarchy? How will the group make decisions? How much responsibility does each team member have? How much authority, influence, and control does each individual on the project team have?
- Am I near or far? This question raises the issues of openness and affection. Team members must decide how close they want to get to each other without feeling stuck with them. Emotions and perceptions may express themselves positively (openly expressed positive feelings and warmth) or negatively (open hostility and jealousy).

A second tool is to analyze the key players in the situation. This analysis should consider the whole project and identify the key players and their personalities. Who are the people or groups contributing to the conflict? Project managers should analyze their personalities, interpersonal habits, values, and convictions. This knowledge will help create a cooperative and accommodating atmosphere. All key players should be willing to accept resolution of the conflict; otherwise it will continue or become even more intense and ultimately reduce project performance. Open communication should be encouraged to help individuals involved in the conflict situation be more objective and prepared to deal with the situation. In planning ahead, the project manager answers the question: "Is the conflict primarily related to goals, authority, or personalities or some combination of these?" Conflicts should be defined in objective terms, with a minimum of personal biases and opinions.

A final planning tool is to prepare for stress management. Conflict can cause stress that varies in intensity, and if it is not managed in a timely manner, it can cause severe physiological and psychological problems.

Facing the Conflict

Although conflict is one of the things most of us dislike intensely, it is inevitable. Most often when we try to avoid conflict, it will nevertheless seek us out. Some people wrongly hope that conflict will go away if it is ignored. In fact, conflict ignored is more likely to get worse, which can significantly reduce project performance. The best way to reduce conflict is to confront it. To face conflict effectively, project managers have several strategies to draw on.[17]

Serve as a Lightning Rod. Hill compared managers of successful projects with those of projects that failed and found that the managers of successful projects did the following:[18]

- Personally absorbed aggression
- Communicated and listened effectively

- Counseled their teams to maximize their output
- Encouraged openness, emotional expression, and new ideas
- Served as role models in planning, delegating, and so forth
- Minimized potential conflict whenever possible
- Stimulated conflict to foster creativity and innovation

The project managers Thamhain and Wilemon surveyed felt that personality conflicts were often disguised as conflicts over other issues, such as technical issues and staffing.[19] These disguises will persist if project managers deal only with facts, and not the feelings themselves. Positive feelings, if expressed, can increase project performance. Even negative feelings, if expressed constructively, may help clarify confusion or remove a bottleneck in a project. To "name without blame," project managers must express feelings as feelings, not as facts. They must accept responsibility for their own feelings and avoid judging people based on feelings and impressions alone.

Surface the Real Issues. Conflicts that remain below the surface can have negative impacts on a project in many ways, such as distorted or withheld information, slipped schedules, unplanned absences from project meetings, lack of initiative to solve problems, or not working together as a real team.[20]

A successful conflict manager should handle these burning issues gently but firmly. Surfacing the real issues can be accomplished by getting all the background information associated with the conflict. This process may uncover important aspects of the project that will lead to serious consequences and even project failure if they are not identified immediately. To surface the real issues, project managers may do the following:[21]

- *Treat the surface issue as "real" two or three times.* Project managers should make every effort to address complaints or issues regardless of how trivial they may seem. They should encourage project personnel to bring the conflict into the open by themselves. However, if this fails, the project manager should approach the person and urge him or her to discuss the conflict in the open with the aim of resolving it as soon as possible.
- *Make the conflict visible to other parties involved.* Project managers can do this by using effective communication techniques and planning and organizing aids such as responsibility matrices, which are quite effective in resolving conflicts over administrative aspects of project management such as procedures, task breakdowns, and assignments of responsibility and authority. Project managers may choose to prepare a responsibility matrix for each phase of the project life cycle.

- *Give ample support.* Block described the importance of support in a work relationship.[22] Most people want to feel secure and worthwhile and receive encouragement, recognition, and praise. Unfortunately, some project managers confuse support with agreement and, consequently, in a conflict (disagreement) situation, they withhold support when it is needed the most.

Resolving the Conflict

Due to the dynamic and sometimes unpredictable nature of projects, a substantial amount of management time is dedicated to resolving conflicts. In some cases, disagreements can be handled by a straightforward decision; in other situations, a combination of time and skills is required. The project manager, the project team, and all other stakeholders involved in a conflict situation must work together to achieve a win-win situation for everyone.

Effective conflict management requires an extensive effort at the front end. Good conflict managers size up possible clashes before contacting the parties, and then they work out appropriate actions to resolve potential problems.[23]

Look for Win-Win Alternatives. Of the interpersonal conflict resolution styles, confronting (negotiating and problem solving) is the most effective approach because it starts with an understanding by both parties that they must search for solutions that satisfy everyone. Project managers must create a cooperative and assertive environment to achieve win-win solutions. These guidelines may be useful:

- *Do the doable.* Project managers must be able to evaluate the situation and spend their efforts and energy in doing only whatever is really possible. "It's no use in trying to teach ducks to sing; it will only frustrate you and confuse the ducks!"
- *Build on earlier market analyses.* Using the strategy of only doing the doable, project managers should build on earlier analyses of situations to give some insight into the conditions that would meet the other party's criteria for a win-win solution.
- *Use the assertive model.* Build on the strengths of all parties while minimizing their weaknesses. Building mutual understanding and trust will help in reaching a win-win solution.
- *Look at things right side up.* It is a mistake to assume that the person is the problem and therefore start attacking the person instead of the problem.
- *Avoid catastrophizing.* It leads to lower team morale and confidence, increased frustration, and possibly project failure. Some of the common catastrophizing remarks that describe inconvenience, difficulty, or frustration are: "This is

going to be a disaster." "We will never get this done on time." "This project is driving me crazy." "I can't stand the project structure." Instead of catastrophizing, encourage project participants to be positive, and suggest solutions that are manageable and helpful.

- *Picture things going well.* Visualize and imagine positive results. It is difficult to move onto something better without knowing what "better" is. To develop a clear picture of "better," the project manager should picture things going as he or she wants them to, enlist the support of others and try to get their commitment, and deal with obstacles positively (using a problem-solving approach).[24]
- *Identify priorities and verbalize them.* Priorities rank highly as a source of conflict throughout the project life cycle. Sometimes people compromise so much in a conflict that no one wins, and everyone is dissatisfied. Successful project managers evaluate the priorities up front and identify the "must haves" and "nice to haves." While resolving conflicts, he or she may compromise on "nice to haves" in order of importance. Project managers can rank priorities by asking which features would contribute most to project success and which features would contribute the least.

Cut Your Losses When Necessary. Sometimes a project may have gotten too deep in the hole, which leads to conflicts. Should the project be continued, or should someone review the situation, try to estimate the bottom line to completion, and then make a rational decision on whether to abandon the project? The project manager should avoid making such decisions based on ego and emotion. Cutting losses can actually yield a savings that can be used for other business opportunities.

In most cases, only senior management or the project director or sponsor is authorized to cancel projects. However, sometimes the project manager may have the authority. Nevertheless, in all cases, the persons with such authority should cut losses and resolve such situations by using the following guidelines:[25]

Keep a mental file of things that do not fit the overall purpose of the project. It is easy to see what you expect to see instead of what is real. Project participants may say one thing but act differently. Project managers must watch out for the degree of real commitment and interest in doing certain parts of a project. When words and behavior do not match, behavior should be believed more—even if it is the words you want to believe.

Project managers should pay attention to the nonverbal components of communication in interacting with team members because actual behavior more closely correlates with the nonverbal component than with the verbal component of communications. For example, a team member may passively resist a project manager's particular suggestion by not showing enthusiasm for it but may not say anything directly against it. Ignoring this nonverbal component will likely lead the project manager to overlook the consequences of this passive resistance—and that is the beginning of a hidden sink hole. (Not all sink holes are hidden, of course; some of them are right out in the open.) But the behavior may be so difficult and complex to measure that project managers may simply not believe their eyes or ears and thereby misjudge the situation completely.

Follow the rule of two (or three). Successful project managers cut their losses before costs skyrocket. They may not be able to recognize the inconsistency right away, but they should confront the situation and address it directly if it occurs a second or third time. For example, always choosing the lowest bidder may lead to problems with schedule and cost overruns.

Establish a system for cutting back investment of money, time, effort, and ego. This follows the common management principle, "Plan your work, and work your plan." When something goes wrong in the project, people may go through the stages of grief: denial, anger, bargaining, depression, stress, and—hopefully—acceptance. Project managers who become emotionally upset over losses on their projects are vulnerable to losing their self-esteem.

People who have planned ahead to handle their losses are better off because they can turn to their written plans and take necessary action accordingly. Although it may be difficult to implement the actions, at least the difficult step of deciding what to do was done when they could think more clearly. To cut losses before it is too late, the project manager's plan should answer the following questions:[26]

- How much money should be invested before expecting some return?
- How much time should be allowed before following another course of action?
- How much energy and ego should be invested before being satisfied that the best shot has been given? (This limits the spillover into personal life as well as the effect on other projects.)

Formulate Conflict Management Strategies. Conflict can be resolved or kept under control by using a proactive approach that anticipates conflict and its impact. When using this approach, it is important to understand the project manager's relationship with other project stakeholders with whom the manager usually interacts throughout the project life cycle—for example, senior management, functional and other managers, clients, and team members.

Project managers must establish good understanding, trust, and rapport with all the stakeholders with whom they interact to minimize the probability of conflict. The ideas for managing conflicts with major project stakeholders are summarized as follows:[27]

Minimizing conflict with senior management involves knowing their requirements. Project managers should put themselves in their boss's shoes and be sympathetic to the challenges, problems, and pressures of senior managers. It also helps to analyze the boss's thinking patterns and to act in ways that are consistent with that pattern (analytically or intuitively, for example). Similarly, it pays to listen and look for verbal and nonverbal components of the boss's message, just as a project manager might do with team members. At the same time, it is important to take solutions as well as problems to the boss and explore alternatives and make recommendations. That makes the boss's job easier.

It is wise to keep the boss informed of progress and plans. That way he or she can act as a mentor, and the project manager can get better support. Consulting the boss on policy, procedures, and criteria will help clarify management philosophy and establish boundaries related to administrative issues (since the project manager may need them to protect himself or herself). Above all, it is advisable to avoid steamrollering the boss; being patient and allowing time for thinking and evaluation will lead to better relationships and results.

Minimizing conflict with project team members means knowing them well and developing rapport and trust. Project managers can begin by discovering team members' personal and professional goals and matching tasks to those goals. That kind of matching is a key to motivation. Being clear about expectations about what is wanted, as well as why and when it is needed, ensures that communication is successful. It is also important to define control parameters through clear performance appraisals and discussions of forms and reports, and to clarify the frequency and intensity of controls with team members. Control should be based on facts, not on opinions.

Successful project managers also develop a tolerance for failure. Everyone makes mistakes; the key is to use mistakes as opportunities for training and improvement—and future success. Postmortem strategy sessions can be particularly useful for learning lessons that can be applied in the future.

Positive feedback, as well as timely praise and recognition, is central to minimizing conflict with project team members. Positive feedback demonstrates the project manager's confidence in the team. If someone has made a mistake, it is appropriate to point it out objectively and balance it with positive feedback. Similarly, appropriate and timely recognition and praise can do wonders to create positive reinforcement and motivate team members to maximize their performance.

Minimizing conflict with a project manager's peers involves respect. As with relationships with senior management, it is important to understand peers' point of view, as well as their personal and professional goals. The best project managers look for ways to support peers' objectives and find areas of mutual interest rather than conflict. Operating in this way establishes a cooperative atmosphere, where everyone realizes that they need each other to succeed. Cultivating informal communication channels can also create many advantages. Whereas formal combinations may be slow and cold, informal communications increase comfort level and understanding, which are important in solving problems. Doing favors for each other without expecting any immediate return, having lunch together, developing social encounters, and talking daily about matters outside work can increase respect and rapport and decrease conflict.

It is also wise to give advance notice when help is needed. Peers may have their own constraints, so project managers will need to justify their requests in terms of project goals and objectives and reciprocate by being accommodating about peers' requirements.

Minimizing conflict with clients and users involves many of the same elements that apply to other participants in a project. The key to working with clients is effective communication and prompt response to their needs and requests. It helps to be supportive of the client's representatives, supplying them with necessary data and information so that they will also be inclined to help with issues that crop up throughout the project. By the same token, maintaining close contact with the client and avoiding communication gaps ensures against clients' becoming demanding—and even unreasonable—in response to too little attention and information. It is important to make sure that contacts with clients mirror their organizational structure; directors should be in touch with directors, managers with managers, engineers with engineers, and so on.

Clients, like everyone else, hate surprises—unless they come in the form of good news. Effective project managers do not let problems build up. They tell clients what the problems are and what is being done to solve them.

Informal relationships fostered through lunches, dinners, and sporting and social events allow everyone to develop a better understanding and a stronger interpersonal sense of each other. Formal relationships need attention too. Regular project status meetings can be used to summarize progress; provide forecasts concerning completion, future problems, and potential needs; and turn everyone's attention to getting the information each party needs and solving problems in a proactive manner.

Use effective negotiation to resolve conflicts. Negotiation is a fact of life in project environments where matrix structures necessitate that responsibility and authority are shared. Negotiation is the process of bargaining and reaching an agreement with project stakeholders concerning the transfer of resources, the generation of information, and the accomplishment of tasks. It is a persuasive process and is one of the most important skills needed to resolve conflicts and manage projects successfully.

The two common methods of negotiation are soft and hard. Soft negotiators are friendly and make concessions readily to avoid conflict and the risk of spoiling future relationships. Hard negotiators, in contrast, take strong positions and try to win, even at the cost of relationships. A third type of negotiation, called principled negotiation, emphasizes deciding and resolving issues based on merits rather than on positions.[28] It results in joint problem solving and often leads to a win-win situation.

Principled negotiation involves understanding the positions, issues, and interests of both parties:

- *Positions:* one party's (usually self-serving) solution to the problem.
- *Issues:* the elements or subject matter of the dispute that need to be negotiated in order to reach agreement.
- *Interests:* factors that motivate the parties to reach their respective positions and the underlying foundation for their positions. These include desires and concerns. Each party's position is intended to meet his or her interests.

Principled negotiation is based on committing to negotiate for mutual gain and to resolve conflicts, separating people from problems and issues, focusing on interests rather than on positions, generating options for mutual agreement and gain, and basing results on objective criteria. The conflict intensity decreases as we move from "positions," which corresponds to Stage 1 (highest conflict intensity) to "options for agreements," which corresponds to Stage 4 (lowest conflict intensity) (see Figure 22.2).

Appreciate cultural differences. In addition to their differences in skills and expertise, project teams may have cultural differences that may significantly influence the project's success, especially in managing joint ventures and international projects. Hofstede describes culture simply as a kind of "mental software": the "collective programming of the mind which distinguishes the members of one group of people from another."[29]

Cultural diversity among team members poses challenges in terms of communication and negotiation and may lead to conflicts. Project managers must appreciate major elements of culture (which include material culture, language, aesthetics, education, religious beliefs and attitudes, social organizations, and political life), what they mean in different cultures, and how they affect the project. There are six critical dimensions of cultural differences:

1. Power distance (how a particular culture deals with inequality)
2. Individualism versus collectivism (the role of the individual versus that of the group)
3. Masculinity-femininity (gender domination patterns)
4. Uncertainty avoidance (tolerance for ambiguity or uncertainty in the workplace)

FIGURE 22.2 RESOLVING CONFLICTS THROUGH EFFECTIVE NEGOTIATION.

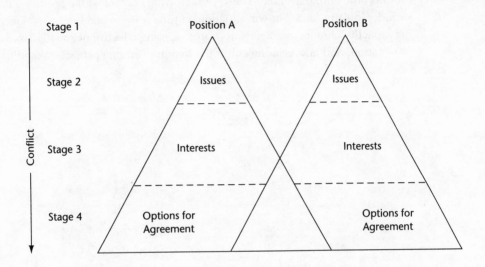

5. Time horizon (long- or short-term orientation)
6. Attitude toward life (value system with respect to desire for material things)

Project participants must be aware of potential cultural differences and demonstrate respect for different cultures of their coworkers. Any failure to show respect and to appreciate culture differences may lead to serious conflicts. Project managers must evaluate the implications of cultural differences and resolve conflicts among team members. They must capitalize on the cultural diversity of project participants by encouraging them to accept others' cultural differences and foster the group's human synergy as well as overall performance by anticipating and resolving conflicts.

Conclusion

Conflict can be healthy if it is managed effectively. Conflict management requires a combination of analytical and human skills. Every project participant should learn to resolve project conflicts effectively. Good conflict managers work at the source of conflict. To resolve it permanently, they must address the cause of the conflict and not just the symptoms of it. They size up possible clashes before "contact" is actually made and then prepare their action plans to handle potential trouble. They should concentrate on building an atmosphere designed to reduce destructive conflict and deal with routine frictions and minor differences before they become unmanageable. The key to resolving conflict with a positive outcome includes looking for a win-win situation, cutting losses when necessary, formulating proactive conflict management strategies, using effective negotiation and communication, and appreciating cultural differences among project stakeholders.

PART FOUR

INTEGRATIVE ISSUES IN PROJECT MANAGEMENT

CHAPTER TWENTY-THREE

CRITICAL SUCCESS FACTORS

Jeffrey K. Pinto
Dennis P. Slevin

The process of developing a method for analyzing and predicting the likelihood of success or failure of an ongoing project is by no means a simple one. There are a number of reasons that this process presents a challenge. One obvious reason is that words like *success* and *failure*, like beauty, are often in the eye of the beholder. Put another way, until we can establish a set of criteria that have some generally accepted basis for assessing projects, at best we run the risk of mislabeling as failures projects that may, in fact, demonstrate the opposite conclusion. A second problem with accurately predicting project outcomes lies in the often incomplete nature of the data themselves. Many times a project's development is surrounded by a great deal of ambiguous and even contradictory data that make midstream assessments problematic. Finally, and closely related to the first reason listed, the often subjective nature of project assessment, depending as it may on individuals' having biases one way or another toward the project, makes it difficult to develop objective measures that offer a reasonably reliable method for judging project outcomes.

In order to address some of these questions, we have developed this chapter as a guide for project managers to use in tracking the status of their projects. The

Note: Substantial portions of this chapter were excerpted from Pinto, J. K., & Kharbanda, O. P. (1995). *Successful project managers.* New York: Van Nostrand Reinhold, chap. 4.

chapter discusses in some detail the various measures of project success and the major causes of ambiguity in assessing project performance, and we offer a set of factors that predict, with good accuracy, the likelihood of a project's success or failure. This chapter concludes with some general points that project managers need to bear in mind when attempting to assess the status of an ongoing project.

The Unique Setting of Project Management

Almost all innovative new products developed within companies arise through the creation of projects and the use of project management techniques. Because projects play such an increasingly significant role in organizational profitability, it is vital that we develop an understanding of their unique properties. What is it about the nature of project management that gives it such a preeminent role?

It is perhaps ironic that attempts to label certain projects as "failures" often pose considerable difficulty. Part of the problem is that while everyone seems to understand intuitively the various component measures of project "success" or "failure," agreement with how to assess various projects in the light of these criteria is often problematic. Put more simply, ugliness, as with beauty, is a highly subjective assessment. This attitude is completely understandable in that project managers' careers often hinge on their ability to deliver successfully completed projects. Consequently, in the absence of dramatic disaster (such as structural collapse in construction or banned or abandoned pharmaceutical development), it seems that for every detractor of a specific completed project there is often a champion singing its praises.

How is this possible? How is it that two equally capable individuals can often view the same results through entirely different frames of reference and come to completely opposite conclusions about a project? Part of the answer lies in the notion that project success is not always as clear-cut as we would sometimes believe. Any one of a number of confounding issues can cloud the ability to view a project's outcome in any sort of objective light. For example, the point in time when a project is evaluated can make a very real difference in its evaluation. Similarly, egos and personal agendas of top managers in a company can serve to obscure the true outcome of a project, as these powerful individuals seek to protect themselves and their turf from the side effects of bumpy projects.

Finally, it is often the case that while successful projects are trumpeted throughout the organization and publicized externally, the majority of project failures are quietly swept under the carpet. People naturally tend to promote the positive; when that is not possible, they adopt a simple philosophy: out of sight, out of mind. The irony, of course, is that all organizations experience project failure far more often than rousing success. Consider the results of a recent study by Peat Marwick of three hundred large companies attempting to implement computer software development projects. Fully 65 percent of the organizations reported experiences where their projects were grossly over budget, far behind schedule, and/or the technology was nonperforming, leading to "runaway" projects. In some cases, the companies experienced all of the above problems. Perhaps more impressive, over half of these firms considered this state as "normal" or "of no concern."[1]

Because of the confusion surrounding the meaning of project success, we need to develop, as systematically as possible, a working definition of project success. In the old days, project managers commonly made use of a concept known as the triple constraint to evaluate a project at completion. This triple constraint offered a three-legged stool for any project's viability: (1) time (the project had to come in on or under its initially scheduled time frame), (2) money (the project had to be completed within its budget limits), and (3) performance (the end result had to perform in the manner that was intended). Seen in this light, it was relatively easy to make some initial value judgments about any project. Project control consisted of tracking the milestones of any particular project. Is it on time? Is it under budget? Does it work? These were the only significant questions to consider. Further, one had only to consult the project's time line to assess schedule constancy, review the cost accountant's report to determine budget adherence, and see if the project "worked" to measure performance.

Although the triple constraint is simple, it unfortunately is also simplistic: it does not work in the modern business world.[2] In an era of tremendous competition and heightened concern for customers, the triple constraint has become a dangerously out-of-date convention. In considering the three components of the triple constraint, it is clear that the primary thrust of each of these measures is internal; that is, they are intended to satisfy some interest group internal to the organization rather than in the environment. For example, satisfying time and budget considerations are often the concern of cost accountants, who are tasked with keeping costs down. Likewise, the performance criterion has often been seen as primarily an engineering concern: the challenge of making a product that works.

Historically, what was lost in the confusion was any real concern for the customer, that is, the desire to satisfy the concerns of the client for whom the project was intended. Within many companies, a fundamental conceit emerged in the assumption that once a project was completed, the public would be offered a fait accompli that they would naturally buy or use. The underlying theme of this position seemed to be an arrogant assertion: *Don't tell us what you need. Trust us to know what you want.* The result of such attitudes was predictable: customers increasingly went to companies whose projects and products reflected a concern for them, as illustrated by the phenomenal success of the Ford Taurus.

The new rules governing global business require that project management adopt a new standard by which future success will be measured: the so-called quadruple constraint. The additional feature of the quadruple constraint requires us to include *customer satisfaction* as one of the pillars of project success. Client, or customer, satisfaction refers to the idea that a project is only as successful as it satisfies the needs of its intended user. This addition has tremendous implications for the way we manage projects and the manner in which the success or failure of both past and future projects will be assessed.[3] With the inclusion of customer satisfaction as a fourth constraint, project managers must now devote additional time and attention to maintaining close ties with and satisfying the demands of external clients.

Among the implications of this new quadruple constraint is its effect on what were viewed as traditional project management roles. Concern for the client forces project managers to adopt an outward focus to their efforts. In effect, they must now become not only managers of project activities, but sales representatives for the company to the client base. The product they have to sell is their project. Therefore, if they are to facilitate acceptance of the project and hence, its success, they have to learn how to engage in these marketing duties effectively.

Assessing Success over Time

One of the truly difficult tasks confronting any project manager lies in making reasonable and accurate assessments of a project's viability early in its development. Part of the problem lies in the fact that many projects do not proceed in a perfectly linear fashion from start to finish, so it is an error to assume that a project's progress can be tracked according to a well-understood path, particularly if that project represents a unique technical challenge or employs features that company has never dealt with before. Figure 23.1 demonstrates the essential differences in development processes that usually exist between the "perfect world" and the world of projects. Notice that the perfect world follows a linear path; that is, when 50 percent of the project's resources are expended, we expect it to be 50 percent completed, and so on.

The true project activity line often follows a far different path. For example, it is not atypical to find that far into the project (from an expense and time point of view), little actual progress has been made. In fact, when 50 percent of the resources have been spent or the schedule has elapsed, it is not uncommon to find less than 20 percent of the activities completed. Such a progress sequence presents a true test of nerves and savvy for many project managers. The natural response to such a state is either to panic, and perhaps find scapegoats and remove

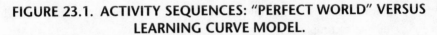

FIGURE 23.1. ACTIVITY SEQUENCES: "PERFECT WORLD" VERSUS LEARNING CURVE MODEL.

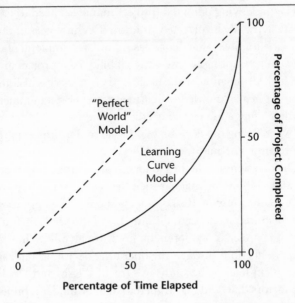

them from the team, or to throw additional resources at the project in the hopes of "buying" progress. Either approach, though understandable, is almost always counterproductive. In his landmark book, *The Mythical Man-Month,* Frederick Brooks describes the sequence of events leading to the development of IBM's 360 operating system in the mid–1960s, a project for which he was responsible.[4] He discovered a fascinating effect caused by belatedly adding resources to ongoing, late activities: additional personnel simply caused the project to slip further and further behind schedule. Rather than make up for lost time, the net effect was to delay the project even more.

The natural project sequence in Figure 23.1 demonstrates Brooks's point: all project activities are subject to delays caused by the learning curve. The rapid ramp-up in progress that occurs near the activity's completion date is a result of the initial learning that had to take place prior to performing the necessary tasks adequately. Assume that the team has just completed this activity, using the learning curve model. If the same personnel were then asked to replicate the process with a new project immediately, in all likelihood their progress line would much more closely match the linear, "perfect world" path. Why? Because they have now charted this activity sequence and learned the appropriate lessons. Hence, any new activities would simply involve replicating the old sequence, with the learning curve completed.

The underlying point that project managers need to understand is that projects, which usually involve new or untried technologies or development processes, require a natural learning curve as part of the implementation process. As a result, when attempting to assess the viability of a project and make a reasonably accurate determination of the likelihood of its successful completion, project managers must first acknowledge that they are operating in uncharted territory, filled with misleading and even contradictory indicators. This point should be kept in mind when facing the decision of whether to terminate a project that is over budget or behind schedule.

The decision of whether to terminate a project is never easy. As Figure 23.1 illustrates, we may be making such decisions on the basis of misleading indicators. A recent study of R&D projects sheds some important light on the termination decision; it shows that many times the seeds of future disaster are sown early in the project's development, not through any technical difficulties the project experiences but through the operating decisions and assumptions of the top management team. The study, by Green, Welsh, and Dehler, measured a number of factors that could be argued to help or hinder a project's development, including the priority the project was assigned, the viability of its commercial objectives, the authority assigned to team members and the project manager, and so forth. The findings are intriguing: within the first six months of an R&D project's existence, there are often clear signs that the project may be a good candidate for termination. For example, their research suggests that terminated projects "were seen by their team members to have a low probability of achieving commercial objectives, did not have team members with sufficient authority, were targeted at fairly stable markets, were given low priority by R&D management, but were managed efficiently and were receiving valuable information from a business gatekeeper."[5]

The final two points are particularly important. Unsuccessful projects may end up that way regardless of the efficiency with which the actual development process is managed. The best "management" in the world cannot obviate the other determinants of project success or failure. Even having someone in top management consistently providing valuable information is not sufficient to ensure that a project will succeed.

Another frequent error that many organizations slip into when assessing the performance of their project development is to make inadequate allowances for the impact of time on a project's viability. To illustrate, consider a real-life situation in which a company was determining the success of a recently completed hardware computer development project. Based on internal cost accounting data, the project looked good: it had come in on time and only slightly over budget. Further, the hardware performed as it was intended to perform. As a result, the project manager was given a performance bonus and reassignment for a job well done. Unfortunately, the story does not end there. This internally efficient project was a disaster in the marketplace from its introduction. The technology that the company had assumed would be adequate turned out to be so user unfriendly that the product was withdrawn within nine months.

This story illustrates a number of the problems in making judgments about projects as either successes or failures. First, it was clear that from the company's point of view, this project was not a failure at all; in fact, just the opposite was the case. The second problem had to do with the incomplete picture of project expectations that top management painted. Obviously client satisfaction was never held up as a concern of the project manager, who naturally devoted his time to the measures that *did* matter for his performance appraisal: schedule, budget, and performance. Finally, the story demonstrates a subtler third point: in the absence of full information, it is important not to assume that a project is a success or failure too early in its life, before the final "returns" have had an opportunity to come in.

This conclusion does not only mean to suggest that many projects deemed successes are in fact failures. The reverse is also true: many projects that give every evidence of being instant failures may actually demonstrate themselves to be long-term successes. One example that comes immediately to mind is the well-known English Channel tunnel project, known as the Eurotunnel, or "Chunnel." Opening in 1994, nearly eighteen months behind schedule, the Chunnel project was originally budgeted for 7.5 billion pounds sterling. The final bill was 15 billion pounds sterling. From an internal auditing perspective, the Chunnel represents a financial nightmare, particularly in the light of recent news that it has defaulted on the bond financing made by the initial investors in the venture. Nevertheless, looking at the project in regard to its long-term potential, one must admit that its contribution to society may be significant, in effect, leaving the judgment of project "success" or "failure" in the hands of future generations.

This case illustrates a central idea regarding project success and failure: the importance of balancing immediate assessment against long-term project viability. Clearly there are definite benefits involved in waiting until after the project has been completed and is introduced to its intended clients before assessing the success and impact of the system. On the other hand, we must be careful in not waiting so long to determine a project's external impact that the possibility exists that other organizational or external environmental factors will influence the organization's operations to the point where we are unable to determine the relative impact of the project in the marketplace.

Critical Success Factors in Project Development

Among the important challenges involved in accurately assessing project status midstream are developing a comprehensive understanding of what exactly are the factors that constitute "success" and how their measurement is confounded by the often misleading information that the project manager receives during the development process, particularly in terms of time and activity completion trade-offs. The larger question, however, and one with which the bulk of this chapter must be concerned, is, "What are the critical factors that ultimately determine the likelihood of successful project completion?" It is simplistic to assume that accurately charting costs and schedules is all that is necessary to ensure that a project will be successfully completed. First, such a mind-set ignores one of our previous points: the quadruple constraint requires that project managers also adopt an external focus on the customer. Time and cost tracking simply do not allow for the external focus that customers demand.

The second problem with the traditional model of project success is that it ignores the findings of important research into the nature of project success. Almost every researcher who has studied the impact of various internal and external factors on project outcomes has concluded that human, rather than technical, factors are the primary determinant of whether a project will succeed.[6] In other words, although no one will deny that computers, scheduling, and budget models are important elements in controlling a project, the research suggests that the larger managerial issues are typically the key determinant of a project's likelihood of success. Project management has always been, and remains, a *people* management challenge first and foremost.

Critical Success Factors: A Ten-Factor Model

Our study of critical success factors (CSFs) in the project implementation process looked at over four hundred projects varying greatly in terms of the basic characteristics.[7] A wide range of representative samples of project type included R&D projects, construction projects, information system projects, and so forth. Our study validated a ten-factor model of critical success factors for project implementation. Further, we confirmed the vital importance of managerial, behavioral, and organization issues in successful system implementation. From this research, we can begin to explore how these factors offer new insights into the "managerial" nature of project CSFs.

Project Mission. The first factor that we developed was related to the underlying purpose for the implementation and was classified as project mission. Most of us intuitively understand the importance of conducting a feasibility study prior to project kickoff. Further, it is vital that project managers answer some fundamental questions, not only at the start of a new project, but throughout its development. Are the goals clear, and can they succeed? Project mission refers to a condition where the goals of the project are clear and understood, not only by the project team but by the other departments in the organization. Some examples of questions for project managers to answer include, "Are the basic goals of the project clear to me?" and "Are the goals of the project in line with the general goals of the organization?"

Top Management Support. Management support is extremely important for the success of any new project. Project managers not only depend on top management for direction and authority in running their projects, they rely on them as a safety valve as well. When the project is undergoing difficulties, it is vital that top management be aware of the problems and willing to offer necessary additional aid or resources for the project manager and team. Top management's support of the project may also consist of the project manager's confidence in their support in the event of crisis. Among the sample issues for project managers to consider when addressing this factor are, "Upper management has provided me with sufficient authority and responsibility to oversee the project" and "I have the confidence of upper management."

Project Schedule and Plans. Project planning refers to the importance of creating a detailed outline of the required stages in the implementation process, including work breakdown, resource scheduling, and activity sequencing. Scheduling is generally understood to refer to the tasks of creating specific time and task-interdependent structures, such as critical path and Gantt charts. Project schedule and plans refers to the degree to which time schedules, milestones, staffing, and equipment requirements are specified. Further, the schedule should include a satisfactory measurement system as a way of judging actual performance against budget and time allowances. A sample of the type of statements considered in this factor include, "I have identified the important manpower skills required for successful project completion," and "I have contingency plans in case the project is off schedule."

Client Consultation. The client is anyone who will ultimately be making use of the final project—either a customer outside the company or a department within the organization. The degree to which clients are personally involved in the implementation process will cause great variation in their support for that project. It is therefore important to determine whether clients for the project have been identified. Once project managers are aware of the major clients, they are better able to determine accurately if their needs are being met. Some examples of statements to consider in the client consultation factor include, "I have solicited input from all potential clients of the project," and "I understand the needs of those who will use the system."

Personnel. Personnel issues include recruitment, selection, and training. An important aspect of the project management process concerns the nature of the personnel involved. In many situations, personnel for the project team are chosen with less than full regard for the skills necessary to contribute actively to implementation success. All current writers on project management understand the role of effective project team personnel in successful implementation efforts. For this discussion, the category of personnel is concerned with developing a project team with the requisite skills and commitment to perform their function. Examples of statements to consider for the personnel factor include, "The personnel of my project team are committed to the project's success," and "The lines of authority are well defined on my project team."

Technical Tasks. It is important that the implementation be well managed by people who understand it. In addition, companies have to ask themselves if they have the necessary technology and training to support the development. Technical tasks refers to the necessity of not only having the necessary personnel on the implementation team, but ensuring that they possess the necessary technical skills and have adequate technology to perform their tasks. Obviously the decision to initiate a new project must be predicated on the organization's ability to staff the team with competent individuals and provide the technical means for the project to succeed. By way of illustration, examples of technical tasks statements would include, "The technology that is being implemented works well," and "Experts, consultants, or other experienced managers outside the project team have reviewed and criticized my basic plans or approach."

Client Acceptance. In addition to client consultation at an earlier stage in the system implementation process, it remains of ultimate importance to determine whether the clients for whom the project has been initiated will accept it. Client acceptance refers to the final stage in the implementation process, at which time the overall efficacy of the project is to be determined. Too often project managers make the mistake of believing that if they handle the other stages of the implementation process well, the client will simply accept the resulting system. In fact, client acceptance is a stage in project implementation that must be managed like any other. Examples of statements referring to client acceptance would include, "Potential clients have been contacted about the usefulness of the project," and "Adequate advanced preparation has been done to determine how best to 'sell' the project to clients."

Monitoring and Feedback. Monitoring and feedback refer to the project control process by which key personnel receive feedback, at each stage of the project implementation, on how the project is comparing to initial projections. Within many organizations that are experienced in running projects, there is little general agreement on how to track projects, what features should be tracked, and how these data should be reported. Making allowances for adequate monitoring and feedback mechanisms gives the project manager the ability to anticipate problems, oversee corrective measures, and ensure that no deficiencies are overlooked. Project managers need to emphasize the importance of constant monitoring and fine-tuning the process of implementation. For our discussion, monitoring and feedback refers not only to project schedule and budget, but also to monitoring the performance of members of the team. Sample statements for the project manager to consider under the monitoring and feedback factor include, "When the budget or schedule requires revision, I solicit input from the project team," and "All members of the project team know if I am satisfied or dissatisfied with their work."

Communication. The need for adequate communication channels is extremely important in creating an atmosphere for successful system implementation. Communication is essential not only within the project team itself, but between the team and the rest of the organization, as well as with the clients. As the factor of communication has been developed for our framework, it refers not only to feedback mechanisms, but to the necessity of exchanging information with both clients and the rest of the organization concerning the project's capabilities, the goals of the implementation process, changes in policies and procedures, status reports, and so forth. Some examples of the issues that are of concern for communication include, "Input concerning the implementation effort's goals and strategy has been sought from members of the project team, other groups affected by the project, and upper management," and "All groups affected by the project know how to make problems known to those who can deal with them."

Troubleshooting. As several project managers have pointed out, problem areas exist in almost every implementation. The measure of a successful project implementation effort is not the avoidance of problems, but knowing the correct steps to take once they develop. Regardless of how carefully the implementation effort was initially planned, it is impossible to foresee every trouble area or problem that could possibly arise. As a result, it is important that the project manager make adequate initial arrangements for troubleshooting mechanisms to be included in the implementation plan. Such mechanisms would make it easier not only to react to problems as they arise, but to foresee and possibly forestall potential problem areas in the implementation process. Some examples of issues to be considered under the troubleshooting factor include, "I spend a part of each day looking for problems that have just begun or have the potential to begin," and "Implementation team members are encouraged to take quick personal action on problems on their own initiative."

What All Project Managers Need to Know

Rather than devote a tremendous amount of space to an in-depth discussion of the results of research on the ten-factor model, we have chosen to offer a set of summary points that project managers need to bear in mind while their project is in its development (they are summarized in Table 23.1). Obviously the value of any of these points lies in the objectivity of the reviewer. In other words, it is pointless to whitewash these issues if, in fact, there is real reason to suspect that one of more of them may be lacking in the project. If that is the case, project managers first need to take the necessary steps to consider how the project got to that point and what action steps can be taken to revive it.

1. *Keep the mission in the forefront.* On the surface, it seems obvious to state that it is important to keep the mission in mind when implementing a project. How-

TABLE 23.1. LESSONS FOR PROJECT MANAGERS.

- Keep the mission in the forefront.
- Balance cost consciousness with project performance.
- Stay well connected to clients.
- Make sure you have the technology to succeed.
- Set up and maintain a scheduling system.
- Put the right people on the project team.
- Make sure top management gets behind the project.
- Continually ask the "what if?" questions.
- Do not be too hasty to judge a project as a success or a failure.
- Any project is only as good as it is used.

ever, the point bears repeating and underlining. The research on the ten-factor model demonstrated clearly that adherence to mission was the number one cause of implementation success. Remember that what "mission" refers to is not simply "having" a mission to implement a project, but conveying exactly what the goals of the implementation effort are to all concerned parties, particularly the other project team members and prospective users of the system. What will the new project do for us and the rest of the organization? How long do we expect it to take to develop and bring it out the door? Does every member of the project team understand and buy into these goals? These are just some of the important questions that need to be asked about the project's mission. Nothing will derail a project faster than establishing ambiguous or contradictory goals that are communicated to all groups affected by the project. When goals change or need updating, that information also needs to be made public.

One well-known problem with getting a project out the door is the potential for the mission to change or metamorphose as the project progresses. There are many examples of projects that, for whatever reason, underwent major specification, technological, or user changes or got off on such tangents that the originally agreed-on goals and purposes became meaningless. Obviously some modifications are bound to occur as a project is customized for a particular client's uses. The point that must be stressed, however, is that the project's underlying purpose must remain clear and important for all members of the implementation team.

2. *Balance cost consciousness with project performance.* There is sometimes a strong temptation to come down on either side of the cost-performance argument, usually with questionable results. For example, organizations that build projects at any cost because they are enamored of technology for its own sake inevitably run into trouble with project financing. We cannot continue to pour money down the gaping hole of a project run out of control. On the other hand, when project development is left in the hands of the accountant (that is, project decisions are ultimately made almost solely on the merits of cost), we run the equally unpalatable risk of stifling crucial creativity and long-term innovation, all in the name of immediate capital constraints.

Clearly a middle ground is needed—somewhere between the excessive controls of cost accounting and the anything-goes mentality of those who would tinker with technology for its own sake. This conclusion forces management to adopt some decision rules for new product development that leave the project team as free as possible to ensure that performance is top-notch while at the same time ensuring that the team does more than simply pay lip-service to cost constraints.

3. *Stay well connected to clients.* Client acceptance, a "selling" activity, is necessary during both the initial planning processes and the termination phase of the implementation. Often the sequence of operations concerned with the client

follows the pattern of (1) consulting to determine specific needs, (2) selling the ideas (including the benefits of the project), budgets, and time frame to completion, and (3) performing a final verification of client acceptance once the project has been completed. This verification may be in the form of a series of formal interviews or follow-up conversations with clients who are intending to use it.

In developing and implementing a project, do not underestimate the importance of "selling" the output to the clients, even after having initially consulted with them about the system. An important truth of project implementation suggests that one can never talk to the clients enough. A corollary to that rule argues that just because the project manager and team members have once spent time consulting with clients about the system, it is absolutely incorrect to assume now that clients will embrace the finished product with open arms. In the time between initial consultation and project development and transfer, too much can change that will alter their perceptions of the product. For example, the technology may be altered significantly, or a great deal of time may have elapsed, changing their basic reasons for even needing the system. Or perhaps one of the department's chief proponents of the project has since left to take another job. The common denominator of all of these issues is that time does not stand still between initial client consultation and final project completion. Do not automatically assume that you fully understand the client's concerns or that once the completed project is transferred, it will now be used.

4. *Make sure you have the technology to succeed.* The successful development and acceptance and use of a project assumes that the organization has the technology or the technically capable people to support the system and ensure that it succeeds. Many small children suffer from the "eyes bigger than the stomach" syndrome, particularly during dessert. No matter how much the child may have eaten to that point, once dessert is offered, it is almost always accepted. Of course, there is no guarantee that the dessert will be eaten. In fact, it is rarely completely finished. The children are simply exhibiting eyes bigger than their stomachs.

Our point is to illustrate a similar characteristic with many organizations: they too suffer from having eyes bigger than their stomachs. A new technology is introduced nationally, and someone within the organization develops great enthusiasm for the concept. The question that needs to be asked at this point is whether the organization can support the successful development and introduction of this project with the personnel and facilities they currently possess. If the answer is no, the organization needs to take immediate remedial steps: hiring additional support personnel who have the necessary technical backgrounds, instituting a department-wide training program to bring potential users up to technical standards, or putting the brakes on the project's development until another time when it can be more fully supported.

5. *Set up and maintain a scheduling system.* Planning is an activity that many project managers would rather avoid. The process can be tedious and involves an activity that does not have immediate visible results. This is particularly true early in the project's life cycle, when top management begins to issue a string of pointed communiqués demanding to know when project development will begin, somehow assuming that time spent "planning" is taken away from time spent "doing." In spite of these pressures for action, it is impossible to underestimate the importance of comprehensive and detailed planning for successful project implementation. There is great validity to the old saying that those who fail to plan are planning to fail. Initiating the action steps in a project without having developed a comprehensive planning and control process may please upper management in the short term, but it is a real recipe for disaster down the road.

6. *Put the right people on the project team.* It is tremendously important that a company spend sufficient time recruiting, selecting, and training people who possess the necessary technical and administrative skills to influence the ultimate success of the project positively. Does the organization currently possess the people capable of understanding the technology and dealing the headaches, deadlines, and conflict that a project implementation can bring? Of equal importance is the question of how project team members are assigned to the group.

In many organizations we have worked with, members are assigned to project teams purely on an availability basis; that is, if managers have subordinates who are currently free, those people are put on the team, regardless of whether they possess the technical qualifications, people skills, or administrative abilities to perform effectively. In some organizations, the picture is even worse. There, members are assigned to projects as a method for getting them out of their departments and making them someone else's problem. In these cases, managers who are dealing with problem subordinates simply use the project as an excuse to ship these troublemakers to other duties. It is easy to imagine the prospects for projects that are continually staffed with castoffs and incompetents. We owe our projects more than simply to make an implementation team the dumping ground for the untrained or malcontents.

7. *Make sure top management gets behind the project.* It is well accepted that top management can either help or seriously hinder a project. Top management grants the necessary authority to the project manager, controls needed resources, arbitrates cross-departmental disputes, and rewards the final results. Its role in the successful implementation of a new project should not be overlooked. However, top management support must go further than simply approving the new system. Their statements of support have to be backed up by concrete actions and demonstrations of loyalty. Actions speak far louder than words and have a way of truly demonstrating how top management feels about the project and, by extension,

the project manager. Are they putting their money where their mouth is, or is their support simply pro forma? This is an important question that needs to be resolved early in the implementation process, before significant time and resources have been spent. Both project managers and their teams need to know that top management will support them in the event of unforeseen difficulties or crises. All implementation efforts encounter difficulties and "fair weather" supporters are likely to be terribly demoralizing.

8. *Continually ask the "what if?" questions.* Problems occur with every project development. Because all projects run into trouble at some point, the mark of a successful project manager is not one who can foresee and forestall problems; rather, the successful project manager is the individual who has taken the time to puzzle out appropriate responses to likely trouble spots. This idea of troubleshooting is particularly appropriate in the implementation of projects with new or not-well-understood technology because there are so many human and technical variables that can go wrong. The successful project manager has to be cognizant of technical issues and difficulties that can arise; further, the behavioral and organizational issues are often more common, pressing, and potentially damaging to implementation success. Therefore, the act of simply troubleshooting the project's technical features will be of only limited usefulness.

9. *Do not be too hasty to judge a project as a success or a failure.* It is the rare project that is correctly judged to be a success or failure immediately following its introduction. The cost accountant may endorse a project's development process as being within budget and schedule constraints, and our organization may have positive feelings about a project's viability in the marketplace, but only time will tell the true story. In reality, many current projects cannot do more than offer imprecise evidence of their future success at the time of their introduction. The obvious problem is that we must make a serious evaluation of the project manager's role based on a project's future expectations. To what set of criteria is it appropriate to hold project managers in evaluating their performance? Clearly, rewarding a project manager on the basis of adherence only to the internally focused triple constraint is inadequate and is in fact likely to send the wrong message to those running current development projects. On the other hand, it may be highly unfair to hold project managers to a standard that is truly beyond their control (for example, the future stream of profits for a project with a ten- or twenty-year market cycle).

Some middle ground is necessary: between the equally misleading guidelines of short-term development and long-term profitability. Companies that are intent on making their evaluations on as clear a set of data as possible must look for methods to evaluate client satisfaction, acceptance, and use of new project offerings in conjunction with the traditional measures of performance, schedule, and budget.

Project managers need to be made aware of the standards that the organization holds with regard to its evaluation criteria so they are willing and even eager to make the investment in client consultation and project marketing that are so important to ultimate project success.

10. *Any project is only as good as it is used.* One of the most important points that past research and experience has taught us is that the client is the ultimate determinant of successful project implementation. This lesson, seemingly so fundamental, is one that nevertheless must be continually relearned by organizations large and small. As long as our gaze remains firmly fixed on the internal criteria for project success, the so-called triple constraint, we will never achieve the full measure of project success.

We live in a culture that is fascinated with the latest technological advances. Organizations that are dominated by their engineering departments are often particularly vulnerable to this bias. The prevailing assumption that one has only to build the latest design with the hottest component properties to ensure client acceptance, use, and subsequent project success is a conceit companies can no longer afford to reinforce. Where marketing and customer service are relegated to supporting cast roles, we will simply recycle the same mistakes again and again. In the drive to innovate, there is a very real danger that we will continue to pursue technology for technology's sake, rather than work to create projects with practical and useful features. Project managers need to devote as much time to networking with potential clients as they do to ensuring that all the technical features of a new project are performing well.

Conclusion

Success is first and foremost a client-based phenomenon. It is the client who is the ultimate arbiter of successful project implementation, not the project manager. Having said this, we would also note that an overemphasis on client concerns, while willingly sacrificing internal constraints such as budgets, schedules, and performance, is not the answer either. A balance is required: an a priori decision rule that allows us to prioritize activities correctly while at the same time ensuring that the project is not done in by a factor we could control but chose not to address. If such a balance is achieved, it will go far toward creating an atmosphere in which project priorities are well understood and serve as guideposts for our efforts, reducing the "manageable" reasons for projects to fail.

CHAPTER TWENTY-FOUR

FOUR FAILURES IN PROJECT MANAGEMENT

Kenneth G. Cooper

The project was slated to design and build an exciting first-of-a-kind product. But during the development effort, unexpected problems emerged: changes in the product specifications, shortages of qualified people, material supply delays. Costs escalated, and work fell far behind schedule. The project's future was threatened, and the work was interrupted. Eventually, project objectives were scaled back, and the work was completed—years late and at a cost more than double the original budget.

Another project conducted just two hundred miles away also aimed to develop a revolutionary product—this one a new software system. Ill-defined design specifications and changes plagued this project as well; here, too, qualified staff were difficult to find. Schedule pressures mounted as months and years passed beyond targeted delivery. Extra staff, more overtime, and tighter schedule targets all failed to bring it under control. It too finished years late, at a cost far more than double its planned estimates.

If only the managers of both projects could have compared notes—talked with one another about solutions attempted and failed—they might have discerned common problems and learned effective solutions. But this seems to be too tall an order even for projects within the same company, let alone for these projects separated by . . . two centuries.

The product sponsor in the first tale of project woes was George Washington; Paul Revere supplied the required copper and brass fittings. The special timber that delayed the work's progress eventually provided the project's product with its nickname, "Old Ironsides." The *U.S.S. Constitution* inaugurated the U.S. Navy and was, in 1794, a new nation's introduction to the challenge of large project management. Today the challenge remains largely unanswered, as evidenced by the problems, failed management efforts, and outcome, all so perfectly duplicated two hundred years later by a prestigious New York banking firm in its effort to develop a financial software system.

If those of us who manage projects have proved one thing, it is that we know how to fail; after all, we do it so consistently. A recent worldwide survey proved what we all suspected: the majority of all development projects fail to meet their time and cost targets.[1] Projects and problems just as those described are lamented regularly in company boardrooms and business publications. For those whose business is projects—construction firms, defense contractors, design agents—the business impacts are obvious, large, and bad. For all other technology-dependent companies, the effects on business—revenue, growth, profits, market share, reputation—are just as large and just as bad.

Computer hardware and software companies miss projected new product introduction dates with such regularity that on-time performance is news. Automobile companies struggle to reduce new car development costs and time, so as to compete more effectively. Banks, insurance firms, and other service institutions conduct in-house or contracted development efforts to improve their operational efficiency and quality. Telecommunications companies compete, in an increasingly complex arena, through system development efforts that aim to reduce costs and broaden product and service offerings.

This chapter is targeted at all the project customers who have sat by, chagrined over the ever-growing cost estimates and ever-slipping completion date targets, or who have jumped in themselves to "help" manage. It is for the company executives who have listened to project managers report first glowingly, then sadly, the state of key development efforts, who set the business policies and environment within which those projects must be executed, and who lead businesses whose survival depends on succeeding with new development efforts. And this chapter is for all project managers who must deal with the aforementioned, while working with independent-minded engineers, matrix department heads who have other incentives, remote vendors, even consultants and lawyers, in a dozen meetings a day, to manage projects that are underfunded, tightly scheduled, understaffed, and closely watched, to develop products that are technically ambitious, ill defined, and critical to the success of the company.

Teams at my firm have conducted analyses of over seventy major projects; their operations touch five different decades, including the next to come. The products of their development and build efforts include power plants, software systems, aircraft, tunnels, electronics, ships, control systems, missiles, and automobiles. Their technologies range from the stable to the unheard of; their locations span half the globe. Some we have helped to succeed; we have retrospectively diagnosed the failure of others. With that mix of products, technologies, and industries among seventy-five projects, we might expect seventy-five different sources of project problems and failures (this vendor, that radar . . .); project-specific excuses abound. Instead, we found four fundamental drivers of project failure. Given the luxury of dispassionate analyses, we saw that how organizations performed on these characteristics determined the magnitude and consistency of project failure. We saw that all four are manageable. Improvement on any one of the four produced improvement in project success, and improving all four yielded dramatic success. None is any surprise to the experienced project manager, but the near-universal tendency to think "but this project is unique" dramatically reduces the appreciation of just how much these manageable, systemic conditions drive project performance and leads managers to repeat these avoidable sources of failure:

Failure 1: Failure to know what to expect, or *Great Expectations*

Failure 2: Failure to know what to watch, or *Half-Blank Tape Measures*

Failure 3: Failure to know what to do (and to do it), or *Counterintuitively Counterproductive Countermeasures*

Failure 4: Failure to know what's what, or *Lessons Not Learned*

Just How Much Difference Does Managing Make?

In a recent opportunity to compare performance on two similar-product system development programs at the same company, the degree of performance difference caused just by the way managers manage became apparent (see Figure 24.1). Program A was a 300,000-hour effort over three years, and Project B was a 400,000-hour effort over four years. Both saw their own peculiar conditions and work scope growth. Program A, the more troubled one, experienced a 200 percent schedule overrun and a 300 percent cost overrun. Program B finished on budget and on schedule, and many reasons for its good fortune were cited by observers: a "better" customer, better tools and hardware, better labor market conditions. Some even noted "better management" as a cause (although the majority with this opinion had themselves managed parts of the program; others discounted the objectivity of that causal diagnosis).

Program A was understandably regarded as a cost and schedule disaster, Program B a success. Despite this perception, the organization's top management was dissatisfied with the extent to which other programs were adopting the processes and practices that the managers of the successful program had employed. Our analysis task was to separate the external causes from the contribution of the internal management practices and to quantify the sources of cost and schedule improvement. Managers of other programs then would know which practices to emulate in order to achieve better performance.

Simulation models of the two programs enabled us to see how they would have performed with equal work scope. Another simulation test removed all "external differences": setting the vendor, hardware, and labor market conditions of the

FIGURE 24.1.

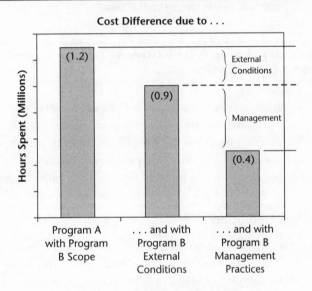

Cost Difference due to . . .

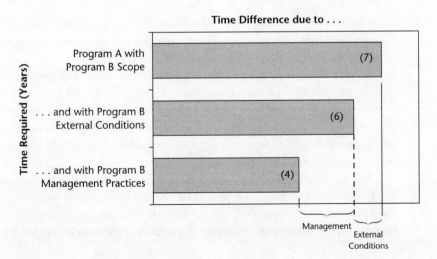

Time Difference due to . . .

poor-performing Program A to those experienced by the on-target Program B. Finally, several model changes were made to reflect the different internal task scheduling, staffing policies, and new work practices implemented by the managers of the on-target Program B.

Together the full set of model changes accounted for all of the actual cost and schedule performance difference between the two programs. After netting out the modest work scope differences, internal management practices caused over 60 percent of the cost improvement (a half-million hours saved) and over 70 percent (about two years) of the schedule performance improvement. Were it not for the improved management practices, the on-target program would have required twice its achieved cost and nearly half again the time.

Failure 1: Failure to Know What to Expect, or Great Expectations

It is axiomatic that if we set project targets poorly (usually meaning overoptimistically), we will perform "poorly" (relative to those targets). If it were just that simple, projects would miss their targets by exactly the amount of inaccuracy in the targets. But the consequences are much worse than any obvious one-for-one linear inaccuracy in the planning of the product and its budget and schedule.

Product Definition

Ask any home-building contractors what they fear most, and you will consistently hear "changes." Ask any defense system developers what got them in so much trouble on that problem-ridden contract, and the answer will likely be "changes." The new automobile development's slow pace? Changes. The slippage in the market date for that new long-awaited software? Changes. Spec changes, feature changes, requirements changes, design changes, change orders, change notices, change paper, late adders, revisions, re-releases, and more.

Rework in all its forms and names is an inevitable part of projects. The instability of the initial product definition is a major contributor to the amount of change that occurs in a project. Devoting more time and effort up front to the product's definition is a high-payback investment. The use of common platforms and objects across multiple development projects is an increasingly common practice to reduce change in product specifications.

The clarity and stability of product definition deserves all the attention it can get. Our analyses of dozens of projects show that for every obvious hour of technical product change avoided, two to four (or more) hours of subsequent effort are saved. This is due to the much-reduced efficiency at which unplanned, out-of-sequence changed work is conducted, as well as the knock-on rework effects of changes (for example, "We'll have to move that wall to reroute that piping so that we can relocate that junction box we need for that new electrical device"). We have seen product definition problems in and of themselves cause 50 to 100 percent growth in projects' time and cost.[2]

If the project is an internal development, the consequences obviously extend even further, as the new service, system, or product is delayed along with its benefits and its revenue-producing life. If an externally funded project, would we not expect the "changes" clause in all such contracts to compensate contractors properly? No. We are universally inept underachievers in estimating and explaining the full impacts of changes. An entire body of contract dispute case law regarding delay and disruption testifies to our collective inability to define correctly and adequately at the time of a change its full costs.

Cost Budget

This one seems pretty obvious: set your budget too low, and miss it by that amount; set it too high, and you become a hero. The latter case is rare, because optimism, competing projects, and budget-tightening pressures usually translate into low-cost budgets for projects. Why should we care? Why, aside from the obvious, is a too-low budget a source of project failure?

Inadequate budgets create two categories of problems: one for the projects themselves and one for the organizations in which the projects are executed. At the project level, a budget that is set too low causes several conditions that actually lead to higher costs than if the project were to have a higher budget. These conditions begin with the inevitably heightened pressure of a too-low budget. Good tools, equipment, and materials needed for a productive effort are more likely to be shortchanged. Worker morale is worsened by excessive budget pressure and the shortsighted actions it often prompts, hurting worker productivity further and driving costs up more.

In no other way are budget pressures more hurtful than in their adverse effect on staffing decisions, especially late in the game. The inadequate project budget is allocated among tasks, becoming inadequate task budgets. As those work tasks near their hoped-for completion, budget pressures are at their worst, depressing the application of staff to the work at hand at the very time they are most needed for finding and fixing rework and concluding a high-quality product that will be used by downstream tasks. This typical budget-induced late staff cutting merely pushes the remaining rework to a later stage, where it will be executed less productively and cause even more rework on dependent items. Total project costs climb further upward.

It need not happen this way. The manager of the tremendously successful Peace Shield air defense program at Hughes Aircraft Company, C. W. ("Chuck") Sutherland, defied tight budget pressures in managing his resources. Where conventional wisdom said otherwise, he chose the seemingly risky path of "overstaffing" the back end of design work stages, expressly for the purpose of finding and fixing rework. His team sought to generate a higher-quality interim product on which later work stages could build. This, with many other such moves, yielded an on-budget project and a high-quality system completed seven months *early*. U.S. Air Force service acquisition executive Darleen Druyun observed, "In my 26 years in acquisition, this [Peace Shield] is the most successful program I've ever been involved with, and the leadership of the U.S. Air Force agrees."[3]

With these cost-affecting project conditions being driven by the budget itself, the organizations in which such projects operate are handicapped. For them, it is even more difficult to budget new work accurately based on their performance on past work. There are always many other possible sources, reasons, and excuses available for the casual causal diagnosis of over-budget projects. The organization has legitimate difficulty sorting out the extent to which (or even if) chronic underbudgeting is contributing to the gap between the project targets and the achievements.

But if there is one thing that drives the business of a project even more than the cost budget, it is the schedule.

Schedule

Setting and achieving an aggressive schedule target is perhaps the most sacred of all sacred cows in the field of project management. It is also the source of some of the most destructive behavior and phenomena in projects.

The quest for early project completion is understandable. New products early to market command a favored position. New systems contribute to business operating efficiency. Early or on-time projects save the costs of marching armies of support personnel, and boost a contractor's standing among customers.

With these laudable outcomes in mind, customers, executives, and managers together routinely agree on overly ambitious project schedule targets, only to see the project spiral downward in an ever-degrading set of conditions induced by the very targets it sought. Indeed, the result is that both schedule and cost targets are typically exceeded by far more than the original amount of inaccuracy. While avoidable, these schedule-induced phenomena are typical and systemic:

- *Excessively overlapped work stages* create low-productivity, high-rework, time-consuming conditions in the downstream stages, which are typically started far too early, in an effort to make (and show) "progress."

- *Schedule pressure* induces a "get the product out" mentality that sacrifices completeness and correctness, even proper task sequence, for the short-term appearance of progress, thus sowing seeds of later problems.
- *Inefficient, costly resource use,* such as costly short-term subcontracting or excessive sustained overtime, generate control and productivity penalties that cost the project both extra dollars and extra time.
- *Worker morale,* especially when schedule pressures are overlaid on budget pressures, suffers when problems mount on an over-target project, further hurting productivity and total project performance.

In the remainder of this chapter, we will examine the operation, and quantify the consequences, of these phenomena.

Failure 2: Failure to Know What to Watch, or Half-Blank Tape Measures

Imagine that you have contracted for your house to be built, and that the standard tape measure used by all the contractors has long segments—half the tape, in fact—that are uncalibrated. What sort of product would you expect from their efforts? We are, in effect, equipping managers with half-blank tape measures as the standard tools for planning and monitoring projects.

When we were first asked by a contractor client to build a computer-based model capable of accurately simulating the performance of a large project from the start of design through the completion of construction, large portions of the project effort simply could not be described or explained by applying the standard available tools. How could this be?

The critical path method (CPM) has long dominated among techniques for project planning. This method provides a framework in which the duration of, and linkages between, individual tasks can be planned. From this, the sequence of tasks may be identified that, if one element on the path were to be delayed, would translate to a delay in the entire project. An accepted, often required, technique for planning projects and testing schedule impacts, it is the basis for virtually every piece of popular project management software offered. Properly constructed and updated, it is an extremely useful planning tool. And yet CPM is an inadequate model for managing complex development projects.

The typical means for monitoring project progress and ongoing cost and schedule performance are variations of earned value systems. These provide for setting work and budget standards for individual tasks. Progress on the tasks, and cost and schedule variations, are assessed by comparing actual effort and cost with the task budgets. The earned value system for project monitoring is, like CPM, an accepted and often contractually required project management technique. Truthfully and faithfully employed, it is a highly disciplined monitoring method. Yet like CPM, earned value is an inadequate model for managing complex development projects. So what is missing?

What is missing, as any experienced project or program manager knows, is rework. For all their utility, conventional methods treat a project as being composed of a set of individual, discrete tasks. Each task is portrayed as having a definable beginning and end, with the work content either "to be done" or "in process" or "done." No account is taken of the quality of the work done, the release of incomplete or imperfect task products, or the amount of rework that will be required. This is particularly inappropriate for development projects, in which there is a naturally iterative process of design and engineering.

Indeed, our analyses have shown that rework can account for the majority of work content (and cost) on complex development projects. Although this varies significantly among projects and project types, it is hardly ever a matter of a single revisiting of a particular task. Instead, several iterations are typical, often far removed in time from the scheduled and actual conduct of the first round of work on the task. This is readily seen in, for example, the release of initial engineering drawings, A revisions, B revisions, C revisions, and so on (for those companies or projects that actually monitor such information). Companies experienced in complex projects know to expect this, and have developed rules of thumb to count on two (or three or more) revisions per engineering product. Even so, this expectation rarely is incorporated explicitly in work planning and management systems— because the techniques do not allow it. Worse are the cases where this rework cycle is not explicitly anticipated or monitored. Here they are not only working with half a tape measure; they are reading it with their eyes closed. These are not unintelligent people or project-naive companies; on the contrary, they include the most technically sophisticated individuals conducting and managing complex developments in firms whose very existence depends on successful project performance. What we need, then, is a different view of development projects, one that recognizes the rework cycle, plans for it, monitors it, and helps managers reduce its magnitude and duration.

We need a method that reflects a more strategic view of projects, one that accounts for the quality of work done and the causes of productivity and rework variations. We need to be able to see more clearly than is allowed by traditional methods how changing external conditions and management actions alter staff productivity and the rework cycle and how the consequences spread through an entire project. We need a new framework applicable across a range of projects, reflecting that which is common and that which is unique among projects. Only thus may we more consistently and rigorously extract, learn, and apply lessons that will yield sustained improvement in project management and performance.

Such a new framework has emerged from the application of system dynamics simulation methods to a wide range of development projects. In a manner quite dissimilar to CPM and program evaluation and review technique (PERT) models, it treats a project not merely as a sum or a sequence of discrete tasks, but as flows of work in which there are multiple rework cycles. Because of the significant rework content of development projects, this framework is able to reconcile with one another a project's person-hours spent, tasks and items performed, elapsed time, and much more. Not only can the rework cycle model structure accurately simulate the actual recorded history of projects, but it can provide powerful forecasting and "what if?" managerial capabilities.

First built for a ship design project at Litton,[4] the rework cycle model has since been applied accurately and successfully to over one hundred different projects: defense electronics systems at Hughes Aircraft, telecommunication software systems at AT&T, aircraft design and production at Northrop, electric utilities' power plant engineering and construction, automobile design at Ford, and dozens of other programs and projects.

At the core of the model structure is a different but straightforward view of project work—one which recognizes the rework cycle. Repeated applications of this more realistic model have proven it to be logically correct and, when codified as a working simulation model, numerically accurate. Its uses have brought benefits (as in dollars) that are large (as in billions) to the businesses that have adopted it. This simple addition to the traditional view of projects has proved to be a powerful diagnostic and management capability.

The Traditional View of a Project

Figure 24.2 recasts the traditional view of a project's (or project stage's) tasks to be done, tasks in process, and tasks done as a more continuous stream of work. The pool of tasks in work to be done is depleted over the course of time, such that at the end of the project, nothing is left there, and all the tasks fill the pool of work done. It is people working at some (varying) level of productivity that cause the work to get done. Changing the number of people along the way, or somehow influencing their productivity, alters the pace of work getting done.

Figure 24.3 displays the shape of some key measures of project performance that would occur under this traditional view. Plotted are graphs of work to do, project (stage) staff, and percentage of work complete, as computed by a simulation model using the diagrammed structure. Such charts may show the way we *plan* the effort to go; this may be the way we *hope* things will go. But how many of us have seen even a remotely ambitious development project actually perform this way?

FIGURE 24.2. PROJECT WORK FLOW.

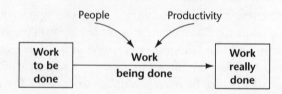

FIGURE 24.3. PROJECT PERFORMANCE IN THE TRADITIONAL VIEW

The Reality

A better view recognizes the existence of rework cycles. In Figure 24.4, what is termed the quality of work executed should be thought of as a valve controlling the portion of the work flow being done that will or will not require rework. View the diagrammed structure as physical pools in which work resides and pipes through which work flows. It is easy to see that a "quality" measure that could vary (over time) in the range of 0 to 1.0 diverts more or less of the work being done into the rework cycle. So long as this measure of quality is less than 1.0, some work being done—even rework itself—will continue to move into and through the re-work cycle. The pool of rework requires staff to expend effort to execute it—that is, to alter, correct, or complete the work items needing revision.

The distinction drawn between productivity and quality is important. Staff may exhibit high "productivity," but be putting out work of low "quality" that re-quires later reworking. In this condition, the net throughput to the pool of work really done is low.[5]

Finally, for that part of work being done that will require reworking, there is a critical way station in which elements of rework linger until being identified as needing rework. We have termed this way station *undiscovered rework*. Undiscovered rework consists of tasks or work products that contain as-yet-undetected errors of commission or omission, and are therefore perceived, and reported by all traditional systems, as being done.

The completed model of the rework cycle yields simulation-generated behavior that is characteristic of all development projects, shown in Figure 24.5. The precise quantities and timing obviously differ among projects, but the behavior is common: as the initial round of work nears conclusion, previously undiscovered errors become apparent, requiring more staff for a longer time; the perceived and reported progress significantly slows as the magnitude of recognized rework grows; and an extended completion effort ensues as the last elements of undiscovered rework emerge.

FIGURE 24.4.   THE REWORK CYCLE.

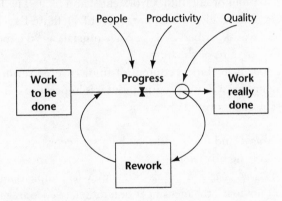

FIGURE 24.5. PROJECT PERFORMANCE WITH THE REWORK CYCLE.

Most rework is discovered by downstream efforts or testing, but months (or even years) may pass before this discovery occurs. During this time, dependent work will have incorporated these errors, or technical derivations thereof, and entered its *own* rework cycle. The more tightly scheduled and parallel the project tasks, the more of a multiplier effect there is on subsequent rework cycles.

This final element of the rework cycle, undiscovered rework, plays a pivotal role in the propagation of problems through a project. Lurking undetected—as a software bug, or design miscalculation, or wrongly placed bulkhead—it causes productivity loss, delays, and more rework on dependent tasks. Undiscovered rework is the single most important source of project cost and schedule crises. It is the great killer of projects (and of new products and of careers), and no traditional systems even acknowledge its existence. Most projects seem to be planned and managed as though it does not exist. Not so for the distinguishably successful, however. The program manager of Northrop-Grumman's Team West (to McDonnell-Douglas's prime role) for the new F/A–18 E/F fighter jet aircraft was Lou Carrier. He propagated throughout the program an awareness of the rework cycle, and the need to monitor and find rework early, and fix it. The E/F program became the first ever to receive the Department of Defense Excellence in Acquisition Award and was described by U.S. Navy officials as "the model for all DoD procurement programs of the future."[6]

The specific technical content of undiscovered rework is by definition unknown at any point in the program. But it is imperative to program management success that undiscovered rework be:

- *Acknowledged* (and plans and schedules set accordingly so as to reduce the disruption of the surprise).
- Actively *sought out*. Earlier discovery may feel unpleasant at the time. It is important not to kill the messenger but, rather, to encourage early technical problem identification. Here, it is what you do not know that hurts you most.
- *Prevented* as much as possible, that is, improving "quality" in the rework cycle. This is easier said than done, since managers cannot mandate by edict the achievement of higher quality. (See Failure 3 for examples not to be followed.)

Failure 3: Failure to Know What to Do (and to Do It), or Counterintuitively Counterproductive Countermeasures

Failure 3 is not knowing what to do as a manager of a challenging project or when faced with the prospect of an ongoing project's missing its targets. Whether it arises from poor planning, monitoring, prior managing, or any changed conditions, the prospect of poor performance means that managers will seek preemptive or corrective countermeasures. In most cases, the countermeasures will be obvious, intuitive, accepted, almost second nature—and wrong.

Although we as managers have little absolute control, we have enormous influence on project performance. Our decisions and actions work through multiple cause-and-effect paths to affect the rework cycle and the project outcome. All too often, the countermeasures we use in response to typical problems along the way are counterproductive. Rather than helping, they aggravate conditions because we so often expect only the obvious impact, and so rarely anticipate the many other cause-and-effect paths by which the decisions influence the project.

As project managers, our most important decisions involve resource management: How much do how many of which resources work when, on what, under what conditions? The sections that follow discuss the most common failings of project resource management and their many consequences.

The $2,000 Hour

We all know managers who have agonized over one or two percentage point differences in salary or wage changes for individuals, amounting to less than a dollar an hour. The same managers will, without a second thought (indeed, without knowing), pay $2,000 or more for each effective hour of work, when that work is performed by project staff working extended overtime.

Figure 24.6 adds to the rework cycle structure a path showing a chain of cause-and-effect relationships, indicated by the thin arrows. Using information from the pools of work in the rework cycle (but without knowing, of course, the size or content of as-yet-undiscovered rework), managers or their aides periodically estimate the progress made to date in the project, or in a stage of the project. Based on this, they assess the extent to which additional staffing is needed to try to finish the remaining work on the prevailing schedule. A common and reasonable response to an indication that one is falling behind schedule is to supplement the effective staffing by the temporary use of overtime. This avoids the cost, hassle, and long-term commitment of bringing in additional people through hiring or transfer.

A few weeks of overtime easily extends into more sustained overtime usage as a key milestone approaches or the schedule gap stubbornly refuses to close (for example, with the continuing discovery of more rework to do). As a purposeful choice or because the "end" remains tantalizingly (and misleadingly) close, the overtime is continued. The intended direct effect of increasing the full-time-equivalent people is achieved. However, the secondary effect (through fatigue) on worker productivity and work quality, though often acknowledged in spirit, is consistently

FIGURE 24.6. PATHS OF INFLUENCE FROM THE USE OF OVERTIME.

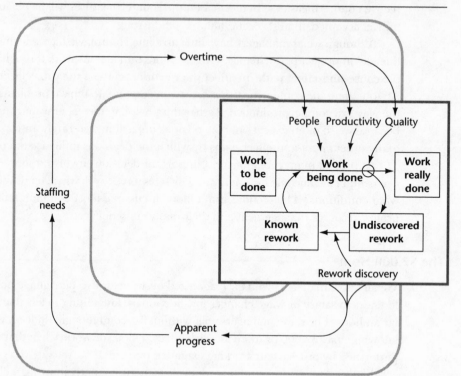

underestimated (this path of unintended secondary influence is shown in Figure 24.6; this is what causes the counterintuitive effect).

We used our project simulation model to generate the performance of a typical four-year, million-person-hour (planned) project under two different conditions. In the first simulation was typical overtime usage, but only with the intended direct effect on staffing; there were no unintended secondary effects on productivity or work quality. In other words, this is an artificial—and unrealistic—world (but one that often seems to be the view of some managers). In the second simulation, we activated the secondary influences of overtime, at the strength of effect that we have observed operating in dozens of development projects.

In this (more realistic) case, the per-person productivity drops and rework increases (by 25 percent) as a result of overtime-induced fatigue. Overall, the same project scope requires 15 percent more effort to complete when using extensive and sustained overtime. "All right, we know it's expensive, but we're trying to meet a schedule here!" might be the proffered explanation. Well, it might be worth the extra cost of the effort, if only it helped the schedule. Instead, though, the work requires an *additional* two months of time to reach completion, as a result of the added rework cycling.

From analyses of several projects, we calculated the cost of each effective full hour of project work output when real productivity and rework penalties were taken into account. Figure 24.7 summarizes the results for typical engineering and production staff working sustained overtime (for two or three months or more) at a level of four, eight, and twelve hours per week (per person).

At a sustained level of four hours per week, both engineering and production staff achieve one to two hours' worth of real, effective extra work output. If managers are paying wages for the overtime hours, perhaps even an overtime premium, the cost for each effective hour of output achieved is staggering. In the most benign condition, achieving about two extra output hours for four overtime hours, each extra output hour costs about $150 (4 hours × $50/hour × 1.5 overtime premium = $300; $300 ÷ 2 output hours = $150/output hour). At 12 hours per week sustained overtime, engineers' extra 0.4 hour of output (1 percent beyond a 40-hour week) means an effective cost of over *$2,000 per hour of gained output.*[7]

In the production efforts analyzed, the crossover point to no net extra work from sustained overtime of appears at about the ten-hour mark;[8] for engineers, the crossover point is (just) beyond 12 hours. Regardless of the precise numbers,

FIGURE 24.7. REAL OUTPUT GAINED FROM DIFFERENT LEVELS OF SUSTAINED OVERTIME.

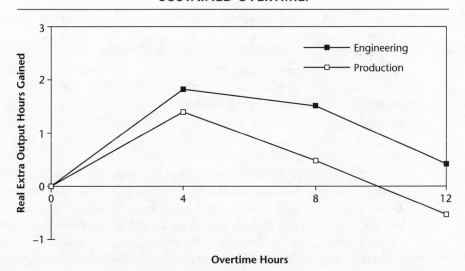

use of sustained overtime is far less productive than widely believed. Even "free" salaried overtime will eventually *hurt* schedule performance.

It's the Law

Unavoidable at the start or in moderation, bringing new people into a project organization (by hiring or transfer) has a degree of counterproductive impact that is, again, widely underestimated or ignored. But the impacts—potentially harsh ones—will occur nonetheless.

In the classic book *The Mythical Man-Month*, the author offers up what he calls "Brooks's Law": "Adding manpower to a late software project makes it later."[9] Admittedly a simplification with exceptions, it still captures the spirit of a very real and damaging set of phenomena.

The diagram in Figure 24.8 shows another set of cause-and-effect paths of influence that work over the course of time, when managers decide to hire in response to a perceived need for additional staff. The obvious intent is to bring in new people who will supplement the staff available to work on the project.

With any substantial hiring or even transferring of people unfamiliar with the project, the new people enter with less experience or skill than those already on board (despite individual exceptions, this holds true, especially for technically demanding work or specialized skill needs). So the average skill level of the growing staff drops, at least long enough for new people to get up to speed (which can take years). Worse, the more hiring that occurs in any constrained labor market, the lower the entry skill level will be (assuming the most appropriately talented are hired first). It is as though you are hiring from a barrel of eligible candidates, and the more you take, the closer you come to scraping the bottom of the barrel.

As if that were not enough, there is an added kicker: newly hired individuals tend to have a higher attrition rate than longer-time experienced people—from mistakes in hiring, recruitment expectations not met, less loyalty, wanderlust. A higher attrition rate requires still more new hiring just to remain even, let alone increase the staff more. So a vicious circle develops, a churning with little forward progress, while new people are hired, departure rates increase, and still more (brand) new people are hired to sustain the organization.

It gets worse still. Any problem response that adversely affects productivity or quality, such as lowered skill levels from hiring (or sustained overtime fatigue, for that matter), can trigger a sinister set of self-reinforcing impacts on a circular path of cause and effect. As Figure 24.8 indicates, the hiring, which yields skill-worsened productivity and quality, slows the pace of progress relative to the schedule (especially as the additional rework generated by less skilled people is discovered).

FIGURE 24.8. PATHS OF INFLUENCE FROM NEW EMPLOYEE HIRING.

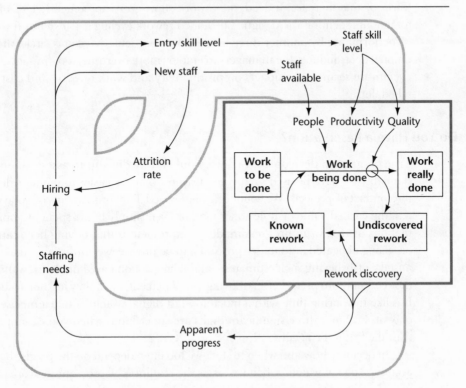

With less than planned progress, we clearly need what? More people! (Thus, more hiring, new people, skill dilution, productivity and quality reduction, and slowed progress result.) Further, there is the extra coaching and training time invested by experienced staff and the disruption of a rapidly growing organization. Lest you think this is an academic concoction, be assured that we have observed this exact phenomenon in many organizations. It starts innocently and builds insidiously, becoming a trap into which one can easily fall.

In engineering control terms, this is called a positive feedback loop ("positive" because it is self-reinforcing), but there is nothing positive about its effect on the project cost. Even the schedule-remedying intent can be thwarted by the addition of a cycle or two of extra rework required as a result of the reduced work quality. Hence, to Brooks's Law we can add the equally simplified and immodestly named Cooper's Corollary: Adding (many) people to a late development project makes it cost more—lots more.

When we activate all of these secondary effects in our typical project model, total hours climb another 45 percent, and more rework accounts for nearly two-thirds of that increase. Indeed, the rework effort grows to be nearly half of the total hours spent on the design. The added rework cycling also extends the time of performance by another three months. In a particularly vicious circle, the additional delay induces the managers to employ more overtime, too, thus incurring even more secondary impacts on productivity and work quality (and cost and schedule).

Do You Have a Reservation?

True progress in development efforts is inherently difficult to assess, so understandably we have devised surrogate measures that are easier to monitor during the conduct of projects. We count drawings issued, lines or segments of code written, the earned value of milestones met, or even simply hours spent as approximations of true work progress made. The problem is that having been taught, or feeling obligated (and under pressure), to be precise, we consistently make the mistake of believing such estimates—and taking action based on them. Although they certainly are precise (793 drawings, 45.2 percent, . . .), they are not accurate. It is like measuring time with a much too-fast digital watch—quite a precise display of 4:52, but three significant digits are superfluous when you cannot even trust the first to be accurate.[10]

In deciding how and when to staff, we too often depend on the precise but inaccurate "digital watch" when we assess the readiness of prerequisite work products to support the execution of the next dependent tasks. The bean count of prerequisite work done may indicate we can staff up on the dependent stage of work. But we need to take better account—even if approximate—of the quality of the work logged as done when making staffing decisions. The quality of that work—the extent to which it will or will not need reworking—is important to gauge because staffing and working dependent tasks will incorporate the same errors, or derivations thereof, and thus create more rework cycling in the downstream efforts as well.

The prerequisite work may take any of several forms—for example, design information on drawings, customer-supplied information or equipment, vendor products, software specs, steel framing, or electronic circuitry. In the case of engineering drawings, some contractors annotate known missing segments or information with a "reservation" (literally the word *reserved*, or a similar notation on the diagram or document). Despite the reservation, however, the drawing is counted as released, and the dependent efforts (within the design stages, or in procurement, or in production) are staffed as though the tally of drawings reflects work really done.

The diagram in Figure 24.9 displays this additional pathway through which management decisions affect projects and their rework cycle. In determining appropriate staffing levels, managers consider the apparent availability of prerequisite tasks' work products. But poor quality of that prerequisite work will cause unintended reductions in subsequent productivity and work quality. And the more aggressively the project (or stage) is staffed in this condition, the more people and work that are subject to these adverse impacts.

When we add to the simulation of the same project these unintended but real productivity and quality effects caused by staffing dependent work while "quality" problems remain in upstream work products, project costs climb an additional 40 percent, and completion time is four months later still. Rework is up disproportionately (it is nearly three-quarters of the total increase in hours; the rest is from reduced productivity), now accounting for over 50 percent of the design effort. In other words, the simulation is now sufficiently realistic as to behave like most difficult development projects.

FIGURE 24.9. PATHS OF INFLUENCE FROM STAFFING ON LOW-QUALITY WORK.

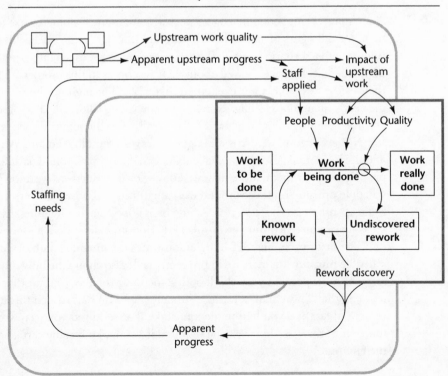

Those of us to whom project managers report, whether inside the organization or as paying customers, are often the most guilty parties. Eager to see progress on an important development, we commit one of two serious errors. The first is that we micromanage, instructing the project manager to staff up (prematurely), not knowing any better ourselves. Or we effectively do so by criticizing the manager (or as a customer, the manager's executive) for failing to staff up (enough, according to plan, or in the face of missing a near-term schedule milestone). We assert that the low staffing will "jeopardize the future of the project," and we lay the basis for, or induce the fear of, retribution. Retribution can take many forms: job loss or demotion, delayed payments, disallowed costs, the prospect of losing future business, intransigence on a variety of to-be-approved or negotiated items, even legal claims—all this when the smartest, best thing to do for the project cost and final completion schedule is to restrain staffing temporarily.

The second thing we do is create an environment or relationship through intimidation in which the project manager, if he or she wishes to remain employed, knows better than to own up to prior work's not *really* being ready. Thus, the project manager staffs as though the prior work had no problems.

Your Parents Were Right All Along

A group of bright young managers were in a company training course to prepare them for the rigors of taking on full program management responsibilities. Confronted with a scenario in which the program they were "managing" was falling behind schedule, they were asked about their responses to this prospect. The glee in their eyes was visible, their excitement palpable. Throughout the responses was the nearly unanimous feeling, expressed by one young fellow who had observed and absorbed the way things really work, "We really turn the screws on the engineers."

Not everything we do as managers involves a tangible action. What we say and the incidental gestures we make influence the people around us, and the people who work for them, more than we know—or is it exactly as we know? To exert schedule pressure on those around us is a natural, and nearly universal, managerial response to lagging progress. A little bit is good, sharpening the senses and increasing productivity. But like unsolicited criticism, a little goes a long way.

The diagram in Figure 24.10 demonstrates the intended path of influence of schedule pressure: an increase in productivity. It also shows the unwanted side effects. At some point in your childhood, someone, probably your mother or father, told you that "haste makes waste"—usually after you had rushed through something, only to find you had made a mistake that required you to rework it with more effort than would have been required if you had taken the care to do it right the first time.

FIGURE 24.10. PATHS OF INFLUENCE FROM SCHEDULE PRESSURE.

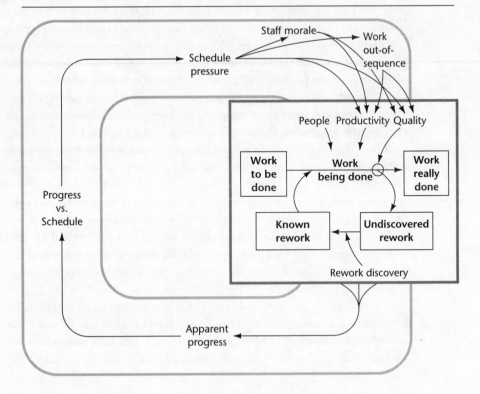

Despite the slogan posters prevalent on the walls of project offices ("If you don't have time to do it right the first time, where will you find the time to do it again?"), it does not seem that we have learned the lesson our parents tried so hard to deliver. "The harder I work, the behinder I get" is the worker's response to the slogan posters. But work hard (and fast) they do, knowing managers want to see product. The quality impact (the later need to do it again) is far less visible but no less real.

Equally real are longer-term impacts of sustained pressures. Every experienced manager has seen the considerable morale impacts when the staff is pressured from all sides to improve not only on the schedule, but also the costs and the quality.

Beyond these secondary effects on productivity and quality, Figure 24.10 depicts yet another cause-and-effect pathway of influence often activated by schedule pressure. In such a highly pressured condition, engineers (or programmers or just about anyone else) are induced to work on something—anything—that will demonstrate "progress" is being made. This usually translates into working more and more out of sequence, that is, on items that plans or cold logic indicate should be done later in the work sequence, when more of their prerequisites (products or information) would be available. "But surely parts of those items could be worked now [even if we aren't quite as efficient in doing them], and, why, we could even release those items [so they will add to our bean count, even if they need to be re-worked later]." So with this familiar refrain, of which we are nearly all guilty, we trigger the desired short-term apparent progress gains and set the stage for even more trouble later when the resulting rework gets recognized.

Once more we will add these effects, at the strengths we have seen them operate in many development projects and programs, to the simulation model. The results should be no surprise. That young manager-in-training and his turn-the-screws plan, though typical, hurts final project performance far more than any temporary gain, through its unintended effects on the rework cycle.

The poorer performance generally shows up in the latter half of the effort, as the pressures mount well into the project. Rework effort now accounts for about 60 percent of the total hours spent on design and causes the vast majority of the 100,000–hour increase.

Indeed, all of the previously cited effects are aggravated as the project performance has become worse (more real)—part of what one of our clients has termed a "death spiral." Oddly, some find that term more descriptive than the "mutually reinforcing interconnection among several causal feedback loops."

It was such an innocent-looking project at the start. Each step along the way added some more troubles and realism. The "normal" managerial responses, all aimed at exerting control, brought unintended side effects and penalties through paths of influence generally not well understood, or at least underestimated. The entire sequence of phenomena described earlier are real consequences drawn from real development projects. The quantitative effects on project performance are shown in the following charts of project simulation results.

Figure 24.11 helps illustrate just how far we "progressed." The counterproductive countermeasures added 600,000 hours to the design effort (a); X plots show the original conditions, P plots the final) through productivity losses (b) and more rework (c), *especially* rework, which alone increased by 500,000 hours. A plan-beating staff profile that had peaked in mid–1992 at *150* people became a serious overrun, with a second peak at *250* people, a year later.

Simulation results plotted in Figure 24.12 show that by mid–1993, when the build effort was under way, the original simulation displayed a perception of design readiness (a) near 95 percent (and accounting for the undiscovered rework, really was at 75 percent; see b). The final, real project simulation displayed a perceived design readiness of 85 percent at the same time (a), but much more undiscovered rework meant the design product was really only 50 percent complete (b).

FIGURE 24.11. THE PROJECT, WITH AND WITHOUT THE EFFECTS OF COUNTERINTUITIVELY COUNTERPRODUCTIVE COUNTERMEASURES.

a: Design Staff

b: Design Productivity

c: Design Staff Allocated to Rework

FIGURE 24.12. MORE ABOUT THE PROJECT, WITH AND WITHOUT THE EFFECTS OF COUNTERINTUITIVELY COUNTERPRODUCTIVE COUNTERMEASURES.

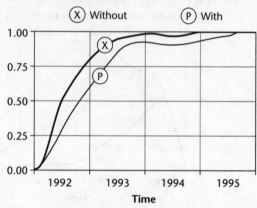

a: Fraction of Design Reported Complete

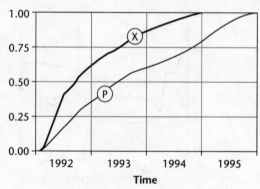

b: Fraction of Design Really Complete

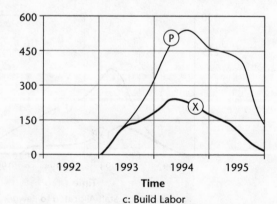

c: Build Labor

While we have focused on the design effort, the build (construction/production) effort has been being simulated all along. And the difference between the two extreme conditions, in terms of engineering readiness and the magnitude of design changes, is enough to cause more than a doubling in build labor costs (see Figure 24.12c) *and* a full year's slippage. Rather than comfortably beating the budget, the labor costs were more than twice the budget (and this does not count the added costs of any support staff incurring more expenditures as such level-of-effort functions are continued for a longer time or any increased unit costs for another year of inflation).

Doing It

If we do know what to do, we certainly are not doing it. Having spent much space diagnosing why common countermeasures fail, let us summarize what *to* do, and ask why we do not:

What to Do

- Restrain the use of real overtime (reported or not) to short bursts—less than 25 percent for no more than two months.
- Hire and use only the most qualified people. Let your competitors have the rest; yours will more than pay back the premium you pay.
- Schedule and plan the phases of work so as to achieve time separation between technically dependent elements. Otherwise, undiscovered rework will thwart the attempted acceleration and add cost.
- Resist pressures to build up staffing at the start of work or work phases faster than you can efficiently deploy them to ready tasks (you will save enormous rework effort later).
- Count on those tasks not being as ready as you think, if they are at all dependent on prior complex work or design activity. There *is* undiscovered rework lurking.
- Find and fix the undiscovered rework as a top priority—the earlier the better. This is one of the few purposes to which extra people, systems, tools, and money can be put to universal benefit. Encourage rework discovery.
- Cut the links from schedule pressure (all projects have it) to productivity and quality. Set clear priorities among work quality, cost, and schedule (preferably in that order; all will benefit). Discourage taking work shortcuts and working out of sequence. Prohibit the release of incomplete work products to (and their use by) dependent work elements.
- Use systems and procedures that acknowledge rework. Behave as though preventing rework is your top priority. It is. A close second is finding the inevitable rework that will still exist.[11]

These represent a cohesive and consistent set of good things to do in managing a project, but they are not common practice (despite being common sense). Why not? There are just two general possibilities: (1) we know what to do but lack the courage or incentive to do it; or (2) we have not learned what to do. We have seen both conditions among the many organizations we have analyzed. There are certainly some individuals who know what to do but operate in companies and project settings that discourage taking the right managerial actions, and so opt instead for short-term (perception of) progress. Such individuals are like candles in the night—a windy night. It takes not too many being snuffed for others to get the message.[12] Even in this setting, however, the real failure is the organization management's or customer's lack of having learned the magnitude of gains achievable by taking the correct, even though short-term painful, actions.

So it is that by far the most common condition that prevails throughout all kinds and sizes of organizations and projects, among all levels of management, is the failure to learn. Without the failure to learn from past successes and past problems, the first three failures would no longer exist.

Failure 4: Failure to Know What's What, or Lessons Not Learned

The failure to learn is the most pervasive failure in all project management, even among organizations dependent on successful projects for income, new products and services, new processes and technology, and thus competitive advantage.

Four different conditions have contributed to and perpetuated this failure. First among these is the misguided belief that all projects are different, that there is little to learn from others. (A common version of this appears in the near-unanimous belief, "But *my* project is different.") The roots of this misconception are in the genuine lack of understanding of the very common dynamics and phenomena shared by virtually all projects (Paul Revere, meet Wall Street).

Second, projects are by definition a transient phenomenon, with a start and an end. Each is time pressured. We are rushed to start, rushed to end, and rushed to start again. Put the past behind us. Failure? No need to point fingers, unpleasant to relive the disaster anyway. Success? Lucky. Easy customer. No challenge. Overbudgeted. Heroic individual effort. There are few companies (there are a few, and they are successful; the software world is beginning to show how, such as at Microsoft) whose organizations and money and systems and practices span projects, for the very purpose of gleaning and improving on transferable lessons of project management.

Even in the absence of organizational learning systems, there are individuals who learn. Great project managers might have three or four great projects that make up their career before they move to different responsibilities or retire. From this we should expect systematic assessment and learning of transferable lessons that get incorporated in subsequent projects? This limited span and career path of good project managers is the third contributor to the failure to learn.

The fourth and final contributing condition is the lingering lack of esteem in which project and program management has been held historically. (Some would assert this is an earned perception, but that is from lack of performance, not lack of importance.) There are no corporate-ego-level mergers or takeovers here, no big-ticket sales. Few business schools feature project management—the exciting worlds of accounting and finance, organization theory, production management, marketing, international business, business law, and statistics, yes—but precious little on the discipline of project management, which requires all of the aforementioned subject skills and more.

Some organizations have begun to recognize that project management is nothing less than the lifeblood of change, the channel of innovation, the definitive source of competitive advantage from which all new refinements, products, and services come to market to create income growth, shareholder value, and societal advancement. Again, look to the software industry, built solely on projects: projects to define, develop, and market new items. Should one ever doubt the value of such projects, take note that Microsoft alone now has a market value that exceeds that of General Motors, AT&T, Sears and CBS combined.[13]

Conclusion

These, then, are the four systemic project failures:

1. *Failure to know what to expect.* Excessive optimism and lack of discipline in defining the product, the cost budget, and the work schedule set the stage for disruptive change, counterproductive pressures, and management actions that worsen performance beyond the inaccuracy in the plans themselves.
2. *Failure to know what to watch.* Understanding the rework cycle in projects is a fundamental requirement for accurate monitoring, progress assessment, and decision making, yet it is absent from all conventional project management systems.
3. *Failure to know what to do (and to do it).* Lack of understanding the multiple cause-and-effect paths through which our decisions cause secondary impacts on productivity, rework, and total project performance leads us to take common counterproductive management actions.

4. *Failure to know what's what.* This failure—the failure to learn—is most critical; it perpetuates the other failures and denies managers and organizations the understanding of the need for, content of, and impact achievable from systemic project management improvement.

Organizations that do not overcome the four failures will themselves fail in a competitive world. Those that do will thrive and grow. To accomplish this, the winning organizations will develop and deploy learning systems for project management. These systems will be used to cull lessons from past projects; disseminate those lessons by training current and prospective project managers; monitor ongoing projects for deviations from expectations; dispassionately and rigorously diagnose the deviations to determine positive and negative lessons and affirmation of prior lessons; feed back that diagnostic information for analysis and subsequent dissemination; plan and schedule new projects based on the rigorous past project performance analysis; educate internal and external customers; and build a culture that sets out incentives and rewards early problem detection, preemptive management, and ongoing lesson transfer and improvement. Organizations operating in this project management learning system will see success build on success and increasingly distance themselves from their failing competitors.

CHAPTER TWENTY-FIVE

THE FUTURE OF PROJECT MANAGEMENT

Jeffrey K. Pinto

What is the future of project management? Clearly, we have no more prescient a crystal ball than do others, but as the chapter authors have demonstrated, we can offer some suppositions based on our experience and the state of the industrial world as we near the millennium. We are convinced that the importance of project management for organizational success will expand rather than wane in the years to come. In this chapter I will discuss some of the reasons that it is possible see a proliferation in project management and subsequent increasing demand for project management skills in the years to come. Finally, I will suggest that companies need to become more systematic in their approach to developing project managers who have the tools and abilities to get the job done.

In the larger context of international business, attempts to make projections regarding the future are often met with skepticism, wariness, and even amusement, as in cases when prognosticators are confronted with their guesses years later. Peter Drucker, the well-known management consultant and writer, is particularly leery of organizations' becoming overly infatuated with the future, arguing that those who forecast the future and make strategic decisions on the basis of probabilities and current trends are generally unlikely to succeed in the

Note: Substantial portions of this chapter were excerpted from Pinto, J. K., & Kharbanda, O. P. (1995). *Successful project managers.* New York: Van Nostrand Reinhold, chap. 18.

long term.[1] Nevertheless, the future does hold out some tremendous opportunities in addition to its threats and uncertainty. For project management organizations, in particular, there are some encouraging signs that point to the likelihood of a tremendous upsurge in market demand for their services and techniques.

The Age of Project Management

"The Age of Project Management" derives from the title of an article by a well-known project management scholar, David Cleland, who painted a convincing portrait of the state of project management in the international sphere and demonstrated the basis for supposing that project management will increase in importance in years to come.[2] We can list the reasons behind the expectation that project management techniques will gain in popularity: dramatically shortened market windows and product life cycles, rapid development of Third World and the former closed economies, increasingly complex and technical products, heightened international competition, and the environment of organizational resource scarcity that has led to downsizing and streamlining operations. Let us consider each of these reasons in turn.

Shortened Market Windows and Product Life Cycles

One piece of evidence of the turbulent changes that are affecting the business world is the degree to which product obsolescence has been advanced. Traditionally, in many industries, product launches could be carefully crafted and planned because companies knew that they had a comfortably wide window of opportunity to develop, test, and market new products. For example, the IBM System 360, which so revolutionized mainframe computing, continued as a viable product for nearly a decade. A more recent example concerns the IBM Personal Computer, the PC. This benchmark 64K RAM microcomputer, launched in the early 1980s, was the industry standard for almost five years. One has only to contrast those examples to more recent PC product announcements and launches to realize that such lengthy product life cycles, particularly in the computer hardware and software industries, are a thing of the past. Indeed, the technology is moving so rapidly today that year-old PCs are often literally passé.

What these and other examples point to is the impact that market timing has made on new product development. I recently spent several months working with a large computer manufacturer's project teams. Their strategic planning and new product development departments routinely prepare for new product delivery and system modification introductions that are sometimes two years into the future.

For example, it was common to hear hardware engineers and project managers developing time frames for future product delivery that had to occur within a three-month market window. If the project was late, it was useless because a rival would have exploited the opening and offered a substitute product.

These time-to-market pressures and shortened product life cycles have had a significant impact on more and more organizations as they seek to counter such threats through the use of project teams. Cross-functional teams and project management techniques have had a major impact on a number of companies and their ability to deliver new products within significantly shorter time frames. For example, in 1989 Honda was touted for its "superfast" approach to new product innovation. Using team approaches, Honda had shortened the time frame for new automobile development from five to three years. While a significant achievement, Honda's team approach was just the beginning of innovative process changes in the automotive industry. By 1994, Chrysler CEO Robert Lutz was able to announce that the Viper Platform (cross-functional) Team had designed, developed, engineered, and produced a new prototype in eighteen months. Less than four years later, the cycle time has dropped to approximately fifteen months.

Other examples abound. Motorola's order-to-finished-goods manufacturing cycle for its pagers has been shortened from three weeks to two hours. Hewlett Packard can now produce electronic testing equipment in five days compared to the old four-week processing time. These innovations have come about through a realization that dynamic changes in the business environment are forcing companies to become more aware of the need to move products to market at a faster and faster pace, in order to take advantage of market windows and allow for technological changes that render products obsolete at an increasingly rapid pace. Embedded in this realization has been the increased use of project teams and project management techniques to maximize organizational resources and creative processes while giving development teams the freedom from bureaucracy and red tape that can often strangle innovation.

Rapid Development of Third World and Closed Economies

One of the astounding by-products of the opening of the former Soviet Union, Eastern Europe, and Asian communist countries has been the explosion in pent-up demand within these societies for all manner of consumer goods and infrastructure development. Wherever one turns in examining the developing sectors of the international economy, it is easy to discover examples of projects either underway or about to be initiated. Vietnam has recently opened its borders to a number of foreign corporations and initiated a massive program for infrastructure and industrial expansion. The People's Republic of China, nominally the world's largest communist state, has been increasingly eager to encourage consumerism and pockets of capitalism within its largest cities. Further, project management groups from major industrial construction firms in the United States, Europe, and Japan are in serious negotiations with the Chinese government for a number of large-scale development projects of every sort.

Eastern Europe stands poised to take advantage of project management in the drive to modernize industries in the wake of a democratic revolution that has replaced the old command economies with market-driven capitalism. Old, inefficient factories are being closed and torn down or upgraded to turn out new products. Although there are very real limits on funding for revitalization of their industries, the nature of the economies of Eastern Europe is such that capital development is likely to continue, albeit slowly at first, for several decades.

Despite the current recession in international economies, the construction industry continues to boom in Asia, which now accounts for over 60 percent of the worldwide construction and continues to grow rapidly. This development has been a positive windfall for Japanese, European, and American contractors.[3] An October 26, 1989, *Wall Street Journal* article described the enormous capital expansion program underway in Japan, a program that is expected to grow at a double-digit pace through the end of the 1990s. It is likely that project management will continue to play a key role in this expansion, not only within the borders of Japan but within other countries that manufacture and market Japanese products.[4]

Not too long ago, the *Asian Wall Street Journal* (April 18, 1994) carried a fourteen–page supplement entitled, "Asian Infrastructure—Asia Transforms Itself." The article went to some length to examine many of the most pressing demands for major infrastructure development and expansion. It is clear that although huge spending on infrastructure in Asia is imperative, the governments of these countries simply cannot pay the enormous cost associated with these megaprojects. Consequently, this situation offers enormous scope for the private sector, both local but particularly, foreign companies, to exploit these needs.

To illustrate the nature of the level of development currently being undertaken or conceived in these Asian countries, consider some of the examples summarized in Table 25.1, each representing a megaproject forecast to cost in excess of $1 billion. And this is just a representational list of some of the more exciting megaprojects that are currently being developed in the Asian world. Perhaps even more intriguing is the list of the largest contractors for these projects.

The rapid development of these countries offers some lucrative possibilities for private companies, including European and American heavy construction firms. Among the top ten list of contractors for these projects are Bechtel Corporation, M. W. Kellog, John Brown/Davy, Fluor Daniel, and Brown and Root.

TABLE 25.1. PROJECT FORECASTS FOR ASIAN COUNTRIES.

Country	Number of Projects	Cost Range ($ Billions)	Largest Project
China	7	1–77	Dam and hydropower station
Hong Kong	3	1–20	Airport
India	2	1–2	Enron power plant
Indonesia	4	1–2.5	Coal-fired power plant
Malaysia	5	1–5.6	Dam and hydropower station
Philippines	1	1.3	Elevated rail system
Singapore	4	1–5	Power station
South Korea	6	1–20	Superhighway system
Taiwan	5	5–17	Mass rapid transit system
Thailand	4	1.5–4.3	Airport

As more companies turn to the developing markets of the Pacific Rim, it is likely that new names will be added to this list.

Several of the projects listed are being rushed through to completion because they are desperately needed by their clients, the governments of the countries. In moving these projects through the pipeline quickly, two differing approaches used by the project organizations are very much in evidence. One model, referred to as BOT, involves the steps (1) build, (2) operate, and (3) transfer, as the contractor completes the facility, brings it to an operating mode, and then transfers ownership to the client. The other variant is called BOOT, referring to the steps (1) build, (2) own, (3) operate, and (4) transfer, in which the contractor takes initial ownership of the facility or project as part of a licensing agreement before eventually turning it over to the government as it is purchased. The latter, in particular, is an exciting concept that has already been translated into reality in several locations.[5]

Increasingly Complex and Technical Products

Many of the products that are being created today in a variety of industries, from children's toys to automobiles, are becoming more technically complex to develop, manufacture, and use. Technologically driven innovation presents a tremendous challenge for organizations in the areas of engineering and design, production, and marketing. As a result, many organizations are relying on project teams composed of cross-functional groups to create and move to market these products in as efficient a time frame as possible.

Rework cycles are expensive and often come about through poor internal communication between functional departments, all of which are expected to co-operate in bringing a new product to market.[6] In many instances, the new product introduction process consists of a series of cycled loops from one functional area to another. For example, consider a simplified case in which a new electronics consumer product is slated for introduction. Typically we would see some sort of causal chain set in motion, in which engineering would first design the product and send the specifications to production. The production department, presented with the design details, might object to certain aspects of the products (perhaps due to manufacturing process limitations that do not allow for all of the features engineering originally included in the product) and will then return the product plans to engineering for rework.

Following this loop, engineering may or may not make enough modifications to satisfy production. Perhaps a couple of iterations of this loop will be needed before production is sufficiently agreeable to the design that they will then begin prototype development. At this point, in many organizations, marketing is finally brought on board and given the opportunity to comment on the prototype. Depending on their experience with and knowledge of other competing products in the marketplace, they may offer suggestions that will once again cycle the product back to engineering for additional rework, all the while holding up development and new product launch.

It is easy to see how unwieldy such a causal chain is when an organization is faced with the pressures of new product introduction. Consequently, many of these companies are scrapping this new product introduction strategy and employing cross-functional teams from the beginning of the process, believing, with ample supporting evidence, that allowing all relevant departments immediate access to and ability to influence new product designs will significantly shorten time-to-market delivery.

Heightened International Competition

Competition drives innovation. It is only in the face of substitutable products that organizations are compelled to upgrade, alter, or develop new and innovative products of their own. In the past, American manufacturers have had the economic playing field to themselves for a variety of reasons, many associated with the impact of World War II on other industrialized nations and the slow industrial advance of developing countries. During this period, U.S. companies had enormous domestic markets to exploit, leading to a sense of hubris, which sowed the seeds for later problems. On the other hand, foreign manufacturing was in its infancy and suffering from the teething problems associated with new start-up companies: poor quality, lack of name recognition, uncertain marketing strategies, and so forth. Although this was truly a golden age for American business, clearly this was not a state that could continue indefinitely, in spite of many companies' belief that in fact it would.

It was not until the late 1960s that any appreciable inroads were made into traditional American markets such as automobiles. However, during the 1970s, the oil shocks and Japanese manufacturing skills combined with lower unit prices served to threaten seriously many strategic and consumer industries, such as steel, computers, electronic data systems (copiers), and electronic consumer goods (television). These economic attacks, although painful, offered a mixed blessing in that they served to shake many U.S. companies out of the inertia and sense of complacency into which they had sunk.

In many industries, domestic counterattacks have been spurred on by increased use of project management. One of the fortunate side effects of the pressures placed on American firms was in forcing them to develop innovative processes for survival in a new, international marketplace for which they were underequipped and did not foresee with accuracy. Project management has a long history in certain industries, such as airframe development at Boeing and McDonnell-Douglas. However, one of the effects of the end of American corporate lethargy was to convince other companies, many with no experience in project management, to look on it as a new and useful tool for competitive advantage. One of the more appealing aspects of my project management teaching and consulting experiences has been the number of companies in a diverse array of industries that are experimenting with project management for the first time. Properly trained and schooled in its techniques, these firms stand to reap substantial benefits within the international marketplace through speedier product development and greater efficiency of operations.

The Environment of Organizational Resource Scarcity

Organizations have never existed in a truly munificent environment in which resource acquisition presented no challenges or concerns. Companies have always been forced to operate in pursuit of a variety of scarce resources: money, trained personnel, plant and equipment, and so forth. Nevertheless, the current uncertain economic conditions have led to a new management philosophy: an age of belief in the need to do more with less. This new approach has had the practical result of leading to many organizations' downsizing and streamlining operations in pursuit of cost savings and efficiency.

From an operations perspective, the impact of such corporate downsizing has been to create increased demands on those who remain to perform as effectively as possible within a resource-scarce atmosphere. In this regard, several of these organizations (Kodak among them) are relying to greater and greater degrees on project management to provide the dual benefits of rapid product development and time to market within greater cost controls and budgetary limitations. These companies, some using project management for the first time in a formal manner, have discovered one of the important features of these techniques: their use gives project teams the ability to be both externally effective in getting products to market and internally efficient in their use of organizational resources.

Project management is predicated on the ability to use resources carefully; in effect, the techniques are themselves resource constrained. Consequently, in an atmosphere of efficiency and streamlining operations, project management offers a valuable tool for companies to exploit, as many currently are doing.

These are some of the compelling reasons that we are likely to continue to witness an increase of interest in and use of project management in international businesses. As Cleland noted, the strategic thrust of many businesses and, indeed, many countries points to a continued drive to improve, upgrade, modernize, and develop their infrastructures, markets, and capital and natural resources bases.[7] In this context, the benefits of project management are substantial and clearly equipped to provide these countries and their business organizations with a powerful tool for effective and efficient operations.

At the same time that we can look with hope to an expansion in the use of project management, it is perhaps ironic to point out the dangers in creating overly optimistic expectations about project management as a business technique. It is true that project management is the management of change, versus traditional functional management, which often solidifies the status quo. As a result, project management is ideally situated to serve as a platform on which many organizations can achieve the degrees of flexibility and efficiency needed for long-term survival and prosperity. Because much is expected from the project management movement, it is also helpful to consider some reasoned words of warning on how to avoid the "flash in the pan" sobriquet so often attached to the latest management technique. As Barnes and Wearne write, "Project management is the management of uncertainty, and its future must itself be uncertain. . . . No technique with a distinctive name achieves what its enthusiasts hope for it or lasts as long as they expect. The same could be true of project management itself."[8]

While we may hope and believe that the authors' concerns are overstated, nevertheless, they strike an appropriate note of caution that must be considered. The worst future for project management would be to create a new organizational buzzword out of the technique, leading too many companies with too high expectations to begin jumping on the bandwagon in hopes of achieving quick and painless solutions to their problems. Like any other useful management tool or technique, project management will work to the degree that organizations employing it do so in a measured and thoughtful approach, understanding its strengths and limitations. Overly ambitious programs without the necessary level of commitment and support could do the worst possible damage to the project management profession by turning the techniques into simply another in a line of faddish techniques that was tried by ill-informed and unprepared companies, failed predictably, and was dismissed as ineffective.

Conclusion

In an environment of soaring costs, rapidly increasing complexity, and diminishing natural resources, organizations find themselves confronted with the specter of having to make do with less and less. Corporate profitability and long-term survival are predicated on their ability to continue to grow, offer the public new and innovative products and services, and find competitive niches that enable them to survive and prosper. It is within this context of diminishing resources, cost cutting, streamlining operations, and slashing overhead and excessive personnel that project management techniques can offer a lucrative form of competitive advantage for those firms that have taken the time to learn and use it well.

Project management, a philosophy and technique based on the ideas of performing to maximum potential within the constraints of limited resources, offers a logical and attractive method for increasing profitability in a number of areas of business. Further, the rapid expansion of Asia, Eastern Europe, and Latin American economies will continue to drive a concomitant expansion in development, building, infrastructure repair and improvement, as well as within the industrial sectors of their economies. Many, if not most, of these pushes for expansion will be fueled by project management techniques.

With the future so bright for expanding the role of project management on a worldwide basis, the only potential clouds on the horizon concern the ability of more and more governments and businesses to perform these techniques well. The lack of formal training for many future project managers is worrisome and must be corrected, particularly through the development of a common skill set and body of knowledge.[9] The rise of project management as a profession is likely to be a key element in these countries' ability to use the techniques to their maximum potential, so key to the continued development and industrial expansion around the world.

NOTES

Chapter One

1. Project management in its modern form was developed almost entirely by the U.S. Air Force, with help from the National Aeronautics and Space Administration and the U.S. Navy. Du Pont and the construction industry developed the critical path method and precedence scheduling. See Morris P. W. G. (1994). *The management of projects.* London: Thomas Telford.

2. Morris, P. W. G. (1988). Managing project interfaces—Key points for project success. In D. I. Cleland & W. R. King (Eds.), *Project management handbook.* New York: Van Nostrand Reinhold.

3. Morris (1988).

4. It was a major issue in developing the recent Construction Industry Board paper on construction strategy, for example. Construction Industry Board. (1998). *Construction strategy.* London: Thomas Telford. It is reflected in the recent report on government building project management: *Construction procurement.* (1995). Report by the Cabinet Efficiency Unit. London: HMSO.

5. Even in these sectors, many companies are now using innovative financing techniques more frequently to fund projects, although the impact on the project's management is less dramatic here than in public sector Build Operate Transfer (BOT) projects.

6. The trend toward private sector financing is just one aspect of a broader trend toward privatization. This trend is driven predominantly by the belief in the greater efficiency of the private sector over the public sector. It is also driven by the desire to reduce public spending and hence ease budgetary pressure and the fiscal burden. BOT schemes are similarly driven by both but, many observers believe, principally by the attraction of short-term fiscal

and budgetary benefits to governments. Certainly there is justified concern that the cost of these projects to the customer over the longer term is higher than the traditionally funded projects. One is essentially substituting lower capital spending today for higher revenue spending tomorrow.

7. There is some confusion over terminology. Generally, value management is taken to cover the five distinct study levels of brief, concept, scheme, detail design, and procurement. The first two are generally called *value planning* in the United States and the last three *value engineering*. In Europe the term *value analysis* is commonly used.

8. Concurrent engineering is the practice of having mixed teams—for example, of marketing, design, and production management—working together to create the best combination of needs definition, design, and production know-how, as opposed to the traditional approach of simply "throwing plans over the wall" from one department to another over the project life cycle. It may involve work proceeding in parallel on several work packages simultaneously. (Here information technology becomes important.) It does not imply beginning production implementation before design is stable, which was the meaning of the old term, much used in defense and aerospace, of *concurrency*.

9. A second major source of difficulty has been inadequate planning and preparation, and a third has been beginning implementation before the design is stable. Prototyping and modeling prior to sanctioning implementation help significantly to manage all these areas of major project difficulty.

10. This has led to the term *portfolio management* in contemporary production management. See, for example, Wheelwright, S. C., & Clark, K. B. (1992). Creating project plans to focus product development. *Harvard Business Review, 70,* 70–82; Pisano, G. P., & Wheelwright, S. C. (1995). The new logic of R&D. *Harvard Business Review, 73,* 93–107.

11. CASE was originally defined as *computer-aided software engineering*. Later it slipped into *computer-aided systems engineering*. The translation was misleading, for the CASE approach, which concentrates on specification of requirements and attributes, analysis, and design, works best in a digital software environment where project performance is relatively closed and predictable. Systems in general may be more analogue with greater openness and unpredictability. CASE tools are then less useful.

12. *Fast track* is used here in a way that purists would say is technically wrong. The purists would contend that *fast track* is the general term for beginning production implementation before the design is complete. In many instances, this is synonymous with *concurrency*. *Fast track* was used in this way in the North Sea in the 1970s through to the mid-1980s. A form of design-production does exist, however, that is relatively secure; this is *fast build*, which is described technically incorrectly as *fast track/fast build*. The practice basically came from the United States but was pioneered in the United Kingdom in the 1980s on major London commercial development projects such as Broadgate and Canary Wharf.

13. A consequence of the need to integrate operations information into the design stage has been the need generally to improve data integration between project stages and between projects. This requires data from many different systems to interact. Arising directly from ILS—strictly from the U.S. CALS (Computer Aided Logistics Support program)—has risen STEP, the international Standard for Exchange of Product model data, which is designed to achieve just this. STEP is at quite an advanced stage of implementation in various project industries, such as aerospace, process engineering, shipbuilding, structural engineering, and building.

14. The fully projectized and the matrix forms of organization are the two basic ways of obtaining resources from within the enterprise. There has been much discussion of the problem that staff working in the matrix organization experience having "two bosses": the functional manager and the project manager. The best way to deal with this conflict is to treat it as a procurement exercise: the project manager should procure, or contract with, the functional department—engineering, for example, or value management—for the supply of so many hours of the functional specialists' time, over what period, and at what price. Formalizing the procurement of services in this way clarifies who is responsible to whom, for what, and at what cost.

15. There is much confusion over terminology. One view is that *partnering* is generally taken to refer to multiproject relationships, *alliancing* to single-project ones. In the U.S. oil industry, however, the definitions would be the other way around. Another view is that *alliancing* refers to partnerships having aggressive cost-saving targets, while *partnering* refers to working together on aligned principles. Framework contracts use project contracts that enable the owner to call off the supplier to do work without having to rebid the package from scratch.

16. The bases of project management are evolution through the common project life cycle, single point integration of all that is necessary to achieve project success, procurement of external resources and/or building of temporary teams, and the use of special planning and control techniques. These bases apply in all project situations, which is why project management is to an extent transferable, and why project management lessons can be learned from looking across and between industries.

17. For example, bill of quantities (BOQs)–based control. While BOQs indeed provide earned value information, they normally cover only the construction contract. They do not provide control over design and engineering, manufacturing and delivery, or project management, for example—areas where it is equally important to control cost and schedule performance.

Chapter Two

1. The material in this section is taken from Cleland, D. I. (1996). *The strategic management of teams.* New York: Wiley. Used by permission of John Wiley & Sons.
2. Description of these components is taken from Cleland, D. I. (1994). *Project management: Strategic design and implementation* (pp. 237–245). New York: McGraw-Hill. Used with permission of the McGraw-Hill Companies.
3. Labich, K. (1994, November 14). Why companies fail. *Fortune*, pp. 52–68.
4. Editorial. (1996, February 5). *Business Week.*
5. Taylor, W. (1993, March–April). Message and muscle. *Harvard Business Review*, pp. 99–100.
6. Jasinowski, J., & Hamrin, R. (1995). *Making it in America.* New York: Simon & Schuster.
7. DeSimone, L. D. (1995, November–December). Perspectives. *Harvard Business Review*, p. 184.
8. Norman, J. R. (1994, October 10). A very nimble elephant. *Forbes*, pp. 88–92.
9. Jasinowski & Hamrin (1995), pp. 61–62.
10. Jasinowski & Hamrin (1995), pp. 163–164.
11. Stewart, T. A. (1996, February 5). 3M fights back. *Fortune*, pp. 94–99.

12. Henkoff, R. (1995, November 27). New management secrets from Japan. *Fortune,* p. 140.

13. Andrews, K. Z. (1995, September–October). Strategic decision making. *Harvard Business Review,* pp. 10–11.

14. Ghoshal, S., & Bartlett, C. A. (1995, January-February). Changing the role of top management: Beyond structure to processes. *Harvard Business Review,* pp. 86–96.

Chapter Three

1. Project Management Institute. (1987). *Project management body of knowledge.* Drexel Hill, PA: Project Management Institute.

2. Frame, J. D. (1994). *The new project management.* San Francisco: Jossey-Bass.

3. Lundin, R. A., & Söderholm, A. (1995). A theory of the temporary organization. *Scandinavian Journal of Management, 11,* 437–455.

4. Lundin, R. A., & Wirdenius, H. (1989). *Företagsförnyelse och kulturskifte: Erfarenheter från Diöskoncernen* [Corporate renewal and cultural change: Experiences from the Diös Group]. Stockholm: Norstedts.

5. Ekstedt, E., Lundin, R. A., & Wirdenius, H. (1992). Conceptions and renewal in Swedish construction companies. *European Management Journal, 10,* 202–208.

Chapter Four

1. Williams, G. (1995, September 4). Enron: Maybe megadeals mean megarisk. *Business Week,* pp. 52–53.

2. Heath, R. (1995, June 3). Hell's highway. *New Scientist,* pp. 22–25.

3. Padgham, H. F. (1991, April). The Milwaukee Water Pollution Abatement Program: Its stakeholder management. *pmNETwork,* pp. 6–18.

4. Pendergast, J. (1993, July). Pioneer Highway. *Civil Engineering,* pp. 36–39.

5. Walker, G., & Myrick, J. (1994, January). Doubling a pipeline. *Civil Engineering,* pp. 50–52.

6. Martin, L., & Green, P. (1995, August). Gaining project acceptance. *Civil Engineering,* pp. 51–53.

7. The techniques described here are paraphrased in part from King, W. R., & Cleland, D. I. (1986). *Strategic planning and policy* (pp. 246–270). New York: Van Nostrand Reinhold.

8. King & Cleland (1986).

9. Padgham (1991), p. 18.

10. Wells, L. T., & Gleason, E. S. (1995, September–October). Is foreign infrastructure investment still risky? *Harvard Business Review,* pp. 44–55.

11. Carey, P. M. (1995, October–November). Urban decay. *Infrastructure Finance,* pp. 22–28.

Chapter Six

1. Hammer, M., & Champy, J. (1993). *Reengineering the corporation.* New York: HarperCollins.

2. Galbraith, J. R. (1971). Matrix organization designs. *Business Horizons, 14* (1), 29–40. See also Knight, K. (1976). Matrix organization: A review. *Journal of Management Studies, 17*(2),

111–130. Larson, E. W., & Gobeli, D. H. (1987). Matrix management: Contradictions and insights. *California Management Review, 29*(4), 126–138.

3. Davis, S. M., & Lawrence, P. R. (1977). *Matrix.* Reading, MA: Addison-Wesley. Denis, H. (1986a). Is the matrix organization a cumbersome structure for engineering projects? *Project Management Journal, 17*(1), 49–55. Galbraith (1971). Kerzner, H. (1984). *Project management: A systems approach to planning, scheduling and controlling.* New York: Van Nostrand Reinhold. Cleland, D. I., & King, W. R. (1983). *Project management handbook* (3rd ed.). New York: Van Nostrand Reinhold.

4. Wall, W. C., Jr. (1984). Integrated management in matrix organization. *IEEE Transactions on Engineering Management, 31*(1), 30–36.

5. Cleland & King (1983). Galbraith (1971). Kerzner (1984). Larson & Gobeli (1987). Meredith, J. R., & Mantel, S. J., Jr. (1995). *Project management* (2nd ed.). New York: Wiley. Might, R. J., & Fischer, W. A. (1985). The role of structural factors in determining project management success. *IEEE Transactions on Engineering Management, 32*(2), 71–77.

6. Larson & Gobeli (1987).

7. Dilworth, J. B., Ford, R. C., Ginter, P. M., & Rucks, A. C. (1985). Centralized project management. *Journal of Systems Management, 39*(8), 30–35. Katz, R., & Allen, T. J. (1985). Project performance and the locus of influence in the R&D matrix. *Academy of Management Journal, 28*(1), 67–87. Larson & Gobeli (1987). Meredith & Mantel (1989). Larson, E. W., Gobeli, D. H., & Gray, C. F. (1991). Application of project management by small business to develop new products and services. *Journal of Small Business Management, 12*(4), 30–41.

8. Gobeli, D. H., & Larson, E. W. (1986a). Project management research program: A status report. *Project Management Journal, 17*(1), 24–25. Gobeli, D. H., & Larson, E. W. (1986b). Matrix management: More than a fad. *Engineering Management International, 4,* 71–76. Gobeli, D., & Larson, E. W. (1987). Relative effectiveness of different project structures. *Project Management Journal, 18*(2), 81–85. Larson & Gobeli (1987).

9. Kerzner (1984). Larson & Gobeli (1987). Might & Fischer (1985).

10. Davis & Lawrence (1977). Galbraith (1971). Kolodny, H. F. (1979). Evolution to a matrix organization. *Academy of Management Review, 4*(4), 543–553.

11. Davis & Lawrence (1977). Kolodny (1979). Peters, T. J. (1979). Beyond the matrix organization. *Business Horizons, 22*(4), 15–27.

12. Lawson, J. W. (1986). A quick look at matrix organization from the perspective of the practicing manager. *Engineering Management International, 4,* 61–70. Wright, N. H. (1980, May). Matrix management—fortifying the organization structure. *Manufacturing World,* pp. 24–26.

13. Ford, R. C., & McLaughlin, S. (1992a, November). Successful project teams: A study of MIS managers. *IEEE Transactions in Engineering Management, 39,* 312–317.

14. Davis & Lawrence (1977). Galbraith (1971).

15. Davis & Lawrence (1977). Denis, H. (1986b). Matrix structures, quality of working life, and engineering productivity. *IEEE Transactions on Engineering Management, 33*(3), 148–156. Kolodny (1979). Larson & Gobeli (1987).

16. Davis & Lawrence (1977). Jerkovsky, W. (1983). Functional management in matrix organizations. *IEEE Transactions on Engineering Management, 30*(2), 89–97. Kolodny (1979). Kur, C. E. (1982). Making matrix management work. *Supervisory Management, 27*(3), 37–43. Larson & Gobeli (1987). Stuckenbruck, L. C. (Ed.). (1982). *The implementation of project management: The professional's handbook.* Reading, MA: Addison-Wesley.

17. Denis (1986b). White, B. (1979). Alternative forms of project organization. In R. Hill & B. J. White (Eds.), *Matrix organization and project management.* Ann Arbor: Michigan Business Papers, no. 64.

18. Denis (1986b). Gobeli & Larson (1987). Jerkovsky (1983).

19. Denis (1986b). Larson & Gobeli (1987).

20. Randolph, W. A., & Posner, B. Z. (1992). *Getting the job done: Managing project teams and task forces for success.* Englewood Cliffs, NJ: Prentice Hall. Katzenback, J. R., & Smith, D. K. (1993). *The wisdom of teams.* New York: Harper Business.

21. Davis & Lawrence (1977). Kolodny (1979).

22. Davis & Lawrence (1977). Galbraith (1971).

23. Kerzner (1984).

24. Davis & Lawrence (1977). Kolodny, H. F. (1980). Matrix organization designs and new product success. *Research Management, 23*(5), 29–33. Kolodny, H. F. (1981). Managing in a matrix. *Business Horizons, 24*(2), 17–24.

25. Kolodny (1980).

26. Barker, J., Tjosvold, D., & Andrews, R. I. (1988). Conflict approaches of effective and ineffective project managers: A field study in a matrix organization. *Journal of Management Studies, 25*(2), 167–178. Denis (1986a). Greiner, L. E., & Schein, V. E. (1981). The paradox of managing a project-oriented matrix: Establishing coherence within chaos. *Sloan Management Review, 2*(2), 17–22. Katz & Allen (1985).

27. Larson & Gobeli (1987). Katz & Allen (1985). Greiner & Schein (1981).

28. Wilemon, D. L., & Thamhain, H. J. (1983). Team building in project management. *Project Management Quarterly, 14*(3), 73–81. Denis (1986a). Kerzner (1984). Katz & Allen (1985). Barker et al. (1988).

29. Barker et al. (1988).

30. Dill, D., & Pearson, A. W. (1984). The effectiveness of project managers: Implications of a political model of influence. *IEEE Transactions on Engineering Management, 31*(3), 138–146. Posner, B. Z. (1986). What's all the fighting about? Conflicts in project management. *IEEE Transactions on Engineering Management, 33*(4), 207–211. Katz & Allen (1985). Joyce, W. F. (1986). Matrix organization: A social experiment. *Academy of Management Journal, 29*(3), 536–561.

31. Davis & Lawrence (1978). See also Wall (1984).

32. Kerzner (1984).

33. Davis & Lawrence (1978). Denis (1986a). Jerkovsky (1983). Pitts, R. A., & Daniels, J. D. (1984). Aftermath of the matrix mania. *Columbia Journal of World Business, 19*(2), 48–54.

34. Jerkovsky (1983). Kerzner (1984). Meredith & Mantel (1995). Larson & Gobeli (1987). DiMarco, N., Goodson, J. R., & Houser, H. F. (1989). Situational leadership in a project/matrix environment. *Project Management Journal, 20*(1), 11–18.

35. Jerkovsky (1983). Stuckenbruck (1982).

36. Denis (1986b).

37. Davis & Lawrence (1977), p. 78. See also Kolodny (1979).

38. Ford, R. C., Armandi, B. R., & Heaton, C. P. (1988). *Organization theory: An integrative approach.* New York: HarperCollins.

39. Randolph, W. A., & Dess, G. G. (1984). The congruence perspective of organization design: A conceptual model and multivariate research approach. *Academy of Management Review, 9*(1), 114–127.

40. Marquis, D. G., & Straight, D. M. (1963). *Organizational factors in project performance* (Working Paper No. 133–165). Cambridge, MA: Sloan School of Management, Massachusetts Institute of Technology. Mee, J. (1964). Matrix organizations. *Business Horizons, 7* (2), 70–72.

41. Ford et al. (1988).

42. Davis & Lawrence (1977). Galbraith (1971). Katz & Allen (1985). Kerzner (1984).

43. Alexander, J., & Randolph, W. A. (1985). The fit between technology and structure as a predictor of performance in nursing subunits. *Academy of Management Journal, 28*(4), 844–859. David, F. R., Pearce, J. A., II, & Randolph, W. A. (1989). Linking technology and structure to enhance group performance. *Journal of Applied Psychology, 74*(2), 233–241. Davis, S. M., & Lawrence, P. R. (1978). Problems of matrix organizations. *Harvard Business Review, 56*(3), 131–142. Galbraith (1971). Kerzner (1984).

44. Cleland, D. I. (1988). The cultural ambiance of project management—another look. *Project Management Journal, 19*(3), 49–56.

45. Cleland (1988). Davis & Lawrence (1977).

46. Anderson, R. E. (1994). Matrix redux. *Business Horizons, 37*(4), 6–10.

47. Davis & Lawrence (1977).

48. Burns, L. R., & Wholey, D. R. (1993). Adoption and abandonment of matrix management programs: Effects of organizational characteristics and interorganizational networks. *Academy of Management Journal, 36*(1), 106–138.

49. Katz & Allen (1985). Kerzner (1984). Knight (1976).

50. Katz & Allen (1985). Larson & Gobeli (1987). Might & Fisher (1985).

51. Larson & Gobeli (1987).

52. Katz & Allen (1985).

53. Ford, R. C. & Rudolph, W. A. (1992). Cross-functional structures: A review and integration of matrix organization and project management. *Journal of Management, 18*(2), 267–294.

54. Davis & Lawrence (1977). Posner (1986).

55. Ford et al. (1988).

56. Davis & Lawrence (1977). Posner (1986). Galbraith (1971).

57. Galbraith (1971). Katz & Allen (1985). Kerzner (1984). Burns & Wholey (1993).

58. Allen, T. J., Lee, D. & Tushman, M. (1980). R&D performance as a function of internal communication, project management, and the nature of the work. *IEEE Transactions on Engineering Management, 27*(1), 2–12.

59. Katz, R. (1982). The effects of group longevity on project communication and performance. *Administrative Science Quarterly, 27*(1), 81– 104.

60. Katz (1982), p. 84.

61. Keller, R. T. (1986). Predictors of the performance of project groups in R&D organizations. *Academy of Management Journal, 29*(4), 715–726.

62. White, K. B. (1984). MIS project teams: An investigation of cognitive style implications. *MIS Quarterly, 8*(2), 95–101.

63. Pinto, J. K., & Slevin, D. P. (1987). Critical factors in successful project implementation. *IEEE Transactions on Engineering Management, 34*(1), 22–27.

64. Randolph, W. A., & Blackburn, R. S. (1989). *Managing organizational behavior.* Homewood, IL: Irwin.

65. McCollum, J. K., & Sherman, J. D. (1991). The effects of matrix organization size and number of project assignments on performance. *IEEE Transactions on Engineering Management, 38*(1), 75–78. Ford, R. C., & McLaughlin, S. (1992b, September). Ten questions and answers

on managing MIS projects. *Project Management Journal, 23*, 21–28. Morris, R. M., III. (1988). Guidelines for project management. *Industrial Management, 30*(3), 2–4. Owens, T. (1988). Effective project management. *Small Business Report, 13*(9), 45–52.

66. Pinto, J. K., & Slevin, D. P. (1988a). Critical success factors across the project life cycle. *Project Management Journal, 19*(3), 67–75. Pinto, J. K., & Slevin, D. P. (1988b). Project success: Definitions and measurement techniques. *Project Management Journal, 19*(1), 67–72. Slevin, D. P., & Pinto, J. K. (1986). The project implementation profile: New tool for project managers. *Project Management Journal, 17*(4), 57–70. Slevin, D. P., & Pinto, J. K. (1987). Balancing strategy and tactics in project implementation. *Sloan Management Review, 29*(1), 33–41.

67. Pinto & Slevin (1987).

68. Batiste, J. L., & Jung, J. T. (1984). Requirements, needs, and priorities: A structured approach for determining MIS project definition. *MIS Quarterly, 8*(4), 215–227. Pinto, M. B., & Pinto, J. K. (1991). Determinants of cross-functional cooperation in the project implementation process. *Project Management Journal, 22*(2), 13–19.

69. Larson & Gobeli (1987, 1988). Larson, E. W., & Gobeli, D. H. (1989). Significance of project management structure on development success. *IEEE Transactions on Engineering Management, 36*(2), 119–125.

70. Larson & Gobeli (1989).

71. Pinto & Slevin (1987, 1988a, 1988b). Slevin & Pinto (1986, 1987). Pinto, J. K., & Prescott, J. E. (1988). Variations in critical success factors over the stages in the project life cycle. *Journal of Management, 14*(1), 5–18. Pinto, J. K., & Prescott, J. E. (1990). Planning and tactical factors in the project implementation process. *Journal of Management Studies, 27*(3), 305–327.

72. Davis & Lawrence (1977).

73. Bartlett, C. A., & Ghoshal, S. (1990). Matrix management: Not a structure, a frame of mind. *Harvard Business Review, 68*(4), 138–145. Katz (1982). Kolodny (1979).

Chapter Seven

1. Stuckenbruck, L. C. (1981). *The implementation of project management: The professional's handbook.* Reading, MA: Addison-Wesley.

2. Cockfield, R. W. (1988). Scope management. In *Project management body of knowledge* (PMBOK). Upper Darby, PA: Project Management Institute.

3. Cockfield (1988), p. A5.

4. Obradovitch, M. M., & Stephanou, S. E. (1990). *Project management: Risks and productivity.* Bend, OR: Daniel Spencer.

5. Cockfield (1988).

6. Cockfield (1988).

Chapter Eight

1. Souder, W. E. (1980). *Management decision methods.* New York: Van Nostrand Reinhold. Souder, W. E. (1983). *Project selection and economic appraisal.* New York: Van Nostrand Reinhold. Sepulveda, J. A., Souder, W. E., & Gottfried, B. G. (1984). *Engineering economics.* New York: McGraw-Hill.

2. Souder (1983).
3. Souder (1983). Souder, W. E. (1988). Selecting R&D projects for profit maximization. In *The project management handbook* (pp. 139–119). New York: Van Nostrand Reinhold. Souder, W. E., & Sherman, J. D. (1994). *Managing new technology development.* New York: McGraw-Hill.
4. Souder (1983, 1988).
5. Souder (1980, 1983, 1988).
6. Gitman, L. J., & Forrester, J. R., Jr. (1977, Fall). A survey of capital budgeting techniques used by major U.S. firms. *Financial Management,* pp. 66–71.
7. Evans, D. A., & Forbes, S. M. (1993). Decision making and display methods: The case of prescription and practice in capital budgeting. *Engineering Economist, 39*(1), 87–92.
8. Dixit, A. K., & Pindyck, R. S. (1994). *Investment under uncertainty.* Princeton, NJ: Princeton University Press.
9. Rao, R. K. S. (1995). *Financial management: Concepts and applications.* Cincinnati, OH: South-Western.
10. Brigham, E. F., & Gapenski, L. C. (1997). *Financial management: Theory and practice* (8th ed.). Orlando, FL: Dryden Press.
11. Madura, J. (1995). *International financial management* (4th ed.). St. Paul, MN: West.

Chapter Nine

1. Construction Industry Institute. (1989, October). Management of project risks and uncertainties. (Booklet). Austin: University of Texas at Austin.
2. Hamburger, D. (1990, June). The project manager: Risk taker and contingency planner. *Project Management Journal, 21*(2), 44.
3. Construction Industry Institute (1989).
4. Brooke, J. N. (1989). Leveraged risk reduction. *Proceedings of Project Management Institute seminar/symposium, Atlanta,* p. 302.
5. Hulett, D. T. (1991). PMP Certification Workshop in Risk Management. Project Management Institute, Orange County Chapter.
6. Fraser, D. C. (1978, May). Risk minimisation in giant projects. Paper presented at international conference, The Successful Accomplishment of Giant Projects, London.
7. Hayes, R. W., Perry, J. G., Thompson, P. A., & Willmer, G. (1986, December). *Risk management in engineering construction.* Special SERC Report by the Project Management Group, University of Manchester Institute of Science and Technology. London: Thomas Telford.
8. Curran M. W. (1990, November 26). Personal letter.
9. Ruskin, A. M., & Estes, W. E. (1982). *What every engineer should know about project management.* New York: Marcel Dekker.

Chapter Ten

1. Following are some additional resources: Cleland, D. I. (1990). *Project management: Strategic design and implementation.* Blue Ridge Summit, PA: TAB Books. Cleland, D. I., & King, W. R. (1988). *Project management handbook.* New York: Van Nostrand Reinhold. Kerzner, H. (1995). *Project management: A systems approach to planning, scheduling, and controlling.* New York: Van Nostrand

Reinhold. Meredith, J. R., & Mantel, S. J., Jr. (1995). *Project management: A managerial approach.* New York: Wiley. Nicholas, J. M. (1990). *Managing business and engineering projects.* Englewood Cliffs, NJ: Prentice Hall. Rosenau, M. D., Jr. (1992). *Successful project management: A step-by-step approach with practical examples.* New York: Van Nostrand Reinhold. Shtub, A., Bard, J. F., & Globerson, S. (1994). *Project management.* Englewood Cliffs, NJ: Prentice Hall.

Chapter Fifteen

1. Sayles, L. R. (1979). *What effective managers really do . . . and how they do it.* New York: McGraw-Hill, p. 194.
2. Baker, B. N., & Wilemon, D. L. (1977). A summary of the major research findings regarding the human element in project management. *Project Management Quarterly, 8*(1), 34–40. Powell, G. N., & Posner, B. Z. (1984). Excitement and commitment: The keys to project success. *Project Management Journal, 15*(4), 39–40. Randolph, W. A., & Posner, B. Z. (1988). What every manager needs to know about project management. *Sloan Management Review, 29*(4), 65–73. Donnelly, R. G., & Kezsbom, D. S. (1994). Overcoming the responsibility-authority gap: An investigation of effective team leadership for a new decade. *Cost Engineering, 36*(5), 33–41.
3. Zemke, R. (1985, August). The Honeywell studies: How managers learn to manage. *Training,* pp. 46–51.
4. McCall, M. W., Lombardo, M. M., & Morrison, A. M. (1988). *The lessons of experience: How successful executives develop on the job.* Lanham, MD: Lexington.
5. Kouzes, J. M., & Posner, B. Z. (1995). *The leadership challenge: How to keep getting extraordinary things done in organizations.* San Francisco: Jossey-Bass.
6. McCauley, C. D., Ruderman, M. N., Ohlott, P. J., & Morrow, J. E. (1994). Assessing the developmental components of managerial jobs. *Journal of Applied Psychology, 79*(4), 544–560.
7. Kotter, J. B. (1982). *The general managers.* New York: Basic Books.
8. Carnevale, A. P. (1990). *Put quality to work: Train America's workforce.* Alexandria, VA: American Society for Training and Development.
9. Kiechel, W., III (1994, April 4). A manager's career in the new economy. *Fortune,* pp. 68–72.
10. Sherman, S. (1994, August 22). Leaders learn to heed the voice within. *Fortune,* pp. 92–93.
11. Sperpa, S. P., Buhrfeind, E. D., & Pennebaker, J. W. (1994). Expressive writing and coping with job loss. *Academy of Management Journal, 37*(3), 722–733.
12. Randolph, W. A., & Posner, B. Z. (1992). *Getting the job done: Managing project teams and task forces for success.* Englewood Cliffs, NJ: Prentice Hall.

Chapter Sixteen

1. Beeman, D. R., & Sharkey, T. W. (1987). The use and abuse of corporate politics. *Business Horizons, 36*(2), 26–30.
2. Graham, Robert. (1989). Personal communication.
3. French, J. R. P., & Raven, B. (1959). The bases of social power. In D. Cartwright (Ed.), *Studies in social power* (pp. 150–167). Ann Arbor, MI: Institute for Social Research.

4. Goodman, R. M. (1967). Ambiguous authority definition in project management. *Academy of Management Journal, 10,* 395–407.

5. Thamhain, H. J., & Gemmill, G. (1974). Influence styles of project managers: Some project performance correlates. *Academy of Management Journal, 17,* 216–224.

6. Graham (1989).

7. Gandz, J., & Murray, V. V. (1980). Experience of workplace politics. *Academy of Management Journal, 23,* 237–251.

8. Lovell, R. J. (1993). Power and the project manager. *International Journal of Project Management, 11*(2), 73–78.

9. Payne, H. J. (1993). Introducing formal project management into a traditionally structured organization. *International Journal of Project Management, 11,* 239–243.

10. Keys, B., & Case, T. (1990). How to become an influential manager. *Academy of Management Executive, 4*(4), 38–51.

11. Thamhain & Gemmill (1974).

12. Keys & Case (1990).

13. Fisher, R., & Ury, W. (1981). *Getting to yes: Negotiating agreement without giving in.* Boston: Houghton Mifflin.

14. Pinto, J. K., & Kharbanda, O. P. (1995). *Successful project managers: Leading your team to success.* New York: Van Nostrand Reinhold.

Chapter Seventeen

1. Engel, M. V. (1997). The new non-manager manager. *Management Quarterly, 38,* 22–29. Thamhain, H. J. (1990a). Managing technologically innovative team efforts towards new product success. *Journal of Product Innovation Management, 7,* 5–18. Thamhain, H. J. (1998). Managing people. In M. Kutz (Ed.), *Mechanical engineers' handbook.* New York: Wiley.

2. Peters, T. J., & Waterman, R. H. (1987). *In search of excellence.* New York: Harper & Row. Kanter, R. M. (1989, November–December). The new managerial work. *Harvard Business Review.*

3. Barner, R. (1997). The new millennium workplace. *Engineering Management Review, 25,* 114–119. Kolody, H., et al. (1996). New technology and the emerging organizational paradigm. *Human Relations, 42,* 1457–1487. Thamhain, H. J. (1993). Effective leadership style for managing project teams. In P. C. Dinsmore (Ed.), *Handbook of program and project management* New York: AMACOM. Thamhain (1998). Walton, R. (1985, March–April). From control to commitment in the workplace. *Harvard Business Review.*

4. Oderwald, S. (1996). Global work teams. *Training and Development, 5.*

5. Bennis, W. G., & Shepard, H. A. (1956). A theory of group development. *Human Relations, 9,* 415–437.

6. Tichy, N., & Ulrich, D. (1984, Fall). The leadership challenge: Call for the transformational leader. *Sloan Management Review,* 59–69. Dumaine, B. (1991, June 17). The bureaucracy buster. *Fortune.* Walton (1985).

7. Gupta, A. K., & Wilemon, D. L. (1996). Changing patterns in industrial R&D management. *Journal of Product Innovation Management, 13,* 497–511.

8. Shaw, J., Fisher, C., & Randolph, A. (1991). From maternalism to accountability. *Academy of Management Executive, 5,* 7–20. Thamhain, H. J., & Wilemon, D. L. (1997). Building high

performing engineering project teams. In R. Katz (Ed.), *The human side of managing techno-logical innovation*. New York: Oxford University Press, 1997. Thamhain, H. J., & Wilemon, D. L. (1987, Fall). Leadership, conflict and project management effectiveness. *Sloan Man-agement Review*. Thamhain, H. J. (1991). Skill developments for project managers. *Project Man-agement Journal, 22*. Thamhain (1993).

 9. Dumaine (1991). Peters & Waterman (1987). Kanter (1989). Thamhain, H. J. (1990b, Au-gust–September). Managing technology: The people factor. *Technical and Skill Training*. Thamhain (1993).

10. Roethlingsberger F., & Dickerson, W. (1939). Management and the worker. Cambridge, MA: Harvard University Press. Dyer, W. G. (1997). *Team building: Issues and alternatives*. Read-ing, MA: Addison-Wesley.

11. Likert, R. (1961). *New patterns of management*. New York: McGraw-Hill. McGregor, D. (1960). *The human side of enterprise*. New York: McGraw-Hill.

12. Nurick, A. J., & Thamhain, H. J. (1993). Project team development in multinational envi-ronments. In D. Cleland (Ed.), *Global project management handbook*. New York: McGraw-Hill. Shonk, J. H. (1996). *Team-based organizations*. Homewood, IL: Irwin. Thamhain & Wilson (1997).

13. Fisher, K. (1993). *Leading self-directed work teams*. New York: McGraw-Hill. Marshall, E. (1995). *Transforming the way we work*. New York: AMACOM. Shonk (1996).

14. Fisher (1993). Ouchi, W. G. (1993). *Theory Z*. New York: Avon Books.

15. Zenger, J. H., Musselwhite, E., Hurson, K., & Perrin, C. (1994). *Leading teams*. Burr Ridge, IL: Irwin.

16. An estimated 90 percent of project managers include the top three factors among the most important measures of project success. The other factors are also often mentioned as im-portant to project success. Together, the seven factors account for 85 percent of all vari-ables of project performance identified in a field study of 1,650 projects (Thamhain, 1990; Thamhain & Wilemon, 1997).

17. For a detailed discussion, see Thamhain (1990). Specifically, a Kendall-tau rank-order cor-relation model was used. These measures yielded an average association of $\tau = .37$ and $p = .03$). Moreover, there appears to be a strong agreement between managers and proj-ect team members on the importance of these characteristics, as measured using a Kruskal-Wallis analysis of variance at a confidence level of 95 percent.

18. Studies by Nurick (1993), Thamhain (1993), and Wilemon (1997) on work group dynam-ics clearly show significant correlations and interdependencies among work environment factors and team performance. These studies indicate that high team performance involves four primary factors: managerial leadership, job content, personal goals and objectives, and work environment and organizational support. The actual correlation of sixty influence factors to the project team characteristics and performance provided some interesting in-sight into the strength and effect of these factors. One important finding was that only twelve of the sixty influence factors were found to be statistically significant. Kendall-tau rank-order correlation was used to measure the association between these variables. Statistical significance was defined at a confidence level of 95 percent or better. All other factors seem to be much less important to high team performance.

19. For more detailed discussions of the field studies, see Thamhain and Wilemon (1997).

20. Senge, P. (1994). *The fifth discipline: The art and practice of the learning organization*. New York: Doubleday.

Chapter Eighteen

1. Parker, G. (1994). *Cross-functional teams: Working with allies, enemies, and other strangers.* San Francisco: Jossey-Bass.
2. Donnellon, A. (1993). Crossfunctional teams in product development: Accommodating the structure to the process. *Journal of Product Innovation Management, 10*(5), 377.
3. Dougherty, D. (1992). Interpretive barriers to successful product innovation in large firms. *Organization Science, 3*(2), 182.
4. Lutz, R. A. (1994). Implementing technological change with cross-functional teams. *Research Technology Management, 37,* 14.
5. Parker (1994), pp. 6–30.
6. Pinto, M. B., Pinto, J. K., & Prescott, J. E. (1993). Antecedents and consequences of project team cross-functional cooperation. *Management Science, 39*(10), 1281–1297.
7. Larson, C. E., & La Fasto, F. M. (1989). *Teamwork: What must go right/what can go wrong.* Thousand Oaks, CA: Sage, p. 27.
8. Parker (1994), p. 81.
9. Meyers, P. W., & Wilemon, D. (1989). Learning in new technology development teams. *Journal of Product Innovation Management, 6,* 79–88.
10. Griffin, A., & Hauser, J. R. (1996). Integrating R&D and marketing: A review and analysis of the literature. *Journal of Product Innovation Management, 13,* 191–215.
11. Donnellon (1993), p. 388.
12. Mower, J., & Wilemon, D. (1989, September-October). Rewarding technical teamwork. *Research Technology Management,* pp. 22–29.
13. McCorcle, M. D. (1982). Critical issues in the functioning of interdisciplinary groups. *Small Group Behavior, 13*(3), 291–310.
14. Loehr, L. (1991). Between silence and voice: Communication in cross-functional project teams. *IEEE Transactions on Professional Communication, 34*(1), 51–56.
15. Donnellon (1993).
16. Gemmill, G., & Wilemon, D. (1994). The hidden side of leadership in technical team management. *Research Technology Management, 37*(6), 25–32.
17. Henke, J. W., Krachenberg, A. R., & Lyons, T. F. (1993). Cross-functional teams: Good concept, poor implementation! *Journal of Product Innovation Management, 10*(3), 218.
18. Katzenbach, J. R., & Smith, D. K. (1993). *The wisdom of teams.* Boston: Harvard Business School Press.

Chapter Nineteen

1. Roberts, E., & Fusfeld, A. (1981). Staffing the innovative technology-based organization. *Sloan Management Review, 22,* 19–34.
2. Barczak, G., & Wilemon, D. (1989). Leadership differences in new product development teams. *Journal of Product Innovation Management, 6,* 259–287.
3. Chakrabarti, A., & Hauschildt, J. (1989). The division of labour in innovation management. *R&D Management, 19,* 161–171.

4. Ferris, G. (1988). Technical leadership: Much discussed but little understood. *Research Technology Management, 31,* 2–17.

5. Kouzes, J. M., & Posner, B. Z. (1993). *Credibility: How leaders gain and lose it, why people demand it.* San Francisco: Jossey-Bass.

6. Allen, T. (1971). Communication in R&D laboratories. *R&D Management, 1,* 14–21. Allen, T. (1984). *Managing the flow of technology: Technology transfer and the dissemination of technical information within the R&D organization.* Cambridge, MA: MIT Press. Tushman, M. (1977). Special boundary roles in the innovation process. *Administrative Science Quarterly, 22,* 587–605. Tushman, M. (1979). Work characteristics and subunit communication structure: A contingency analysis. *Administrative Science Quarterly, 24,* 82–98.

7. Clark, K., & Wheelwright, S. (1992). Organizing and leading "heavyweight" development teams. *California Management Review, 34,* 9–28. House, C., & Price, R. (1991, January–February). The return map: Tracking product teams. *Harvard Business Review,* pp. 92–100.

8. Ancona, D., & Caldwell, D. (1992). Bridging the boundary: External activity and performance in organizational teams. *Administrative Science Quarterly, 37,* 634–655.

9. Ancona & Caldwell (1992).

10. Ancona & Caldwell (1992).

11. Kouzes, J. M., & Posner, B. Z. (1995). *The leadership challenge: How to keep getting extraordinary things done in organizations.* San Francisco: Jossey-Bass.

12. Kohn, A. (1986). *The case against competition.* Boston: Houghton Mifflin.

13. Tjosvold, D. (1986). *Working together to get things done.* Lexington, MA: Heath, p. 25.

14. Randolph, W. A., & Posner, B. Z. (1992). *Getting the job done: Managing project teams and task forces with success.* Englewood Cliffs, NJ: Prentice Hall.

15. Kouzes & Posner (1993).

16. Clark & Wheelwright (1992).

17. Kouzes & Posner (1993).

Chapter Twenty

1. Adams, J. S. (1963, November). Toward an understanding of equity. *Journal of Abnormal and Social Psychology, 2,* 436.

2. Vroom, V. H. (1964). *Work and motivation.* New York: Wiley.

3. Ferster, C. B., & Skinner, B. F. (1957). *Schedules of reinforcement.* New York: Appleton-Century-Crofts, 1957.

4. Locke, E. A. (1968, May). Toward a theory of task motivation and incentives. *Organizational Behavior and Human Performance, 3,* 157–189.

5. Locke, E. A., & Latham, G. P. (1990). *A theory of goal setting and task performance.* Englewood Cliffs, NJ: Prentice Hall.

6. Klein, H. J. (1989). An integrated control theory model of work motivation. *Academy of Management Review, 14,* 150–172.

7. Hackman, J. R., & Oldham, G. R. (1976). Motivation through the design of work: Test of a theory. *Organizational Behavior and Human Performance, 16,* 250–279.

8. Olson, M. (1965). *The logic of collective action.* Cambridge, MA: Harvard University Press.

9. Janis, I. (1982). *Victims of groupthink: A psychological study of foreign policy decisions and fiascos* (2nd ed.). Boston: Houghton Mifflin.

10. Latane, B., Williams, K., & Harkins, S. (1979). Many hands make light work: The causes and consequences of social loafing. *Journal of Personality and Social Psychology, 37,* 822–832.

11. Thoms, P., and Greenburger, D. B. (1998). A test of vision training and potential antecedents to leaders: Visioning ability. *Human Resource Development Quarterly, 9*(1), 3–20.

Chapter Twenty-One

1. A more detailed description of the steps involved in preparation for negotiation can be found in Lewicki, R. J., Litterer, J. A., Minton, J. W., & Saunders, D. M. (Eds.). (1994). *Negotiation* (2nd ed.). Burr Ridge, IL: Irwin.

2. Lax, D. A., & Sebenius, J. K. (1993). Interests: The measure of negotiation. In Lewicki et al. (1994).

3. Lewicki et al. (1994).

4. Pruitt, D. G., & Carnevale, P. J. (1993). *Negotiation in social conflict.* Pacific Grove, CA: Brooks-Cole.

5. Fisher, R., Ury, W., & Patton, B. (1991). *Getting to yes: Negotiating agreement without giving in.* New York: Penguin Books.

6. Magenau, J. M., & Pruitt, D. G. (1979). The social psychology of bargaining: A theoretical synthesis. In G. Stephenson & C. Brotherton (Eds.), *Industrial relations: A social psychological approach.* New York: Wiley.

7. Fisher et al. (1991).

8. Pruitt & Carnevale (1993).

9. Pruitt & Carnevale (1993).

10. Fisher et al. (1991), p. 88.

11. Lewicki et al. (1994).

12. Kennedy, G., Benson, J., & McMillan, J. (1983). *Managing negotiations* (Rev. ed.). Englewood Cliffs, NJ: Prentice Hall.

13. Pruitt & Carnevale (1993). Lewicki et al. (1994).

14. Pruitt, D. G., & Rubin, J. Z. (1986). *Social conflict: Escalation, stalemate and settlement.* New York: McGraw-Hill.

15. Pruitt, D. G. (1983). Strategic choice in negotiation. *American Behavioral Scientist, 27,* 167–194.

16. Pruitt & Rubin (1986).

17. Bazerman, M. H. (1983). Negotiator judgment: A critical look at the rationality assumption. *American Behavioral Scientist, 27,* 211–228.

18. Pruitt & Carnevale (1993), pp. 36–46.

19. Fisher et al. (1991). Lewicki et al. (1994). Pruitt & Carnevale (1993).

Chapter Twenty-Two

1. Williams, M. (1987, September). How I learned to stop worrying and love negotiating. *Inc. Magazine,* p. 132.

2. Robbins, S. P. (1974). *Managing organizational conflict: A nontraditional approach.* Englewood Cliffs, NJ: Prentice Hall.

3. Robbins (1974).

4. Baker, S., & Baker, K. (1992). *On time/on budget: A step by step guide for managing any project.* Englewood Cliffs, NJ: Prentice Hall.

5. Thamhain, H. J., & Wilemon, D. L. (1975). Conflict management in project life cycles. *Sloan Management Review, 16,* 31–50.

6. Kezsbom, D., Schilling, D., & Edward, K. (1989). *Dynamic project management: A practical guide for managers and engineers.* New York: Wiley.

7. Thomas, K. W., & Schmidt, W. H. (1976). A survey of managerial interests with respect to conflict. *Academy of Management Journal,* 315–318.

8. Graves, J. (1978). Successful management and organizational mugging. In J. Papp (Ed.), *New direction in human resource management.* Englewood Cliffs, NJ: Prentice Hall.

9. Allison, G. T. (1971). *Essence of decision.* Boston: Little, Brown.

10. Robbins (1974).

11. Coser, R. A., & Schwenk, C. R. (1990). Agreement and thinking alike: Ingredients for poor decisions. *Academy of Management Executive,* no. 4, pp. 69–74.

12. Starke, F. A., & Sexty, R. W. (1992). *Contemporary management in Canada.* Englewood Cliffs, NJ: Prentice Hall.

13. Womack, D. F. (1988). Assessing the Thomas-Kilman conflict mode survey. *Management Communication Quarterly, 1,* 321–349.

14. Blake, R. R., & Mouton, J. S. (1964). *The managerial grid.* Houston, TX: Gulf Publishing.

15. House, R. S. (1988). *The human side of project management.* Reading, MA: Addison-Wesley.

16. Schutz, W. (1958, July–August). The interpersonal underworld. *Harvard Business Review,* pp. 123–135.

17. House (1988).

18. Hill, R. E. (1977). Managing interpersonal conflict in project teams. *Sloan Management Review, 18*(2), 45–61.

19. Thamhain & Wilemon (1975).

20. House (1988).

21. House (1988).

22. Block, P. (1981). *Flawless consulting.* Austin, TX: Learning Concepts.

23. Sievert, R. W., Jr. (1986, December). Communication: An important construction tool. *Project Management Journal, 77.* House (1988).

24. House (1988).

25. House (1988).

26. House (1988).

27. Dinsmore, P. C. (1990). *Human factors in project management* (Rev. ed.). New York: AMACOM.

28. Fisher, R., & Ury, W. (1991). *Getting to yes: Negotiating agreement without giving in* (2nd ed.). New York: Penguin Books.

29. Hofstede, G. (1993). *Cultures and organizations: Software of the mind.* New York: McGraw-Hill.

Chapter Twenty-Three

1. Cringley, R. X. (1994, August 29). How to forfeit millions for nothing. *Forbes,* pp. 61–64.

2. Pinto, J. K., & Rouhiainen, P. (1998). Developing a customer-based project success measurement. In *Proceedings of the 14th World Congress on Project Management,* Ljubljana, Slovenia, pp. 829–835.

3. Shenhar, A. J., Levy, O., & Dvir, D. (1997). Mapping the dimensions of project success. *Project Management Journal, 28*(2), 5–13.

4. Brooks, F. P. (1995). *The mythical man-month: Essays in software engineering* (3rd ed.). Reading, MA: Addison-Wesley.

5. Green, S. G., Welsh, M. A., & Dehler, G. E. (1993). Red flags at dawn, or predicting R&D project termination at start-up. *Research-Technology Management, 36*(3), 10–12.

6. Baker, B. N., Murphy, P. C., & Fisher, D. (1988). Factors affecting project success. In D. I. Cleland & W. R. King (Eds.), *Project management handbook* (2nd ed.) (pp. 902–919). New York: Van Nostrand Reinhold. Morris, P. W. G. (1988). Managing project interfaces—Key points for project success. In D. I. Cleland & W. R. King (Eds.), *Project management handbook* (2nd ed.) (pp. 16–55). New York: Van Nostrand Reinhold. Pinto, J. K., & Slevin, D. P. (1987). Critical factors in successful project implementation. *IEEE Transactions on Engineering Management, EM–34*, 22–27.

7. Pinto, J. K., & Slevin, D. P. (1988a). Critical success factors across the project life cycle. *Project Management Journal, 19*(3), 67–75. Pinto, J. K., and D. P. Slevin, (1988b). "Project success: Definitions and measurement techniques," *Project Management Journal, 19*(1), 67–72. Pinto, J. K. and Slevin, D. P. (1992). *The Project Implementation Profile.* Tuxedo, NY: Xicom, Inc.

Chapter Twenty-Four

1. Roberts, E. B. (1992, December 10). Strategic management of technology: Global benchmarking. Results of a survey sponsored and conducted by the Massachusetts Institute of Technology, Cambridge MA, and PA Consulting Group.

2. For a delightful example, see the Cary Grant–Myrna Loy movie classic, *Mr. Blandings Builds His Dream House,* wherein the I've-seen-it-all contractor explains the ballooning house building cost stemming from a "simple" midproject change the Blandings wanted. The example is a fictional house, but you can get a similar, albeit less humorous, explanation from any experienced manager of big construction, defense system development, shipbuilding, automobile design, electronic systems, or software projects.

3. Kausal, B. A., IV. (1996, March–April). Peace Shield—a study in motivation. *Program Manager,* pp. 22–24.

4. Naval ship production: A claim settled and a framework built. (1980, December). *Interfaces, 10*(6).

5. This distinction of productivity, quality, and rework has the added benefit of making all of these factors measurable and monitorable. Total throughput of work items in a project stage (lines of code, tons of steel, drawings, numbers of units, tests conducted, and so forth) can be measured over time much as in traditional systems and compared to the number of hours spent in the same time frames, so as to monitor a legitimate measure of productivity. Numbers of revisions and rounds of revisions, can be monitored over time so as to derive a tangible measure of quality, as described in "Benchmarks for the Project Manager" in the March 1993 issue of *Project Management Journal.*

6. Advanced hornet milestone. (1995, May). *Northrop Grumman Review,* no. 1.

7. 12 hours × $50/hour × 1.5 overtime premium = $900; $900/0.4 output hour = $2,250 per output hour. Use your own company's wage rates and overtime pay premium to calculate your projects' real overtime output costs.

8. The most recent analysis we found elsewhere, a November 1980 report of a Construction Industry Cost Effectiveness Task Force, "Scheduled Overtime Effect on Construction Projects," published by the Business Roundtable, showed similar, even some more extreme, phenomena among construction workers. Interestingly, the same crossover point, ten hours weekly overtime (sustained for two months), was identified as yielding no extra real output; more overtime than that produces *less* than a standard work week.

9. Brooks, F. J. (1975). *The mythical man-month: Essays on software engineering.* Chapel Hill: University of North Carolina Press.

10. Better to have a good working analog watch, with just the hour hand! We offered up "Progress Ramps" as approximately accurate translators of monitored progress in Cooper, K. G. (1993, February). The rework cycle: Benchmarks for the project manager. *pmNETwork.*

11. This is precisely why well-implemented integrated product teams are producing such good results. Representative toolers and builders who would normally wait to receive design product, for example, are actively engaged early in the design, helping to prevent, find, and improve what would otherwise linger as undiscovered rework.

12. In this setting, managers can fear knowing "too much." I have had project managers (happily a small minority) express their wish to use the rework cycle modeling capability, but explain that they could not because they would then "know too much" about the project's future (and need to disclose it, and get fired...). The concept of foreknowledge and the power of preemptive action eludes such dolts. They shall remain anonymous; they get fired later anyway.

13. Who among the S&P 500 has the most on the ball? Our growth rankings offer surprising insights into America's most closely watched companies. (1998, March 30). *Business Week.*

Chapter Twenty-Five

1. Drucker, P. (1992, July 22). Planning for uncertainty. *Wall Street Journal*, p. A12.

2. Cleland, D. I. (1991). The age of project management. *Project Management Journal, 22,* 19–24.

3. Construction industry remains buoyant. (1994). *Asian Review, 31.*

4. Cleland (1991).

5. Kharbanda, O. P., & Stallworthy, E. A. (1992). *Lessons from project disasters.* Manchester, England: MCB University Press, pp. 25–27.

6. Cooper, K. G. (1994). The $2,000 hour: How managers influence project performance through the rework cycle. *Project Management Journal, 25*(1), 11–24.

7. Cleland (1991).

8. Barnes, N. M. L., & Wearne, S. H. (1993). The future of major project management. *International Journal of Project Management, 11,* 138.

9. Pinto, J. K., & Kharbanda, O. P. (1995). *Successful project managers: Leading your team to success.* New York: Van Nostrand Reinhold.

INDEX

A

Abandonment decisions, 130
Accommodation. *See* Smoothing
Accounting rate of return (ARR), 126
Acquisition control, 116
Action focus: of 4T framework, 43; task definition and, 44; teams and, 45; transition and, 45
Activities: crashing, 217, 220; defining, 179–180; loops of, 183; network diagramming, 181–187; precedential relationship of, 183; reducing duration estimates of, 215–216, 218–220, 221, 230–231; scheduling, 187–203, 213, 215–216; sequence of, "perfect world" versus learning curve model, 382–384; time-cost trade-off and, 217–220, 221. *See also* Work breakdown structure (WBS)
Actual finish time (AF), 209
Actual start time (AS), 209
Administrative conflict, 356, 357, 358

Advisory and review team, for proposal development, 78–79
"Age of Project Management, The" (Cleland), 426
Airport extension example, 157
Alignment, in cross-functional teams, 296
Alternative analysis, in conceptual development, 111
Alternative dispute resolution, 24
Ambassador activities, 302–304, 305
Ambiguity, in matrix organization, 100–101
American Management Association, 357
American Society for Training and Development, 253
AT&T, 281, 405, 423
Amount at stake, risk assessment and, 140, 143–144, 147
Ancona, 302–304, 306
Anderson, W., 158
Apple Computer, 33
Approvals, 12–13, 113–114
Arab oil embargo of 1973, 154

Arnold, H., 162–163, 164, 165, 175
Asea Brown Boveri (ABB), 38
Asian countries, rapid development in, 427–429
Asian Development Bank, 71
Asian Wall Street Journal, 428
Assertive model, 369
Authority, 258–260, 263
Authority changes, 360–361
Authority conflicts: in cross-functional organization, 96, 98; between functional and project managers, 96, 98, 100, 263, 294, 360–361
Authority to commit resources, assessing customer's, 75, 76
Automobile industry, partnering in, 19
Avoidance. *See* Withdrawal

B

BAA, 8
BANC criteria, 75–76
Barczak, 300
Bargaining. *See* Compromise